The Encyclopedia of

Glass Paperweights

The Encyclopedia of Glass Paperweights

Paul Hollister, Jr.

PAPERWEIGHT PRESS

SANTA CRUZ • CALIFORNIA

To my wife,
who suggested this book
and then
put up with it

ALL COLOR PICTURES WERE TAKEN BY THE AUTHOR
EXCEPTING FIGURES 3, 7, 8, 10, 12, 15, 16, 28, 41, 62, 63, 64
BLACK-AND-WHITE PICTURES WITHOUT CREDITS ARE BY THE AUTHOR
DRAWINGS ARE BY THE AUTHOR
COVER PHOTOGRAPH BY PAUL SCHRAUB
PHOTOGRAPH OF PAUL HOLLISTER BY BILL RAY

Library of Congress Cataloging-in-Publication Data

Hollister, Paul M., 1918–
   The encyclopedia of glass paperweights.

   Reprint. Originally published: New York:
C. N. Potter, © 1969 (1970 printing)
   Bibliography: p.
   Includes index.
   1. Paperweights.   I. Title.
NK5440.P3H6   1986   748.8'4   86-30351
ISBN 0-933756-10-0

Acknowledgments

THIS BOOK COULD NOT HAVE BEEN WRITTEN without help from many sources. The author wishes to thank for information, advice, and speculation, Mme. Yolande Amic, Conservateur, Musée des Arts Décoratifs, Louvre, Paris; Mrs. Frank Barger; Mr. Roland Barker; Mr. and Mrs. W. Dale Barker; Mr. Geoffrey W. Beard; Mr. John Bunyan, Director, the Medical Engineering Development Trust, London; Sir Hugh Chance; Mr. Robert J. Charleston, Keeper of Ceramics and Glass, Victoria and Albert Museum, London; M. Henri Dessalle, Administrateur Général, Cristalleries du Val-Saint-Lambert, S.A., Val-Saint-Lambert, Seraing, Belgium; Mrs. John Dorflinger; Mr. Paul V. Gardner, Curator, Division of Ceramics and Glass, Smithsonian Institution, Washington, D.C.; Mrs. William Godsman; Mr. Lloyd J. Graham; Mr. Bill Hahn; Dr. Joseph S. Hepburn, Ph.D., M.D., Franklin Institute, Philadelphia; Mr. Amory Houghton; Mr. James Houston of Steuben Glass; Mr. Walter L. Hyde, Director, Institute of Optics, University of Rochester, Rochester, New York; M. Gérard Ingold, Compagnie des Cristalleries de Saint Louis, Paris; Mrs. Robert Kershaw, Director, Sandwich Historical Society Museum, Sandwich, Mass.; Mr. C. A. Kilner; Dr. Junius Langston; Mr. J. M. D. Legge; Mr. B. H. Leffingwell; the late Mr. Victor E. Lutz; Mr. Louis Lyons; Mr. Lawrence J. Majewski, Associate Professor of Conservation, Institute of Fine Arts, New York University; Mr. Fred A. Nagel; Mrs. Viola Neiman; Mr. Donald F. Nesbitt; the late Mr. S. Weldon O'Brien; Mr. Andrew Oliver, Jr., Assistant Curator of Greek and Roman Art, The Metropolitan Museum of Art, New York; Orrefors, Orrefors, Sweden; Mrs. Clara Peck; Mr. Edwin L. Popper; M. Joseph Philippe, Secrétaire Général des Journées Internationales du Verre, Musée du Verre, Liège; Mr. James Key Reeve, Curator of American Art, The Toledo Musum of Art, Toledo, Ohio; Mr. Norman S. Rice, Curator, Albany Institute of History and Art, Albany, New York; Mr. Stephen T. Riley, Director, Massachusetts Historical Society, Boston; Mr. Millard F. Rogers, Jr., former Curator of American Art, The Toledo Museum of Art; Mrs. Stephen H. Sampson; Miss Vivian J. Scheidemantel, Associate Curator of Decorative Arts, The Art Institute of Chicago; Mr. Ray Winfield Smith; Mrs. George W. Stedman; Mr. W. A. Taylor, City Librarian, Birmingham Reference Library, Birmingham, England; Dr. Libuse Uresová, Museum of Industrial Art, Prague; M. André Vulliet, Baccarat, Inc., New York; Mr. Hugh Wakefield, Keeper of Circulation, Victoria and Albert Museum; Miss Hermione Waterfield, Christie's London.

Special thanks for service beyond the call of duty are given to Miss Edith Adams of The Cooper Union Museum Library; Mr. Louis Biancolli; Mr. Melvin Billups; Mr. J. P. Boore; Dr. Robert H. Brill, Administrator of Scientific Research, Corning Museum of Glass; Mr. T. H. Clarke, Director, Sotheby & Co.; Mrs. E. Campbell Cloak, Curator of Paperweights, Bergstrom Art Center and Museum, Neenah, Wisconsin; Miss O. D. Dahlgren; Mrs. Jessie McNab Dennis, Assistant Curator, Department of Western European Art, The Metropolitan Museum of Art; Miss Reta Farnham, formerly librarian, Corning Museum of Glass; Mr. Paul Harvey; Mr. Charles Kaziun; Dr. Seymour Z. Lewin, Professor of Chemistry, Conservation Center, Institute of Fine Arts, New York University; Mr. Edward J. Mazerski; Mr. Paul Perrot, Director, Corning Museum of Glass; Mr. Joseph Rapport, Museum Assistant, New-York Historical Society; Dr. George S. Richardson; Miss Carolyn Scoon, Assistant Curator, New-York Historical Society; Mrs. Charles H. Watkins; Mr. Kenneth M. Wilson, Curator, Corning Museum of Glass. It was through their suggestions, tireless cooperation, and encouragement that this book finally took shape.

For the use of photographic illustrations I am indebted to The Art Institute of Chicago; The Bergstrom Art Center and Museum; Christie's; Corning Museum of Glass; Dr. Seymour Z. Lewin; The Metropolitan Museum of Art; Musée du Verre, Liège; Old Sturbridge Village; Parke-Bernet Galleries, Inc.; Sotheby & Co.; Taylor & Dull; James C. Ward; and to the private collectors whose paperweights grace these pages.

CONTENTS

Acknowledgments   v

Introduction   1

I. PAPERWEIGHT GENESIS   5

    1. Egyptian Mosaic and Roman Millefiori   7

    2. The Part Played by Venice   12

    3. Bohemian-Silesian Millefiori and Paperweights   24

    4. The Victorian Context   35

II. THE INDIVIDUAL MAKERS   45

About the French Makers   46

    5. Baccarat   47

    6. St. Louis   85

    7. Clichy   123

    8. Other French Factories   145

About the English Makers   151

  9.   Bacchus and Islington   152

  10.   Whitefriars   164

  11.   Other English Factories   174

         Color Section   [following 184]

  12.   Belgian Factories   185

About the American Makers   192

  13.   The New England Glass Company   194

  14.   Sandwich   211

  15.   Gillinder   223

  16.   Other American Factories   233

  17.   Sulphides   254

  18.   Modern Paperweights   268

III.   EXAMINATION OF PAPERWEIGHTS   283

  19.   Testing For Refractive Index   285

Bibliography   290

Glossary   299

Some Museums Having Glass Paperweights   305

Index   307

Introduction

THOUGH THE ELEMENTS THAT COMPOSE THE INTERIOR DESIGNS of glass paperweights generally derive from glass materials, forms, and procedures discovered in ancient Egypt and perpetuated in Hellenistic practice, their use in those millennia was for practical and decorative domestic and religious purposes. It required a clear glass magnifying lens above a glass design to round out both literally and figuratively the concept of a paperweight. A decorative motif rendered more vivid and yet more mysterious by the magnifying and light-refracting properties of a thick glass covering lens became a possibility with the introduction of lead glass by Ravenscroft in the 1670's. But the concept of a glass paperweight embodying these features had to await the productive, inventive European environment of the mid-nineteenth century. The glass conglomerate of the Venetian ball, cylinder, or cube of the early 1840's is not a paperweight in the Classic sense.

The Classic period of paperweight-making begins about 1842, possibly simultaneously in Bohemia-Silesia and in France, reaches its height by 1851, and runs another decade in Europe. In America, it begins and ends some ten years later.

The Classic period is followed by a decline in both quantity and quality of paperweights, then in the late 1870's by a revival in which three-dimensional forms are stressed. Afterward, there were a series of revivals at different times in different countries. We are at present in the midst of a large-scale, worldwide revival that began after World War II. The current revival is embodied in production by glass artists and artisans who have tried, with varying degrees of ingenuity and success, to approximate the flat millefiori designs of the Classic period or the three-dimensional flora and fauna of the post-Classic revival. Only a few makers, particularly in Sweden, seem to have been aware of the anomalous relationship of such designs to our own time, and they have at least tapped modern-glass technology in the search for new approaches to a now old and static form.

Though it includes all periods, this book is primarily concerned with the paperweights of the Classic period, partly because they categorically represent the best that has been done, and also because heretofore they have been largely ignored in print and relegated historically to a minor subheading in the dusty, dog-eared archives of the decorative arts. The obscurity of the millefiori glass paperweight in the annals of art stems from the Victorian period, when it was considered merely another minor novelty item of trade in Venetian or Bohemian style, something that was exhibited as an addendum to other flamboyant glass, and found its way into the stationery shops of Europe and those other bauble or "fancy" shops that displayed for the elite the wonders of glass toiletry and decorative knickknackery. With few Victorian exceptions, most of which are cited in this book, paperweights were critically ignored; naturally enough, since in the Victorian emporium of objects of unparalleled hideousness, of aesthetic horribilia on the grand scale, paperweights were almost the only genuinely beautiful objects made and, being small, were easily passed over. But for collectors we might never know they existed.

Collectors rescued paperweights from the menagerie of neglected objects, and later they gave them to the museums, those mausoleums of art and artifact, which Maurice Rheims has so aptly called "the churches of collectors." Aside from such eclectic aesthetes as Oscar Wilde, the first big collectors were probably members of royalty and the nobility, for we know collections were made by Empress Eugénie, wife of Napoleon III, Carlotta, wife of Emperor Maximilian of Mexico, the Duke of Cardoza, the Princess Murat, the Marquis de Bailleul, and, later, King Farouk of Egypt, whose collection after his abdication formed one of the first big public auctions of paperweights.

At the great glassworks of Baccarat, Clichy, and St. Louis in France, paperweight-making was for a few years an intensive line of manufacture. Bacchus in England, the Boston & Sandwich Company, New England Glass Company, and Gillinder in America are also known to have made and exhibited paperweights commercially. Yet in most other factories they were "offhand" work done by glassworkers in their own free time, which usually meant the lunch hour because many factories operated in shifts around the clock and there was no such thing as "after hours." However, if the making and cutting of the canes, the final assembly and annealing of paperweights had to be done at the factory, the making of flowers, leaves, and fauna could be done at home in a process known as lampwork. Lampwork refers to the cutting and shaping of leaves, petals, and other small parts from rods of glass and to their assembly with the aid of a tallow torch, blow torch, blast lamp, or Bunsen burner. A man could assemble his floral motif at home and keep it until he had time to reheat it and enclose it in glass at the factory. Often he found no time, as we know from the lampwork of Nicholas Lutz, who made many more flowers than he was ever able to use. Interestingly enough, flowers seen in glass paperweights do not follow the popularity order found broadcast through the Victorian decorative arts; in fact, except for the ubiquitous pansy, the order of frequency of appearance would seem almost to have been reversed. The ever-popular rose and morning glory are seen infrequently, the lily of the valley only rarely, the poppy never. Paperweight flowers tend to be shorthand flowers, simplified and stylized as one finds the emblems of heraldry, with the flower fully opened and seen always in the same position, one type of leaf serving all flowers.

Offhand paperweights were frequently made by glassworkers as wedding or anniversary presents, or as tokens of affection to members of their families or to other glassworkers. Offhand glasswork of all sorts, though occasionally done with the encouragement of the management toward developing special skills, was often done without the knowledge of the company whose expensive colored glass the glassworkers were using, and when shortages were traced, the practice was frequently stopped. Such a situation was recorded at the New England Glass Company, though paperweight-makers were not cited among the culprits.

From start to finish, from the first bundling together of the first rods to make the first cane right through to the final annealing, a complicated millefiori paperweight might take several months to make, though once a pattern was established a series of similar weights might be made. The production figures of Baccarat paperweights made as recently as the early 1960's are of interest. It took three or four months to build up a stock of canes sufficient to make 150 millefiori weights. Each weight comprised from 180 to 220 canes, but these, of course, were only thin slices from very long rods. The actual making of a single paperweight took seven hours. And these were simple, close millefiori weights.

Traditionally, glassmaking has been done in relative secrecy. The glassmakers of medieval Venice, who were set up like princes on Murano, were forbidden on pain of death to leave that glass island with their secrets. Today an eager but ignorant public may watch glassblowing at Murano, Steuben, and a number of other places, but formulas are carefully guarded everywhere. Paperweight-makers are among the most secretive of glassmen. The great contemporary paperweight-maker Charles Kaziun speaks of his friendship with Emil Larson, maker of the Larson rose paperweight. When they were together, Kaziun and Larson talked glass, but Larson never gave Kaziun a clue as to how he made his rose. "Since he did not volunteer any information on the subject, I knew better than to ask," said Kaziun. A few written sources of information about the making of simple types of paperweights are listed in the bibliography, but one cannot learn to drive a car by reading about driving in the *Encyclopaedia Britannica,* and the real secrets of the art are in the minds and hands of the paperweight-makers, living and dead. This author is in no position to understand all the complexities involved. One can only say that a paperweight is all glass and art.

The impetus for this book stems from a childhood fascination with paperweights that never waned, reinforced in later life by a regret that no comprehensive study of their history had been undertaken to relate them to the culture of their time, and place them where they belong—high in the history of art. I am convinced that in the plethora of its products and in the conscious ease with which everything stored in the warehouse of history was considered legitimate for modernized aping, the World's Fair culture of the Victorian period closely parallels our own. It is certainly not remarkable that paperweights, with their wholesale use of old glass techniques were made, but it is almost miraculous that men would have applied these techniques in new directions with such instantaneous and consummate success, creating something at once completely new, beautiful, and unique.

Perhaps the most remarkable thing about glass paperweights of the Classic period is not the technical achievement, which places them at the pinnacle of all glassmaking, but the curious process itself of alternate diminution and enlargement whereby the canes are begun big, then pulled out to minute cross-section, then again enlarged by the convex lens of the crown and reduced by the concave printies in a series of reverse transformations whose final result is one of unceasing mystification to the eye of the beholder. Precisely what is it, one asks, that is inside this paperweight? And continues to ask even when one knows it is simply colored glass. The mystery of the interior glass design is further complicated and enhanced by the continuity of a single refractive index, which renders every element of the glass design without that surface reflection or shine we tend to associate with glass. We are gazing into a mystery whose true dimensions and physical composition our senses are unable to pinpoint, a mystery sealed away in perpetuity. You may look at it but you cannot touch it. When the continuity of the refractive index is interrupted, as it is in sulphide paperweights, a new mystery is created that, like an alchemist's dream, turns china clay and supersilicate of potash into silver.

In all, perhaps 50,000 paperweights of good quality were made. Of these, probably not more than a third to a half survive. Many are now in museums, and before too long most of the best of them will be off the market. This is good because the competition of affluence has turned them into symbols of status, when in truth they are simply objects of extraordinary beauty. As intrinsically beautiful objects they represent the important exception to the mediocrity of Victorian taste and they cry out for a recognized place in the hierarchy of beautiful objects made by man. For the finest of them, created by true and great artists, rank with the finest illuminated manuscripts, the bronzes of Cellini, the boxes of Fabergé, or the portraits of the greatest of the miniaturists.

Introduction to the Paperweight Press Edition

WRITTEN IN 1969, Paul Hollister's *Encyclopedia of Glass Paperweights* was the first comprehensive study of antique glass paperweights. This well-researched reference book encouraged my early interest and later fascination with paperweights. I carried it with me to shops and auctions, studying it regularly. It provided the framework for my education in the field and greatly influenced my collecting career.

Today, even with the many new books being published on the subject, *The Encyclopedia of Glass Paperweights* is still one of the most important basic references available. Out of print for several years, this classic has become highly prized by scholars and collectors alike, even finding its way into the major auction houses where it has sold for high prices.

It is a privilege for us at Paperweight Press to be able to make this landmark publication available once again to all interested in learning about the history and art of paperweights. We feel that this comprehensive study has significant and lasting value to all collectors, students, and experts in the field.

Lawrence Selman

I

Paperweight Genesis

Figs. 1, 2. Millefiori bowls, Roman 100 B.C.–100 A.D. *Courtesy Corning Museum of Glass.*

1

EGYPTIAN MOSAIC

AND

ROMAN MILLEFIORI

GLASS PAPERWEIGHTS have their genesis deep in the matrix of history.

As a starting point the Eighteenth Dynasty of the New Kingdom in Egypt will serve, partly because it is a convenient marker in the history of glass but mainly because it is the ultimate source of those elements which three thousand years later would become paperweight-making.[1] These basic precursive elements include the glass bead, the glass rod, and the glass and millefiori cane mosaic. These elements intermingle in the history of early glass as they do later in paperweight-making, forming mixed techniques.

Before the Eighteenth Dynasty, that is before 1570 B.C. and back as far as the fourth millenium, glass usage seems to have been confined to the making of beads and other ornaments and to the glazing of tiles and stones. No vessels are known to have been made of glass. Beginning early in the Eighteenth Dynasty new possibilities of three-dimensional use for glass were exploited in the first hollow ware, vessels derived from stone and ceramic models and formed about a core mold of sand or clay. The point about these sand-core vessels is that the predominantly opaque glass (usually a dark blue) was decorated by trailing or festooning threads of glass of other colors (usually yellow or light blue).[2] The glass was then combed with a sharp instrument to achieve zigzag, looped, or feathery effects.[3] These designs illustrate a new variety and flexibility of glass decorative practice, and some of them have spirally trailed rims and panels of diagonally inclined color that strongly suggest in appearance, though not in technique, filigree and latticinio effects that were to become, many centuries later, staples of paperweight design.[4] Occasionally, vessels are found with preformed mosaic elements.[5]

A more direct antecedent is the glass rod itself. Glass rods were made in Thebes dating from the Eighteenth Dynasty and are thought to have been in use long before, along with glass blanks (blocks, bricks), in trade among glassmakers as basic units of manufacture.[6] Glass rods were to become the basic unit of paperweight design-making, but in ancient Egypt they were used for making beads. Sometimes they were simply heated, and drops snipped off, which became beads;[7] sometimes they served as the core about which other threads were twisted in rudimentary filigree fashion. In the early years of the New Kingdom there was inventiveness in bead construction with simple, effective color combinations. Another paperweight rod prototype is a pierced black rod with an opaque white spiral band dating from the thirteenth century B.C., probably from Mesopotamia or Persia. It was used as a door decoration and is easily recognizable as a filigree rod.[8]

The glass rod as an item of trade and as isolate decoration is simple enough, and easy to visualize. What is more difficult is the intricate and developing function of the glass rod during the Egyptian centuries as a raw material and tool for fashioning increasingly intricate designs in beads, and in the fused mosaic plaques of the second and first centuries B.C. and the first century A.D., that period conveniently known as the Roman period from the domination involved, but whose glass heritage centered in Egyptian Alexandria and was influenced by Syrian and eastern Mediterranean production and Hellenistic style.

Mosaic plaques were a development of the New Kingdom cloisonné mosaics,[9] with the metal cloisonné stripping replaced by glass stripping. Glass formerly separated by metal was now fused to glass,[10] a process which simplified construction and created material homogeneity of method and texture. Colored glass rods, easy to hold, easy to draw a thread line from, easy to extend and slice, must have played an important role in mosaic construction, a role roughly equivalent to the combined roles of tubes and brushes in painting. Canes also played an important part. To quote Ray Winfield Smith, "The essential feature of the best Alexandrian fused mosaic plaques in the first century B.C. is their microscopic fineness. A 'cane' was laboriously prepared by successively adding molten elements, apparently often preformed in a mold, to form the desired design. The artisan then pulled out the hot canes as one would do with taffy candy, reducing the cross-section to the desired small scale. Slices were then cut from these reduced canes for use in adorning jewel caskets, furniture, etc."[11] Seen in their original form before slicing, mosaic canes are often several inches long, that is, they extend deep behind the frontal plane, the design running all the way through. And it is this running all the way through that distinguishes true millefiori cane from the shallower marvering in of threads in the New Kingdom sand-core vessels. Mosaic colors were chiefly the primaries plus green, black, and white, with the background color usually blue and the glass usually opaque or slightly translucent, though later background glass was more transparent.[12] To the mosaic glass artist, Proculus of Perinthus, the Alexandrian merchants erected a statue.[13]

The term "millefiori," an Italian nineteenth-century term coined from *mille* (thousand) and *fiori* (flowers), refers to the visual effect created by closely assembled canes and their subdivisions (rods) of different colors or patterns. However, its retroactive usage here follows historical precedent and is essential to the understanding of paperweight elements and techniques which stem from the sources and times I have indicated. Practically speaking, the term "millefiori" is too literal, for there is no such thing as glass simulating a thousand flowers. Neuburg says, "The term millefiori glass can only be used in its proper sense when a large number of tiny flowers—even if not literally a thousand—completely or almost completely occupies the surface of the glass."[14] Actually, what millefiori refers to is not literal representations of flowers but the final visual result of a process that begins with the bundling together, like a fasces, of various colored glass rods which, after being fused together to form canes, pulled out, sliced, and the slices arranged close together in an overall pattern, give the effect of a flower bed or a field strewn with flowers.

Apart from its limited use in beads and mosaic,[15] the chief and most striking use of millefiori is found in the wonderful glass bowls, made first in Alexandria in the second century B.C., undoubtedly with an eye to the tremendously expanding glass market of the Roman period, and later in Rome itself by natives and imported Alexandrian glassmen, continuing through the first century A.D.[16] They were made of slices of millefiori cane, arranged either on a flat clay support or in a mold, and while ductile, pressed (in a mold) not blown (Figs. 1, 2). Knowledge of these bowls, substantiated by archeological finds, indicates that they were popular in western Roman provinces, and used in such far-removed places as Luxemburg and Scandinavia. The Luxemburg find, a ribbed bowl, had been placed in a bronze vase enclosed in a ceramic container.[17]

At first glance, and compared to the extraordinary delicacy of some of the fused mosaics, these millefiori bowls appear primitive and crude. However, the impact of their simple designs repeated over the entire surface is ample justification for their creation. They are effective in the same way Scotch plaids and French checkered tablecloths are effective, and possess, in addition, a quality of variation within uniformity that is due to the difficulty encountered in their making. A color-texture they get from the glass and the polishing makes them appear, to modern eyes at least, objects of great dash and charm. Some of the designs combining several different millefiori elements are as bold as the background of a Matisse painting, and others as timid as faded calico. In one dish from Alexandria a checkerboard pattern alternates millefiori canes of which every other one is a butterfly. The simple millefiori cane patterns of these bowls include the whorl [1]; the star [2]; the lozenge, which shows several variations [3]; the single rod seen obliquely and in profusion (the forerunner of the carpet ground) [4]; and the cane bundle sliced longitudinally [5]. Some bowls show the diaper pattern [6], and some contain reticuli stripes. One example in the Boston Museum of Fine Arts has lozenges of goldstone submerged in the background glass between other elements.[18] Others contain shattered gold foil. Background colors of the millefiori bowls include lilac,

[1]

[2]

[3]   [4]   [5]   [6]

purple, various shades of blue and green, blue-green, while cane colors include amber, manganese red, and the other colors mentioned. These bowls generally have spiral twist rims, and one bowl includes human portrait canes.

Near relations to the millefiori bowls are the color-band bowls and vessels; the colored loopings of some of these resemble marbrie paperweights, and of others, Victorian slag glass. In the splashed ware there are the appearance and indeed the method of making the paperweight mottled grounds, as well as the late nineteenth-century art glass confusingly called murrhine.[19]

Conclusions

It would be pure nonsense to conclude that any of the objects and methods discussed in this chapter were attempts by ancient glassmakers toward the making of paperweights. They were not. The nineteenth-century paperweight was an unpremeditated end result of a long historical series of contests with the basic technical elements discussed in this chapter. Half a millenium devoid of such glass was to elapse before a revival of interest in these ancient possibilities took place, and half as long again before the possibilities were sublimated in paperweights.

The important thing is not the time connection—at best a chain with most of the links missing—but the design connection. For, extraordinary as it may appear upon first confrontation, the imprint of the design technique of Victorian paperweights, the brand, so to speak of the design itself, is Egypto-Roman. It is not Victorian and bears only a slight ephemeral relationship to other Victorian arts and crafts. Except for the device of the magnifying glass crown above the motif, whatever is Victorian about paperweights is cultural and belongs to cultural history, not to design. Paperweight design is ancient, formal, and symbolic, the end result of ancient possibilities. It required the Renaissance to refocus attention upon these ancient possibilities. That focus and its results are the subject of the next chapter.

N O T E S

[1] Eighteenth Dynasty (1570 B.C.–1349 B.C.); New Kingdom (1570 B.C.–1086 B.C.).

[2] Haynes E. Barrington, *Glass*, Penguin A 166, 1948, p. 19.

[3] Ray Winfield Smith, *Glass from the Ancient World*, Corning, New York, 1957, p. 14.

[4] They were incorporated flush into the surface on a marver, that is to say, marvered in.

[5] Smith, p. 19.

[6] Frederic Neuburg, *Glass in Antiquity*, London, 1949, p. 14.

[7] Frederic Neuburg, *Ancient Glass*, Toronto, 1962, p. 18.

[8] Ray Winfield Smith, *Glass from the Ancient World*, Corning, 1957, item 47, p. 37. ill.

[9] *Ibid.*, p. 47.

[10] Smith (p. 47) says fusion had already been done in the fourth century B.C.

[11] Smith, p. 47. How often have we read this description of cane making in connection with paperweight canes!

[12] In a sense, the history of glass has been the history of progression from opacity to transparency. In general, full transparency coincided with thin walls made possible by glass blowing.

[13] Gardner Teall, "The Glass of a Thousand Flowers," *House & Garden*, Jan., 1913, p. 21.

[14] Frederic Neuburg, *Glass in Antiquity*, London, 1949, p. 14.

[15] Glass historians and specialists are very careful to distinguish among beads and among mosaics, labeling them rigidly according to method of construction. A bead that to the casual glance may appear to be millefiori may actually be an eye, Aggry, a chevron or mosaic bead, according to how it was made.

[16] Alexandria founded by Alexander the Great, 331 B.C. Conquest of Alexandria by Rome 30 B.C. After this time Alexandrian glass reached Rome in quantity. Honey (p. 24) says that part of Augustus' conquest of Egypt was paid in glass.

[17] Ray Winfield Smith, *Glass from the Ancient World,* Corning, 1957, p. 81.

[18] Goldstone too was to enjoy a revival in Venice, indeed to become, along with filigree, a trademark of Venetian work.

[19] Confusingly, because the ancient murrhine were either of stone or of glass in imitation of stone, and were more likely to have resembled madrepore or chalcedony, or the nineteenth-century agata or slag than splashed ware. Honey (p. 22) says it is possible that the Alexandrian-Roman bowls were imitations of the fabled murrhine.

2

THE PART
PLAYED BY VENICE

ACCOUNTS OF GLASSMAKING contemporary to the Venetian Renaissance leave
little doubt as to the revival of the millefiori technique. In his *De Situ Urbis
Venetae,* written about 1495, Marc Antonio Sabellico, the learned librarian of
St. Marks', speaks of the multifarious glass of the period. "A famous invention
first proved that glass might feign the whiteness of crystal, soon as the wits of
men are active and not slothful in adding something to inventions, they began to
turn the materials into various colours and numberless forms. . . . there is no
kind of precious stone which cannot be imitated by the industry of the glassworkers, a sweet contest of nature and of man . . . But, consider to whom did it
first occur to include in a little ball all the sorts of flowers which clothe the
meadows in spring. Yet these things have been under the eyes of all nations as
articles of export . . . Nor has invention been confined to one house or one
family, the street glows for the most part with furnaces of this kind."[1] Perrot
says, "The word 'ball' might refer to a type similar to the late 15th century
enameled *millefiori* globe at the Sigmaringen Museum, Germany, or it could be
translated as 'column' and refer to the *millefiori* canes themselves."[2] Sabellico's
allusion to Venetian glass as being "under the eyes of all nations as articles of
export" indicates clearly the difficulties in attempting to attribute specific
examples to Venice, a difficulty compounded in the sixteenth century by the
exodus of Venetian glassmakers to other parts of Europe—which all enticements
and even the threat of death could not stop—and the spread of the *façon de
Venise.*

   The glass literature of the nineteenth and twentieth centuries abounds in
casual, assumptive, passing references to the revival of the ancient millefiori
techniques in Venice during the Renaissance, and a very few books such as
Schmidt's *Das Glas* even illustrate millefiori vessels said to be Venetian work
of about 1500.[3] Yet, in recent years glass experts have begun to question these
assumptions and to update some of the supposed Renaissance pieces, as, for
example, the ewer at the Victoria and Albert Museum, which Honey in 1946
suggested was "probably of much later date," without specifying how much

later.[4] The ewer was acquired in 1855 from the Bernal Collection, which contained many fine Venetian glasses whose authenticity is unquestioned. In a letter to me about this ewer, Robert J. Charleston, Keeper of Ceramics and Glass at the Victoria and Albert, does not exclude the possibility of its being a Victorian copy.[5] Three other millefiori examples from the Bernal and Soulages Collections are, Charleston says, "without provenance."[6] In his recent book, Vavra illustrates in color, without dating, a millefiori vessel with bronze bands and decor.[7] In other words, very few examples of authenticated Venetian Renaissance millefiori exist for study, and most early millefiori now appears to date from the seventeenth and eighteenth centuries. The term, "millefiori," meaning thousand flowers, appears first not during the Renaissance, as has been thought, but in early nineteenth-century Germany and, according to the shorter *Oxford Dictionary,* in the English language in 1849, where Apsley Pellatt uses it in his *Curiosities of Glass-Making*, dated that year.[8]

While it is certainly to be hoped that the historical chronology of glass millefiori will eventually be filled in by the experts, in a larger sense it seems appropriate to suggest that from Roman times onward representation of flowers in one medium or another never left the cultural scene. One has only to note the use of the term "millefleurs" in connection with tapestries, or to recall the lovely floral embellishments of the medieval manuscripts, of Romanesque and Gothic architecture. In such a contextual inheritance it is not illogical to suggest that glass millefiori objects of one sort or another may have been made from time to time since the early Renaissance.[9]

Latticinio and Aventurine, Fruits, and Flowers

Quite the opposite situation exists with regard to the other component parts of what were one day to be glass paperweights, for if old millefiori from Venice is scarce, old latticinio, the hallmark of sixteenth and seventeenth-century Venetian glass, is plentiful. The term comes from *latte*, the Italian for milk. Opaque white glass, or milk glass as we know it today, was called *vetro biancho de smalto* by the old writers, and was made from oxide of tin (*calcina di stagno*).[10] In its threaded form, milk glass was so called according to the way it was arranged and the effect created. Latticinio (or latticino) refers to glass produced with the aid of a mold vertically lined with evenly spaced rods of opaque white glass which are then fused to a gather of clear glass blown into the mold. The result could then be simply reblown to the desired shape, twisted to create a spiral effect, or blown into another mold lined with glass rods of another color or an opposing spiral. In his *Guide du Verrier* of 1868, Bontemps devotes a chapter to the procedures for making these threaded glass twists which in France are called *verres filigranes,* or filigree glass. Too lengthy to discuss here, the procedures involve a predetermination of pattern in the spacing of opaque white and clear glass rods within the molds. Bontemps' explanations should be read by anyone mystified by the twists and torsades found in glass paperweights of the

Classic period. Haynes compiled a pictorial glossary of the many types of spiral twists found in the stems of drinking glasses that can serve equally well in defining the various forms of the paperweight torsades.[11] By the late sixteenth century latticinio glass was already being made in Silesia, Bohemia, and Saxony, and though Venetian production continued into the eighteenth century, when Giuseppe Briati (died 1772)[12] specialized in it, Venetian dominance in history and glass was already on the wane. By 1773 there were only 383 glass artisans left in Murano.[13] By 1800 the art of making latticinio had almost died out, and it remained for Pietro Bigaglia to try to reestablish it.

Aventurine (*avventurina*) was a secret of the Miotti family from about 1700, so carefully guarded that the formula died with the family and was only rediscovered after many experiments in the nineteenth century by Dal Mistro Barbaria & Co. and Bigaglia.[14] The term "aventurine" is derived from the Italian *avventura*, implying the mystery or chance (accident) provided in an adventure. Aventurine was rediscovered by chance. Gasparetto says of it, "Avventurina: this enamel of the gracious feminine gender, which recalls the capricious ladies of Goldoni's comedies, has all the bizarre traits of the gentle sex, in fact, it sometimes happens that despite careful preparation of all the ingredients, the composition fails."[15] The less mysterious component of aventurine glass is the relatively opaque glass itself, in which are interspersed small particles of copper, crystallized in the form of flat segments of a regular octohedron, which give to the glass its soft sparkle.[16] Specimens of the glass show enough variation to warrant speculation that several formulas may have been successful. In one such, Fremy and Clemandot succeeded with a recipe that called for a mixture of three hundred parts pounded glass, forty parts copper scales, and eighty parts iron scales, cooked for twelve hours and then slowly cooled.[17] Aventurine glass was to be a prominent element of Venetian paperweights of the nineteenth century, notably those of Bigaglia, where it shows as a sparkling coppery gold mixture referred to colloquially as goldstone, whose texture resembles maple syrup laced with fine golden sand. Goldstone, conspicuously absent from Bohemian paperweights and in this coppery tone from French weights, travels to America, perhaps via Nicholas Lutz and certainly by importers of glass rods, to show up most notably at Sandwich and in some of the later art glass. In French paperweights, especially from St. Louis (where Lutz worked), it shows up as the softly sparkling green glass ground of a few rare flower weights, and in sparsely distributed copper or iron flakes found on the yellow ribbons of a very few crown weights. It should be added that aventurine goldstone has been used continuously in Venice and Murano, and appears as a design element in many paperweights being made there today.

From the mid-eighteenth century realistic glass flowers and fruits have been a noticeable if not major Venetian product. Mariacher illustrates in color a spectacular chandelier of the Rococo period with carnations and other flowers which rival the finest from Meissen, and which are unequaled in paperweight flower work until we come to the rare rose weights of late nineteenth-century France and Mt. Washington.[18] A group of *70 fruitti di diverse sorte,* now in the

Museo Vetrario, Murano, is listed in an inventory of Ettore Bigaglia, dated 1714.[19] One wonders if these blown Venetian fruits were seen by the fruit-blowers at the New England Glass Company, whose work in turn inspired the Peachblow of Hobbs, Brockunier and others?

Nineteenth-century Venetian Millefiori Other than Paperweights

It has been noted that Venetian glass, like Venice itself in 1800, was at a low ebb. The Venetian *cristallo,* for all its boasts of clarity and its supremacy for a time over the common glass of northern Europe, was still only a soda-lime glass, readily fusible and easy to manipulate, but also thin, too brittle to engrave, and never without a slight yellowish, brownish, or even a blackish cast. Northern Europe had long since appropriated the *façon de Venise,* and this in turn had given way to the new *façon de Bohême.* And from England in the 1670's had come lead glass, the clearest of all glass, which in its turn had undercut the Bohemian and would soon adapt the *façon de Bohême* to its own purposes.

Pietro Bigaglia came from a long line of glass craftsmen. As early as 1674 the Bigaglias had three workshops, run by the brothers Ettore, Marino, and Bernadino Bigaglia, the last being called "illustrious maker of mirrors." The former virtual Venetian monopoly in mirror-making had been broken by the French in the time of Louis XIV, but Pietro Bigaglia made mirrors in addition to white and colored glass lamps, round window panes decorated with latticinio, and the latticinio and aventurine glass which he revived in an attempt to stimulate the lagging Venetian industry.[20] In 1864 Bigaglia's work was shown in the first big exhibit of Venetian and Muranese glassmakers in the Murano Glass Museum.[21] Another exhibitor was G. B. Franchini whose portrait canes appear in Venetian paperweights.

The millefiori revival continued late into the nineteenth century in the work of Salviati & Company, founded in 1864, and its offshoot, the Venezia-Murano Company formed about 1866. In this year we find the *Art Journal* striking a cautionary note:

> It is necessary to warn collectors that many of the modern productions of Salviati are selling as veritable antiques. Those who are not experienced connoisseurs may be easily deceived, for the imitations—or rather copies —cannot be at once distinguished from the old. They are as light and as soft to the touch; the semi-transparency has been preserved, the colours are often brilliant, and the designs are, in nearly all instances, after veritable models.[22]

The millefiori of Salviati and Venezia-Murano stood in contrast to other Venetian work, for in his report on the Paris Exposition of 1878, Colné says, "The colors shown by the Italians, with a few exceptions are so dull and wanting in the brilliancy of other nations, that the difference becomes apparent on comparison. The wares are blown very badly and indicate the work of artisans who are not skilled in their art."[23] To this exposition the Venezia-Murano Company sent "vases in millefiori, showing the patterns in sections at the sides."[24]

James Jackson Jarves, the son of Deming Jarves of Sandwich and a collector and writer on art, visited Murano in 1881 or 1882 and brought back millefiori bowls of the Venezia-Murano Company, which he gave to The Metropolitan Museum of Art in New York (Fig. 3). The walls of these bowls are thicker than the walls of the old Roman millefiori, the surface of the glass duller, and the patterns in most instances are jazzier. They would not deceive the student today as they did the writer in the *Art Journal* of 1866. Nevertheless, in their own terms they are exciting creations and some of them are signed with a cane [7], while others contain mosaic heads. Jarves writes, "The chief specialty of the Venezia-Murano Company is their successful reproductions of the famous antique murrhine glass, mentioned by Pliny, in imitation of fluor-spars, gems, and precious stones of transparent colors, in the form of cut and polished cups, bowls, and dishes."[25] Interestingly enough, Jarves' belief in Renaissance millefiori was not shaken by these late nineteenth-century examples. He writes:

[7]

> In the 15th century, or perhaps earlier, began the attempts to revive the varieties of the old Roman and Etruscan mosaic glass, or that known as millefiori, or thousand flowers, which is made by the combinations of canne, or rods, in fusion and union of colors in divers patterns. . . . The old Venetians were successful but not to the extent of quite equalling the taste and beauty displayed by the Romans in this line of art.[26]

The Origins of Millefiori Paperweights

Inherent in the successive revivals of the ancient millefiori is the more obscure question of when the first paperweight was made. A discussion of this matter always tends to begin with the quotation from Sabellico given at the beginning of this chapter: "But consider to whom it did first occur to include in a little ball all the sorts of flowers which clothe the meadows in spring." This millefiori ball (or column) obviously must have been made before the 1490's, though it is hardly likely it was a paperweight. A later reference appears in a letter dated December 25, 1756, written from Rome by the Abbé Barthélemy (1716-95) to the Comte de Caylus: "I am especially pleased with a little ball of a pale yellow color, with clusters of white enamel ranged inside perpendicularly around the circumference."[27] Here we have what sounds like the first crown paperweight, though we are not told the origin of the object or its intended use. Probably it was a mere bauble. The spherical glass shape which was to suggest the inclusion of Sabellico's millefiori, Barthélemy's latticinio, and the somewhat modified shape for use as a paperweight, not to mention a hand cooler, may have had a

Fig. 3. Two millefiori bowls, Venetian, 19th century. *Courtesy The Metropolitan Museum of Art, gift of James Jackson Jarves, 1881.*

Roman origin. In an interesting old book, *Glass in the Old World* by M. A. Wallace-Dunlop, I came across the following description:

> Roman ladies used glass balls to cool and whiten their hands; as the glass grew heated, they changed the ball. The poet Propertius, 51 B.C., describes "Cynthia demanding the present of a peacock feather, fan, and cooling balls for her hands." An alabaster urn, which was found in Rome, contained sixty glass balls, which gave rise to many discussions as to their probable use; they were most likely the cooling balls of a Roman belle. The female figure found on an amphora found at Nola, apparently throwing coloured balls in the air, is most likely playing with her own cooling balls, and not with worsted as has been suggested.[28]

This charming book was written sometime in the late nineteenth century, and it is both amusing and sad that the author was apparently unaware of the speculations of Minutoli, whom she mentions several times, that the ancient (and probably solid) glass spheres in his famous collection were used to cool people's hands. Minutoli acquired these spheres in Italy where they had been found in various archeological sites. They were sold with his collection in Cologne in 1875. The information on Minutoli was given me in a letter from Ray Winfield Smith, who writes further that the 1875 catalogue of Minutoli's collection has no plates. "However, there is a section of items labeled 'Ancient Glass Spheres (*Glaskugeln*).' These may well be solid, because one of them is described as 'drilled through (*gebohrte*).' Another *kugel* is listed with a diameter of 7.5 centimeters."[29] Whatever their beginnings, like many other things, paperweights were simply an old form adapted to a new use.

Nineteenth-century Venetian Millefiori Paperweights

The first Venetian paperweights are generally considered to have been of the type called the Venetian ball, described by Pellatt as a "collection of waste pieces of filigree glass conglomerated together, without regular design: this is packed into a pocket of transparent glass, which is adhesively collapsed upon the interior mass by sucking up, producing outward pressure of the atmosphere."[30] Such a process seems to me to fit Pellatt's own cameo incrustation process but not the Venetian ball, which appears to be nothing more than an aspic of waste filigree, aventurine, and canes picked up with a gather of clear glass, covered with a thin glass coating and then marvered. The rarest and perhaps earliest examples (some dated 1845) are cylindrical and cubical, the others shaped like most paperweights and flat on the bottom. They are nothing more than scrambled weights. The glass is inferior, quite light (being soda-lime glass) and rough on the outside, and the jumble of rats and snails and puppy dogs' tails inside is usually not attractive. Yet the Venetian ball or scrambled weight accounts for nearly all Venetian paperweights.

That the first examples may have been made about 1843 is indicated in the workmanship of weights dated from 1845 through 1847, which show a definite improvement year by year. Weights signed PB, by Pietro Bigaglia, including one cube weight, are dated from 1845 through 1847, though it is not possible to tell if he was the first Venetian to make weights. Other examples are dated through 1852 and signed F or GBF, presumably for G. B. Franchini (who made mosaic silhouettes and included some of them in paperweights), FC, B, R, CW, MR, and AC. Some weights are dated 1845 in several places, and at least one is dated both 1845 and 1847. This weight, which also contains silhouettes, has one cane inscribed *IX Congresso Degli Scienziati in Venezia 47.* This refers to the last of a series of science meetings held in Venice in 1847 and attended by a record number of 1778 scientists.[31] Another weight dated 1846 has a central cane bearing the initials FI (for Ferdinand Imperator) and the insignia of the Austrian Emperor Ferdinand (1835-48). This weight, which remained in the family of the Emperor until recently, is a reminder that the former Republic of Venice was for a time a part of the Austrian Empire.

Venetian canes of the 1840's show a limited variety of designs based on plain tubes, crimped tubes, star rods, and cogs. Only the cane composed of a circle of hair-thin rods appears to derive from Roman millefiori; the others may be taken from Renaissance or Bohemian millefiori of the late 1830's, as will be seen in the next chapter. A refinement of color in glass has never been a Venetian strong point, and the millefiori canes are no exception—the greens, reds, and blues are mostly hard and lifeless, and the chrome yellow is particularly unattractive. There is a great variety of silhouette canes including a running figure similar to the St. Louis devil; a Negro with black face, yellow eyes and hair, dressed in striped pantaloons; a crouching dog; a horse; a white goat; a pelican; two birds; a chessboard; a rose bush; the railway causeway leading to Venice (built in 1846 and appearing in a paperweight dated 1847); a gondola floating on water with one or two gondoliers; what appears to be the prototype for the Clichy rose; a number of bold designs based on stars and spokes; designs based on military medals; and, finally, the portrait canes, usually of women, said to have been made by Bigaglia and G. B. Franchini. These last are somewhat cruder than the later Franchini and Moretti portrait rods of Garibaldi, La Marmora, Cavour, and others dating from 1869, which are thought to have been constructed from a fusion of rods containing individual facial features.[32] The bottom of one gondola cane is dated 1846. The finest millefiori canes appear in a plaque bearing Franchini's initials and dated 1846, and it is likely that he made as many of the better scrambled weights as Bigaglia (Col. Fig. 1).

Pietro Bigaglia's paperweights were exhibited at the Exhibition of Austrian Industry in Vienna, May, 1845, where they were noticed and briefly described by Eugène Péligot, professor at the Conservatoire des Arts et Métiers in Paris, who was sent by the Paris Chamber of Commerce (Fig. 4). And it is interesting to note that in 1851 Bigaglia was listed in the Austrian section at the Great Exhibition in London, Venice being still part of Austria-Hungary until it was reunited with the Kingdom of Italy in 1866.

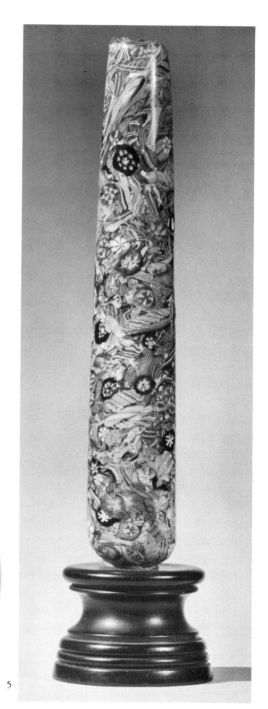

4   5

Fig. 4. Scrambled weight signed "P.B.," 1845. *Courtesy Sotheby & Co.*

Fig. 5. Scrambled millefiori shaft, Venetian-Murano 19th century. *Courtesy The Metropolitan Museum of Art, gift of Henry G. Marquand, 1883.*

A crown paperweight in the Bergstrom Museum is possibly Venetian of this period. If it is, it is the finest Venetian weight ever made. Not only is it well done, but the latticinio (filigree) form suggests the ball referred to by the Abbé Barthélemy and is characteristic of the Venetian latticinio idiom.

Related Millefiori Items

Other millefiori work of the period comprises a snuff box (F. C. 1846); a cane handle dated 1847; a multiple desk series of joined trays with jars and other receptacles; several paper knives; a set of six dessert knives, forks, and spoons; and a number of small amphora-shaped scent bottles with chained caps. These items contain portrait and date canes in addition to millefiori, filigree, and aventurine (Fig. 5).

Conclusions

Nineteenth-century Venetian millefiori paperweight work probably began about 1843 and ceased in 1852, showing some improvement over this decade, though even the best of it was crude in comparison with contemporary French and Bohemian work. It seems never to have occurred to Franchini, Bigaglia, and the others that the chief feature that distinguishes the paperweight form from other millefiori work should be the magnifying crown of clear glass over the inner material, which brings it into focus and lends it mystery. In Venetian scrambled weights the soda-lime glass is tinted and unclear, though sometimes it appears watery wet, and the impromptu motif is set too close to the rough, mottled surface. This very neglect of the surface shows that the Venetians did not understand the paperweight effect and were merely concocting in a new shape what they had used in making up vessels. On this ground alone one can discredit them with the invention of the Classic paperweight. Though the revival of the millefiori technique undoubtedly belongs to the Venetian Renaissance or the following two centuries, there is no certainty that the Venetian paperweights of the 1840's were the first paperweights made. On the contrary, evidence presented in the next chapter will show that Bohemian millefiori work was being carried on about 1835 and that Bohemian paperweights were coeval with and far superior to their Venetian counterparts.

NOTES

[1] Translation used by Paul Perrot, *Three Centuries of Venetian Glass,* Corning, New York, 1958, p. 17.

[2] *Ibid.*

[3] R. Schmidt, *Das Glas,* Berlin & Leipzig (2nd ed., 1922), figs. 51, 54.

[4] W. B. Honey, *Glass: A Handbook,* Victoria and Albert Museum, 1946, p. 57.

[5] Letter to me dated May 4, 1966. Charleston says of the 1855 acquisition, "This is a fairly early date to be thinking of contemporary Venetian copies, although such a possibility is by no means excluded merely on the grounds of date."

[6] *Ibid.* He refers to Bernal collection Nos. 1910 and A-1855, & Soulages collection No. 5518-1859.

[7] Jaroslav R. Vavra, *5000 Years of Glassmaking,* Prague, 1954, col. plate **XXVIII**.

[8] Letter from Paul Perrot, April 7, 1966, who received corroboration in correspondence with Astone Gasparetto.

[9] I am indebted for this suggestion to James Reeve, Curator of American Art, The Toledo (Ohio) Museum of Art.

[10] Edward Dillon, *Glass,* New York, 1905, p. 204.

[11] E. Barrington Haynes, *Glass,* London, 1948, *et seq.,* Plates 56, 57 in the 1948 Penguin edition; figs. 86, 87 in the 1964 edition.

[12] Honey, *op. cit.,* pp. 59, 64.

[13] Astone Gasparetto, *Il Vetro di Murano,* 1958, p. 131.

[14] *Ibid.,* p. 215.

[15] *Ibid.* Translation by Louis Biancolli.

[16] Charles Tomlinson, ed., *The Cyclopedia of Useful Arts and Manufactures,* New York, 1854, vol. 1.

[17] *Ibid.*

[18] Giovanni Mariacher, *L'Arte del Vetro,* Verona, 1954, plates 69, 78.

[19] Gudmond Boesen, *Venetian Glass at Rosenborg Castle,* Copenhagen, 1960.

[20] Gasparetto, *op. cit.,* pp. 131, 158, 171. Translation by Louis Biancolli.

[21] *Ibid.,* p. 134.

[22] *Art Journal,* vol. 28, 1866, p. 290.

[23] Colné, *U.S. Commission Reports,* vol. 3, 1878, p. 304.

[24] *Ibid.,* p. 305.

[25] James Jackson Jarves, "Ancient & Modern Venetian Glass of Murano," *Harper's New Monthly Magazine,* 1882, vol. 64, p. 183. According to Oliver, however (See Andrew Oliver, Jr., "Late Hellenistic Glass in the Metropolitan Museum," *Journal of Glass Studies,* 1967, p. 29), Gasparetto believes the VM monogram stands for Vincenzo Moretti.

[26] *Ibid.,* p. 184.

[27] A. Sauzay, *Wonders of Glass-Making in All Ages,* New York, 1885, p. 219. Sauzay uses the quote to show that the Venetians may not have invented filigree glass.

[28] M. A. Wallace-Dunlop, *Glass in the Old World,* London, New York, n.d., p. 36

[29] Letter to me from Ray Winfield Smith, dated May 15, 1966.

[30] Apsley Pellatt, *Curiosities of Glass-Making,* 1849, pp. 109, 110.

[31] Information obtained from the Italian Consulate in New York.

[32] Albert Christian Revi, "Miniature Portraits in Glass Rods," *The Glass Industry,* June, 1957.

3

BOHEMIAN-SILESIAN MILLEFIORI
AND PAPERWEIGHTS

Bohemian Glass

GLASS WAS MADE IN BOHEMIA from at least the fourteenth century, and geography helps explain its success—a country bordered by mountains whose forest cover provided resinous pine for fuel, whose limestone provided the lime, and whose granite walls and torrents provided the quartz veins and pebbles for the glass itself. From the great Carpathian forests of nearby Hungary came the potash washed down from trees that had been set afire as they stood. By the sixteenth century there were thirty-four glassworks.[1] Once the Venetian monopoly was broken and the *façon de Venise* latticinio had run its course in the Netherlands and Germany, the thick, hard, engraved glass of the eighteenth-century Baroque and Rococo came into its own. Yet, the competition from the English lead glass, from the porcelain of Wedgwood, Vienna, and Meissen, and from the antiquated nature of the Bohemian glass industry itself, forced the development of new forms. By 1725 gold and silver foil were being enclosed in a glass sandwich of two walls; by 1800 the Bohemians had come up with "lithalyn" as a reply to the Wedgwood basalt, and with facet-cutting of glass, finally augmented by overlay.

The Bohemian introduction of incrustation, or the enclosure of sulphides in glass, is discussed in Chapter Seventeen, but we must now consider Bohemia's rightful place in the history of millefiori paperweights. For our purposes, it begins in Braunschweig (Brunswick), Germany, in 1786, with the suggestion by a man named Brückmann of a method for reproducing Roman millefiori.[2] As so often happens with suggestions, Brückmann's appears to have been tabled for nearly half a century until 1833. In that year in Silesia, a Dr. W. E. Fuss, with the support of the Prussian authorities, succeeded in making millefiori at the Hoffnungstal works in the Silesian Reisengebirge. He exhibited this millefiori at his home near Magdeburg and later showed more of it in Mainz in 1842.[3] His first attempts included such objects as small flower vases, a milk jug, drinking glasses, sword hilts, and decorative stones framed in precious metal. Prices

24

were listed for a silver-plated set of tableware with millefiori handles, a bracelet, brooch, and pair of earrings. Millefiori, now an important medium for small objects such as small bottles, ornaments, buttons, and the like, was produced in the neighborhood of Gablonz in northern Bohemia. A recipe book of F. Egermann giving various color combinations for mosaic and millefiori glass is dated 20 October, 1837, and was found at the Zenker works in the Antoniwald.[4]

In 1839 the Association for the Encouragement of Industries in Prussia organized a prizewinning contest for Venetian type glass. The prize was won by Franz Pohl (1813-84) of the Josephine works, whose submission included as test pieces two cups (glasses) and one small bowl, made with the assistance of the glassmaker Alwin Seidel, which were heavier than the best Venetian work. Pazaurek illustrates Pohl's sketches of latticinio technique and also three latticinio tumblers and a plate from the Josephine works about 1845.[5] By 1844 both the Karlsthal and Josephine works were listing millefiori in their catalogues. And Reis adds the factory of Neuwelt.[6] The author is indebted to The Metropolitan Museum of Art for the opportunity to study a millefiori bottle with stopper attributed to the workshop of F. Pohl about 1835-40 in Karlsthal in the Silesian Riesengebirge (Fig. 6). The glass is considerably thicker than Venetian work. The scrambled millefiori canes in a rather dead cobalt blue, soft reds, pinks, and pale yellow are mostly composed of petal-shaped rods circled about a similar central rod. They are interspersed with rather heavy long strips and tubes of opaque white glass and filigree, with a faintly yellowish cast to the amalgamating glass. The illustration of this bottle should be studied with care, because it shows so unmistakably the type of cane that with some variation appears in nearly all Bohemian-Silesian paperweights.

Further evidences of Bohemian-Silesian millefiori activity comes via Minutoli. Lt. Gen. Heinrich von Minutoli was an archeologist and an early student of ancient glass, particularly millefiori, and the first to publish a treatise (1836) with chemical analyses. Smith says that he was "instrumental in arranging for the production by Silesian factories of modern millefiori."[7] Minutoli's own vast collection included much ancient millefiori and was "the point of departure for the rediscovery of the lost technique which at first was employed by several Silesian glass factories, and then found further expansion in other countries."[8]

In 1843 M. L. P. Debette made a tour and close study of the glass factories of Bohemia. Of the 67 factories with 30,000 workers then operating, only one (in Neuwelt) made flint (lead) glass. The rest, except for the thirteen factories making window glass which may have used soda, made a lime-potash glass that shows a wide range of formulas. Debette shows fine crystal with a density of 2.892. The silica used was crystalline quartz found mostly as rolled pebbles of the Bohmerwaldgebirge torrents. These were pounded in wooden mortars with heavy pestles, each pestle capable of pounding 90 pounds of quartz in twelve hours. The finest Bohemian crystal contained 100-200 parts pulverized quartz, 10-18 parts quick lime, 8-24 parts carbonate of lime, a trace of arsenious acid and peroxide of manganese, and sometimes cullet. The pine fuel came from the

Bohmerwald and Riesengebirge forests, the tallest trees being cut in summer and floated down the mountain streams or snow slides in winter. When a forest was denuded, the small glassworks moved to a new source of fuel. The melting pots were made of fire clay mixed with dry-pounded quartz or a cement made of old potsherds, and each held 140-220 pounds of glass. In Bohemia the annealing was not done in a "progressive furnace" as it was elsewhere, but the glass object was placed in a crucible covered with sheet iron, and stowed in a quiet corner of the annealing furnace, which was heated by flame from the melting furnace.[9] Debette's fascinating discussion of glass colors, together with a listing of the chemical ingredients of each, includes those colors we find in Bohemian paperweights. His warnings are interesting. Too much potash, he says, makes a greenish tint, too much manganese a bluish tint which sunlight makes violet, too much lime shows up milky, too much charcoal turns glass a topaz yellow to purple.

Bohemian-Silesian Millefiori Paperweights

The question of when millefiori paperweights were first made in Bohemia-Silesia is conjectural, yet, as in the case of Venice, it is related to the overall picture of millefiori production and to dated paperweights. Pazaurek puts the paperweight production of F. Egermann as early as 1845, noting that the millefiori was often combined with enamel painting and foreign inclusions.[10] Presumably this may be a reference to sulphides or medals. In 1843 Debette refers to the recent recovery of the Bohemian art of incrustation. "At present," he says, "they incrust in a great deal of glass, while making it, small objects in white clay, which have, when the glass is finished, a deceptive lustre and appearance of mat silver."[11] So Pazaurek's date of 1845 seems completely reasonable for the incrustation of sulphides in paperweights.

The first dated paperweight does not appear until 1848, yet by this time Bohemian-Silesian paperweight production was on a par with the French and far superior to anything from Venice. Paperweights dated 1848 show a sophistication that must have taken several years to achieve, though, of course, by 1846 there were French models to emulate. In fact, the range of Bohemian paperweight types is proof that either the Bohemians were imitating the French or the French were improving upon the Bohemian, with the latter more likely. For French glass production at this time, particularly that of Baccarat, St. Louis, and Clichy, was characterized by the expropriation of foreign (Bohemian and Venetian) styles which it improved upon while adapting them to its own trade. An unmistakably Bohemian white overlay vase with faceted paperweight base in the Sinclair Collection at the New-York Historical Society bears a label which reads, "Purchased in Paris by a prominent Bostonian in 1847" (Fig. 7). The canes in this weight place it with many other Bohemian weights whose motif is scattered millefiori canes on filigree ground. Aside from the characteristically Bohemian cutting of the overlay vase itself, this paperweight could not possibly have been

Fig. 6. Millefiori bottle with stopper, F. Pohl's workshop (1835–40). *Courtesy The Metropolitan Museum of Art, Musham Collection, Munsey Fund, 1927.*

Fig. 7. Bohemian paperweight vase, c. 1847.
Courtesy The New-York Historical Society.

made in the Venice of 1847—it is simply too well made. Furthermore, the advance in its execution over some of the other Bohemian scattered millefiori indicates progress that must have begun at least as early as 1845, when the first dated Venetian and French weights appeared. Yet, in the light of evidence of millefiori work from Bohemia-Silesia in 1837 or 1839, it seems reasonable to assume a date at least as early as the first paperweights from Venice and France. It seems most likely that the idea for the inclusion of millefiori in paperweights was one of spontaneous generation, occurring practically simultaneously in the three countries which had access to one another's styles and whose products were widely exhibited in Venice, Paris, Vienna, and Berlin.

Paperweight Types and Characteristics

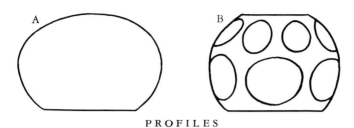

PROFILES

Bohemian profiles show two basic shapes. Shape A is typical of most paper-weights, while Shape B is more compact and higher domed. Bases show a flat rim about a shallow concavity, except in some overlays which are flat bottomed. The lime-potash glass is hard and lighter than lead glass, frequently showing a slight yellowish cast.

Millefiori cane types are relatively simple, as has been stated above, usually consisting of six or more rods about a slightly larger rod. The rods may be shaped like the petals of tiny flowers, or they may be plain or crimped tubes, star-centered or marked with an arrow like Baccarat's. More elaborate double bundles of rods or bundles of rods of alternating colors are also seen, sometimes with the elements so reduced in size as to appear incredibly detailed when actually they are very simple. A rare cane is circled with one or two rows of extremely thin, opaque white or yellow rods, a feature also seen in a few Clichy, St. Louis, and in Chinese weights of the 1930's. Millefiori cane colors cover a range of colors far more extensive and softer than the Venetian, but more limit-ed and less bright and colorful than the French, including wine red and scarlet, pink, cobalt and robin's egg blue, forest green, pale yellow, and occasionally lav-ender, and other pale tints. Greens and reds are frequently rather dense, while the other colors are often applied so thinly as to lack power.

More important are the silhouette canes and the cabbage rose. Silhouette canes include the German or Austrian crowned eagle (longer legged and necked than the American eagle of Sandwich and the New England Glass Company), large laterally striped bee, running white rabbit with pink eye, red rabbit, horse, a dog almost indentical with the St. Louis dog of the 1848 weights, white monkey, and dancing devil. The pink cabbage rose is similar to the cane from Clichy, though the color is less opaque and cooler, and one wonders who bor-rowed the idea from whom, since it also occurs in somewhat more primitive form in Venetian weights. Like the Clichy rose, the Bohemian rose appears frequently, sometimes as the central cane or as an important row in a concentric weight.

The only dated cane known so far shows the date 1848, which is sometimes topped by the lower-case initial "j." For this reason and want of a better, these weights have sometimes been referred to as J-weights. One indication that these paperweights are not likely to be Venetian is that the letter "j" is seldom used in Italian, which substitutes the letter "g" (Fig. 8).

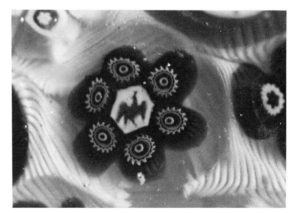

Fig. 8. Bohemian canes. *Courtesy J. P. Boore.*

SCATTERED MILLEFIORI—Referred to as scattered millefiori rather than as spaced millefiori because the canes are almost casually scattered, these comprise most of the Bohemian-Silesian paperweights. The haphazard canes, frequently with silhouettes and dates, appear on white filigree muslin (lace) grounds which they deeply indent. The rather well-done white lace, including fragments of colored spiral, may be given a slightly dirty cast by the lime-potash glass. What we have here is a Baccarat form, but with inadequate spacing between canes. The canes spread slightly at the base but without the contour of French canes (Figs. 9A, 9B). Some weights have vases on top, shaped and cut in Bohemian single and double overlay style, or latticinio in the *façon de Bohême*. Pairs of vases are known.

CONCENTRICS—Very few of these. They are usually enclosed in a basket of staves of one or more colors, the staves being semiopaque tubes compressed so that their tops show a flattened rectangle. Concentrics are likely to feature roses and generally have a Clichy look about them that is not quite Clichy.

SWIRL—At least one example is known: a pink and white swirl miniature, centering a Clichy-like rose within a circle of small canes. It is this added circle of canes that distinguishes Bohemian swirl and crown weights from Clichy equivalents, though the individual canes also differ from Clichy.

CROWNS—These are a cross between the Clichy swirl weights and the St. Louis crowns; that is, they are constructed like a crown weight, but the balloon of striped tubes is opaque like the members in a swirl weight, as if the spokes of a swirl had been straightened. A departure from both swirl and crown is the small circle of canes about the usual central cane, frequently a silhouette. Stripes are alternately deep pink and white, or deep blue and white (Fig. 10); (Col. Fig. 2).

OVERLAYS—These fine weights run smaller (2½-2¾ inches in diameter), higher crowned, and more compact looking than the French overlays. The overlay may be cobalt blue flash with numerous small circular printies, or a fine double overlay of royal blue, scarlet, or green over white, cut with printies in the usual Baccarat-Clichy manner. The interior design may be a spaced millefiori or a concentric, both on lace grounds, or a mushroom, most making frequent use of Clichy-like roses and figure canes, especially the dog. They are always mistaken-ly called Baccarat, Gilliland, or Clichy (Fig. 11). When their smaller size, the relative lightness of the non-lead glass, and the difference in cane forms are noted there should be no confusion with Baccarat. And as Gilliland is not known to have made any paperweights, there should be no indentification prob-lem there. One green overlay mushroom in stave basket might be confused momentarily with a similiar Clichy, but here the difference in staves should be noted.

9A

9B

Fig. 9A. Bohemian scattered millefiori. *Courtesy J. P. Boore.*
Fig. 9B. Bohemian scattered millefiori with latticinio vase. *Courtesy Sotheby & Co.*

10   11

12

Fig. 10. Bohemian crown weight. *Courtesy Louis Lyons.*
Fig. 11. Bohemian overlay, lace ground. *Courtesy Sotheby & Co.*
Fig. 12. Bohemian basket weight. *Courtesy Sotheby & Co.*

RARE BASKET—An extremely rare and perhaps unique Bohemian three-dimensional basket nearly fills a compact, high-domed, 2½-inch weight of light, slightly tinted glass, the flat base deeply star cut to the very edge. The concentric motif in wine red, deep green, pink, and white rests in a basket of white staves that is trimmed top and bottom with a red-and-white twist ribbon and an arched handle of the same (Fig. 12). It sounds spectacular, but the color is rather hard and flat; the execution was beyond the technique of the artist, and somehow it doesn't quite come off. Comparison with the great St. Louis basket is unflattering.

Conclusions

Because they have been confused with weights from other sources, including Venice, Bohemian paperweights have been largely neglected, as nothing more than unusual examples of one make or another. Thus, no serious study of them as a group has been undertaken that might lead to a determination of their factory or factories of origin. Some glass scholars in present-day Czechoslovakia, formerly Bohemia, seem willing to help, but admit a lack of knowledge about Bohemian paperweight history. It remains for someone to visit the museums like the one at Kašperské Hory, and the great factories at Harrchov, Rejštejn, Lednické Rovné, and Bor, where paperweights may have been made.[12] Perhaps the illustrations in this book will provide a stimulus.

Bohemian paperweights appear to be contemporary with Venetian and French work of the Classic period of paperweight-making, but closer to the French in feeling and quality of workmanship. It is not yet possible to say which way paperweight influences traveled between France and Bohemia, if they did not travel both ways, but the similarities in figure canes and types of motif are so striking that some connection between glassworkers from the two countries seems inescapable. The best of the Bohemian weights show superior workmanship and great charm; if they are somewhat pallid beside the French, it is because all non-French weights lose something in that comparison.

NOTES

[1] The factory figure comes from *Bohemian Glass,* Victoria and Albert Museum, 1965, p. 5.

[2] Gustav E. Pazaurek, *Die Gläser der Empire-und Biedermeierzeit,* Leipzig, 1923. p. 289.

[3] *Ibid.*

[4] *Ibid.,* p. 290.

[5] *Ibid.,* pp. 284, 285; figs. 254, 255.

[6] Albert Christian Revi, "Millefiori, Filigree, and Striped Glass," *The Spining Wheel,* Jan., 1958.

[7] Ray Winfield Smith, *Glass from the Ancient World,* Corning, New York, 1957, pp. 79, 80.

[8] Translation from German by R. W. Smith of a reference in the introduction to the Minutoli Auction catalogue. Minutoli collection sale, Cologne, Oct. 25, 1875, communicated in a letter to me from Smith, dated May 15, 1966.

[9] M. L. P. Debette, "On The Manufacture of Glass in Bohemia" (translated from the *Annales des Mines,* Dec., 1843, for the *Franklin Journal*), vol. 9, 1845.

[10] Pazaurek, p. 290.

[11] Debette.

[12] These names were given me in a letter dated Dec. 15, 1966, from Dr. Libuše Urešovâ, Museum of Industrial Art, Prague.

4

THE VICTORIAN CONTEXT

The Great Exhibition, 1851

"Really in London—the big, beating heart of the British Empire
and the emporium of the civilized world."[1]

EXHIBITIONS AND TRADE FAIRS per se were nothing new; the idea of an exhibition is as old as the desire to display, to impress, perchance to sell. Nor was the size and international character of some of them the invention of one country or one century. But the nineteenth century with its Industrial Revolution, its improved communications, its nationalism and internationalism, its free trade, its sense of competition and progress, was the right time and the right culture in which the idea of periodic, large, housed exhibitions could take root. Looking backward, the nineteenth century, particularly the latter half, seems to have been as much the century of the great world fairs as of the factory and the railroad. Yet, until 1849 no prognosticator would have dreamed it.

In France there had been national exhibitions since 1798, first at irregular intervals and later every five years. An idea of their progress is inherent in the figures. The 1798 exhibition lasted three days and had 110 exhibitors; the exhibition of 1849 lasted six months and had 4,532 exhibitors.[2] In England the situation was at first altogether different. The Society of Arts, founded in 1754 for the Encouragement of Arts, Manufactures and Commerce, had put up small exhibits, beginning in 1756. But it was not until 1847, the year it received its Royal Charter, that it staged the first of a series of annual exhibitions, aimed partly to reverse the annihilation of aesthetics by industrialization.[3] Premiums for excellence of design were offered. Behind the scene of these London exhibitions was Henry Cole, a man of moderate position with enormous and varied talents and boundless energy. This nineteenth-century Renaissance man was into everything. Facing an indifferent public and suspicious manufacturers, he triumphed over both. The 1847 exhibition netted 20,000 visitors, the one the next year, 70,000, and the 1849 exhibition, 100,000. In that year there were two other exhibitions, one held in Birmingham under sponsorship of the British Association. Both Bacchus and Islington showed their glass there, and the catalogue of Bacchus exhibits included "letter-weights."[4]

But 1849 was also the year of a quinquennial national exposition in Paris, and Cole, who had his own ideas about national expositions, went to Paris to size it up. A proposal for an international exhibition made by the French Minister of Agriculture Buffet had been rejected by the French Chamber.[5] But Cole heard about it, and when he returned to England his ideas were focused on an international exhibition to be held in England. When Prince Albert, who loved Progress and the Arts, heard about it, he proposed "a great collection of works of Industry and Art to be held in London in 1851 for the purposes of Exhibition, Competition and Encouragement."[6]

So far so good, but before the essential royal sponsorship could be obtained there must be some certainty of success in so vast an undertaking. It is not within the scope of this book to go into the voluminous details of the dangling fate and shifting character of the exhibition during the next year. Suffice it to say that the gigantic dream of an international exhibition of historic proportions became a reality. Exhibitors the world over were rounded up, money was raised, a site was chosen in Hyde Park, and on March 13, 1850, the Building Committee, pressed for time, opened a public competition for a design to house the vast inventory. The competition lasted less than a month, yet by April 8, 245 designs had been received. The Building Committee then commended many, but rejected all 245 submissions. Instead, it substituted a building design drawn up by one of its own members, the great engineer Isambard Kingdom Brunel, who was later to build that fabulous, fated steamship, *Great Eastern*. Brunel's monstrous and costly design, which called for a building of 15,000,000 bricks and a dome larger than the dome of St. Peter's, caused an immediate public outcry that put the committee and the Royal Commissioners on the spot and nearly stopped the Great Exhibition in its tracks. What happened next made exhibition, industrial, architectural, and glass history.

The Crystal Palace

In 1826 the Duke of Devonshire made Joseph Paxton, who was then twenty-three, head gardener at Chatsworth, his country home.[7] In this milieu Paxton was free to study and improve the botanical features of the various greenhouses at Chatsworth. Glass at this time was still taxed by weight, and the thick, heavy, expensive glass of the greenhouses lay in short, overlapped sheets on a heavy wooden framework which let in little of the precious English sunlight. Paxton began by beveling off the sides of the heavy sash bars. He invented a light, grooved sash to hold the glass and prevent the putty from washing away with each rain. He developed the ridge and furrow principle for glass roofs, which regulated the penetration of the sun, causing its rays to pass straight through when the sun was slanting, but obliquely when it was overhead. Paxton went to observe the new sheet-glass process recently introduced from France by Robert Lucas Chance, and eventually persuaded Chance to make him thin sheets 4 feet by 10 inches, thus reducing wasted overlap and cost.[8]

From 1837 to 1840 Paxton built the great conservatory at Chatsworth, the largest glass building known up to that time. In the Victoria Regia house that followed in 1850, Paxton replaced wood with iron, the iron columns, rafters, and sash bars doing double duty as drainpipes. "Paxton's remarkable ingenuity had by now given practical demonstrations of the principles that were soon to be embodied in the Crystal Palace."[9]

The Building Committee for the Great Exhibition at a standstill, Paxton drew up his own plan in a week of whirlwind activity. With the help of the great Robert Stephenson and the blessing of Prince Albert, Paxton's plan was submitted to the Building Committee, who by this time had no choice but to consent to consider it. But Paxton was taking no chances. He had his plan published in the *Illustrated London News*, circulation 200,000, and public opinion did the rest. Three weeks later it was formally adopted by the committee and the Royal Commissioners. It was Douglas Jerrold of the *Times* who christened it the Crystal Palace.[10]

Living as we do in an age of technological miracles, it is difficult for us to realize what the Crystal Palace was and what it meant in 1851. First of all, the building itself and the bare facts of its construction: The contract with Messrs. Fox and Henderson, whose low bid of 79,000 pounds was accepted, called for a building 1,851 feet long (over ⅓ mile), and 450 feet wide, enclosing some 18 acres and 33 million cubic feet of space with 956,195 square feet of sheet glass in panes 49 by 10 inches. The panes were only 1/13-inch thick and weighed exactly one pound per square foot. The plan of the building was to be a long rectangle three tiers high, intersected at midpoint by a barrel-vaulted transept. The main axis of the building was a nave flanked by aisles and courtyards, and, above them, galleries over the aisles connected by bridges over the courtyards. Mathematically conceived to the last detail, the entire building was calculated in units of 24 feet and their subdivisions. This was to be the first entirely mass-produced building in history, planned to a scale seldom exceeded even today and never exceeded in the extent and quantity of glass used. It was to be done in glass and iron, materials new to building, and on a gridiron plan that was to become the basis of skyscraper construction a half-century later. No cathedral without massive buttressing could have supported the transept this building was to have.[11]

Erection of the building proved to be as remarkable as its plan: The Crystal Palace was completed in seventeen weeks; its construction was the sight of London. Iron columns were tested for strength right on the spot by a special machine; truss girders were slipped into slots provided for them; and huge sections of prefabricated transept vaulting were hoisted into position by cranes and pulleys. "Paxton witnessed the erection of three columns and two girders in 16 minutes."[12] Then came the covering of the iron skeleton with a skin of glass weighing 400 tons, or 1 pound per square foot. The glass was fitted into the 205 miles of sash at an incredible rate. In one week, 18,392 panes of glass were installed by 80 men, and one glazier put in 367½ feet of glass in a single day.[13] To install the glass the glaziers used wheeled cars which ran in wooden gutters later used to carry off the rain; the scaffolding on which they stood had been a fence built about the building tract in the initial stages. Nothing was left unthought of, nothing wasted. When the sun was too hot, Paxton had devised a canvas cover for the entire roof. Should a sudden shower occur, the seams of the canvas let the water through into the gutters, and thence down the iron columns into 34 miles of pipe beneath the floor which both locked the columns in place and carried the water away. High winds? The weight of 18 acres of snow? The Crystal Palace was foolproof. No one was killed in its construction and no one died in the building during the 141 days of the exhibition, though "3 petticoats, 2 bustles, 3 pincushions and 12 monocles were lost and never claimed."[14]

The Great Exhibition of The Industry of All Nations, 1851, to give it its full title, was a howling success. During its 5 months and 11 days, the 100,000 exhibits from 13,937 exhibitors, British and foreign, were seen by 6,039,195 people. Total profits: 186,437 pounds.[15] In smaller figures, an eighty-five-year-old Cornish fish-woman walked from Penzance to Hyde Park to see the Crystal Palace, a distance just short of 300 miles.[16] "The exhibition," wrote Queen Victoria in her diary, "goes to prove that we are capable of doing almost anything."[17] It was a triumph of engineering, mass production, speed, economy, opulence, cooperation, competition, nationalism, internationalism, Free Trade, romanticism, medievalism, science, everything. Coming at the time of the Gothic revival, the Crystal Palace which housed it defied the Gothic revivalists. An observer wrote of it:

> It asserts loudly that it is glass and iron. . . . It reports the state of nature and the weather. Thus, also, it has a poetry of its own—the poetry of fact and of nature rather than of fantasy. It is the poetical product of a materialistic age—it is a realized idealism worked out in a century of reality—it is fiction grown into fact, with a tinge of its old fabulous poetry about it.[18]

Glass and Paperweights at the Great Exhibition

But what of the contents of the Crystal Palace, the exhibits themselves and, in particular, the glass? Yvonne ffrench writes caustically that there were "examples of the bastardisation of taste without parallel in the whole recorded history of aesthetics. If any lesson is to be drawn from the Great Exhibition solely with reference to taste it must be that design in the hands of a machine-minded, money-seeking generation tends to take a downward curve, losing its purpose in a senseless smother of irrelevant detail. . . . 1851 is the first collective opportunity for assessing the damage done to the arts in one generation alone of philistine freebooting; it marks the high water of hideosity."[19] The Victorian of 1851 at the Great Exhibition was adrift in a sea of products that were the

combined result of improved technology with heterogeneous tastes. The architect Nickolaus Pevsner writes:

> It is known that the sources of inspiration used by Victorian
> designers grew in a certain order. First, still in the eighteenth century,
> the Gothic and Greek were added to the Roman style, then some
> occasional Egyptian, Hindoo, and so on. By 1830 the Italian Ren-
> aissance and the Elizabethan and Jacobean styles reappeared, and
> occasionally even a Neo-Louis Quinze for specially festive occasions.
> At the time of the Great Exhibition the styles available had become
> unlimited. Richard Brown's "Domestic Architecture of 1841" lists
> and illustrates everything from Cottage Ornée and Swiss Cottage to
> Norman, Lancastrian, Tudor, Stuart, Anglo-Grecian, Italian, French,
> Persian, Moorish-Spanish, and Chinese.[20]

These are the criticisms of today's hindsight. The state of culture today in
the United States, flourishing as we tell ourselves it is, is a striking parallel to
the culture of the Great Exhibition. A cultural critic with hindsight is likely to be
a critic with tunnel vision of the culture of his own time. The critics of 1851
were no exception, especially in the area of glass. It did not occur to them that
the majestic simplicity of the use of glass for the Crystal Palace bore any relation
to or stood in any conflict with the plethora of meaningless manipulation of
glass that produced the revolting chaos of the glass exhibits.

Many thousands of words were written about glass in the *Jury Reports* of
the exhibition, in magazines, books, and journals of artistic opinion, and nearly
all of them in praise. We have to look hard to find any weather eye to what was
happening. Exceptions to the general assent were Ruskin, who lambasted cut
glass while his own vice was Gothic, and the *Journal of Design and Manufactures,* which in 1850 commented on the glass of Lloyd & Summerfield, Bacchus,
and Rice Harris:

> We can safely praise all the articles here engraved for their excellence of
> manufacture. The specimens of pressed glass nearly approach in appear-
> ance cut glass, whilst the latter for sharpness and mechanical skill they
> exhibit are most commendable. But we greatly doubt if the present state
> of public taste, in its preference for heavy, massive forms cut all about,
> is not misleading the glass manufacturers from the true and natural
> principles which really should regulate the application of glass to use . . .
> Every material has its own peculiar treatment and glass is certainly no
> exception to this rule.[21]

With English glass, at least, the exuberance of forms and styles was the result of
the removal of the century-old excise duty seven years before. English
manufacturers were making up for precisely one hundred years of lost time. But
the excesses were not confined to English glass; in fact, the English glass of the

Great Exhibition was largely in imitation of foreign excesses.

When we come to the question of the paperweights among the exhibits we find them typically and almost completely ignored. When I began doing the research for this book I thought the Great Exhibition would be a gold mine of information. How wrong I was! In the complete official catalogue of the exhibition there is one brief classification listing, which in itself is proof that paperweights were exhibited. Under the glass subheading, "Flint glass, or crystal, with or without lead," there appears Category No. 5, "Glass mosaic, millefiori, aventurine and Venetian glass weights." The glass exhibits were in the Central North Gallery—would we had been there. In the *Jury Reports*, tangential references to the glass of those factories we know made paperweights are in abundance, but in this exhibition no reference to the paperweights themselves. They seem to have been treated with complete indifference by everyone whose official capacity with the exhibition required comment. A prize medal was given T. F. Bautte of Geneva for a paperweight, but it was "a Paper-weight of gold, the base being ornamented with scenery painted in enamel. From this a stem ascends, and is surmounted with a small casket which opens and closes by means of clock-work. When the cover is turned back a most beautiful and perfect little bird is discovered, which is apparently singing, and at the same time fluttering its minute wings and twirling about in different directions."[22] Lovely, no doubt, but hardly in a class with the millefiori paperweights that must have been on exhibit. It might be added that some marble paperweights, made by Boyd of Van Diemen's Land, Tasmania, were also exhibited. Pellatt was listed as exhibiting incrustations (sulphides), but whether any of these were paperweights is not stated. Pellatt's "letter-weights" were not paperweights in our use of the term. (See Chapter Seventeen.)

Part of the trouble was due to the position of the French at the Great Exhibition. As Eugène Péligot of France, professor at the Conservatoire des Arts et Métiers and one of the glass jurors, explains in his extensive report on the work of the French Commission, "While the glass people of England, Germany, Belgium, and the United States made great efforts to see to it that their industry was worthily represented in this great industrial gathering, the French glassmen for the most part stayed home." He says that Saint Gobain and Clichy sent some suitable things at the last moment, but that Baccarat and St. Louis refrained from sending anything.[23] Clichy, however, walked off with the Council Medal awarded for the new boracic glass optical lenses of Maës, which were very clear and free of striae, bubbles, and foreign matter. The Council Medal, designed by W. Wyon, R. A., and struck by the Royal Mint, showed Victoria and Albert in profile with dolphins and trident. It was adapted as a flat glass intaglio paperweight by the New England Glass Company of Cambridge, Massachusetts. A paperweight now in the Corning Museum of Glass is proof that Clichy sent at least one *presse-papier* to London. It is a large, spaced millefiori in clear glass. The type was common enough, and there is nothing special about the workmanship, an indication of the haste or indifference with which Clichy selected its exhibits. But on the back of the weight appears a crown above the monogram, V.

A. (Victoria-Albert), and the date, Londres, 1851 [8]. The weight even has its own hinged leather case. No doubt of the destination of that paperweight. Another Clichy weight, a faceted sulphide of Queen Victoria on a black ground, has on its bottom a sticker that reads, "Exhibition, Hyde Park, London 1851."

Péligot's report does mention "filigree and millefiori glass of the most varied designs," but we are not told anything more.[24] Similarly, the *Jury Report* says of the crystal section, "The coloured glasses of Bohemia, of which Count Harrach, Count Schaffgotsch, and others have exhibited very beautiful specimens, and their imitations in Germany, France, and England, are comprised in this section; and likewise the *millefiori* style of work, adopted for making *presse-papiers* and other ornaments, and sold by hundreds of thousands, which, by the extent of the trade, have become a very important branch of manufacture."[25] This provocative figure, "hundreds of thousands," has an interesting history. In the *Art Journal* of 1849 we read, "In France at the manufactory of Choisy-le-Roi, under the able superintendence of M. Bontemps, have been produced some clever imitations of *millefiori* fused in crystal glass; in one article alone, viz. paper-weights, they have distributed over Europe hundreds of thousands of these elegant table-ornaments."[26] Yet Choisy-le-Roi folded during the Revolution of 1848. By the time the *Jury Reports* for the Great Exhibition were being written, Bontemps had already joined Chance in Birmingham as Director of Works to help perfect the quality and manufacture of Flint optical and sheet glass.[27] But the notion that Bontemps had made and distributed hundreds of thousands of paperweights over Europe had taken root. In a piece, "Modern Enamel Mosaics and the Reproduction of Venetian Glass in the Nineteenth Century" by W. C. (William Chaffers) that appeared in the *Art Journal* for 1866 (vol. 28, p. 257), we find the above passage verbatim, but without quotation marks, giving the impression that this was the situation in 1866, which it certainly was not. Some writers today credit Bontemps himself with the quotation. Since Péligot was on the glass jury and Bontemps a glass associate at the Great Exhibition, it could have originated with either, but was certainly meant to apply to paperweights in general and not simply to Choisy-le-Roi, for as Péligot says of French crystal, "Almost all our crystal is made at Baccarat, St. Louis, and Clichy."[28]

Péligot reports on all the glass shown at the Great Exhibition and he has a great many complimentary things to say about glasshouses, some of which made paperweights, if nothing about the paperweights themselves. Of Pellatt he says, "It is difficult, in fact, to make whiter or more sparkling crystal." Of Rice Harris (Islington), that they "are occupied with some success in making colored crystal which is less advanced in England than in France and Bohemia. The assortment of their colored glass is complete enough, but we must say that it is due to French workers who learned this kind of work at Clichy." Of Bacchus, "Their crystal is white and well cut; their glasses thinly engraved and reaching to filigree knees bent with pincers, have succeeded and present a pleasing effect."[29] Péligot also praised Gilliland, the only American glass exhibitor to win a medal. But there is no evidence as yet that Gilliland made any paperweights. Aside from the Clichy weight already mentioned, the only paper-weights indelibly associated with the Great Exhibition are the Allen and Moore sulphide of the Crystal Palace itself (see Chapter Seventeen) (Fig. 13) and the painted weight showing the Crystal Palace (south side), patented by Berens Blumberg & Company, St. Paul's Churchyard, London, October 31, 1851.[30]

As may be noted from the quotations already given, the influence of Bohemia permeated the glass exhibits. In the case of paperweights, however, there was confusion as to the original sources of inspiration. While some of the millefiori references, particularly those appearing in the *Art Journal* of 1849 refer to Bohemian influence, most cite Venice in connection with millefiori. For example, *The Cyclopedia of Useful Arts and Manufactures,* referring to the Great Exhibition, says, "The varieties of coloured ornamental glass are very numerous, and many of them are derived from the Venetians." It proceeds with a description of the "Venetian ball," lifted from Pellatt's *Curiosities of Glass-Making* or some such source, and continues, "Millefiori glass (the manufacture of which has recently been revived by M. Bontemps) is formed by fusing together a number of tubes of various colours, sections representing stars, flowers, &c: slices of these tubes are imbedded in white transparent glass, the whole forming a pleasing ornament which may be used as a letter-weight. Many of the patterns are, however, very tasteless."[31] To further confuse the problem of millefiori origins, Bigaglia was listed under the Austrian section, but got a prize medal for his Venetian glass.

If paperweights were lost in the shuffle it was because they were made as novelties for stationery shops, accessories in the pen-and-ink line, mere baubles of the day, and there was simply too much else to see. In the museum-emporium of the Crystal Palace everything clamored for attention. How could Pellatt's cameo incrustations compete with its 24-foot cut-glass chandelier, or the latter

Fig. 13. Allen and Moore sulphide of the Crystal Palace. *Courtesy Sotheby & Co.*

with the gigantic Osler crystal glass fountain, 27 feet high and weighing 4 tons, that occupied the focal point of the entire exhibition? By 1851 the decorative arts had become, as one wit recently termed them, *"des arts trop decoratifs."*[32] One must be thankful on the one hand that so much was there, for, as the *Illustrated London News* of May 10, 1851, put it, "Had this exhibition taken place seven years ago, the examples of glass manufacture on the British side would have been so ridiculous as to have provoked contempt." Yet on the other hand it must be regretted that so little written and illustrated record was kept of the one glass object in it which exceeded all others in imagination, workmanship, and beauty.

On Saturday, October 11, 1851, the *Illustrated London News* wrote, ". . . and we suppose that in a few months the glittering palace of iron and glass, the most unique and remarkable building in the world, will be entirely a thing of the past as the ice-palace of the Empress of Russia that thawed in the summer sun."

NOTES

[1] A Traveller & Teacher, *Crests from the Ocean World,* Boston, 1853.

[2] Kenneth W. Luckhurst, *The Story of Exhibitions,* London, 1951, p. 220.

[3] The date of the charter, 1845 or 1847, and the acceptance of the presidency of the society by Prince Albert varies with the source consulted.

[4] For contemporary comment, see Chapter Nine.

[5] Yvonne ffrench, *The Great Exhibition, 1851,* London, n.d., p. 19.

[6] *Ibid.,* p. 22.

[7] *Ibid.,* p. 90.

[8] Material in this paragraph from McGrath and Frost, *Glass in Architecture & Decoration,* London, 1937, p. 120. A lavish and informative study of the subject. However, according to Guttery, in 1778 George Ensell of Amblecote near Stourbridge had already made glass sheets 36" x 26" for which he received a Premium from the Society of Arts. D. R. Guttery, *From Broad-Glass to Cut Crystal,* London, 1956, p. 96. In 1832, Chance, in collaboration with Georges Bontemps (formerly of Choisy-le-Roi), had imported French and Belgian sheetworkers to the works at Smethwick. —Guttery, p. 98.

[9] McGrath and Frost, p. 121. New evidence from James Reeve of The Toledo Museum of Art indicates that some of the work at Chatsworth credited to Paxton may instead have been the work of the architect Decimus Burton, or at least joint undertakings.

[10] Christopher Hobhouse, *1851 and The Crystal Palace,* London, 1937, pp. 29–37.

[11] McGrath and Frost, Hobhouse, ffrench, and others. Individual statistics vary somewhat from source to source.

[12] Hobhouse, p. 44.

[13] McGrath and Frost, p. 122.

[14] Hobhouse, p. 145.

[15] C. H. Gibbs-Smith, "The Great Exhibition of 1851, A Commemorative Album," Victoria and Albert Museum, 1950.

[16] *Illustrated London News,* 1851. Her name was Dolly Pentreath and she carried mackerel on her head to pay for her lodging. She was one of the last to speak the old Cornish dialect and she is buried near Penzance.

[17] Gibbs-Smith, p. 16.

[18] McGrath and Frost, pp. 126, 127, and quoted from *The Athenaeum,* when the Crystal Palace had been dismantled and reassembled at Sydenham.

[19] ffrench, pp. 230, 231.

[20] Nickolaus Pevsner, *High Victorian Design,* p. 50.

[21] *The Journal of Design and Manufactures,* Vol. III, 1850, pp. 16–18.

[22] *Jury Reports,* 1851.

[23] Eugène Péligot, *Travaux de Commission Français sur l'Industrie des Nations,* Paris, 1854, Vol. 6, XXIV Jury, pp. 1–58.

[24] *Ibid.,* p. 50.

[25] *Jury Reports,* 1851, p. 528.

[26] *Art Journal,* Vol. II, 1849, p. 257.

[27] *Jury Reports,* 1851, p. 529.

[28] *Travaux de Commission Français,* etc., Paris, 1854, p. 43.

[29] *Ibid.,* p. 40.

[30] Albert Christian Revi, "English Patented Paperweights," *Bulletin,* 1964, p. 43.

[31] *The Cyclopedia of Useful Arts and Manufactures,* New York, 1854, Vol. I.

[32] Raymond Ysay, *Revue de Deux Mondes,* Dec. 1936, p. 584. He says this of the Paris Exposition of 1855.

II

The Individual Makers

ABOUT THE FRENCH MAKERS

ALTHOUGH THE NUMBER OF GLASSWORKS of all kinds in France had risen from 54 in 1800 to 185 in 1830, it verges on the fantastic that in the brief span of five years a foreign specialty of Bohemian-Muranese origin, however deliberately appropriated and methodically pursued, should have reached a zenith of perfection surpassing anything offered by the models appropriated. Yet this is what happened in France between about 1843 and 1848 when French paperweight-makers set the standard high for the world to follow.

Not only was every possibility of the millefiori technique explored and bettered, but new motifs such as lampwork flora and fauna were introduced and perfected almost overnight. At Baccarat and St. Louis the glass had a high lead content; that at St. Louis higher and more consistent in range. The early Clichy weights also show a high lead content, while later the content appears to have been reduced when a new formula using boric acid as a flux was substituted. By 1885 Clichy had passed from the scene, but Baccarat and St. Louis continued, however sporadically, to make paperweights, and are still making them.

The range of paperweight designs in France during the Classic period was enormous, far greater than in any other country. And it is interesting to note that while millefiori and silhouette canework, although more finely executed, ran parallel to foreign counterparts, the new flower work was indigenous and had, in fact, no apparent counterpart in the foreign or domestic decorative arts.

If one surveys the decorative arts of England and France as a whole the disparity becomes evident. About 1837 the poppy and rose are especially popular. By 1840, when France imported the camelia from China, the cosmos, morning glory, aster, and iris appear frequently. Add by 1844 the columbine, and from 1845-50 the hydrangea, tulip, narcissus, pansy, dahlia, marigold, lily of the valley, passion flower, with the rose and poppy continuing popular. At the Great Exhibition, flowers in fabrics, wallpapers, china, and other materials included the aforementioned and the petunia, sweet pea, carnation, and bleeding heart. Soon afterward, the thistle, foxglove, and acanthus leaves appeared with frequency. In 1862 nicotine was popular and in 1876 the iris again. Yet among all of these flowers only the pansy and the symbolic Clichy rose appear frequently in French paperweights and most of the others are never used.

There would seem to be no ready, satisfactory explanation for this, unless the extreme difficulty of accurate representation in glass that in turn was immersed in glass put it beyond all but the master craftsmen. Or perhaps the explanation, at once more vague yet more basic, lies in the imaginative leap embodied in the realization of a new art form and the restraints imposed upon it in the formulation of a classical approach. In any case, the three-dimensional realism of the baroque phase is not apparent before 1878.

But early or late, the look of the glass paperweight as we conceive it is French.

46

5

BACCARAT

THE DATES, GEOGRAPHY, AND HISTORY OF BACCARAT and St. Louis, two of the three major French glasshouses ultimately to be associated with paperweights, are closely related. Founded only two years apart in Alsace-Lorraine, they were originally and still remain competitors. Alsace, lying between the Vosges and the Black Forest, is a mountainous, heavily wooded area that has been fought over for centuries by France and Germany. Originally a part of Belgian Gaul, in the fifth and sixth centuries Alsace was invaded by the Alemanni. Later and successively it was a buffer state, then part of the Holy Roman Empire until 1648, then French under the treaties of Wesphalia and Aix-la-Chapelle, then German from 1871 to 1918, and since then, French.[1]

In 1764 Baccarat began as a small glassworks when the Verrerie de Sainte Anne was established on the right bank of the river Meurthe opposite the hamlet of Baccarat by a prelate named Monseigneur de Montmorency-Laval.[2] From 1764 to 1815 the Verrerie de Sainte Anne produced industrial glass, that is to say, windowpanes, mirrors, bottles, and the like. In 1800 D'Artigues, the former director of the St. Louis factory, started another glassworks in Vonêche, France, and began making a successful glass in the "cristal" or English style. The Treaty of Paris in 1815 made Vonêche part of Belgium. The next year D'Artigues transferred the operation to the Sainte Anne works, and in 1819, according to Imbert and Amic, a furnace was lit for the production of flint glass. The Verrerie de Sainte Anne continued to make the staple window glass, and in 1824 Robinet, a glassblower, invented a pump which made it possible to blow cylinders for sheet glass larger than human lungs could blow. For his ingenuity Robinet won a medal from the Société d'Encouragement and a pension from Baccarat.[3] In 1822 D'Artigues sold out to a triumvirate who founded the Compagnie des Cristalleries de Baccarat. From then on Baccarat appears to have been recognized as the preeminent French glasshouse.[4] There was competition, particularly with St. Louis, though in one instance Baccarat and St. Louis joined forces in 1832 to buy up and extinguish another competitor, the Creusot factory.[5] It must also be recalled that though rivals, Baccarat, St. Louis, Choisy-le-Roi, and Bercy shared Launay, Hautin & Company as their Paris distributor.[6]

The periodic exhibitions in Paris, whose jurors tended to respond to the number and variety of products, were the ideal place for Baccarat to bring a large selection of fine crystal before the public. Winning a medal in 1823, Baccarat exhibited again in 1827, 1834, and 1839. It was one of 3,960 competitors in 1844,[7] the year that Bontemps of Choisy-le-Roi exhibited millefiori and latticinio glass. In 1845 Péligot saw the millefiori paperweights of Bigaglia at the Exhibition of Austrian Industry in Vienna. Baccarat again exhibited in Paris in 1849, but refused to send its products to the Great Exhibition in London two years later, partly, it seems likely, through fear of international competition. The success of that exhibition must have changed its mind, for it exhibited frequently thereafter.

During roughly the decade (1845-55) of its paperweight manufacture, Baccarat seems to have gone unlisted and unmentioned in the catalogues and jury reports of the various exhibitions. We have to remember that in spite of the fierce rivalry among glasshouses and the interest it engendered in new forms, paperweights were at no time considered the important objet d'art this book claims them to be. Except for the few donations of paperweights to museums during this period, the only public record we have seems to be the dating of the paperweights themselves.

Baccarat exhibited again in 1855 and in 1867. In connection with the Exposition Universelle at Paris in 1878, we find an interesting appraisal. Writing the report on glass as secretary to the United States Commissioners to that exposition, Charles Colné considered Baccarat the most important exhibitor, with Clichy next. Yet of Baccarat he says, "The reputation of this house is as good as ever, but it cannot be denied that some of the glass works around Paris are producing goods fully equal, and sometimes superior."[8] In spite of Colné's evaluation of Baccarat, this was the Exposition at which Baccarat and Thomas Webb & Sons were awarded the only Grand Medals for glass. It was also the exposition at which Pantin showed its flower, fruit, and lizard weights in great profusion; these Colné describes in tantalizing generalities. (See Chapter Eight.) But Colné makes no mention of any paperweights from Baccarat, and one wonders whether Baccarat was making any similar weights at this time or if it did not take up the challenge offered by Pantin until around 1900 when, as has been suggested, Baccarat made lizard paperweights. This suggestion will be considered under "Lizards" in this chapter.

As I said in Chapters Two and Three, revivals of the millefiori technique are nothing new. Baccarat was a leader in the revival of the 1840's and again in the late 1950's. Yet a company memorandum of 1914 states that by that time there was no craftsman capable of making the old millefiori and nothing in the archives to reveal the process.[9] Was the century then a blank between revivals? Evidence has come to light that it was not. As an outlet for its products, Baccarat used to operate a small retail shop next door to the Hotel Montalembert in the Seventh Arrondisement. From 1931 until about 1934 it sold pansy and millefiori garland paperweights in three sizes, made by an old man named Dupont who worked in great secrecy at the factory in Baccarat. My informant, Miss O. D.

Dahlgren, lived in Paris during these years and often visited the shop, where she purchased two of these paperweights. Being very much interested in glass, she also visited the Baccarat factory, where the manager refused her request to meet old Mr. Dupont, who he said was very irascible, believing that he alone knew the secrets of millefiori and that when he died the secrets would be gone forever. Mr. Dupont died about 1934 and the little retail shop ceased carrying his weights.

The pansy weights that Mr. Dupont made are like the Baccarat pansies of the Classic period, except that they are a gelatinous yellow that shows translucent when held to the light. Some of them bear unrealistic dates such as 1815 or 1837, and though these dated weights were not sold in the retail shop, they are in every respect identical to the work of Mr. Dupont. Miss Dahlgren says that the miniature-size pansy was very popular. The millefiori garland weights made by Dupont employ canes undoubtedly made from the old Baccarat molds, but pulled out longer and so reduced somewhat in size; and some canes that must have been made by Dupont himself from molds of his own design.[10] There is a distinctly Baccarat feeling about all the canes, though the colors are often a bit harsh and raw and they tend to bleed. The base of the weight is broad in relation to the diameter, and the sides consequently rise straighter. Some garlands are dated in the center also with unlikely dates. These Dupont-Baccarat garland weights are generally incorrectly referred to as "Bristol," a quaint notion since no paperweights are known to have been made in Bristol. The notion probably stems from the days after Dupont's death when the French claimed the weights were English and the English said they must be French.

On October 30, 1951, a paperweight dated 1853 was found in the cornerstone of the church at Baccarat, which had been bombed in World War II. Its discovery set off another millefiori revival at Baccarat, which is recorded by Chaumeil.[11] The Chaumeil report completes the sparse history of Baccarat's involvement with paperweights. One can only regret that the commercial enterprise expended on behalf of an historically isolated and outmoded art form has not in its enthusiasm exposed more information to the light of historical inspection.

Baccarat Paperweights

PROFILE

The typical Baccarat profile illustrated here shows a curve that is somewhat flatter on the sides than the Clichy curve. Nor does it go in as far at the base, which means that the diameter of the base averages somewhat greater than Clichy, or about $1\frac{7}{8}$ inches for a weight with a diameter of 3 inches. The thickness of the basal rim varies from $\frac{1}{8}$ inch to a mere sharp edge left by the hollow grinding. The shallow grinding of the basal concavity has usually but not always removed all trace of the pontil mark in unadorned examples. But decoration of the slightly concave (and occasionally flat) base with star-cutting in sixteen or twenty-four rays is a Baccarat characteristic. The star rays follow the concave curvature and are deeply and precisely cut. When seen from above, their catching of the light enhances the flowers in flower weights and increases the mystery of the design in faceted millefiori, particularly the overlays, whose windows multiply the star.

With a refractive index range of 1.562-1.600 (see Chapter Nineteen), the heavily leaded glass forms a clear, magnifying lens over designs placed about 1/3 of the way up from the base in flower and patterned millefiori weights, and about 2/3rds of the way up in spaced and close millefiori examples. Viewed from above, the image shows minimal distortion in examples that have not been reground, and when viewed at an angle about the same blurring as weights from St. Louis but more blurring than those from Clichy.

DATES AND SIGNATURES—Perhaps a third to a half of Baccarat weights are dated. Dates include 1846 through 1849, 1853, and 1858, and are usually topped by a "B."* The dates and letter appear in red, blue, and green on the ends of opaque white rods fused together. The variety of combinations possible with the five rods and three colors is 243, which gives an idea of the variety found in arrangements of the hundreds of different millefiori canes. Today we know that the "B" stands for Baccarat, for it was a company policy not to let individual workmen sign company products. But not so many years ago the "B" was thought to stand for a variety of things such as Bristol, Birmingham, and Bigaglia.

One of the more intricate assumptions was the Battestini theory. This theory proposes that two Italians named Battestini, a father and his son, left Venice about 1815 to live and work in Baccarat, changing their names to the more French-sounding Batest. Batest père is said to have taken great pride in his work and great pains to teach it to his son. It was the father who conceived the idea of signing his weights with a "B" and of including in them the flora and fauna silhouette canes. Young Batest designed the elephant cane, and his paperweight efforts were distinguished from his father's by its inclusion. Then in 1850 the old man died and the son went on to make even finer paperweights including these canes.

The one element in this theory which has a ring of truth is the distinction

---

* The tazza and the close millefiori paperweights dated 1846 show a sophistication and a detailed excellence of cane structure that could not have been achieved from scratch in 1846. Baccarat must have begun making weights in 1844 or 1845 at the latest, which means at the same time as the Bohemians and Venetians.

between the elephant and the other animal canes; for the elephant is as amateur-ishly delineated as the other canes are professionally designed, implying two creators. Yet this distinction is perhaps more effectively made by the Gridel account, which says that the silhouette canes were decided upon by Jean-Baptiste Toussaint, a nineteenth-century industrialist and general manager of Baccarat, who discovered his eight-year-old nephew Emile Gridel making paper cutouts of animals—"so falteringly made."[12] That was in 1846. Gridel, appropriately enough, grew up to become a hunter and painter of animals and a student of animal life. The animal cutouts he made as a boy remain today in the possession of his granddaughter, Mme. de Thuault.[13]

Occasional Baccarat paperweights carry the date without the "B." The close millefiori weight discovered in the cornerstone of the Baccarat church is an historically significant example. Dated 1853, the year the cornerstone was laid, it was made by "Master Craftsman" Martin Kayser who was thirty-nine at the time.[14] Martin Kayser (1814-60) went to work for Baccarat in 1827 when he was only thirteen.[15] The last two numbers in the 1853 cane are unlike the first two, indicating that perhaps weights were only made during the 1850's to commemorate special occasions. This is borne out by the only other weights known to date from that decade, the close millefiori weights, of which several were made to commemorate the visit of Maréchal Canrobert to Baccarat in 1858 (Fig. 14A). In these, a large, opaque white, tooth-edged cane bears in blue the inscription, "Baccarat, 21 Avril, 1858" above a sprig of laurel. Maréchal Canrobert (1809-95) had recently distinguished himself in the Crimea and was to gain further honors in the Franco-Prussian War of 1870. Some of this edition of paperweights are as fine as the best of the earlier close millefiori, but one contains a large blob of glass saliva.

One undated Baccarat rock ground weight is inscribed on the dome, "Souvenir de Baccarat."

MILLEFIORI CANES—Owing to elaborate variety of form and color combinations, Baccarat canes are impossible to catalogue in detail, and one can only make a few generalizations and point to a few characteristic rod elements. When, for example, a Baccarat and a Clichy close millefiori are placed side by side a great similarity in cane parts or rod combinations will be noted. The chief difference is in the coloring, for while the Clichy will show a warmer overall tonality, the Baccarat will appear cooler, with less aquamarine or robin's egg blue and more cobalt blue, less pink, and more coral red. Though rich, the Baccarat color is somewhat deader.

Characteristic Baccarat rods include the stars, whorl, arrowhead (crowsfoot), trefoil, quatrefoil, honeycomb, and one I call the fortress. The stars show a great variety of elaboration, size and color, but one immediately recognizable is the prominent star at the inner junction of whose five points tiny star tips appear [9]. The whorl rod may be distinguished from its Clichy counterpart because it is really a spiral open at one end, and not a series of tubes one within another [10]. Whorls

[9]

[10]

Fig. 14A. Baccarat close millefiori dated 1858. *Courtesy Corning Museum of Glass.*

[11]

[12]

may be small rods or ½-inch canes. The arrowhead (crowsfoot) rod is a three-pronged affair with prongs usually straight and coming to a point [11]. not anchor-shaped as in St. Louis. The trefoil and quatrefoil are simple enough to identify, but should not be confused with the shamrock which has a short stem and in special concentrics is used as a separate cane[12], [13]. The honeycomb cane looks like this [14]. The fortress or castle rods may appear four in a square formation, forming one cane, or singly and enlarged to cane size where, in one such instance, it forms the center of an all-stardust ground mushroom [15].

[13]

[14]

[15]

SILHOUTTE CANES—Also called figure canes, these are by no means unique with Baccarat. We have already come across them in Venice and Bohemia, and we will encounter them at St. Louis, Bacchus, Islington, Sandwich, Cambridge, Gillinder, while they are conspicuous in their absence from Clichy. At Baccarat, silhouette canes include the dog, squirrel (or kangaroo), deer, horse, goat, elephant, monkey; a variety of fowl such as the dove, rooster, stork (or crane), swan, pheasant, pelican, and a pair of small birds set face to face.[16] There are also the moth (mistakenly described as a butterfly), a hunter with gun, a dancing devil, and several flower canes. The silhouettes may be blue, plum, white (white monkey and rooster) or, in the case of the devil, red, but not black as has been assumed. Except for the elephant, which looks like a child's drawing of a mastodon, it seems unlikely that the animal canes were taken directly from the cutouts of eight-year-old Gridel, for the drawing of the others is too sophisticated.[17]

One of the more elaborate silhouettes is the swan, which swims in a halo of rods on wavelets that appear to flow right out of the cane. In one case the waves come forward as blue honeycomb rods. Flower silhouettes are also complicated because they are so small. A collector friend of mine was tickled when I pointed out to him that the tiny flower in one of his canes was actually a complete camomile reduced to a few millimeters. Occasional canes actually contain two tiny camomiles, in delicate flesh pink. Other flower silhouettes include a variety of arrow, star, and other rods arranged as petals, and there is still another made of a seemingly endless kneading of glass.

Finally, mention must be made of the Clichy rose, which occasionally appears in the center of a close millefiori miniature or a spaced millefiori on muslin ground. Make no mistake about it, it is the Clichy rose in that marvelous flesh color of the camomiles described above—seldom seen in Clichy roses—but with a non-Clichy center composed of star stigma and anthers.

It is important to note that Baccarat flower canes are not, like the larger flowers, the result of lampwork. They are canes made in molds with the silhouette running right through from top to bottom.

Paperweight Types and Characteristics

SCRAMBLED—Baccarat scrambleds are easily distinguishable from all other scrambleds because the filigree twists are set at right angles to one another, abutting in a casual mosaic. Scrambleds come in all sizes but are few in number. One containing silhouette canes is dated 1847, an experiment unsatisfactory to the eye and probably therefore not repeated afterward.

CLOSE MILLEFIORI—This Baccarat staple is one of the most consistently interesting weights ever made, always revealing something new. The range is from miniature to magnums of 4-inch diameter, and they are dated in all sizes, from 1846 through 1849, 1853, and 1858, with 1848 and 1847 respec-

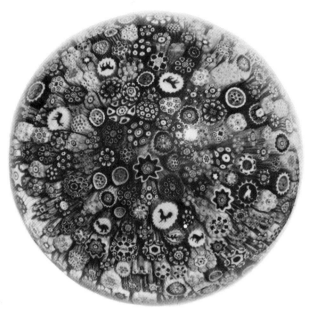

Fig. 14B. Baccarat close millefiori. *Courtesy Sotheby & Co.*

tively the most common dates (Fig. 14B). Most dates are topped by the letter "B," standing for Baccarat. The canes, often including silhouette canes, are tightly packed in a cushion that occupies two-thirds of the inner space of the weight, appearing, when viewed from above, to fill it to bursting. The lower canes are usually but not always drawn toward the center of the base. The interior of the cushion, invisible from the top or side, is usually stuffed with filigree twists which prevent a seepage of light between the canes, thus enhancing the effect of opaque solidity. A complicated process appears to be involved here with regard to the filigree fill and the shaping of the cushion of canes around it. Rarely does one see a close millefiori shaped like a low powder or patch box with projecting lid, though the object is all one piece. The lid is painted with gold floral decoration.

S P A C E D   M I L L E F I O R I—Here the same millefiori and silhouette canes are spaced apart on a muslin (lace) ground cushion which, as in the case of the close millefiori, occupies about two-thirds of the volume and height of the weight. The white filigree, when viewed at right angles to its long axis, spirals counterclockwise, a phenomenon first recorded by J. P. Boore.[18] Fragments of cane, colored filigree, and the blue spiraling over gauze cable (seen in mushroom weights) are frequently interspersed with the white filigree. The large millefiori florets and silhouette canes are sunk at approximately even intervals between the bits of filigree, their tops flush with or very slightly above the cushion. The moth cane most often appears in or near the center of the motif. The separation of the large canes gives them a breathing space they do not have in the close millefiori and makes their colors look

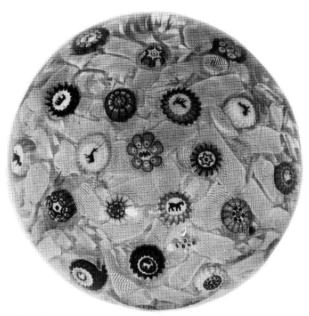

Fig. 15. Baccarat spaced millefiori signed and dated "B 1848." *Courtesy Sotheby & Co.*

as bright as Clichy. Dated examples are from 1847-49 (Fig. 15). Sizes are from miniature to magnum. In one faceted example the spaced canes stand up above a green and white jasper ground that lies at the base of the weight. In another they are spaced in a smoky green ground.

C O N C E N T R I C S—In these medium-sized weights (2⅜ inches to 2⅝ inches), the simple motif of from two to four concentric circles about a central floert is usually set in clear glass on a gently curved, invisible cushion. The precise rows are likely to include canes composed of arrowhead rods in alternating colors and canes whose exterior is striped with tiny star rods. Cane colors are generally restrained, though some weights have rows of Naples yellow and cadmium green. About half the examples are faceted, with the concave top window so cut as to show a reduction of the entire design.

A few concentrics rest on lace beds and can easily be mistaken for Clichy, until it is noticed that the gauze twists run counterclockwise and that the projections of the pastry mold canes are sharper pointed and tighter pleated than their Clichy counterparts.

G A R L A N D S—The basic pattern of most Baccarat garlands is the intertwining of two trefoils, each of differently colored canes [16]. But spaced circlets of canes and an open, six-loop are also known [17]. Most garlands are set in clear glass (even in the translucent overlay weights), though a few appear on lace, carpet, or color grounds, where the canes take on more life. In the circlet garlands each circlet is likely to be centered with a large cane. Perhaps a silhouette, and the trefoil gar-

[16]

[17]

lands usually place a similar cane in the loops (Fig. 16). The remarkable six-loop garland in red, white, and blue appears on a white stardust ground like a formal garden whose flowers are set in a ground of white pebbles (Col. Fig. 7).

SPECIAL PATTERNS—These rare weights, peculiar to Bacarrat, are of two sorts. In one, the motif always rests on a muslin ground and there is always a very large central design, usually of complicated construction. About this central design there may be a couple of widely spaced concentric circles of canes, or several widely spaced very large canes (Figs. 17, 18). Large, deep, cane folds are characteristic, as is the use of the shamrock and moth as integrating design elements. These are weights of power and impact, whose design must have taken considerable thought.[19]

The other kind of weight features separated concentric rows of canes in red, white, and blue about a large central floret, each cane extending toward the base in a long, inward slant which gives the weight the appearance of a sky-rocket burst. To block off the passage of light that might dilute the opacity of the long canes and thus weaken their coloring, wads of white filigree (lace) have been stuffed into the bottom of the clear glass space between each row of canes, the procedure generally used in the close millefiori.

Designs that probably occur only once in Baccarat are the six-pointed star of canes (see "Clichy Star Weights," Chapter Seven), and one where the canes form four hearts. A St. Louis example is known with a field of canes in the form of a heart.

CHEQUER—Among the rarest Baccarat weights. Unlike the ubiquitous Clichy chequer which is basically a spaced concentric or a radiating affair, the Baccarat is a chequerboard of straight rows of large silhouette and other canes, each separated by a grid of continuous, straight, tubular rods. The two examples known to the author are almost identical. Both measure 3¼ inches in diameter, both are dated 1849 but without the "B," and the separating rods in both are a robin's egg blue (Col. Fig. 3).

MUSHROOMS—So-named for their resemblance to the fruiting fungi. The standard Baccarat mushroom is a close millefiori tuft usually with a high-crowned cap, sharply undercut around the bottom edge, where the long canes retreat inward and downward in a column or stem that reaches the base. Just above the base the mushroom is encircled by a torsade consisting of a fine-mesh gauze cable enclosed in a blue spiral thread that runs counterclockwise. The tubular form of the torsade appears to have caused the artist the same air bubble trouble as caused by the snake, and the torsade frequently appears like a life belt floating in roily waters or an inner tube half out of the tire casing. The most successful torsades are those that show no bubble at all and ride level and comfortably above the base, so that they may be seen from above (Fig. 19). Close millefiori mushrooms occasionally appear with a pink or red spiral torsade, and are

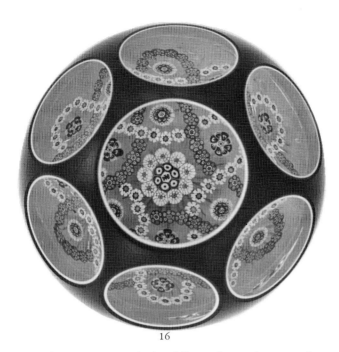

16

Fig. 16. Baccarat double overlay garland of trefoils, moth cane in center. *Courtesy Old Sturbridge Village. Photograph by James C. Ward.*

Fig. 17. Baccarat special pattern on lace. *Courtesy Sotheby & Co.*

Fig. 18. Baccarat special pattern on lace. *Courtesy Parke-Bernet Galleries, Inc.*

Fig. 19. Baccarat close millefiori mushroom with torsade. *Courtesy Christie's.*

17

18

19

Fig. 20. Baccarat concentric mushroom. *Courtesy Sotheby & Co.*
Fig. 21. Baccarat concentric mushroom. *Courtesy Sotheby & Co.*
Fig. 22. Baccarat concentric faceted mushroom. *Courtesy Sotheby & Co.*
Fig. 23. Baccarat concentric mushroom. *Courtesy Sotheby & Co.*
Fig. 24. Baccarat concentric all-white mushroom. *Courtesy Sotheby & Co.*

the motif of most double overlays, where they appear minus the torsade. Finer mushrooms are the concentrics with even rows of the most subtly tinted canes, and these frequently have pink or red torsades (Figs. 20, 21, 22, 23; Col. Fig. 4). Only very rarely do they appear in double overlays. There are a small number of all-white caned concentric mushrooms (Fig. 24), and rarest of all are the white stardust mushrooms of which there are probably less than half a dozen. They have a purity and a simplicity that one associates with the unattainable (Fig. 25).

Other interesting mushroom weights are a faceted miniature, a mushroom pedestal weight 3 ½ inches high with the mushroom above a filigree basket, a close millefiori mushroom with silhouette canes, and one with Clichy roses among Baccarat canes.

CARPET GROUNDS—These rich, juicy paperweights take three forms (Col. Fig. 5): the spaced millefiori with silhouette canes and florets; the garland in which touching circles of tightly packed canes surround a central circle (Col. Fig. 6); and the garland of intertwined trefoils. A six-loop garland on

Fig. 25. Baccarat white stardust mushroom. *Courtesy Old Sturbridge Village. Photograph by James C. Ward.*

white stardust ground has already been mentioned (Col. Fig. 7). (See "Garlands.")
The grounds themselves are composed of canes in a variety of colors packed so
tightly against one another that the ground frequently appears as an overall field of
rods. The rod units are stars (Figs. 26, 27), single tubes and honeycomb tubing,
and whorls (in the cauliflower grounds). Carpet ground colors include a medium
cobalt blue, a mottled red and white that looks like raw hamburger, pale aqua
(honeycomb) (Col. Fig. 8), lime green, apricot, and several subtle grounds of no
predominating tonality that have the quality of needlepoint (Fig. 28). In these,
each rod may be composed of two colors against white, such as blue and red, or
pink and green, with the color dispersed by the surrounding white. A *choufleur*

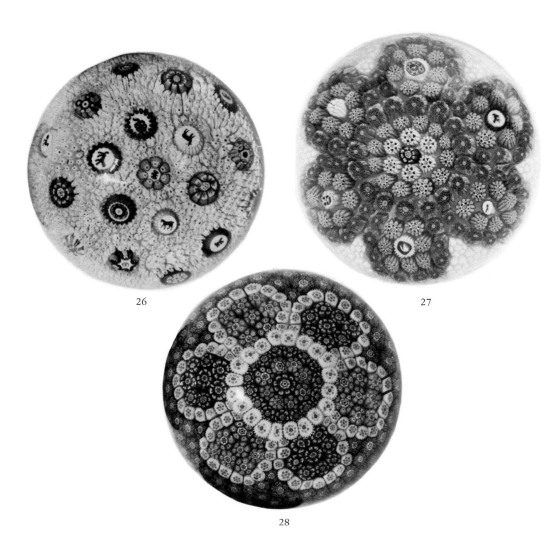

26   27

28

Fig. 26. Baccarat stardust carpet ground, spaced millefiori. *Courtesy Sotheby & Co.*
Fig. 27. Baccarat carpet ground. *Courtesy Sotheby & Co.*
Fig. 28. Baccarat carpet of clusters. *Courtesy Sotheby & Co.*

(cauliflower) ground is made up of canes that, unlike the canes in other grounds, are set loosely and with a bit of a twist. These canes are composed of opaque white whorl rods lined in lilac and lemonade. The overall tonality is cauliflower white (Fig. 29).

COLOR GROUNDS—Aside from the carpet grounds and sulphides (see Chapter Seventeen), color grounds are rare in Baccarat. An occasional red, blue, or green translucent ground appears beneath a garland, and a plain opaque white ground and one or two jasper grounds are known (Fig. 30).

Fig. 29. Baccarat *choufleur* carpet of lilac and pale yellow whorls. *Courtesy Sotheby & Co.*

Fig. 30. Baccarat jasper ground, spaced silhouette and other canes. *Courtesy Sotheby & Co.*

PEDESTALS—Except for the mushroom example mentioned above, these infrequent weights are concentrics with even, tightly packed rows of typical Baccarat canes; the pedestal with latticinio and twist ribbons of pink, red, blue, or white. One delicate specimen has pale canes in rows spaced apart in clear glass. Another is a magnum with a pink corkscrew ribbon on the flange.

UPRIGHT BOUQUETS—Rare as a class; perhaps one for every twenty from St. Louis. As with St. Louis, this is not just a flat bouquet standing vertical, but a three-dimensional bouquet of leaves, canes, and small, unidentifiable flowers that can be viewed from all sides. Torsades with blue, pink, or red spirals are the rule, but these cannot always be seen clearly from above (Col. Fig. 9). One large weight is cut with three graduated tiers of round printies and a large top printy. Another type of cutting leaves the instepped domed top untouched, while the sides from the waist down are cut with large diamond-shaped facets [18]. In this type of weight the upright bouquet is shaped like a square funnel.

[18]

FLOWER WEIGHTS—These include several Victorian favorites, but in most instances mix realism with symbolism. The flower center, for example, is usually a standard Baccarat millefiori cane. Most flowers are flat.

Pansy—The most common of the quasi-realistic flowers. About 25 percent of all Baccarat flowers are pansies. Most appear in clear glass with bright green leaves and one bud. Rarer arrangements include a circle of millefiori canes, the same on a lace ground, other flowers (see "Floral Groups"), but rarely a butterfly. One pansy weight is engraved on top with ears of wheat.

There are three basic forms of Baccarat pansy which, until now, have been widely assumed to date from different periods. However, an illustration from Baccarat archives (*Bulletin,* 1966-67, p. 37) shows sketches of two of the three types of pansy adjacent on the same plate, an indication that they may have been produced simultaneously. 1) The earliest has two large purple (over opaque white) petals above three small blue petals striped with white arrows and bordered in serrated white (Figs. 31, 32). Except for this border, these are the usual Baccarat arrow rods seen large because they have not been drawn out to their usual reduced size. The same petals are also seen composing complete flowers in some of the floral groups. The rod was simply handy to use. 2) The scarce intermediate type of pansy has the same two top petals, though they may be a dusky burgundy or plum color. But the lower three petals are now the heavily banded, blunt-cornered yellow and blue petals we find in blue and white or red and white in the Baccarat primroses—another instance of interchangeable parts. There must be a primrose somewhere with yellow and blue petals that were originally made up for a pansy. 3) In the final, most realistic, and most common type of pansy, the bottom three petals again change. Here we have an opaque white underlay similar to but slightly flatter than the large buttercup petals (see "Buttercup"), with the perimeter slightly upturned to contain the opaque yellow petal which fills its shape to just short of the opaque white edge. The ensemble is then cased in clear

31

32   33

Fig. 31. Baccarat early pansy in clear glass. *Courtesy Sotheby & Co.*
Fig. 32. Baccarat early pansy on muslin ground. *Courtesy Sotheby & Co.*
Fig. 33. Baccarat later pansy with star-rod center, star-cut base. *Courtesy Christie's.*

glass and the black or deep purple veining is laid in stripes on the clear glass. The yellow is the yellow of fresh butter and not the rancid amber we find in the Baccarat pansies of Dupont made around 1930 (see Chapter Eighteen). The opaque white sometimes shows on the back side and on the petal edges. By now the disposition of stem, leafage, and bud has become standardized, appearing the same in weight after weight. The millefiori center of the weight is usually a honeycomb, or a red whorl surrounded by white star rods (Fig. 33).

[19]

[20]

Primrose—A stylized flower superficially resembling the primrose. Colors: blue and white, red and white, pink and white, pale sulphur yellow and white, purple, blending to blue. Petal shapes show considerable variations [19], [20], [21], [22]. Coloring is strong in these large attractive flowers, and leafage is standardized. Weights come in all sizes to about 3⅛ inches (Figs. 34, 35, 36).

[21]   [22]

[23]

Primrose-related Flowers—Show a wide variety of petal forms and colors that must have been made up as lampwork [23], [24]. Some of the petals appear to be made up of flattened tubes fused together and bent into the desired petal shape like the multiple ply in the head of a tennis racket [25]. (Col. Fig. 10). Others consist of a petal of one color placed over a larger petal of another color, as in one wheat-flower that has daisy petals above it.

Fig. 34. Baccarat primrose. *Courtesy Sotheby & Co.*
Fig. 35. Baccarat primrose. *Courtesy Christie's.*
Fig. 36. Baccarat faceted primrose. *Courtesy Parke-Bernet Galleries, Inc.*

[24]

34

35   36

Wheatflower—The common name given to flowers of the field, consisting of about ten petals in pale yellow with, alternately, two and three black dots to each petal, or white petals with the same dots in pale blue. It appears with and without bud, alone or in floral groups. A variation is mentioned just above (Fig. 37).

Clematis—These only vaguely resemble the clematis flower. The long, veined petals with pointed tips come in single or double ranks and in several colors, including white, pink, aquamarine blue, pale yellow, chrome yellow, red, and amethyst. A lilac-colored petal may be striped with orange veins, or a white petal with lilac [26]. In the very formal arrangement the flowerhead wears a tiara of leaves and is flanked low down by two long, horizontal, tulip-like leaves and two buds whose stems cross, one in front of and one behind the flower stem [27]. A high proportion are miniatures (Fig. 38).

[26]

[27]

Fig. 37. Baccarat wheatflower. *Courtesy Sotheby & Co.*
Fig. 38. Baccarat clematis. *Courtesy Sotheby & Co.*

37   38

Some large and often handsome clematis weights are composed entirely of buds arranged symmetrically in tiers on long stems. Buds of different colors occasionally turn up in the same weight. These flowers have mistakenly been called tulips, whereas they resemble the closed clematis (Fig. 39A; Col. Fig. 11).

Bellflower—In another symmetrical arrangement these graceful flowers hang in threes from a central stew with long leaves above and below. Colors are salmon, white, aquamarine. A neat but static performance (Fig. 39B) [28].

[28]

Fringed Gentian—Shaped more like the canterbury bell than the bellflower, these cleverly placed blossoms in ultramarine blue, light scarlet, or alizarin crim-

Fig. 39A. Baccarat clematis buds in tiers. *Courtesy Sotheby & Co.*
Fig. 39B. Baccarat bellflowers. *Courtesy Bergstrom Art Center and Museum.*
Fig. 40. Baccarat buttercup. *Courtesy Sotheby & Co.*

[29]

son have a white fringe at the bottom. A flower book of the time says of them, "All the gentians require abundance of free air, and will not grow well in the smoky atmosphere of a town." The flowers in these weights ring like bells in country air (Col. Fig. 12) [29].

Dahlia—Set about with leaves like other Baccarat flowers, this rare type is smaller than the St. Louis dahlia. Petals in one example are two shades of lavender, bordered by white.

THREE-DIMENSIONAL FLOWERS

[30]

Buttercup—These single blossoms come, logically enough, in yellow, but also in blue and white, plum and white, or rich aquamarine. The bowl-shaped, three-dimensional flower is composed of deeply cupped petal segments. The petals in one are white at the center and orange-red in the outside row. Even where the colors are fanciful, the shadows caught in the bowl of the flower give it a look of sculptural reality [30]. Sometimes included in floral groups (Fig. 40; Col. Fig. 13).

Fig. 41. Baccarat camomile. *Courtesy Sotheby & Co.*

Fig. 42. Rare Baccarat camomile, mottled blue and white petals. *Courtesy Old Sturbridge Village. Photograph by James C. Ward.*

Camomile—The same petal form as seen in the buttercups is used for the camomile but in greatly reduced size and great profusion. The petals in the outer row do not feather or bleed into the surrounding clear glass as they frequently do with St. Louis, but instead turn their collars up as if to catch the rain. Much scarcer than their St. Louis counterparts, these Baccarat flowers come in white, mottled blue and white, peach, rose, and a wonderful copper tone, with leaves and sometimes a bud of another color. These rare flowers are obviously something special (Figs. 41, 42; Col. Fig. 14).

Rose—About as scarce as the Baccarat camomile. The realistic features of these three-dimensional flowers are the way the petals remain closed in the center, suggesting a half-opened flower, and the lovely rose coloring which ranges from softest pink to dusty velvet red (Figs. 43, 44, 45).

Floral Groups—These are large, flat arrangements of flowers appearing in weights that run over 3 inches in diameter. The flowers may be arranged as a bouquet, or individual blossoms may be spaced in a big circle about a central blossom. Any of the flowers already mentioned may be included and several usually are. Where the flowers in a weight are limited to red, white, and blue, the weights are commonly called tricolore in commemoration of the Revolution of 1848—a likely notion, though unsupported by instances of dating (Figs. 46, 47, 48, 49; Col. Fig. 15).

Fig. 43. Baccarat soft pink rose. *Courtesy Sotheby & Co.*
Fig. 44. Baccarat red rose with bud. *Courtesy Corning Museum of Glass.*
Fig. 45. Baccarat rose. *Photograph by Taylor & Dull.*
Fig. 46. Baccarat floral group with star-cut base. *Courtesy Sotheby & Co.*
Fig. 47. Baccarat floral group with middle-period pansy. *Courtesy Corning Museum of Glass.*
Fig. 48. Rare Baccarat floral group with five camomiles. *Courtesy Corning Museum of Glass.*
Fig. 49. Baccarat floral group, buttercup center, arrow petals. *Courtesy Old Sturbridge Village. Photograph by James C. Ward.*

43

44

45

46

47

48

49

Leafage—Though Baccarat leaves show some variation, they are easy to identify from the form and color. The special Baccarat green is more emerald than the St. Louis yellow-green, and lighter and brighter than Clichy green. Usually a rich emerald, it is sometimes a pale emerald, almost a malachite green. Leaves may sometimes be pointed at the end, but are usually blunt [31]. While the serration varies from fairly pronounced (it is never so pronounced as St. Louis) to indecipherable, the opaque white underlay is nearly always flooded with the green coating that spills over the edge of the leaf like frosting over a cake, flooding the serrations and leaving an outline that is smooth and rounded [32]. Like most French leaves these look as if the white underlay had been blown and then collapsed and then modeled before the green coating was applied. Perhaps they started as opaque white tubes that were heated, then flattened. In any event, considerable lampwork appears to have been involved. The long, tulip-like leaves, already mentioned in connection with the clematis, may be distinguished from Clichy by their color and the fact that they are, while sometimes veined, less reedy looking than the same from Clichy.

[31]

[32]

Once the arrangement of leaves most enhancing to each flower is worked out it is retained almost without variation, like a design in corsage by a florist.

FRUIT WEIGHTS—It is doubtful if all the fruits attributed to Baccarat are Baccarat; in many the leafage, the only telling factor, is uncharacteristic.

Strawberry—Though the leaves here have scalloped edges, they show the characteristic Baccarat shape, and their careful but lively arrangement in relation to the strawberries themselves leaves little doubt as to their origin (Fig. 50). The Baccarat strawberry is a remarkable creation. Look closely at how the three-dimensional strawberry is made. It is composed of a bundle of opaque white hexagonal rods fused tight together, cut off, and then rolled into a sphere perhaps as beads or marbles were rolled. Each hollow hexagonal rod has a red filler in the center [33], and when the opaque white sphere is coated with red those red fillers show up as the deep red pores of the berry. In a typical weight containing three berries one is usually made to look unripe, and this is done with a coating of green glass over the white, red-filled sphere. It should be noted that while the bract leaves as the base of the berries are likely to be small versions of the other leaves, they are also sometimes little green clematis petals, still another example of interchangeable parts (Col. Fig. 16). Strawberry weights are about as rare as snake weights.

[33]

Pear—These are infrequently seen but finely done, with the emerald green leaves and the full fruits arching off the graceful stem in a carefully balanced yet natural arrangement. The blossom ends of the pears are convincingly indented and detailed. These appear to be blown fruits, yet they are probably solid glass that was shaped under the lamp and then coated. Usually one or two fruits per weight.

Fig. 50. Baccarat strawberry. *Courtesy Corning Museum of Glass.*

Apricot—I have seen one example in a private collection: the twin fruits without a doubt look edible.

BUTTERFLY WEIGHTS—These interesting and frequently unsuccessful weights constitute a laboratory for the use of prefabricated, interchangeable parts to create the symbol of a butterfly. The body of the butterfly is nothing but the gauze cable from the mushroom torsade; the perfunctory wings—only the overlap suggests a butterfly's wings—are nothing more than a simple millefiori cane sliced thin and introduced to a tortoise-shell bed of fused colored chips; the antennae are threads with which to stripe a pansy; only the concave oval eyes seem to have been created especially for the butterfly. It is an ingenious use of spare parts and one senses the standardization of the performance once the design is approved, but what a nerve-wracking task the assembly must have been—covering the antennae with crystal, for instance, without letting them become detached from the head!

The standard butterfly appears in clear glass or on muslin with a ring of canes (Fig. 51). Sometimes it hovers over a flower (wheatflower, primrose, clematis, pansy, etc.) or two or three flowers (Fig. 52; Col. Fig. 17). The wings are always opened flat, except in one case where the butterfly appears in profile, wings folded in the "at rest" position on a sprig of mauve bellflowers—the same color as the butterfly's gauze body.

A few superb and many poor examples exist. Diameters run about 3 inches.

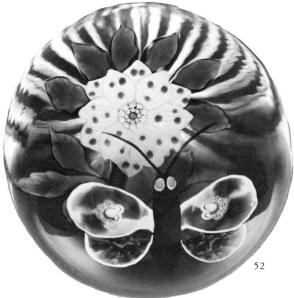

Fig. 51. Baccarat butterfly on muslin ground. *Courtesy Sotheby & Co.*

Fig. 52. Baccarat butterfly over white flower. *Courtesy Old Sturbridge Village. Photograph by James C. Ward.*

ROCK GROUNDS—These uninteresting weights are like those beds George Washington purportedly once slept in—George is missing. The rock grounds are the ones upon which snakes coil and lizards slither—only the snakes and lizards are missing. The ground itself appears as a stagnant pudding concocted of pulverized clay used for sulphides, unmelted sand, mica, and algae-green glass. These weights are reminiscent of a fish tank on cleaning day, though one specimen, curiously enough, has an upright rose with green leaves growing from the sand. Sizes range from miniature to magnum.

SNAKES—Presumably the rock grounds are trial runs for the snake weights, though Baccarat snakes also appear on muslin grounds, and one serpent with the forbidden fruit in its mouth is coiled above spiral latticinio that is centered by a typical Baccarat arrow cane. The tubular bodies of the snakes lie coiled above whatever ground is used in one and a half or two turns, the head usually resting on a coil, the tiny button eyes with an expression of benign asininity if the eye is black pupil on white, or drunken bliss if it is black pupil on red or orange. The coiled body comes in colors including black mottling on crimson, brown mottling on green, black or pink, green, white and pink (Fig 53). One snake is made of green latticinio gauze cable. The big problem seems to have been to place this lampwork snake upon the ground and cover it with glass without creating an almost continuous bubble between the coils—the same problem as with the torsades. No matter how skillfully the markings of the snakeskin are done, this annoying bubble or series of bubbles ruins the appearance of the weight (Figs. 54, 55).

Weights on lace grounds are frequently faceted like the brilliant-cut diamond, with a flat top table and elaborately cut girdle that chops the snake into little segments. Snakes are not dated. Weights generally run just over 3 inches. They are uncommon but not as rare as Baccarat camomiles, or upright bouquets.

LIZARDS—It is not yet possible to identify with certainty the great lizard weights. The choice is narrowed to three glass factories: Baccarat, St. Louis, and Pantin, who could have made the lizard weights sometime between 1878 and 1900 or shortly thereafter. But the choice of each of the three factories is fraught with difficulties, the delicate balance of provenance shifting with the addition of each new factor for consideration. The dates mentioned appear to be the only constant factor. Paperweight-making of the Classic period offers no counterpart to these great lizard weights. The first eyewitness account comes in the Colné report on the glass of Pantin at the Paris Exposition of 1878 (see Chapter Eight).[20] Colné's long report, which describes all the paperweights he saw at the exposition, makes no mention of any from Baccarat. But Imbert and Amic considered that the lizard was made by Baccarat around 1880, the "period in which high relief was in fashion." [21] Imbert and Amic also say that a simplified version of it appears in the Baccarat 1907 price list, which closes the period of its possible manufacture. [22]

The amphibians in these weights have frequently been called salamanders, the emblem, incidentally, of King Francis I of France. The only resemblance these wonderful creatures bear to the salamander is their mythical ability to endure fire without harm. The salamander has a smooth skin, whereas these convincing portraits of various lizards are stenciled and studded with scales and spots in green, sulphur yellow, amber, and silver. One bright green example is probably intended to represent the sand or green lizard. Others—the ones with shorter bodies and fat tails—look like the gila monster, though they lack the

53

55

54

Fig. 53. Baccarat snake on rock ground. *Courtesy Sotheby & Co.*
Fig. 54. Baccarat snake on muslin, note large bubbles. *Courtesy Corning Museum of Glass.*
Fig. 55. Baccarat snake on snake-algae ground. *Courtesy Parke-Bernet Galleries, Inc.*

spinal ridges. Green, black, or silvery, infant or fully grown, these fully three-dimensional creatures probe and bask in their sandy, herbivorous habitat (Figs. 56, 57; Col. Fig. 18).

The sandy ground is heavily mottled with dark green algae, and supports tall flowers on straight stems accompanied by much leafage. The flowers in various reds, white, or blue are similar to but more realistic than the flowers of the Baccarat and St. Louis upright bouquets, while the straight stems and long, naturalistic leafage suggest the aloes appropriate to this environment. These long leaves, frequently yellow-edged, show a longitudinal grooving (perhaps combed, perhaps the effect of parallel rods) that is as pronounced as tire treads. A second type of leafage is the old Baccarat leaf writ large. A third type is a big leaf convoluted and puckered. In all cases the leaves spring naturally from the stem, bending and curling this way and that, even falling over the body of the lizard.

The important thing about these various leaves is that severally they are identical to the leaves found in the rare, three-dimensional, naturalistic flower weights of unknown origin. The long leaves are seen in the lily of the valley weight whose blossoms are three-dimensional, and also in the Bergstrom Collection weight on spiral latticinio, where two white blossoms are like the lizard weights' aloes blossoms. The large, Baccarat-serrated leaves and the large puckered leaves are found in several of the "unknown" rose and other flower weights on color grounds. Like the lizard aloes blossoms, the flower centers of most of these other unknown flowers are composed of opaque, sulphur yellow filaments.

The connection between all these unknown flower and fruit weights to the

56   57

Fig. 56. Gila monster with aloes on sand-algae ground. *Photograph by Taylor & Dull.*
Fig. 57. Baccarat gila monster. *Courtesy Sotheby & Co.*

great, four-inch lizard weights is unmistakable. Revi, basing his assertions simply upon the Colné report, has presented a strong case for Pantin origin. But a study of the component parts of these weights points toward Baccarat of a somewhat later date. One must await some historical document or chemical analysis for a fuller answer.

DUCKS IN THE POND—Another weight precariously attributed to Baccarat. Enormously valued because of their scarcity, these are really nothing more than glass curiosities or friggers in which from one to three blown ducks, two ducks and a swan, or two swans swim on a ground of green algae (sometimes flecked with mother of pearl) under a hollow, faceted glass dome, the fused base forming a small pedestal. In some examples the fowl have come loose or are decapitated. The whole idea of contiguous glass magnifying the image is ignored in these weights. In this book they are but one step up from the hollow weight with the turtle that wiggles its legs (Figs. 58, 59).

Fig. 58. Ducks in the pond. *Courtesy Corning Museum of Glass.*

Fig. 59. Swans in the pond. *Courtesy The New-York Historical Society.*

OVERLAYS—For precision of design, these are among the finest paper-weights, though the interior coloring is apt to be a bit bland. The exterior over-lay coloring, however, is on a par with and very similar to that from Clichy. The single overlay is a coating (thicker than mere flash) of translucent ruby red, deep emerald green, or royal blue glass (Fig. 60). The double overlay is a coat-ing of opaque white beneath a coating of robin's egg blue, sky blue, cobalt blue, pale pink, or rose pompadour. The weights may be cut with six or more circular printies, the largest on top, with sometimes a lower row of oval printies or vertical flutes. The white margin encircling each printy where the inner overlay extends beyond the outer colored overlay may be fairly prominent or it may be hair thin. Some double overlays retain painted gold vermiculation or floral decoration.

Interior motifs are about equally divided between garlands of circles or interlocked trefoils and mushrooms that may be close millefiori or concentric but lack the torsade. The motif and basal star-cutting are repeated in each printy to great effect, and the soft, interior light created by the inner white overlay is one of great mystery (Col. Figs. 19, 20).

Fig. 60. Baccarat single overlay with millefiori garland.
    Courtesy Sotheby & Co.

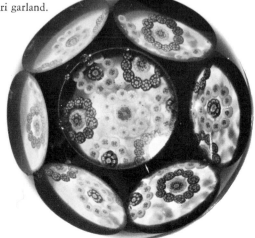

TRIPLE WEIGHTS—These are two known cases where three weights have been fused, one on top of another with the smallest on top. The large bottom weight in both is a spaced millefiori on muslin with silhouette canes. The middle weight in one is a scrambled, in the other a concentric. The top miniature weight in both is an upright bouquet, with a primrose in one and a wheatflower in the other. Technically interesting because the weights must have been made separately and then reheated so they could be fused together, they are, nevertheless, aesthetically too much of a good thing. Seldom, as here, do Victorian excesses in design extend to paperweights (Fig. 61).

PLAQUE WEIGHTS—The central motif of these rare weights is a circular, opaque white glass plaque to which has been transferred by lithography or some such process a picture, the plaque encircled by canes. In two different versions a blue chiaroscuro transfer picture shows a horse at full gallop (Col. Fig. 21). Another picture in lake red shows a blindfolded cupid holding an arrow, the bow beside him on the ground. These weights are cut with large printies. They are unmistakably Victorian.

PAINTED WEIGHTS—Attributed to Baccarat, these are thick, opaque white overlays with no faceting—the entire surface is opaque white and painted with flowers and foliage, including the rose, poppy, canterbury bell, cosmos, and anemone, a veritable lexicon of popular Victorian flowers (Figs. 62, 63).

A possibly unique painted weight shows a very realistic pansy with leaves, enclosed by a circle of little pink flowers and leaves. The motif here was etched into the base of the weight, then painted in, and afterward backed with more glass to seal in the painted design. The clear glass dome is faceted with six large printies. Again very Victorian, but also very attractive because the design is seen through the magnifying glass (Col. Fig. 22).

MEDAL WEIGHTS—Generally these feature the Légion d'Honneur or weights showing relief portraits of Napoleon. One medal is inscribed "Bonaparte I, Consul 1802" (Fig. 64), another, "Napoleon I, Roi des Français." The medals are made of thick gold leaf and, though lying flat, appear to be suspended from ribbons. Both ribbon and parts of the medal are enameled in various colors. The effect of a real medal is remarkable, though the object may actually be no more than half an inch in diameter. Another subject is the Grecian lyre in gold leaf that is brightly enameled in red, blue, and green.

SULPHIDES—(See Chapter Seventeen)

Millefiori By-Products

Include those objects tangent to paperweights, such as tazzas, shot glasses, handcoolers, goblets, vases. A beaker with double ogee bowl shows engraved foli-

Fig. 61. Baccarat triple weight. *Courtesy Parke-Bernet Galleries, Inc.*
Fig. 62. Baccarat painted weight. *Courtesy Sotheby & Co.*
Fig. 63. Baccarat painted weight. *Courtesy Sotheby & Co.*

Fig. 64. Baccarat medal weight, Bonaparte I, Consul, 1802. *Courtesy Corning Museum of Glass.*

age set with single florets as flowers: a close millefiori paperweight with silhouette canes and dated 1849 forms the base for a vase with flared rim, decorated with filigree spirals and cables in white and blue. A pair of vases with engraved garlands of leaves, the flowers again represented by millefiori canes, are set in gilt metal base holders (Fig. 65). A tazza with flattened, cup-shaped bowl and circular foot, both of close millefiori canes, connected by an inverted baluster stem with opaque white spiral tapes is dated 1846, the earliest known Baccarat millefiori date (Figs. 66, 67). As with Roman millefiori bowls, the canes run right through bowl and foot. A wine glass with millefiori base, a goblet with rigaree molding and millefiori canes, a candlestick with faceted staff and close millefiori base are other examples.

Baccarat handcoolers are usually hollow, blown, egg-shaped double overlays with many small printies, the printy on the broader end permitting them to stand. Occasional examples are deeply star-cut on top or cut generally to suggest foliage. One odd handcooler is stuffed with muslin. Another rare example is a double upright camomile, with the pink and the white blossoms placed back to back. (For the origin of the handcooler see Chapter Two.)

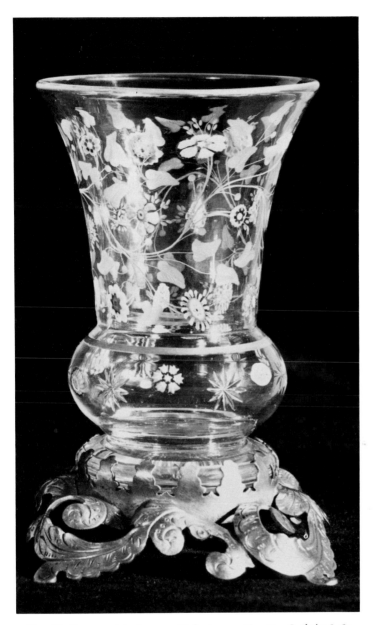

Fig. 65. Baccarat etched vase, millefiori canes. *Courtesy Sotheby & Co.*

Fig. 66. Baccarat tazza dated 1846 (side view). *Courtesy Corning Museum of Glass.*

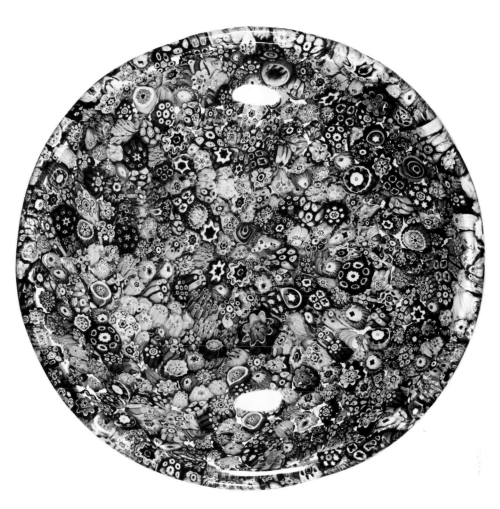

Fig. 67. Baccarat tazza dated 1846 (top view). *Courtesy Corning Museum of Glass.*

NOTES

[1] *Encyclopaedia Britannica,* 14th ed., vol. 1, pp. 701–2.

[2] The date is sometimes given as 1765, but 1764 is the date the company celebrates. See Guillaume Chaumeil, "The Rebirth of Millefiori at Baccarat," *Bulletin,* 1965, p. 41.

[3] A. Sauzay, *Wonders of Glass-Making in All Ages,* New York, 1885, pp. 87–88.

[4] This is a pastiche of historical information derived from a variety of sources.

[5] This old glasshouse, once called Manufacture de Cristaux et Emaux de la Reine (also known as La Cristallerie Lambert et Boyer, and more popularly as Cristallerie de Saint Cloud), moved in 1785 to Montcenis near Creusot and was afterward referred to simply as Creusot. Among other things it made sulphides.

[6] Ingold gives the inclusive dates of this association as 1830–1850, while Barrelet, p. 138, says Baccarat and St. Louis had a disagreement in 1855 and separated.

[7] Kenneth W. Luckhurst, *The Story of Exhibitions,* London, 1951, p. 220.

[8] Charles Colné, *Paris, Exposition Universelle 1878, Reports of the Commissioners,* vol. 3, pp. 243-387.

[9] Chaumeil, *op. cit.,* pp. 39–41.

[10] Most of the old cane molds at Baccarat disappeared during World War II.

[11] Chaumeil, *op. cit.,* pp. 39–41.

[12] J. de Poncins, "The Story of the Baccarat Figured Canes," *Bulletin,* 1956.

[13] *Ibid.*

[14] For an account of this weight see J. de Poncins, "The Odyssey of a Paperweight," *Bulletin,* 1954, pp. 15–17.

[15] Chaumeil, *op cit.,* pp. 39, 40.

[16] One single weight has nine of these pairs.

[17] Fred A. Nagel, "A Date with Silhouettes," *Bulletin,* June 1957; J. P. Boore, "Baccarat Silhouettes," *Bulletin,* June 1964, pp. 16–18.

[18] J. P. Boore, "Was There a Glass Conspiracy?" *Bulletin,* 1963, p. 19.

[19] Weights featuring the shamrock are said to have been made for the Dublin Exhibition of 1853, though I find no paperweights mentioned or listed in catalogues or accounts of this exhibition.

[20] 1878, *U.S. Commission Reports,* vol. 3, pp. 252–53.

[21] Imbert and Amic, *Les Presse-Papiers Français de Cristal,* Paris, 1948, p. 75.

[22] Some have attributed these weights to St. Louis, presumably on the basis of the mold-made lizards from that factory.

6

ST. LOUIS

CLOSELY PARALLEL AND RIVAL TO THE CAREER OF BACCARAT was, and still is, St. Louis, the second of the great French glasshouses associated with the making of paperweights. The factory was established three years after Baccarat, in 1767, at St. Louis near Bitche in the Munzthal of Lorraine. Like its neighbor Alsace, Lorraine, which runs from the Vosges to the Ardennes, has changed allegiance many times. From 511 A.D. to 925 A.D. it belonged to the Franks. It was successively part of the Germanic Holy Roman Empire (962-c.1300), then nominally independent until 1766, then French until 1870. After 1871 Lorraine became part of France; and it was always more French than Germanic in speech. For centuries Lorraine had been the center for the manufacture of "broad" glass, that is, sheet glass for windows and mirrors made from blown cylinders which were opened out and flattened. In the sixteenth century many of the "Lorrainers" emigrated to England where they became an important part of the glass industry.

In the early part of the eighteenth century the making of glass vessels in France was inferior to that being achieved elsewhere in Europe, which meant a dependence upon imports. But factories were springing up in the Lorraine in an attempt to compete with the then preeminent English and Bohemian crystals. In 1760 the French Academy of Sciences offered a prize to stimulate suggestions on how the situation in France might be improved. Almost from the first the Verrerie Royale de Saint-Louis, under the protection of the King, achieved a glass comparable to the Bohemian.[1] In 1781 came its first attempt to duplicate English flint glass, and the next year the first samples were submitted to the Academy of Sciences, which declared it the equal of the English glass. The crystal department expanded with its success, and by 1788 it was said to employ 76 workers.[2]

In 1829 the name of the company was changed to Compagnie des Cristalleries de Saint-Louis, an indication of where its specialties lay. A decade later St. Louis took up multicolored, overlaid glass[3] and the first paperweights must have been made soon after, though the first dated cane appears in 1845, a year before the same from Baccarat. There was, as I mentioned in Chapter Five, the joint purchase with Baccarat of the Creusot factory in 1832 in order to suppress that rival establishment, and the sharing for some twenty years of Launay Hautin & Company as Paris distributor. Through the decades of the last century and continuing into the present, the two companies have remained friendly rivals, especially, for our purposes, in the field of paperweights.

The correspondence of Launay contains several passages in which he encourages, cajoles, or berates St. Louis about its paperweights, suggests new forms such as desk sets and toothpick holders, and spells out exactly how he thinks they should be done. "Paperweights seem to sell well but they must be well made," Launay writes in 1847. "We believe you made an error in sending poorly made paperweights like certain ones we have received from you. This item of manufacture has no sales merit unless it is well done." [4] In a communication of 1848 to St. Louis he refers to fine bouquet weights:

> Amongst those we have received from you we have chosen one which is a fine composition and which will sell well. This type is generally well made; but it is still necessary to look for a way to improve it so as to create as much lightness as possible in the composition of the bouquet. If we are returning it to you it is so that you may notice how the white enamel flower detaches itself from the other colors. Return it to us as soon as you can and those which we will want from you will generally have the white flower. [5]

He goes on to advise that they should try cutting one with printies and that, if the flower is placed higher, it can reflect in the printies. "This is Mr. Laroche's idea who wants to see the effect this cutting will have before ordering newel posts with bouquets." [6] Laroche was the owner of the famous Escalier de Cristal, a shop in the Palais Royale that offered the finest in French crystal.

In another communication Launay criticizes the fruit weights as very poor. We have in the Launay correspondence the rare good fortune to glimpse the intimate details of what were great creative acts done with practical business ends in view. At the same time the letters provide a solid rebuff to the frequently expressed notion that glass paperweights were made without the knowledge of the factory management. For these paperweights and related millefiori were a new line of merchandise for St. Louis in its effort to eclipse the supremacy of Baccarat. The situation suggests a parallel in the relationship of the New England Glass Company and the Boston & Sandwich Glass Company, friendly rivals for almost sixty years. And, coincidentally, the weight-makers of the two American companies were men who learned their craft at the two great French works.

St. Louis exhibited at the Paris expositions of 1834, 1839, 1844, and possibly others in the following decade. Like Baccarat, St. Louis refused to send to the Great Exhibition of 1851, thus enabling Clichy to walk off with the Council Medal, the top prize. However, the *Jury Report* on glass for the Great Exhibition does refer to St. Louis: "Another manufactory of crystal or silicate of lead, using wood fuel and open pots, was established . . . It has continued to carry on a very extensive business during the last thirty years, and only yields in importance to the glass works at Bacarat[sic]." St. Louis exhibited in the Paris Exposition of 1867. Writing in the official catalogue, George Wallis of the South Kensington Museum observes how much more decorative glass was shown there than had been shown in the Paris Exposition of 1855. But in general very little notice was taken of the glass in the 1867 exposition and I find no useful discussion of St. Louis products. Nor is St. Louis mentioned among the *cristalleries* at the Paris Exposition of 1878, though Baccarat, Clichy, and Pantin were.[7]

St. Louis continued to make fine crystal and after World War II revived the art of making paperweights. A discussion of these will be found in Chapter Eighteen.

St. Louis Paperweights

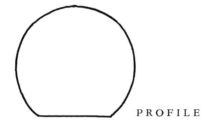

PROFILE

St. Louis paperweights show a good deal of variation in profile but on the average resemble those of Clichy. The thickness of the basal rim varies greatly from a thin edge to fairly wide, and the basal depth also varies. The constant factor appears to be the glass itself, which is very heavy and has a very high refractive index, and is usually very clear, "white," and free of striae. Bases, less frequently star-cut than at Baccarat, are nevertheless the usual thing with mushrooms, the upright bouquets, and some floral groups. The design is generally placed low and appears without distortion as the weight is viewed from different angles, except at the perimeters of latticinio baskets, which tend to blur in prismatic colors.

DATES AND SIGNATURES—A few of the finer St. Louis weights and related millefiori are dated 1845 through 1849, the commonest date being 1848. No other dates are known. The figures may be red, mauve, cobalt blue, or a deep purple, and the large letters "S.L." in black or blue above the figures. Again it should be stressed that the 1845 date almost certainly does not mark the beginning of St. Louis paperweight production. Dated weights are usually mushrooms, concentrics, or those weights that center silhouette canes. But, curiously, scrambled weights are occasionally dated, as are vases (one is dated 1845), a seal (dated 1846), and a magnum of 3¾ inches in diameter (dated 1848). Some concentrics and others are not dated but bear the large initials "S.L."

[34]

[35]

[36]

[37]

[38]

CANES—St. Louis canes show far less variety than those of Baccarat and Clichy and are therefore easier to recognize. The rods of which they are composed are generally stars, tubes with a colored filler, or crimps—a variation of the star being a blossom-like six-petaled rod [34]. Canes comprise these elements in a variety of combinations, but the crimped, coglike cane is the hallmark of St. Louis [35]. An anchor-shaped variation of the Baccarat arrow or crowsfoot cane turns up now and then [36], the anchor rods likely to be bundled every which way. In most of these, the Bohemian influence of a circle of rods about a central rod is evident. Less frequent are the cylinder with colored center, the large crimped cane whose center is a square filled with tubes [37], the Catherine Wheel of medieval infamy [38], and a fortress cane similar to Baccarat's. The commoner rod elements must have been made up in great quantities for they are ubiquitous.

Silhouette canes include a stylized flower; among the fauna, a walking duck with duckling, a hyper-lumpy, rubber-kneed camel, a plausible turkey, and a dog. The dog is sometimes a typical predatory French mongrel, at other times it seems to be a large, unshorn poodle. Neither dog has the pedigree of the Baccarat dog. Human canes include at least two of girls dancing alone, one of whom wears a skirt with a flounce. There is also, more happily, a cane with a dancing couple, and one of a dancing faun. And to keep these festivities in their proper perspective there is a red devil who appears to be figure skating. And then there is a cane that seems to me ambivalent, perhaps even anthropomorphic. It is a white silhouette on deep navy blue that is likely to appear at the very center of the finest carpet grounds. Look at it one way and it is a portrait of Punch, of some besotted dandy, or circus clown. Turn the weight ninety degrees and it becomes a very realistic aardvark or anteater; take your choice. These silhouette canes appear usually in the concentrics and carpet grounds, but occasionally serve to identify scrambleds. Rarest of the silhouettes is a sulphide profile of a woman some say is Pauline Bonaparte, the Princess Borghese with "empire" hairdo. Whoever she is, she is not Victoria. This lady appears in the center of a large, thick, jelly-like tube of swimming red glass that forms the center of a few superb carpet grounds and imparts to the lady the surrealistic look of a recently severed head. (See "Carpet Grounds".)

An equally rare pictorial motif is a delicate floral bouquet painted on a circular sulphide or one that is rectangular with cut corners, both plaques with stippled borders. These appear as the central motif of a very few carpet grounds and one marbrie.

COLORING—If St. Louis millefiori canes, limited in variety to begin with, show up with monotonous regularity, this is compensated for by the coloring which sets this glasshouse apart—and this in spite of the fact that the same colors are used over and over again for the same canes. A casual study of Victorian fabrics, wallpapers, and painted decoration indicates varying degrees of color subtlety. On the lowest level there are the floral pinks, reds, and greens seen boldly against brown or black. More daring yet more subtle are the colors used in the English calico prints of the period before 1856, when analine dyes were discovered. Made for the West Indian trade, these calicoes are unaccountably uncontaminated by the bad taste of the period.

The coloring of St. Louis paperweights points ahead to Degas and Kate Greenaway—lake red against Persian blue; lime green against powder blue and eggplant; coral, peach, and Naples yellow in proximity; sulphur yellow against raspberry; patriotic red-white-blue but with a dash of chartreuse. And all the colors are fine and clean and luminous over the opaque white base color, never watery or detached from it. Most of the time, to be sure, we do not see this; we see instead sloppily set rows (there is usually one cane that has slipped out of place and breaks up the next row) of unexciting canes, the colors not well balanced from row to row. But when the rows are even and the colors daring yet harmonious, there is nothing in paperweight-making like it, and one is left thinking of Monet's Rouen Cathedral series.

Paperweight Types and Characteristics

E A R L Y   W E I G H T S—From the look of these close millefiori weights we can be sure that they were made before 1845. For one thing they are close millefiori, a type not often made at St. Louis after 1845. The dome of canes almost reaches the surface of the glass, filling the whole weight as in the Venetian ball—once the magnifying effect of a lens above the motif was appreciated this procedure was abandoned. Though sometimes tightly packed, the canes are often loosely and carelessly placed, their outer edges squashed or fused into almost any shape but circular, and the weights studded with bubbles. Two canes infrequently seen in later weights are a sort of heraldic cross [39] and an opaque white cane set with petal-shaped blue rods [40]. Coloring, generally pale, includes powder blue and pale yellow. One weight is predominantly yellow.

[39]

[40]

S C R A M B L E D—Like Clichy these are often (one suspects in earlier examples) real scrambleds in Venetian ball style, a fruit jello of diced canes, latticinio, and colored twists, the mass close to the surface; though often we find the ground set lower, especially in faceted examples (Fig. 68A). Curiously, scrambleds are frequently the bases to shot glasses and tazzas of formal design, and some contain a real, end-of-the-run slag mixture with wild stripes of color, a kind of fricassee of macaw parrot. One fantastic weight has a large centered figure cane, the scrambled design suspended over a blue and white torsade which in turn is suspended over a white spiral ring. The letters "S.L." appear with and without a date.

C L O S E   M I L L E F I O R I—Aside from the earliest weights these appear very infrequently as mushrooms and pedestals.

C R O S S   W E I G H T—In this, the close millefiori is divided into quadrants by a cross of like canes enclosed in or bordered by spiral threads, with a central floret at the crossing. The large millefiori canes used here are the subtlest and most delicately colored, and the spirals are likely to be chartreuse yellow. Rare. (Col. Fig. 23.)

CONCENTRIC—One of the more common millefiori weights, these range in execution from sloppy to superb, and in size from just above miniature to 4-inch magnums with nine or ten rings (Fig. 68B; Col. Fig. 24A). One would presume signed and dated examples to be among the best done; yet, curiously, the insertion of the large signature and date assembly appears frequently to have disturbed the symmetry of a row, causing a cane to slip from the formation. But a well-done St. Louis concentric is a joy to behold (Figs. 69, 70, 71, 72, 73). One unique concentric in The Art Institute of Chicago centers a small sulphide pansy inside a thick, tawny-port tube. The outer row has red and plum-coated white rods in a border that suggests the edge of a marsh. Another probably unique concentric has a center of deep blue canes enclosed in a ring of white canes enclosed in an outer ring of brick red (Fig. 74). It is really a cross between a concentric and a carpet ground, a red, white, and blue target that, once seen, cannot be forgotten.

PATTERNED MILLEFIORI—Compared to their counterparts at Clichy and Baccarat, these common weights are not very exciting. A few large florets are spaced in a circle about a central floret, with an outer ring of similar or contrasting canes, the ensemble appearing in clear glass, or on a lace or jasper ground (Fig. 75). The delicately colored canes in pale blue, salmon pink, and chartreuse yellow are lost in the clear glass and on the jasper grounds, but show up well against the lace. A royal blue ground is rarely seen (Fig. 76). There are many miniatures showing a single cane in the center of a red, blue, or green and white jasper ground, the cane frequently misshapen. One extremely rare pattern shows a field of rods in the shape of a heart, enclosed in a field of rods and canes, a black devil sihouette in the center of the composition; all this on a green ground.

JASPER GROUNDS—A St. Louis specialty. The ground is composed of partially pulverized glass in two colors: opaque white and light cadmium green, garnet red, or cobalt blue. The amalgamation is shaped like a cushion or flattened balloon, with the bottom opening touching the base. Frequently cruder in texture than its Sandwich–New England counterpart, it forms the ground for single and double flowers, spoke weights (see "Jasper Paneled"), and a few others (Fig. 75).

JASPER PANELED — These are, happily, restricted to St. Louis. The ground is divided into eight panels of jasper in alternating red and green or blue and red by eight thick, opaque white spokes, each pie-shaped panel set with a large floret or silhouette cane; the axle of this wheel design is a silhouette cane or a miniature, turban-shaped swirl of tiny latticinio threads. Most examples have a delicate torsade of pink ribbon around white thread which can be seen only from the side. Not a successful conception, since the turban is almost impossible to decipher without a magnifying glass, and the florets are lost against the crude jasper (Fig. 77).

68A

68B

Fig.   68A. St. Louis scrambled with dog silhouette. *Courtesy Lloyd J. Graham.*
Fig.   68B. St. Louis concentric pedestal weight. *Courtesy Corning Museum of Glass.*

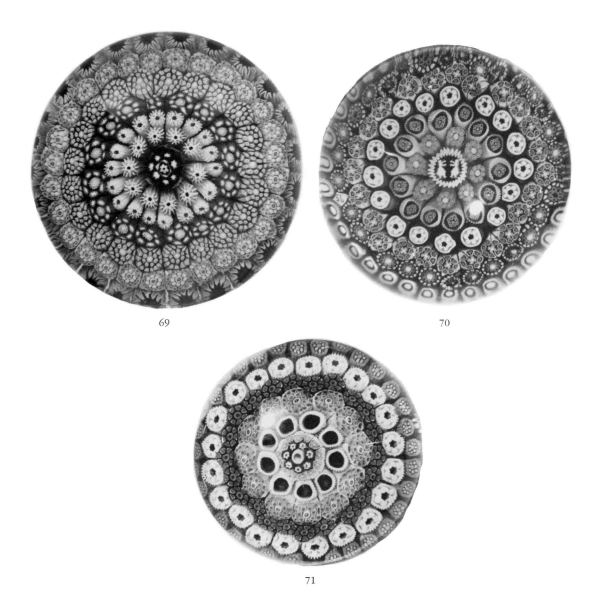

69

70

71

Fig. 69. St. Louis concentric. *Courtesy Sotheby & Co.*

Fig. 70. St. Louis concentric. *Courtesy Sotheby & Co.*

Fig. 71. St. Louis concentric. *Courtesy Sotheby & Co.*

Fig. 72. Signed St. Louis concentric, devil silhouette. *Courtesy Corning Museum of Glass.*

Fig. 73. Signed and dated St. Louis concentric, horse silhouette, rare arrow, quatrefoil canes. *Courtesy Corning Museum of Glass.*

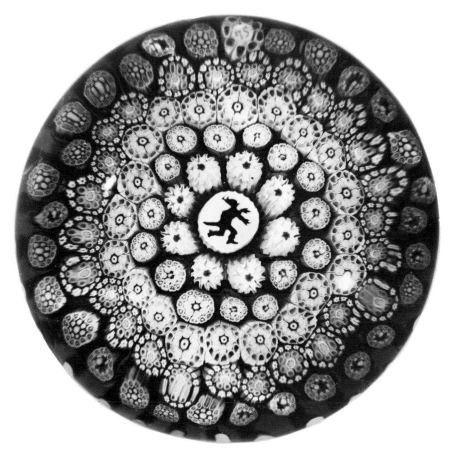

72

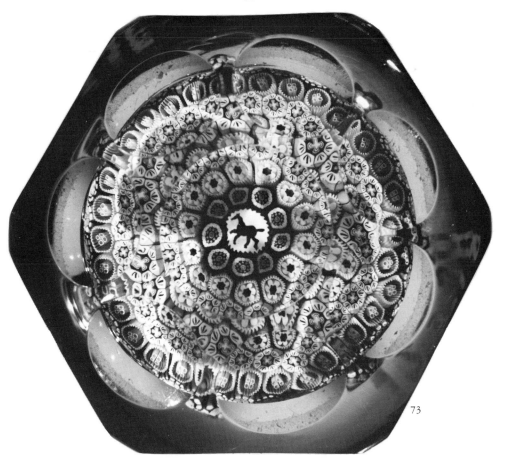

73

74

77

75

76

Fig. 74. St. Louis red, white, and blue concentric. *Courtesy The New-York Historical Society.*
Fig. 75. St. Louis spaced florets on jasper ground. *Courtesy Sotheby & Co.*
Fig. 76. St. Louis spaced florets on royal blue ground. *Courtesy Sotheby & Co.*
Fig. 77. St. Louis jasper paneled weight, turban swirl center. *Courtesy Sotheby & Co.*

GARLANDS ON COLOR GROUND—Rare with St. Louis, but generally not as effective as the same from Clichy, partly because the rather pale canes are overpowered by the bright grounds, and partly because the diamond-shaped or propeller-blade garlands are somehow uncomfortable to look at [41], [42]. The grounds are, of course, double, with a layer of opaque white beneath the intense salmon pink, aquamarine and sky blues, apple green, lemon, and chartreuse yellow (Figs. 78, 79A, 79B, 80; Col. Fig. 24B). The problem seems to have been to block the hole in the top center of the otherwise solid ground with a floret; a problem not always solved. However, the grounds are almost fluorescent in their brightness, and the weights are much sought after. A very rare blue ground is divided into four panels by amber and blue twist ribbons, each panel set with a garland of millefiori canes. Another particularly effective garland shows closed horseshoe-shaped loops of canes fitted to a bright yellow ground, which is composed of thick, looped sections set close together—a remarkable job of engineering that probably will remain some artist's secret. He appears to have made only one or two [43].

[41]

[42]

[43]

78

79A

79B

Fig. 78. St. Louis garland on color ground. *Courtesy Sotheby & Co.*
Fig. 79A. St. Louis garland on color ground. *Courtesy Sotheby & Co.*
Fig. 79B. St. Louis garland on color ground. *Courtesy Sotheby & Co.*

Fig. 80. St. Louis garland on color ground. *Courtesy Parke-Bernet Galleries, Inc. Photograph by Taylor & Dull.*

[44]

[45]

M U S H R O O M S—Though occasionally close millefiori, these usually lovely and sometimes ravishing concentric weights show daring color juxtapositions such as sapphire blue next to chartreuse yellow, coral against forest green, Prussian blue against amber, long-spined cerulean crimps filled with lake red (Figs. 81, 82). The high-domed, steeply undercut mushrooms may be large or quite small, and a few take the shape of a capstan, with the canes studding the entire bulbous surface [44], [45]. Mushroom weights are more frequently unfaceted but usually have a star-cut base, occasionally amber-flashed. The distinctive torsades contain a variety of opaque white chaplet beads, corkscrew and gauze twists encircled clockwise by the most delicate coral, pale orange, saffron yellow, blue or white spirals, which are sometimes flared or hooked (Col. Fig. 25). Occasional torsades are all white. One unusual torsade has a red corkscrew surrounded by an eight-strand spiral of flat white threads (Fig. 83). Most examples run under three inches and some are signed and dated. A lovely weight indeed.

Fig. 81. St. Louis mushroom, torsade with chaplet bead twist. *Courtesy Sotheby & Co.*

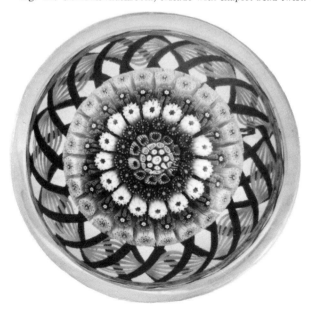

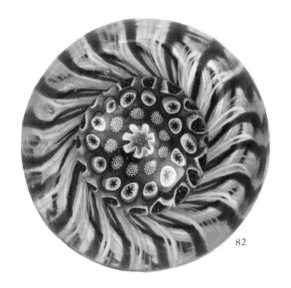

82

83

Fig. 82. St. Louis mushroom, unusual torsade. *Courtesy Sotheby & Co.*
Fig. 83. St. Louis mushroom, eight-strand spiral torsade. *Courtesy Corning Museum of Glass.*

CARPET GROUNDS—These weights are generally distinguishable from Baccarat by the presence of crimped or cog canes and the soft pink or green fields they create (Figs. 84, 85; Col. Figs. 26, 27). Subtle carpet tonalities are created by close color juxtapositions such as thalo blue and red, rich aquamarine and amber, or red, white, and blue as in at least two superb grounds which have to be seen to be believed. These, except for the central floret, are composed of large white crimped canes, lined with a glowing red about a single opaque thalo blue rod (Col. Fig. 28). In most examples, however, the carpet is accented with a few large florets, which may consist of the same carpet canes in contrasting colors (such as green florets in a pink carpet) or of silhouette canes; there is often a prominent central floret (Fig. 86). All-white stardust carpet grounds are known (accented with florets), and an extremely rare carpet is composed entirely of close-packed florets which are made up of white stars arranged about blue tubes, with a central red tube to each floret (Fig. 87).

Most extraordinary are the carpet grounds whose center is the profile sulphide of Pauline Bonaparte, the Princess Borghese (see Chapter Seventeen). In the Bergstrom example the carpet is divided into six panels of ravishing tonality that is alternately pink and blue, but composed of red, white, and blue rod elements; the crimps about the sulphide have chartreuse yellow centers (Fig. 88; Col. Fig. 29). Other similar fields are divided by festooning that recalls the marbrie festooning from St. Louis. A final example shows a white cog carpet accented with four large cog florets about a central square grouping, bordered by blue and yellow barber-pole twists. This remarkable weight is flat-faceted like an octagon.

Usually three inches or more, the large carpet grounds rank with the finest weights made.

CROWN—Undoubtedly suggested by Venetian filigree work and perhaps one or two crown paperweights made in Venice, this interesting and effective form varies in Bohemia (see Chapter Three), is perfected in France only at St. Louis, and travels to New England. As noted in Chapter Two, the form of the crown may have received its first notice in a letter written from Rome by the Abbé Barthélemy to the Comte de Caylus on Christmas Day, 1756: "I am especially pleased with a little ball of a pale yellow color, with clusters of white enamel ranged inside perpendicularly around the circumference."[8]

The St. Louis crown weight is a hollow, somewhat flattened ball whose walls are composed of a perpendicular series of white filigree twists alternating with twisted, colored ribbons that together follow the curve of the ball. The apex where these meet is capped with a floret (occasionally a silhouette cane), which, though it serves no structural purpose such as the keystone in a groined vault, nevertheless gives cohesion to the design and covers up any mismeeting of members. It seems plausible that these crown weights are hollow because of the way in which they were made, which may have been similar to the process used for making filigree goblets or bowls, that is, with the twisted filigree and ribbon rods lining a cupped mold into which a gather of glass is blown. It should be no-

Fig. 84. St. Louis carpet ground. *Courtesy Sotheby & Co.*
Fig. 85. St. Louis carpet ground. *Courtesy Sotheby & Co.*
Fig. 86. St. Louis carpet ground silhouette canes. *Courtesy Sotheby & Co.*
Fig. 87. St. Louis white stardust carpet ground. *Courtesy Sotheby & Co.*
Fig. 88. St. Louis paneled carpet ground, sulphide plaque center. *Photograph by Taylor & Dull.*

ticed that while these perpendicular rod elements meet at the apex of the weight, they do not quite join at the bottom; in fact, the bottoms occasionally show a hole—big enough to poke a pencil through—leading to the hollow chamber. It is as if the blow iron had been cracked off with enough force to take some of the delicate glass wall with it.

The ribbons, opaque white underneath, have been coated with a different color on each side, and thus show up as two-colored when twisted, a thin line of the opaque white showing only at the edges. Ribbon colors may be red and green, orange and blue, or blue and yellow (Figs. 89, 90, 91). Sometimes one sees three alternating color schemes instead of two, or a random arrangement of

Fig. 89. St. Louis crown. *Courtesy Sotheby & Co.*
Fig. 90. St. Louis crown, twenty-six ribbon and filigree twists. *Courtesy Sotheby & Co.*
Fig. 91. St. Louis crown, superbly done. *Courtesy Parke-Bernet Galleries, Inc.*

89

90   91

Fig. 92. St. Louis crown with thirty ribbons and filigree twists. *Courtesy Sotheby & Co.*

colors with some filigree in color, though this is more usual in American crowns. The aventurine is the rarest of all St. Louis crowns. Here all the twisted members are ribbons of chrome yellow, flecked with flakes or crystals of copper, giving a golden luster. There are at least two of these weights (Col. Fig. 30).

Crown-weight sizes run from miniature to a 3¾-inch mammoth that has thirty twisted members (Fig. 92).

FLOWER WEIGHTS

Flat Bouquet—Also called posy, this is the standard symbolic flower weight, usually consisting of three or four canes (symbolizing flowers) accompanied by four or more leaves of fresh spring green with deeply serrated edges, typical of St. Louis foliage. In its simplest arrangement the flat bouquet appears alone in clear glass (Fig. 93). More elaborate arrangements add a ring or two of canes, an amber

Fig. 93. St. Louis faceted flat bouquet. *Courtesy Sotheby & Co.*

94

95

Fig. 94. St. Louis flat bouquet, strawberry-diamond cut, amber-flashed base. *Courtesy Sotheby & Co.*

Fig. 95. St. Louis flat bouquet faceted with printies. *Courtesy Sotheby & Co.*

flash base; faceting, or all three (Figs. 94, 95). Faceting may include strawberry-diamond cutting on the base and multiple round, square, or hexagonal printies above. In these weights one sees the evolution of an idea from its simplest to its most complicated expression. The St. Louis flat bouquet and the spiral latticinio ground are the two greatest influences on American paperweight-making.

Special Flat Bouquets—Seldom seen, these appear with a cornucopia-like grouping of the stems in one example, in an opaque white vase with handles in another. Early examples have translucent dark green leaves and Bohemian-style canes (see Chapter Three). These very heavy weights have a low, flat dome and a very delicate torsade that is not clearly visible from the top. One is set in clear glass, another on a stippled white ground (Fig. 96). Both weights have flat bases.

Bouquet Garlands—These uncommon weights show a big circle of small flat bouquets, clematis, or other blossoms, or pansies, usually in clear glass (Figs. 97, 98A). One maverick example shows six single canes, each attached to a single leaf, about a similar center—blossoms blown by the wind. Three rarities show a circle of small bouquets about a central flower, all on a rich ruby to cranberry red translucent ground (Fig. 98B; Col. Fig. 31). These intense weights are faceted with three tiers of small oval printies.

96

97

98A

98B

Fig. 96. St. Louis early flat bouquet, stippled white ground. *Courtesy Sotheby & Co.*

Fig. 97. St. Louis bouquet garland in clear glass. *Courtesy Sotheby & Co.*

Fig. 98A. St. Louis bouquet garland, star-cut base. *Courtesy Old Sturbridge Village. Photograph by James C. Ward.*

Fig. 98B. St. Louis garland, ruby ground. *Private collection. Photograph by Taylor & Dull.*

Pansy—More like the viola than the pansy from Baccarat, these blossoms are not often seen. The flower center is likely to be a sulphurous dot like a kitchen matchhead. Pansies are usually seen alone, but one is repeated as a garland (see reference above), another comes in tandem with another small flower and leaves on latticinio double swirl ground, and still another appears on a red and white jasper ground.

Clematis—The prominently veined petals appear to be made from deflated tubes whose white ends frequently show at the tips. These are more casually contoured than with Baccarat, and come in pale and deep cobalt blue, pink, white, and occasionally mauve. Grounds may be clear glass, jasper, or most often latticinio swirl (Fig. 99). The thick white latticinio, tightly knit and superbly laid out,

99

100

101

has often rescued a mediocre flower (or fruit) (Fig. 100). The quality of the latticinio and the deeply serrated bright green leaves serve to distinguish these weights from the American. The finest from St. Louis, usually in blue, are cut about the sides with big printies, but the top is left round, which creates an interesting pattern (Fig. 101). An extraordinary example shows a white double clematis above a *single* latticinio swirl ground in turn above a closed dome of translucent cobalt (Col. Fig. 32).

In rare instances, the clematis appears on a deep green aventurine ground surrounded by a red and white or pink and white torsade (Col. Fig. 33). One fabulous weight contains six clematis blossoms in blue, pink, white, and orange on a deep green aventurine ground. This diamond-faceted weight has a deeply concave top, as if it were intended as a wafer holder. Another pink and white petaled clematis with leaves rests on a black or deep mulberry ground whose center perforation unfortunately reveals the white underlay (Fig. 102).

[46]

Anemone—Also called geranium, this handsomely simple flower in deep rose or blue is the St. Louis equivalent of the Baccarat primrose. The five petals bear short black stripes and the large black flower center shows sulphurous dots [46]. The flower can be seen across the room (Fig. 103).

Camomile—Perhaps the finest St. Louis flower, the feathery camomile is set with bud and leaves on a latticinio double swirl ground; the flower is most commonly white on pink ground; sometimes, the reverse (Figs. 104, 105). Unlike Baccarat, the flower petals here are carefully often bled out into the surrounding clear glass, giving the blossom a gossamer quality that is one of the triumphs of pa-

102   103

Fig. 99. St. Louis clematis on fine jasper ground. *Courtesy Sotheby & Co.*
Fig. 100. Pink St. Louis clematis on double spiral latticinio. *Courtesy Sotheby & Co.*
Fig. 101. Blue St. Louis clematis, printies but round top. *Courtesy Corning Museum of Glass.*
Fig. 102. St. Louis, two clematises on color ground. *Courtesy Sotheby & Co.*
Fig. 103. St. Louis anemone on thick latticinio ground. *Courtesy Sotheby & Co.*

teristically simple, usually consist of a yellow cog cane with pale blue center. Most weights are large, but miniatures are known. The tendency has been to call all dahlias St. Louis, but quite distinct Clichy and Mt. Washington examples are known (Col. Figs. 37, 38).

Fuchsia—These beautiful flowers, generally given a passing nod, are as rare as snakes. The presentation of this realistic flat flower on double-swirl white lattici nio is worked out with Baccarat precision. In addition to the main blossom, the orange stem supports two small upper leaves, two larger lower leaves, one or two small buds, and a larger bud. The smaller buds also do duty as the cherries in St. Louis fruit weights. The stem is placed intentionally off center to accommodate the extension of the large blossom, whose delicate green stem curls about the larger stem (Col. Fig. 39). The detailing of the large scarlet and blue blossom with buds in two stages and primary and secondary leaves combines to make an ensemble whose valentine grace and ravishing color are not soon forgotten (Fig. 112). One faceted miniature, believe it or not, rests on a pale blue latticinio ground.

Chrysanthemum—So-called for want of a better approximation. One probably unique example has long blue petals with a broad pink stripe down the center, set with leaves on double spiral latticinio. Another (that may be St. Louis) has pink-striped white petals and rests above a rich amethyst cushion in a weight whose sides have been squared off.

Other Flowers—Appear singly or in groups but are not specifically identifiable.

Large Flat Bouquets—These are large, informal groupings of various flat flowers, including the snowdrop, clematis, anemone, pansy, one even includes a fuchsia and other buds, as well as blossoms with leaves in clear glass with star-cut base. Effective as they are, they need no ground embellishment. They are slightly less natural looking than Clichy bouquets, and the foliage is sparingly

Fig. 112. St. Louis fuchsia on double-swirl latticinio ground. *Courtesy Sotheby & Co.*

has often rescued a mediocre flower (or fruit) (Fig. 100). The quality of the latticinio and the deeply serrated bright green leaves serve to distinguish these weights from the American. The finest from St. Louis, usually in blue, are cut about the sides with big printies, but the top is left round, which creates an interesting pattern (Fig. 101). An extraordinary example shows a white double clematis above a *single* latticinio swirl ground in turn above a closed dome of translucent cobalt (Col. Fig. 32).

In rare instances, the clematis appears on a deep green aventurine ground surrounded by a red and white or pink and white torsade (Col. Fig. 33). One fabulous weight contains six clematis blossoms in blue, pink, white, and orange on a deep green aventurine ground. This diamond-faceted weight has a deeply concave top, as if it were intended as a wafer holder. Another pink and white petaled clematis with leaves rests on a black or deep mulberry ground whose center perforation unfortunately reveals the white underlay (Fig. 102).

Anemone—Also called geranium, this handsomely simple flower in deep rose or blue is the St. Louis equivalent of the Baccarat primrose. The five petals bear short black stripes and the large black flower center shows sulphurous dots [46]. The flower can be seen across the room (Fig. 103).

[46]

Camomile—Perhaps the finest St. Louis flower, the feathery camomile is set with bud and leaves on a latticinio double swirl ground; the flower is most commonly white on pink ground; sometimes, the reverse (Figs. 104, 105). Unlike Baccarat, the flower petals here are carefully often bled out into the surrounding clear glass, giving the blossom a gossamer quality that is one of the triumphs of pa-

102

103

Fig. 99. St. Louis clematis on fine jasper ground. *Courtesy Sotheby & Co.*

Fig. 100. Pink St. Louis clematis on double spiral latticinio. *Courtesy Sotheby & Co.*

Fig. 101. Blue St. Louis clematis, printies but round top. *Courtesy Corning Museum of Glass.*

Fig. 102. St. Louis, two clematises on color ground. *Courtesy Sotheby & Co.*

Fig. 103. St. Louis anemone on thick latticinio ground. *Courtesy Sotheby & Co.*

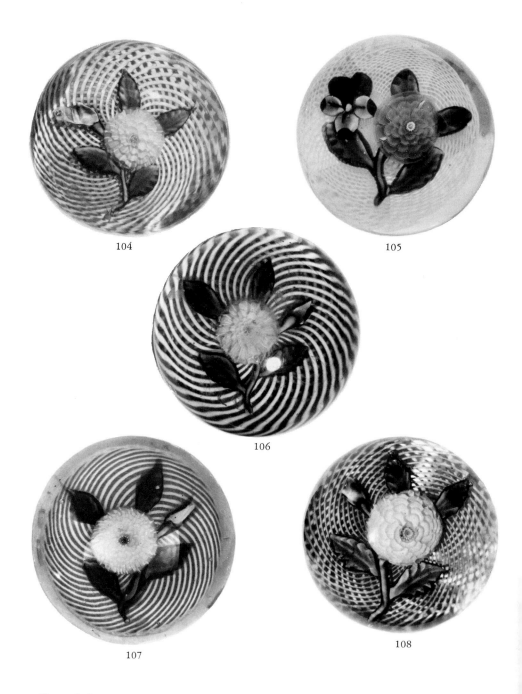

104

105

106

107

108

Fig. 104. St. Louis camomile on white over pink latticinio swirl. *Courtesy Christie's.*

Fig. 105. St. Louis pink camomile and pansy on white latticinio. *Courtesy Sotheby & Co.*

Fig. 106. St. Louis feathery white camomile. *Courtesy Sotheby & Co.*

Fig. 107. St. Louis camomile on double swirl that appears to be single. *Courtesy Sotheby & Co.*

Fig. 108. St. Louis camomile, note typical serrated leaf edge. *Courtesy Sotheby & Co.*

Fig. 109. St. Louis lilac-colored dahlia, striped petals. *Courtesy Sotheby & Co.*

Fig. 110. St. Louis dahlia, starred center. *Courtesy Corning Museum of Glass.*

Fig. 111. St. Louis dahlia with orange and brown-striped yellow petals. *Courtesy Corning Museum of Glass.*

perweight-making (Figs. 106, 107, 108). The strikingly colored latticinio double swirl runs from a soft pink to a tomato red, a rare example showing tomato red over white, and another, a ruby alternating with white. Sometimes the two layers of white latticinio have a layer of translucent red glass between them. A pair of pink blossoms on white latticinio are known (Col. Fig. 34).

Dahlia—Really a big clematis with three or more ranks of petals, this flower nearly fills the weight—only the leaves peek out. Petal tonality is deceptive because the petals, which may be flattened crimped tubes, are striped with various colors. What may at a glance appear to be a deep lilac color is in fact the impressionistic (I use this term in its historically technical sense) merging of parallel threads of red, white, and blue (Fig. 109; Col. Fig. 35). A petal that appears amber may have mauve, pink, and yellow stripes. Some petals are all pink, and some are yellow, striped with orange and brown (Fig. 111; Col. Fig. 36), but the mauve dahlia is the most common (Fig. 110). Flower centers, charac-

109

110   111

teristically simple, usually consist of a yellow cog cane with pale blue center. Most weights are large, but miniatures are known. The tendency has been to call all dahlias St. Louis, but quite distinct Clichy and Mt. Washington examples are known (Col. Figs. 37, 38).

Fuchsia—These beautiful flowers, generally given a passing nod, are as rare as snakes. The presentation of this realistic flat flower on double-swirl white lattici nio is worked out with Baccarat precision. In addition to the main blossom, the orange stem supports two small upper leaves, two larger lower leaves, one or two small buds, and a larger bud. The smaller buds also do duty as the cherries in St. Louis fruit weights. The stem is placed intentionally off center to accommodate the extension of the large blossom, whose delicate green stem curls about the larger stem (Col. Fig. 39). The detailing of the large scarlet and blue blossom with buds in two stages and primary and secondary leaves combines to make an ensemble whose valentine grace and ravishing color are not soon forgotten (Fig. 112). One faceted miniature, believe it or not, rests on a pale blue latticinio ground.

Chrysanthemum—So-called for want of a better approximation. One probably unique example has long blue petals with a broad pink stripe down the center, set with leaves on double spiral latticinio. Another (that may be St. Louis) has pink-striped white petals and rests above a rich amethyst cushion in a weight whose sides have been squared off.

Other Flowers—Appear singly or in groups but are not specifically identifiable.

Large Flat Bouquets—These are large, informal groupings of various flat flowers, including the snowdrop, clematis, anemone, pansy, one even includes a fuchsia and other buds, as well as blossoms with leaves in clear glass with star-cut base. Effective as they are, they need no ground embellishment. They are slightly less natural looking than Clichy bouquets, and the foliage is sparingly

Fig. 112. St. Louis fuchsia on double-swirl latticinio ground. *Courtesy Sotheby & Co.*

used. They are purely decorative and have an indefinable peppermint quality that one associates with the best American weights (Col. Fig. 40).

Upright Bouquets—These three-dimensional, thick, tight groupings of canes and real flowers with foliage are, except for the cane types and the simple flower centers, very similar to Baccarat. Generally, the bouquets are so sculptural that it is necessary to turn the weight about to see all the little buds and canes which pop out here and there in bright primary colors and white. The thick trunk tapers to a very fine point at the base of the weight where the star cutting is, often touching the very center of the star. Except in the handcoolers, where they are frequently seen, in a few heavily faceted magnums (Figs. 113A, 113B) they usually come surrounded by torsades, whose outer spirals may be blue, red, coral, pale yellow, pale green, or white. Even more than with the mushrooms, the torsades here show a great variety of filigree, and a corkscrew of several white strands is also popular (Fig. 114). Weights are usually faceted, some with

113A

113B

114

Fig. 113A. St. Louis upright bouquet with torsade, side view through flat facets. *Courtesy Parke-Bernet Galleries, Inc.*

Fig. 113B. St. Louis upright bouquet with torsade, side view through flat facets. *Courtesy Sotheby & Co.*

Fig. 114. St. Louis upright bouquet with corkscrew torsade. *Courtesy Sotheby & Co.*

diamond or other cutting, and bases are frequently strawberry-diamond cut (Figs. 115, 116). A floral variation stands about halfway between the flat and the upright bouquet, the relief flowers surrounded by a flat, spokelike arrangement of leaves whose serrations are apostrophized with tiny bubbles in the Sandwich manner; these fine formal arrangements usually have all-white torsades (Figs. 117, 118). One appears on amber flash base with initials, probably of the giver and the receiver. A most unusual mixed example has the counterclockwise spiral torsade of Baccarat and a circle of canes from both factories, recalling the Baccarat-Clichy mixtures and the fact that canes of one factory did occasionally stray into the province of another.

Fig. 115. St. Louis upright bouquet, diamond faceted. *Courtesy Sotheby & Co.*

Fig. 116. St. Louis upright bouquet with tight torsade enclosed in printies. *Courtesy Sotheby & Co.*

Fig. 117. St. Louis upright bouquet with wheel of leaves. *Courtesy Sotheby & Co.*

Fig. 118. St. Louis upright bouquet, white torsade, wheel of leaves with bubbles. *Courtesy Sotheby & Co.*

115   116

117   118

Fig. 119. Chinese copy of St. Louis basket weight. *Courtesy Bergstrom Art Center and Museum.*

There are a very few upright bouquets in double-swirl latticinio baskets with red and white twisted ribbon handles, the sides of white latticinio bands, extending down to blue and white stardust finials. These triumphs of the paperweight art were copied, probably by the Chinese, and with surprising success (Fig. 119; Col. Fig. 41). Upright bouquets with torsade are complete and nearly perfect in themselves and should not be considered as dress rehearsals for the encased overlays.

F R U I T W E I G H T S—Chemical analyses or testing of refractive indices would be required to determine if all the fruit weights attributed to St. Louis really belong there. Yet four well-established types from this glasshouse include fruit baskets, strawberries, cherries, and grapes.

Baskets—The term "basket" must be construed here as referring to a funnel-shaped double-swirl latticinio ground in which small fruits are displayed in a casual or formal arrangement. Casual arrangements include three pears, or two pears and an apple, a few cherries on stems, and leaves; or with one large pear among the rest; or cherries alone (Figs. 120, 121, 122, 123, 124). Some arrangements might be called upright, with the fruit and stems going far down into the funnel basket. One example substitutes four spiral torsades for the basket. The formal arrangement has six white, mauve, and/or pink turnips arranged in a stiff circle, leaf end out, like so many pigs at the trough (Fig. 125A).

Strawberries—A fine weight indeed, and easily distinguishable from Baccarat, it shows two strawberries suspended from a stem with leaves and, at the top, a white strawberry flower. Of the semirealistic but flat fruits one is sometimes not yet ready for picking. The motif here rests above a slightly convex latticinio

120

121

122

123

124

Fig. 120. St. Louis fruit in latticinio basket. *Courtesy Christie's.*
Fig. 121. St. Louis fruit in latticinio basket. *Courtesy Sotheby & Co.*
Fig. 122. St. Louis large pear and cherries in basket. *Courtesy The New-York Historical Society.*
Fig. 123. St. Louis fruit in looser latticinio basket. *Courtesy Sotheby & Co.*
Fig. 124. St. Louis miniature pear. *Courtesy Sotheby & Co.*

125A

125B

Fig. 125A. St. Louis turnip weight. *Courtesy Sotheby & Co.*
Fig. 125B. St. Louis strawberries. *Private collection. Photograph by Taylor & Dull.*

double-swirl ground. One weight shows a single-swirl ground that is very attractive. If anything, these weights turn up less often than the fuchsia (Fig. 125B; Col. Fig. 42).

Cherries—Like the fruits already referred to, one weight has ten small cherries on yellow threadlike stems with leaves tossed into a double-swirl basket. But most cherry weights come with two cherry-sized cherries on stems in clear glass. The various faceting treatments give the illusion of fifty or more cherries on a bough (Figs. 126, 127). This is imaginative paperweight-making. One cherry weight (or is it a plum?) is a miniature on pedestal. Another has a three-dimensional cluster of Queen Anne cherries, their long stems tied by a cord.

Fig. 126. St. Louis two-cherry, faceted strawberry-diamond base. *Courtesy Sotheby & Co.*
Fig. 127. St. Louis two-cherry. *Courtesy Sotheby & Co.*

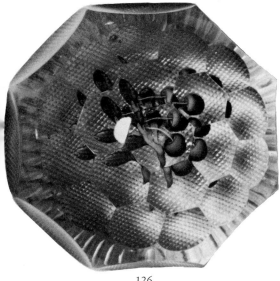

126

127

Mulberries or Currants—These show the same form as the small cherries, but are arranged in a thick, natural cluster with winding yellow tendrils. Some appear with pale acid green leaves on opaque white grounds and are possibly from the Pantin factory or elsewhere.

Grapes—In my opinion, the loveliest of all the fruit weights from St. Louis. A bunch of tiny purple and blue grapes hangs from an orange woody stem from which spring realistic grape leaves (a departure for St. Louis, which generally uses one kind of leaf for everything) and delicate tendrils. Delicate faceting in concave squares enhances the picture (Fig. 128A).

Pears and Apples—Some may be St. Louis but some are not. These fruits in high relief are usually found in doorknobs or in miniatures, some of which may be small knobs that were reground as paperweights. Not very interesting and not always well done.

DOUBLE OVERLAYS—A few with upright bouquet as motif are double exterior overlays such as one sees from Baccarat.

ENCASED OVERLAYS—In form these are upright bouquets minus torsade, but elaborately overlaid. First the double overlay is applied in two dippings like any double overlay, and one must assume that the weight was then

Fig. 128A. St. Louis bunch of grapes, on stem with leaves and tendrils. *Courtesy Sotheby & Co.*

cooled or annealed to permit the cutting of the printy windows. These are well cut, showing an even white margin about the printies where the first opaque white overlay meets the cobalt blue, cadmium green, rose pink, or chartreuse yellow overlay (Col. Fig. 43). Some weights are single opaque white overlays. But unlike all other overlays, except those from Bacchus, the process does not end here, for the weight has again to be taken up on the pontil rod, reheated, and given a third overlay in the form of a heavy coating of clear crystal that seals off and preserves the color overlays. One wonders why it was done, for there must have been something in the reheating process that infected these upright bouquets with bubbles and glass saliva that is not present to anything like the extent in the upright bouquets embedded in clear glass.

Some of the overlay work is notable for the way it has been cut. A single white overlay is cut with a dog and a stag. A few pink and white, and apple green and white overlays have oval panels which frame silhouette cutouts of a fox and a hound (Col. Figs. 44, 45). A fantastic royal blue over white overlay is cut with six windows shaped like flower blossoms through each of which may be seen the upright bouquet—perhaps the finest of all St. Louis encased overlays. All these, like other overlays, derive from the Bohemian overlay work then in fashion, but with the striking difference that they are themselves encased in clear glass. One very special weight in the collection of the Corning Museum of Glass is a triple overlay: royal blue over opaque white, but with the inner surface of the white flashed with a flamingo shade that gives the interior of the weight the ethereal quality of a Renaissance dome.

MARBRIE—Unrelated to the encased overlays are the remarkable marbrie weights. They are hollow and must have been blown. The single white overlay, which covers the whole weight except for the small floret or cane motif at the apex, is festooned with trailed swags of another color, such as medium thalo blue, blood red, or red and green together (Col. Figs. 46, 47). Festooning takes various forms, but the surface is usually divided into quadrants of festoons which may arc inward toward the apex or outward from the apex of the weight [47], [48]. One possibly unique example centers a rectangular sulphide plaque with painted bouquet. Some marbries have a large molded lizard perched on top. As a class, these weights are rare.

[47]

[48]

The term "marbrie" derives from the French *marbre* (marble), but the idea of the festooning may derive from the earlier decoration of witch balls in the Bristol area. A Sandwich marbrie weight is known, and the festooning can be found in a few Sandwich and Somerville flower weights as an interior decoration to frame the flower.

BUTTERFLIES—A colorful but not very successful weight, with the yellow, blue or mauve body of the butterfly sloppily done, the eyes misplaced, the feelers thick and watery. The canes which decorate the wings are easily identifiable as St. Louis and the butterfly invariably rests (though like as not off center) on a double-swirl latticinio ground. One unique example also shows a realistic, three-dimensional frog on its latticinio ground.

SNAKES—It is likely that the snakes on green and white or red and white jasper grounds are St. Louis (Col. Fig. 48). In other respects they are as uninteresting as the same weights from Baccarat, with the same big bubble trouble. One wonders how they ever got to be so valued in competition with rarer, lovelier weights.

LIZARD—This cast-molded reptile, like a miniature life cast, is fused to the top of hollow-blown paperweights. While the lizard is almost always gilded (the gilt showing various stages of wear), the weight itself comes in a variety of colors such as opaque white with marbrie festooning in medium thalo blue or blood red, green and white jasper, china blue, and Nile green, sometimes decorated with gilded foliage or vermiculation. Some overlays, particularly apple green over white, are cut with foliage that is typical of mid-century St. Louis overlay cutting. Part Victorian, part Rococo, part Empire Egyptian, the lizard weight is nevertheless a noble object (Col. Fig. 49).

FISH—This is more than just another sulphide. The three-dimensional, molded sulphide fish resembling a fully grown carp is so long that it nearly bisects the weight. We see it nibbling at what looks like a piece of red bait or a smaller goldfish, for, according to Lee McLean, carp eat all sorts of other fish. One carp hovers over a blue and white jasper ground, but a few examples are double overlays—blue over white or green over white—the scallop-edged, flute-cut overlay covering only the lower half of the weight, leaving the top clear, as if we were looking into a circumscribed pool.

BIRDS—Sometimes called parrots, these few, long-legged, colorful birds perch on a branch with leaves of the early St. Louis variety (see "Special Flat Bouquets"). Low crown is slightly flat; flat base is strawberry cut; and there is a spiral torsade that is not visible from the top of the weight (Fig. 128B).

DOG—Probably unique. The flat motif shows a fine, large, retriever-type dog white with brown and black ears and a long, plumed tail pointing in profile against a bold green and white jasper ground, a blue and white torsade that cannot be seen from the top. This bold weight reminds one of work from Millville, though it is doubtful anyone from Millville ever saw this unique specimen.

Related Millefiori Objects

HANDCOOLERS—These are of four types: 1) Close millefiori extending almost to the surface, all in the shape of an egg. These are sometimes made in

Fig. 128B. St. Louis bird on branch. *Courtesy Sotheby & Co.*

two sections fused together, the joining place easily visible about halfway up (Fig. 129). In the finer examples a floret crowns one end of the design. These handcoolers are solid. 2) Hollow blown and vertically ribbed, with various filigree rods fused together but lacking an outer clear glass casing, so that the rods can be felt as ribs (Fig. 130). 3) Upright bouquets in clear glass with thumb printies, these handcoolers will usually stand on the basal printy (Fig. 131). 4) Two flat flowers of different colors upright and back to back in clear glass. One example is flank cut. Rare.

TAZZAS—These infrequent items usually have scrambled paperweight bases and a bowl with a spiral twist rim in white or color. Sizes vary. One superb wafer dish has a spaced millefiori paperweight base to a six-knopped stem, the bowl above delicately engraved with grapes, their leaves and tendrils, and rimmed with a corkscrew twist—one of the most handsomely proportioned and detailed desk articles ever made (Fig. 132). Crown-weight bases are almost as common as scrambled.

SHOT GLASSES—These also come with millefiori or crown bases. The cup that holds the shot may be spirally threaded or basket woven with latticinio and filigree; it may be clear, flashed or single overlaid, or faceted.

VASES—Vary greatly in height and shape, the vessel again showing a variety of treatments similar to the shot glasses. Some trumpet-shaped examples with elaborate faceting have gorgeous concentric paperweight bases, some dated.

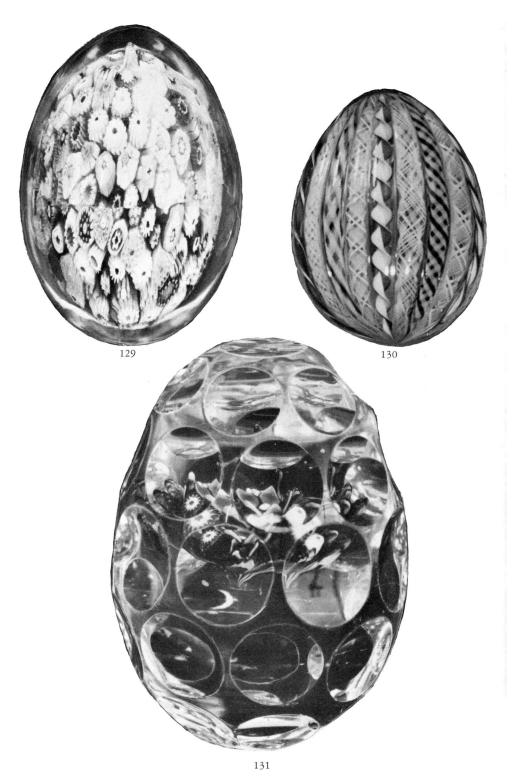

129

130

131

Fig. 129. St. Louis close millefiori hand cooler. *Courtesy Parke-Bernet Galleries, Inc.*
Fig. 130. St. Louis filigree and twist ribbon hand cooler. *Courtesy Parke-Bernet Galleries, Inc.*
Fig. 131. St. Louis upright bouquet with thumb printies. *Courtesy Parke-Bernet Galleries, Inc.*

Fig. 132. St. Louis tazza, knopped stem, etched grapes and leaves. *Courtesy Old Sturbridge Village. Photograph by James C. Ward.*

Other bases are crown weights, the filigree and ribbon members repeated in the vase with powerful effect. Vases are sometimes seen in pairs (Fig. 133A).

S E A L S—Usually faceted, these small objects sometimes show a tiny upright bouquet in the clear glass handle.

B O T T L E S or D E C A N T E R S—Most are faceted and flashed, or latticinio swirled. Stopper may enclose a miniature upright bouquet. One remarkable toilet bottle has a paperweight ground in its base, decorated with an eight-flower garland (Fig. 133B).

S T A T U E S—A pair of bronze figures of women, one apparently representing France and the other Algeria or Morocco, carrying baskets on their heads which contain miniature, faceted upright bouquets of the utmost delicacy in clear glass. A charming idea beautifully carried out.

S U L P H I D E S—(See Chapter Seventeen.)

Questionable Attributions

In recent years a group of weights previously classified as unknown has been attributed to St. Louis. These include the single example of a squirrel (Col. Fig. 50), two or three gaily colored birds, and a grasshopper, all of them flat motifs in flat-bottomed weights with low, flattened crowns, some with delicate torsades that cannot be seen easily from the top, some with strawberry-diamond cutting on the base, but all pretty much part of one group. Still more recently, Revi has attributed these, along with many other sorts of weight, to Pantin (see Chapter Eight). My thought is that while Pantin may very well be the source of many types of weight whose provenance has heretofore been listed as unknown, the weights mentioned above show a group consistency that sharply differentiates them from the various other weights potentially attributable to Pantin. In fact, they show a great affinity in profile, torsade, flat base, and heaviness of glass, even in leafage to those few weights described in this chapter under the heading, "Special Flat Bouquets." No one really knows where they all belong. A more reliable determination must await further historical research or some sort of scientific analysis as yet unavailable.

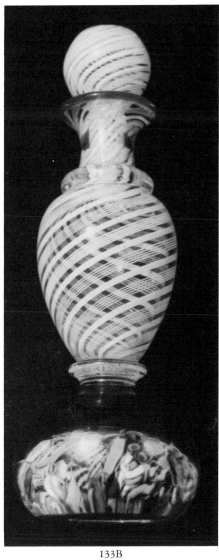

133A

133B

Fig. 133A. St. Louis etched vase with crown weight base. *Courtesy Sotheby & Co.*
Fig. 133B. Latticinio bottle with scrambled base. *Courtesy Bergstrom Art Center and Museum.*

NOTES

[1] James Barrelet, *La Verrerie en France,* Paris, 1953, p. 108.

[2] *Ibid.*

[3] *Ibid.,* p. 131.

[4] R. Imbert and Y. Amic, *Les Presse-Papiers Français de Cristal,* Paris, 1948, P. 32, footnote 2. This is my translation of a letter of Launay's, Sept. 22, 1847.

[5] My translation of the Launay letter of Oct. 21, 1848, as given in French by Imbert and Amic, p. 35.

[6] The idea for the little newel posts must have been abandoned, for to my knowledge they never were made.

[7] See Colné report.

[8] A. Sauzay, *Wonders of Glass-Making in All Ages,* New York, 1885, p. 219.

7

CLICHY

COMPARED TO BACCARAT AND ST. LOUIS, both of which had eighteenth-century origins, Clichy was a latecomer to paperweight-making. There is a difference of opinion as to the founding date. Imbert and Amic say it was founded at Sèvres about 1838 by Rouyer and Maës and moved to Clichy, then a suburb of Paris, shortly before the Paris Exhibition of 1844,[1] while Barrelet places the founding at Billancourt (Pont-de-Sèvres) in 1837 and the transfer to Clichy as early as 1839.[2] The earlier dates seem more plausible, since *Les Beaux-Arts*, published in Paris in 1844, lists Maës of Clichy-la-Garenne as having already exhibited *cristaux variés* in the exhibition of 1839 held in the Champs-Elysées.[3] The Clichy factory had begun by making cheap glass, mostly for export[4]—probably what was meant by *cristaux variés*. But in the exhibition of 1844 Clichy was represented along with St. Louis, Baccarat, and Choisy-le-Roi; and Maës and his new associate Clemandot were praised for their colored overlay crystal.[5]

The Clichy factory prospered, as evidenced by its participation in the big expositions. Sometimes it was referred to as Clichy-la-Garenne and sometimes as M. Maës, Clichy-la-Garenne, but its wares were discussed with enthusiasm and praise and its growth apparently worried older houses like Baccarat and St. Louis. And here, with specific reference to its paperweight production, I quote Imbert and Amic's translation of a letter of 1849 from Launay of Launay, Hautin and Company, agents for St. Louis and other glass factories, in which Launay reproaches St. Louis for not giving enough attention to the paperweight line:

> The selling of weights is now gone mostly [in part] to Clichy which cannot fulfill all the orders received. This article has given a great importance to this factory by the contacts that were established through it with buyers who were not in the habit of applying there. Two furnaces are now permanently burning; a third one shall probably be lit soon.[6]

The point is clear enough: paperweights were a regular part of Clichy's stock in trade.

At the exhibition of 1849, which ran for six months in the Champs Elysées, 4,532 exhibitors showed their wares.[7] Clichy exhibited a new kind of glass, soda-based with zinc oxide, in which boric acid was used as a flux. It was called boracic glass and intended primarily, according to Barrelet, for use as optical glass.[8] The exhibition jury praised it as being "without doubt the clearest, most limpid glass yet obtained, and which rivals for whiteness the most beautiful lead-based crystals."[9] Though it has been widely assumed that the greater the lead content the clearer the glass, this is not necessarily true. Too great a proportion of lead tends to turn the glass yellow. The lighter Clichy weights, presumably of boracic glass, are certainly as clear as any from Baccarat or St. Louis.

In 1955 an historically important Clichy paperweight came up for sale in London. Though in form—a spaced millefiori in clear glass—it was common enough, this was a 3¾-inch magnum (the size of a newel post) which had its own specially shaped leather case. The important thing about it was the flat base, which was incised with the initials "V.A." in monogram below a royal crown, and beneath it, "Londres, 1851." It was obviously made to commemorate Victoria and Albert and the Great Exhibition in London, the first "world's fair." Since Clichy weights, though signed, are undated, this is the only known dated example. (See page 41.)

Unlike Baccarat and St. Louis, Clichy exhibited at the Great Exhibition of 1851 and its glass was awarded a prize. Eugène Péligot, reporting on glass for the French Commission, notes the admirable quality of Clichy colored glass: overlays in all shades, gold and copper red, multicolored, opaque white, pink, green, blue, yellow, black, painted opals, "rose overlays recalling the Du Barry pink of old Sèvres china, and flawless turquoise blue, muslin, filigree, and millefiori glass in the most varied designs."[10]

Two years later Maës again exhibited, this time at the Crystal Palace in New York, located at Fifth Avenue and 42nd Street and named for the great London building. Horace Greeley speaks about it at great length:

> In ornamental glass, Venice excelled, especially, in that variety termed millefiore, in which a number of colored flowers and glass ornaments are embedded in a lump of transparent white glass. This ornament has been revived lately in the form of letter-weights, and beautiful specimens are exhibited from the French Department.

Then he says:

> The collection of Mr. Maez of Clichy, near Paris, is a very extensive and beautiful one. Besides being a manufacturer of glass, he is also well acquainted with the chemical department of his art, as is evinced by the beauty and novelty of some of his productions, for which he has received two medals from his own country and from

England at the London Exhibition. The latter was given for lenses and glass for optical instruments; a Council medal for novelty of chemical application, and a prize medal for a prism of zinc glass. . . . Not only is the ornamentation and coloring of Mr. Maez's collection of great merit, but in the design and form of the vessels there is great taste: . . . The paper-weights, already alluded to, are here in innumerable variety.[11]

In the official catalogue for the New York exhibition of 1853, Clichy, listed as "L. Joseph Maës, manu. de Clichy, Paris," is mentioned as exhibiting "fancy paper-weights of crown glass, cologne and essence bottles, vases of pure and fancy crystal, glass door plates and door knobs; vinaigrettes."[12]

Clichy glass continued to be exhibited, usually with the glass of the other great French factories, but, curiously, alone with Apsley Pellatt at the London exhibition of 1862. Here the catalogue listing was "L. J. Maës of Clichy-la-Garenne (Seine)." Maës is again mentioned in connection with the Paris Universal Exhibition of 1867, but this time as exhibiting fine flint glass.[13] As a footnote to changes in taste, 1867 was the time of the Japanese craze. The period 1840-70, as Boore puts it, was the good period for Clichy.[14] After that, quality fell off and the jury of 1878 wrote in their report that "This establishment was living on its past glory."[15] In 1885 the Clichy factory was taken over by the old glasshouse of Sèvres, run by the Landier family,[16] an old glassmaking family specializing in colored glass.[17] Though it became known as Cristalleries de Sèvres et Clichy, "its products no longer had anything in common with those of Maës and Clemandot."[18]

Clichy Paperweights

PROFILE

This is a profile sketch of a bisected Clichy scrambled weight on exhibit in the Bergstrom Museum. In many examples the evenly flowing profile curve is terminated abruptly at the base. The rather shallow but wide basal concavity is circled by a flat rim whose width may vary in the same weight from 1/16 inch to 1/8 inch, and frequently has a frosted appearance as if ground on a fine stone, which may have been done at the factory, an effect which is not to be confused with unscrupulous attempts to make a new weight look old. The most easily recognizable feature of many but not all Clichy weights is a slightly depressed ring near the base that can be felt with the fingers, often coinciding with the edge of the ground and suggesting a ring or mold mark not eliminated in later working of the glass. The clear glass is colorless, free of striae in the better examples, and generally lighter in the hand than Baccarat or St. Louis. In the double overlays the base is nearly always flat and may be decorated with star rays, strawberry-diamond cutting, or a fine graph of lines crossing at right angles, which was unique with Clichy until Murano recently began to make crude copies.

THE CLICHY ROSE—Since roses in cane form turn up in about 30 percent of all Clichy paperweights, they have been considered a Clichy trademark.[19] Yet it is an uncopyrighted trademark appropriated from public domain, especially when one considers the ubiquitous persistence of the rose's popularity. One has only to recall the widespread use of the rose in heraldry; the Wars of the Roses—the House of Lancaster with its red rose and York with its white rose; Dutch flower painting; and the paintings of Fragonard, Boucher, and Redouté. Or to browse through books on nineteenth-century fabrics, wallpaper, china, and whatnot. More specifically, the Clichy rose may have been appropriated from a Venetian plaque signed "G.B.F." (for Franchini) and dated 1846.[20] Or from Bohemian paperweights where it appears frequently.

The Clichy rose floret is a rose in abstraction, a conception halfway between the large, formal Clichy flowers and the floral geometry of the cane itself, as close to the formal rose of heraldry as to that in nature. Its small size, defying instantaneous analysis, gives it the budlike illusion of a real rose seen in miniature, a rose something like the cabbage rose of Provence from which rosewater was produced.[21] The Clichy rose is really a cane like other canes. Its petals are composed of flattened tubes bundled together about a core of thin rods symbolizing pistil and anthers that appear to have been assembled much as other canes are assembled; or composed of cabbage-like strands of glass that may have been formed in a rose cane-mold [49]. The proof that these are canes is furnished by weights containing more than two roses of the same color, for here we can see the repetition of identical petal patterns that mean the roses were snipped from one cane.

[49]

The earliest Clichy rose centers are cylinders whose cross-section resembles a slice of lemon, or rods with a cross design. Later we find "whorls," bundles of pale yellow or green rods. The rose usually comes with sections of green casing apparently symbolizing the little sepal leaves. Colors show several shades of pink ranging from palest salmon to deep rose, white, white with an outer row of red petals, pale Naples yellow, pale aquamarine, lilac, pale cinnabar green, amethyst, and deep wine red.

CANES—The variety of Clichy canes is equal to Baccarat and greater than St. Louis. The predominant cane is the pastry mold. In a spaced millefiori sample of thirty-eight canes there are twenty-four pastry molds. The characteristic pastry-mold cane (or floret) has an outer casing that is often loosely and deeply serrated or ruffled, though sometimes tightly so. Though the top diameter of these canes is usually about the same as other French canes, they appear larger because they have been squashed into place in such a way as to spread the contour profile [50] like a full skirt settling on the floor. Next in frequency are the canes composed of rod bundles, the rods including crimped rods, star rods, and "whorls." The crimped rods are as delicate as those from St. Louis. The star rods are often arranged in alternating colors. And it is interesting to note that while the whorls from Baccarat are scrolls with a beginning and an end [51], those from Clichy are usually made from concentric tubing [52].

[50]

[51]

[52]

Though most Clichy canes are composed of a center, an outer sheathing, and the part in between, the whole design is often so reduced in size, so beautifully executed, and so subtle in coloring as to defy comprehension. Some canes, for example, composed simply of a bundle of star rods with an outer sheath, resemble (according to coloring) barnacles or mountain laurel. Square canes are seldom seen, but a few weights have designs composed of them. Green moss canes are rare.

Cane colors are actually similar to those found in St. Louis and Baccarat, but cobalt blue is used sparingly, and opaque pink, brilliant deep aquamarine or medium thalo blue (not turquoise), warm cadmium green, ivory, lilac, and deep ruby or deep cherry red are seen in abundance, giving the weights a warmth and richness not found elsewhere. If Baccarat paperweights appear to be seen in shade, Clichy seem to be always in broad sunlight.

Though Clichy weights, with the exception already mentioned, are not dated, they are occasionally signed with an opaque white rod that forms the center of a cane and bears the letter "C" in red, blue, green, or black, the serifs making the letter resemble a horseshoe [53]. In a very few instances the name is spelled out in rods, one such occurring on the bottom side of a moss ground.

[53]

Paperweight Types and Characteristics

SCRAMBLED—With one notable exception this form is restricted to paperweights—no tazzas, shot cups, etc. The exception is a superb pair of vases 9⅝ inches high in the Corning Museum of Glass, each signed "Clichy" on a small cane. (Fig. 161) Scrambled paperweights come in all sizes and are very attractive in miniatures. The only slightly curved cushion is usually placed fairly high and, though composed of a variety of colored canes, has a predominance of green that makes it resemble a tossed salad, the roses chopped up like red cabbage, bright yellow canes diced like hard-boiled egg, etc. Pale yellow and lilac-colored roses are also seen. A few examples are signed with a "C" rod.

CLOSE MILLEFIORI—These are not too common. The cushion in one form is shaped like a dome, the long outside canes irregularly broken off on the bottoms and moving toward the center of the base, the inside of the dome stuffed with scrambled filigree or long rods of filigree to give the top view opacity. In the other form the slightly curved ground is enclosed by staves, the motif consequently being placed very high (Fig. 134). Some close millefiori are mushrooms or pedestal weights. Coloring is warmer and richer than Baccarat and more decisive than St. Louis. Clichy rose canes are numerous and may appear in variety and quantity in a single weight. A few examples are elaborately faceted with polygonal tables or vertical or spiral flutes.

S P A C E D   M I L L E F I O R I—These come in clear glass (also newel posts), on muslin and translucent and opaque grounds. The florets (usually pastry molds) are evenly spaced in straight rows or concentric circles, but unequal floret sizes and unequal distances between outer florets and weight circumference account for the mistaken notion that they are "scattered," random settings (Fig. 135). They are patterned weights and some even balance in cane form and coloring, especially on the color grounds (Col. Fig. 51). These weights are samplers for Clichy canes, and against such color grounds as bright thalo blue, white, or (rarely) purple, the richly colored canes stand in sharp relief. Unlike the muslin and translucent ground examples, where the canes rest on top of the ground, in the opaque grounds the canes indent the ground in pockets that may frequently be seen on the underside, their tops lying flush with the ground. Above certain translucent red or blue grounds one sees straight rows of barnacle, starfish, or urchin-like canes in pale colors.

One spaced millefiori is engraved on its flat bottom with the only dating known at Clichy; this is the weight sent to the Great Exhibition in London. It shows the date 1851 beneath the letters "V.A." (for Victoria and Albert) in monogram surmounted by a crown.

C H E Q U E R—Really a spaced millefiori with the canes separated by filigree cables. Some chequers have been done precisely enough to have been called "radiating chequer," but this is a relative term and many chequers are boldly but indifferently executed, the canes cut off by or sinking beneath the separating filigree. A few examples with small canes are so poorly done as to suggest that they may have been tried by the same apprentice. However, usually, the very large florets, including fine Clichy roses in various colors, stand out rich and bold against the white filigree, the ground's opacity reinforced by parallel filigree rods placed beneath it (Figs. 136, 137, 138). The peripheral canes tend to be tremendously magnified but not distorted by the glass. In newel posts the chequer design is shaped as a hemisphere and shows up handsomely in this form which, incidentally, closely resembles a human cell magnified 275,000 times.

Fig. 134. Clichy close millefiori. *Courtesy Sotheby & Co.*
Fig. 135. Clichy spaced millefiori on opaque ground. *Courtesy Sotheby & Co.*
Fig. 136. Clichy chequer with Clichy rose center, large florets. *Courtesy Sotheby & Co.*
Fig. 137. Clichy chequer nicely set and faceted. *Courtesy Parke-Bernet Galleries, Inc.*
Fig. 138. Clichy chequer magnum. *Courtesy Sotheby & Co.*

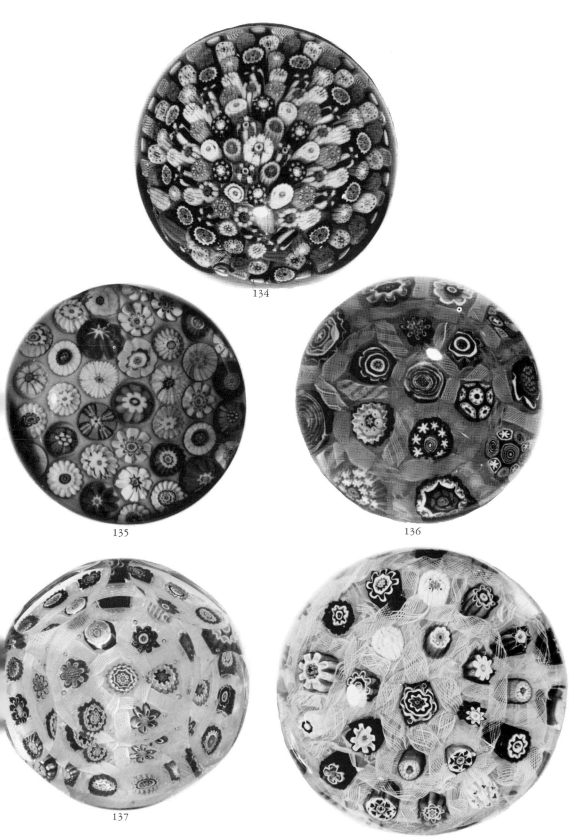

134

135

136

137

138

While white filigree separations are the rule, the more uncommon weights show twisted rods about which spiral colored threads and filigree, the threads being cobalt or thalo blue, peppermint pink, red, or green, the underside of the ground lined as usual with parallel filigree rods (Col. Fig. 52). Somewhat rarer are those weights whose separations are gauze cables in sherbet pink, aquamarine, powder blue, and pistachio green. One chequer has underneath the cushion an open swirl of pale milk glass, as if the maker had been experimenting with a new effect (Col. Fig. 53).

CONCENTRICS—A wide variety here, ranging from the very common, rather plain miniatures and doorknobs in which one or two concentric rings of canes are set in clear glass or on muslin to the large, tightly packed baskets, pedestals, mushrooms, and overlays. Roses are common in all and complete rings of roses are frequently seen in the finer weights. Two-ring concentrics in the 2- to 2½-inch range are likely to be on opaque peacock blue (thalo) or red grounds that range from flamingo pink through deep scarlet, some being so tinged with brown or even with a gold overcast that one suspects the red was overcooked. Where the central cane has slipped, the white underlay of the ground can be seen. For precision and color harmony the finer concentrics are unsurpassed—one looks down upon a formal garden bordered by vertical staves in alternating colors, a garden of pink with blue and lavender, eggplant purple against mid-summer green, aquamarine against wine red, all centered, perhaps, about a big Clichy rose (Fig. 139). One concentric pedestal weight has an opaque blue base (Col. Fig. 54). A massive early example with a diameter of 4⅝ inches, possibly the largest Clichy weight, has two rows with a total of sixty-four Clichy roses (Col. Fig. 55).

BASKET STAVES—Used as the containing sheaths of close millefiori, concentric and mushroom weights, they are composed of opaque white tubes that have been flattened and arranged vertically about the periphery of the motif like a board fence. In mushroom weights they take the curve of the mushroom below the cap. Staves may be all white, white alternating with red, blue, green, mauve, yellow, and, rarely, all blue.

COLOR GROUNDS—Occasionally translucent ruby, cranberry, or cobalt blue, Clichy color grounds are usually opaque, that is, opaque white covered by a translucent overlay. The opaque ground may perhaps be double, that is, blown and then collapsed upon itself like the latticinio swirl grounds, a possibility accounted for by the fact that indentations caused by canes in the top of the ground are sometimes not visible on the bottom. In addition to opaque white grounds as ground color, colors over opaque white grounds include, among the reds, turkey red, scarlet, wine red, alizarin crimson, rose pompadour, salmon, flamingo; among the blues, pale cerulean, sky blue, aquamarine, peacock, deep thalo, cobalt or sapphire; among the greens, pistachio, lime, apple, emerald, forest (the color of the moss canes), and sap; plus pale and deep amethyst. One

Fig. 139. Clichy concentric, eight pink, fifteen white roses. *Courtesy Corning Museum of Glass.*

Clichy ground is an all-white stardust carpet. A lovely miniature has a single giant cane on a deep ruby cushion.

G A R L A N D S—This very attractive Clichy motif is seen on a white muslin or color ground, and, occasionally, in clear glass (Col. Figs. 56, 57, 58).

        [54]

The variety of garland patterns [54] composed from such simple design elements as the circle, trefoil, quatrefoil, and loop, combined with the many color grounds, make this perhaps the most continually surprising of all paperweights, for it can almost be said that there are no two garland weights alike. The nearly total success of such a variety of arrangements is astounding—seldom is a chain broken, a circle minus a cane, a garland curve distorted; even when garlands are intertwined in canes of different color sequences all goes smoothly. Many garland weights contain both simple pastry-mold canes and complex florets with extremely detailed, minutely reduced interiors in a close association that is striking in its contrasts. Great care has been taken in the setting of cane color against ground color, so we may find amethyst canes on a sky-blue ground, or royal blue and flesh-colored canes against an apple-green ground, to name just two instances (Figs. 140, 141, 142, 143, 144, 145, 146).

Unusual garland weights include a continuous looped chain of sixty-six pink Clichy roses (Fig. 147), an opaque white ground completely covered with aquamarine bubbles, a weight whose royal blue ground is humped in waves beneath a humped and wavy garland, the crown glass a cloudy opaline, a garland weight with a central enameled plaque of a bird and flowers, a garland of six circles of canes, each circle centered with a sulphide bust, the weight centered with a plaque painted with a schooner, and several garland weights on green moss grounds (Col. Fig. 59). Occasional examples are faceted with large printies separated by vertical flutes.

One problem with these weights today is that so many garlands have been reground, which frequently obscures or distorts the outer canes in the design and brings to the side surface of the weight the white base on which the color ground is laid, like a slip that shows below the hemline of a dress.

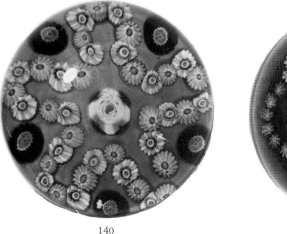 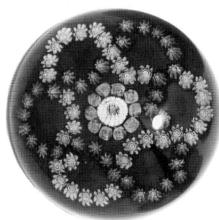

140   141

Fig. 140. Clichy cinquefoil on colored ground, rose center. *Courtesy Sotheby & Co.*
Fig. 141. Clichy interlaced trefoil garland. *Courtesy Sotheby & Co.*
Fig. 142. Clichy garland of circles on muslin. *Courtesy Sotheby & Co.*
Fig. 143. Clichy interlaced quatrefoils on muslin. *Courtesy Sotheby & Co.*
Fig. 144. Clichy garland chain on muslin. *Courtesy Sotheby & Co.*
Fig. 145. Clichy garland of circlets. *Courtesy Sotheby & Co.*
Fig. 146. Clichy unusual garland on dark ground. *Courtesy Parke-Bernet Galleries, Inc.*
Fig. 147. Clichy sixty-six rose garland. *Courtesy Sotheby & Co.*

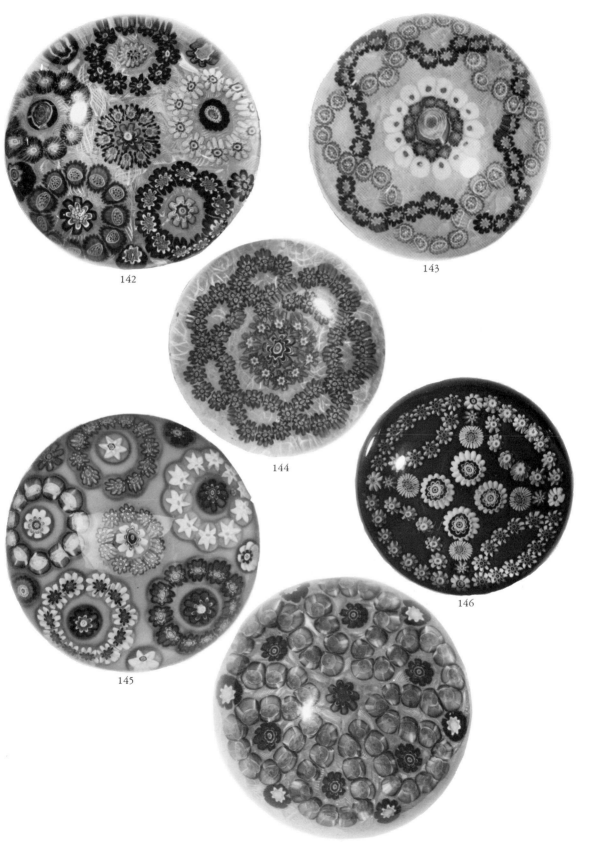

142

143

144

145

146

147

[55]

[56]

C-SCROLLS, STAR WEIGHTS, AND PANELS—Closely related to the garlands, these usually large (rarely, miniature) weights are about equally set with muslin and color grounds. The C-scroll is just that: several canes are arranged in the shape of a large "C" [55], the shape repeated about a central motif (Fig. 148). One lovely example appears on a moss ground. In the star weight two or three large but concentric stars, each composed of different canes form the bold but difficult motif—difficult because the star lines are not always even or parallel and the star points are somewhat blunted (Figs. 149, 150). Panel weights feature up to eight clusters of tightly packed canes, the canes identical within each cluster [56]. A miniature is known. Ground colors in all three types of weight are varied and rich (Fig. 151).

One Clichy weight has as its motif four large letter "A's" instead of "C's," one of the "A's" made up of Clichy roses.

[57]

SWIRL—Perhaps originally suggested by the Bohemian crown weight of tubes or by latticinio, the Clichy pinwheel of opaque tubes is really nothing but a single-ply latticinio greatly enlarged—even the clear glass between the colored tubes is plain to see. The swirl form in two or three alternating colors: pale green, pink, and opaque white, or thalo blue and white, or purple and white—a large floret holding the design together like the axle of a wheel—is simple and effective [57]. When that floret is the Clichy rose the effect is particularly charming—picture a pink Clichy rose at the center of a pink and white swirl. Rarest are those with a circle of canes, including Clichy roses, in the center. Swirls come in miniature size up to 3¼ inches. Uneven repolishing is particularly disruptive to this kind of weight where the slightest deviation in the crown curve breaks the swirl of the design. Heavy grinding in an attempt to make a 2¼-inch swirl a miniature is apt to expose the tube ends (Col. Fig. 60).

Fig. 148. Clichy C-scroll on dark opaque ground. *Courtesy Sotheby & Co.*

Fig. 149. Clichy star weight, faceted with printies and vertical flutes. *Courtesy Old Sturbridge Village. Photograph by James C. Ward.*

Fig. 150. Clichy star weight. *Courtesy Old Sturbridge Village. Photograph by James C. Ward.*

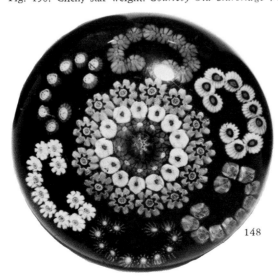

148

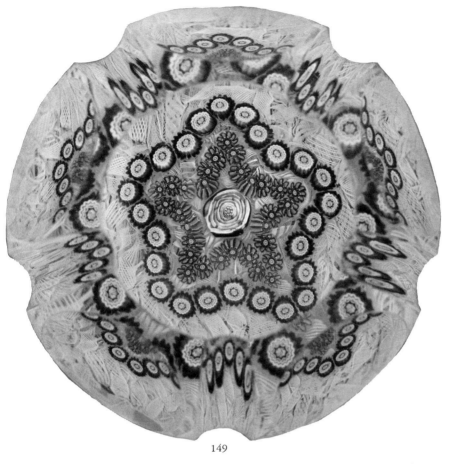

149

150

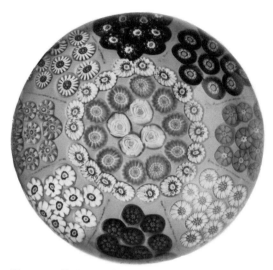

Fig. 151. Clichy panel weight, note divisions. *Courtesy Sotheby & Co.*

[58]

SPOKES—Similar to the swirl, except that the tubes radiate straight out from the center like spokes (Col. Fig. 61) [58].

PEDESTAL (PIEDOUCHE)—This is simply a close millefiori, concentric, or chequer weight with a short columnar or footed base, the motif enclosed by vertical staves reaching to the base, or the base decorated by latticinio in the best Venetian manner (Fig. 152). One magnificent example has a circle of pale Naples yellow roses, another of lavender roses, reminding one of baskets of flowers at La Madeleine.

FLOWER WEIGHTS

Flat Bouquets—Seldom seen, this flat arrangement of three or four canes symbolizing flowers with leaves and stem are reminiscent of the same from St. Louis. In one example, leaves are deep cadmium green but the stem is malachite green. Generally, there are clear glass or lace grounds, the latter with a circle of canes.

Pansy—No two are more than superficially alike; some look like pansies, some look like the viola, some look just plain tipsy. Upper petals run from red to blue violet, lower petals from pale yellow to deep amber, with black veining. Seldom seen alone, they are usually combined with other flowers. Like all Clichy flowers they are flat. Clear glass or double-swirl latticinio grounds (Fig. 153).

Other Single Flowers—These include a variety of blossoms resembling no particular flower. They appear flat on double-swirl latticinio, or bright blue, or red grounds. The flower petals, sometimes pointed like the clematis petal but frequently rounded, are likely to be strongly veined or striped in a variety of colors (Fig. 154). Yet some opaque white petals without veining look as soft

152

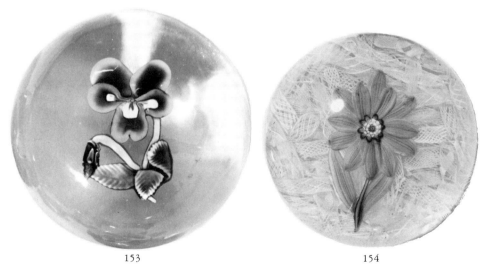

153   154

Fig. 152. Clichy pedestal weight. *Courtesy Old Sturbridge Village. Photograph by James C. Ward.*

Fig. 153. Clichy pansy with bud. *Courtesy Sotheby & Co.*

Fig. 154. Clichy flower on lace. *Courtesy Sotheby & Co.*

and pure as a gardenia petal (Col. Fig. 62). The center of all these flowers is a delicate floret or pastry-mold cane, and the petals of some flowers are nothing but large florets (Col. Fig. 63). Leafage is more casual than at Baccarat. (See "Leafage".) Against colored grounds these flowers are magnificent. In one rare weight a white bird hovers beside the flower (Fig. 155).

Convolvulus (Morning Glory)—Rarely seen, this lovely flat, realistic flower comes in clear glass or on double-swirl latticinio, usually alone on a long stem with two long leaves (Fig. 156). Blossom colors include white, pale blue, pale pink, pale yellow, or white touched with bands of these colors. One enormous double-swirl latticinio ground has upon it two convolvulus blossoms, one blue lined with white, the other white banded with blue, yellow, and purple, plus an imaginary flower in white and pink (Fig. 157).

Mignonette or Scabiosa—This extremely rare and not specifically identifiable flower comes in mauve pink and is set in clear glass (in one miniature) or on a green moss ground (Col. Fig. 64), where it stands out as one of the finest flower weights ever made.

Fig. 155. Clichy gardenia with bird. *Courtesy Corning Museum of Glass.*

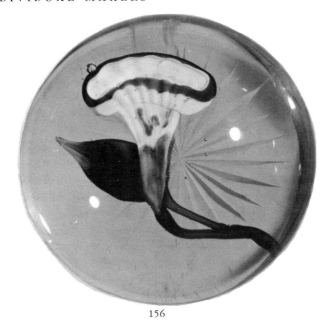

156

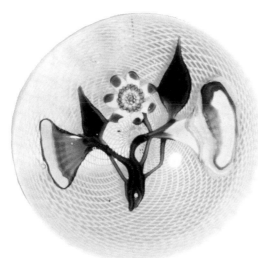

157

Fig. 156. Clichy convolvulus, star-cut base. *Courtesy Parke-Bernet Galleries, Inc.*
Fig. 157. Clichy morning glory group on latticinio. *Courtesy Sotheby & Co.*

Large Flat Floral Bouquets—So different from their Baccarat counterparts, these casual groups look as if the flowers had just been picked and laid down before being put in a vase. Some groups, however, show an arrangement like an old-fashioned bouquet, the stems emerging from a pink or blue cornucopia, or brought together and tied with colored or white ribbon (Col. Fig. 65). The casual leafage shows great variety of form and texture. Except for the convolvulus and mignonette or scabiosa, all the flowers mentioned above are seen, plus the Clichy rose and a flower that is like a thistle or a clover, though it has always been called a tulip (Fig. 158). Some fantastic flowers have petals fashioned

158   159

Fig. 158. Clichy floral bouquet with Clichy rose, pansy, clover. *Courtesy Sotheby & Co.*
Fig. 159. Clichy double overlay close millefiori. *Courtesy Sotheby & Co.*

from lengths of cane that have been sliced through lengthwise, exposing the interior of the cane, the petal tips showing the bisected cane ends, a remarkable feat
and an exercise of imagination that represents paperweight-making at its best
(Col. Fig. 66). These are generally large, clear glass weights—no ground was
needed—but a few are on latticinio swirl (Col. Fig. 67).

L E A F A G E—Clichy leaves and stems, usually a rich, deep cadmium green,
though occasionally pea green, pale malachite, or thalo green, come in a variety
of forms: some long and thickly veined, some deeply serrated like St. Louis,
some sharp as holly and some round-tipped, some waffle-stamped, and some
simply green but amorphous. Stems leading to the rose and the clover may be
long, green crimped tubes. Seldom placed with the stylish precision of Baccarat,
Clichy leaves are, nevertheless, very natural looking.

O P A L I N E—The name given to a single flower or a small, flat bouquet of
canes and leaves set in an oval, slightly raised center of a rectangular opaline
glass plaque measuring about 2¼ inches by 3¼ inches, sometimes shaped
like a book. Here the exquisite floral design is seen in its true size because there
is no magnifying lens of glass above it. One is looking, in effect, at the ground
of a paperweight. Very Victorian and very lovely.

F R U I T S—While it cannot be stated with any precision that Clichy made any
fruit weights, one weight with two strawberries in relief branching from a stem
topped by a white flower in relief, accompanied by leaves, might possibly be a
late Clichy product. The points for and against such an attribution are too complicated to detail.

OVERLAYS—Though one or two are single overlays, nearly all are double, the inner, opaque white overlay showing a narrow, even margin about the printies where it meets the rich pink, medium thalo blue, royal blue, dark green, or bright vermilion of the outer overlay. Though occasionally shaped and faceted like Baccarat overlays, the typical Clichy double overlay is a rather high, pentagonal polygon with a squarish profile, the large printy windows cut flat or very slightly concave, the top window usually a flat circle (Fig. 159; Col. Figs. 68, 69). A very few examples have vertical flutes cut between the printies. The usually flat base may be star cut, strawberry-diamond cut, crosshatched with fine close lines, or plain. The interior motif is a close millefiori or concentric arrangement of close-packed canes enclosed in a stave basket that resembles in profile an urn or vase more than a mushroom, the staves all white or alternately white and another color. The finest canes in subtle, color-row juxtapositions, including Clichy roses in various colors and shades, are neatly arranged, and the view of them through the top window is breathtaking.

A unique weight shows the single white overlay cut in melon-rib style with ten deep vertical flutes that run from base to the apex of the weight, where a lovely Clichy rose cane right on the surface crowns the whole design. Inside is a low-ground, close millefiori that can only be seen in narrow glimpses through the clear glass flutes (Fig. 160).

UNIQUE BASKET WEIGHT—This great object is, in my opinion, the finest paperweight ever made (Fig. 161; Col. Fig. 70). The weight is made in the shape of a basket with vertical white staves for the sides and red and white twist ribbons marking the top and bottom perimeters, the nearly circular millefiori motif swelling gently at the top of the basket, its curve indented on either side where the handle of a basket would be. There actually was a red and white twist ribbon handle, and one can see where it was broken off. The fantas-

Fig. 160. Clichy unique melon-rib overlay, Clichy rose at top center. *Private collection. Courtesy Louis Lyons.*

Fig. 161. Clichy unique basket of flowers. *Private collection. Courtesy Louis Lyons.*

160

161

tic motif itself, like a basket full of flowers, is covered only with a thin film of glass, giving one of the illusion of being able to touch the tops of the flowers. The motif is a concentric with rows of Clichy roses, moss, and other canes, in turn surrounded by a carpet ground of moss canes in which are set fifteen clusters of identical canes in different colors. The audacious concept has been carried through with total success and one can only marvel at the result, for surely this is the high point of Victorian paperweight artistry. As an art object it can hold its own with any made by man.

Related Millefiori Objects

In addition to the newel posts already mentioned, millefiori motifs are seen in faceted inkwells and perfume bottles, where the millefiori motif may appear in both base and stopper, in the scrambled millefiori vases at the Corning Museum of Glass, in seals and in doorknobs, and, in one instance, in a paperweight fused to the top of a solid, faceted clear glass block in the shape of a perfume bottle. Some of these objects come in pairs (Fig. 162).

NOTES

[1] Imbert and Amic, *Les Presse-Papiers Français de Cristal*, Paris, 1948, pp. 49, 83.

[2] James Barrelet, *La Verrerie en France*, Paris, 1953, p. 133.

[3] *Les Beaux-Arts*, Paris, 1844.

[4] Jules Barat, *Exposition de l'Industrie Française, Année 1844*, Paris, n.d.

[5] Imbert and Amic, *op. cit.*, p. 83. According to Imbert and Amic, Clemandot was the owner, Maës the director. Barrelet, p. 172, calls Clemandot the director of Clichy.

[6] Imbert and Amic, *op. cit.*, pp. 49, 50.

[7] Kenneth W. Luckhurst, *The Story of Exhibitions*, London and New York, 1951, p. 220. The *Art Journal* notes 4,494 exhibitors.

[8] Barrelet, p. 138, gives the year as 1851.

[9] My translation of Imbert and Amic, *op. cit.*, p. 50.

[10] *Ibid*. My translation.

[11] Horace Greeley, "Art and Industry as Represented in the Exhibition at the Crystal Palace, 1853–4," *New York Tribune*, edited and revised by Horace Greeley, New York, 1953, p. 126.

[12] Official Catalogue of the New York Exhibition of the Industry of All Nations, 1853, p. 165.

[13] *Reports of Artisans Selected by a Committee Appointed by the Council of the Society of Arts to Visit the Paris Universal Exhibition 1867*, London, 1867, p. 127.

Fig. 162. One of a Clichy signed pair of scrambled millefiori vases 9⅝″ high. *Courtesy Corning Museum of Glass.*

[14] J. P. Boore, "Old Glass Paperweights. Clichy, Part I," *Hobbies,* Aug. 1961, pp. 90, 91.

[15] Imbert and Amic, *op. cit.,* p. 50.

[16] Barrelet, *op. cit.,* p. 138.

[17] *Ibid.,* p. 177.

[18] Imbert and Amic, *op. cit.,* p. 84.

[19] This is Elville's figure and it seems correct. E. M. Elville, *Paper-Weights and Other Glass Curiosities,* London, 1954, p. 35.

[20] Mary A. and S. Weldon O'Brien, "Old Glass Paperweights," *Antiques,* Nov. 1949, illustrated, p. 352.

[21] *Encyclopædia Britannica,* 14th ed., vol. 19, p. 554.

8

OTHER FRENCH FACTORIES

The Question of Choisy-Le-Roi

GEORGES BONTEMPS (1799-1884) was passionately interested in the history and techniques of glassmaking. By the time he was twenty-five this descendant of the valet of Louis XIV was a director of the glasshouse at Choisy-le-Roi, a suburb of Paris. The factory was built on land bought by M. Ponce Grimblot in 1820, and the next year had in operation three furnaces for ordinary glass and four for crystal. In 1825 Claudet and Bontemps were named directors, and two years later the jury of the exposition of 1827 commended Choisy for the number and variety of its products. Choisy exhibited again in 1834, 1838, and for the last time in 1844. Writing of French glass at the time of the Paris Exposition of 1849, the *Journal of Design and Manufactures* says, "The establishment of M. Bontemps at Choisy-le-Roi is the great centre of activity, and to him the Parisians are indebted for their supply of all the thousand and one imitations and originalities which decorate their chimney pieces and sideboards."[1] Yet Choisy was seriously disrupted by the Revolution of 1848 and Bontemps had already left for England to work with Chance of Birmingham on the perfection of optical glass. The fires of Choisy went out finally in 1851, the year of the Great Exhibition in London.

Barrelet speaks of a new line of French multicolored, overlay glass introduced by Choisy-le-Roi in 1825, and at Baccarat and St. Louis only in 1839.[2] This was the famous French *façon de Bohême* glass appropriated from Bohemia, a style that traveled quickly to England (especially to Birmingham) and was all the rage at the time of the Great Exhibition. It was commented upon by Bontemps, who was very much interested in opaline, in his report to the Jury of the Paris Exposition of 1844[3] Barrelet goes on to say that Choisy took up millefiori from 1844, when Bontemps rediscovered its secrets.[4]

Georges Bontemps has been widely credited with the rediscovery of the secrets of making filigree and millefiori glass. As to the filigree, his work is well established. In the museum at Sèvres an elaborate filigree pitcher by him shows how well he understood its secrets. And in his *Guide du Verrier* of 1868 there is a whole chapter devoted to the methods of constructing the various types of filigree rods. But what about millefiori paperweights? In the *Guide du Verrier* there is practically nothing on the subject. How many millefiori paperweights could Bontemps or Choisy have made if a discussion of millefiori techniques does not appear in Bontemps' own glassman's guide? We know from Bontemps' reports to the juries of the French Exposition of 1839 that filigree glass by Choisy was shown, which in his opinion was lacking in craftsmanship, and that in the Exposition of 1844 millefiori vases were also shown. But paperweights?

The idea that glass paperweights were made at Choisy-le-Roi was first brought out, as far as I can determine, in 1849, when Choisy was already on its last legs. On page 257 of Vol. 11 of the *Art Journal* for 1849, we find the following remarks:

> In France at the manufactory of Choisy-le-Roi, under the able superintendence of M. Bontemps, have been produced some clever imitations of *millefiori* fused in crystal glass; in one article alone, *viz.* paper-weights, they have distributed over Europe hundreds of thousands of these elegant table ornaments.

Unfortunately, it was not stated who was responsible for these remarks, which are followed without a break by a discussion of the constituents of flint glass. Curiously, these identical remarks turn up again on page 257 of Vol. 28 of the *Art Journal* for 1866. But here they are incorporated in a piece signed "W. C." (for William Chaffers) and entitled "Modern Enamel Mosaics and the Reproduction of Venetian Glass in the Nineteenth Century." Chaffers' cribbing includes verbatim the remarks on flint glass appearing in the earlier *Art Journal.* Then, when we come forward in time to Barrelet, we read on page 136 of his *La Verrerie en France*, "Bontemps, who rediscovered the Venetian procedures of filigree and millefiori decoration, had already declared in 1851 that 'A single article, millefiori paperweights, has been sold by the hundreds of thousands.'"

Perhaps it was Bontemps who first made this statement. If so, he must have made it before the *Art Journal* got hold of it in 1849. And this would make sense, for Bontemps was already in England by 1849. But that Bontemps was referring to paperweights made at Choisy-le-Roi is very doubtful; that factory would not have had much time to perfect the art before running into the vicissitudes that closed it down, and certainly it could not have turned out paperweights in the hundreds of thousands, for that many paperweights were never made by all the glasshouses put together. If Bontemps made the statement, he must have been speaking of the popularity of paperweights in general and he must have had his figures misquoted.

Furthermore, Bontemps himself was probably too preoccupied with other matters to have made more than a few token paperweights. Since before 1828 Bontemps had been working on problems of perfecting optical glass that had occupied John Dolland, Faraday, and others. Specifically there was the question of devising some method to free the flint glass lens of the achromatic telescope object glass from striae so that it would not distort the image transmitted. Experimenting along the lines of a system devised by a Swiss watchmaker named Guinand, Bontemps and one of Guinand's sons succeeded in 1828 in producing good flint glass disks of up to 14 inches in diameter.[5] Apsley Pellatt, in whose glassworks Faraday experimented with flint glass, was familiar with the efforts of Bontemps. "M. Bontemps," he writes, "a scientific French Glassmaker, has succeeded in making good flint optical glass also on the principle of mechanical agitation; and was rewarded for his process by the French Society of Arts in 1840."[6] Pellatt even gives Bontemps' formula for flint glass: sand-43.5; red lead-43.5; carbonate of potash-10; nitrate of potash-3; totaling 100 parts. The formula for flint glass given by the gentleman in the *Art Journal* of 1849 who spoke of Choisy-le-Roi paperweights having been distributed over Europe in the "hundreds of thousands" comprises 100 parts of "purified Lynn sand," litharge (red lead) 60 parts, and purified pearl ash 30 parts—quite a different recipe.

Since it was partly to continue the manufacture of flint optical glass and sheet glass that Bontemps went to Birmingham in 1848, we may assume that he had more pressing concerns during the Choisy years than the making of millefiori paperweights. If paperweights of flint glass containing as much red lead as sand were made at Choisy, they would have been so heavy as to be easily recognizable. Yet the only group of paperweights containing French-looking millefiori dating from the early days that have not yet been attributed to a French factory are those weights that have been called, for want of information, "Factory X." But these are light weights, probably made of lime-potash glass in Bohemia (see Chapter Three). Thus its early demise, its flint glass, and the preoccupations of its director, all make it unlikely that Choisy-le-Roi made many paperweights.

The Question of St. Maude

The quotation from the *Journal of Design and Manufactures* of 1849, excerpted in its reference to Bontemps at Choisy-le-Roi, has a continuation. The writer says:

> The works at St. Maude rather confine themselves to the specialité of Venetian glass, more particularly as applied to those fanciful objects which swarm in the windows of the shops of the Palais Royal and on the toilette tables of the exquisites. To descend from gay to grave, from lively to serene, from elegancies to comforts, from paper weights to wine bottles, etc.

What have we here? A factory at St. Maude producing paperweights on sale in the shops of the Palais Royale, possibly in the Escalier Crystal? It sounds like it.

Pantin

In an article titled "Thoughts on French Paperweights," Yvonne Sohn Revelli, who was born and raised in France, writes:

> The first time I came in contact with French glass paperweights was during the year 1915. I was then one of the teachers at the boys' school of Pantin (suburb of Paris). One of my pupils brought me, as a present, a lovely glass paperweight inkstand of brilliantly colored glass, quite similar in shape to the ones on the market today (1941). His father, a worker at the glass factories (of Pantin), had made it for me after working hours.

The Cristallerie de Pantin was a latecomer in glass. A. C. Revi did a thorough research of this company's history which he presented first in the *Bulletin of the Paperweight Collectors' Association* in 1965 and, in a somewhat enlarged version, in the *Spinning Wheel* for October, 1966. Briefly, the glassworks of Monot and Company was established in 1850 at La Villette, then near but now part of Paris. There were several moves, accompanied by changes of name to Monot and Stumpf; Monot, Père et Fils, et Stumpf (at Pantin); Stumpf, Touvier, Violette and Company; and finally, about 1900, to Cristallerie de Pantin, operated by Saint-Hilaire, Touvier, de Varreux and Company.[7]

Revi found his information on paperweight production at Monot, Père et Fils, et Stumpf, as it was known in 1878, in the report of Charles Colné, the assistant secretary to the U. S. Commissioners reporting on the Exposition Universelle, Paris, 1878. Colné reported on the Pantin factory's paperweights as follows:

> Paperweights of solid glass, containing glass snakes, lizards, squirrels, and flowers; air bubbles are distributed in the mass, looking like pearl drops. . . . A coiled snake, with head erect, of two colored glasses, cut in spots to show both colors, mounted on a piece of mirror; an interesting piece of workmanship, showing great dexterity in coiling the snake. . . . Paperweights in millefiori of roses, leaves, and fruit, embedded in lumps of clear glass . . . a paperweight containing a lizard of colored glass, which had been cut in several parts before being inclosed in the glass.[8]

No illustrations were included in the report, so we are left to guess what all this means (Col. Figs. 71, 72, 73).

Colné's reference to the lizard "which had been cut in several parts before being inclosed in the glass" would seem to indicate a three-dimensional lizard, the result of lampwork involving assembly of body members. This being before the days of Dada, what else could it mean? A three-dimensional, sculptural motif would be in keeping with other paperweights at this 1878 Exposition remarked upon by Colné, as for instance from Schindler and Veit of Gablonz, Austria-Hungary, "paperweights in acid-polished glass representing cat heads, with mouth and eyes painted in enamel," or, from C. Dressler of Gablonz, "paperweights of depolished statues, mounted on bases of colored glass."[9] Or from another exhibitor, "Paperweights of hollow balls filled with water, containing a man with an umbrella. These balls also contain a white powder which, when the paperweight is turned upside down, falls in imitation of a snowstorm."[10] This was the age of the three-dimensional paperweight motif.

Then we have Colné's mention of air bubbles "distributed in the mass, looking like pearl drops." These would seem to be the concomitant of the three-dimensional object enclosed in glass. We have already seen how bubbles in varying degrees accompany the St. Louis upright bouquets. And we note that they appear also in the great lizard-iguana paperweights previously referred to as possibly late Baccarat (see Chapter Five). In the light of Colné's descriptions these lizards may well be Pantin products. Whichever factory they belong to, the late date of 1878 seems a likely one, though a later date at Baccarat is indicated.

The same likelihood as to date would seem to apply also to the lifelike, three-dimensional flowers as yet unattributed to any specific factory (Figs. 163, 164, 165). But what about the squirrels Colné mentions? Wouldn't they also be three-dimensional? Yet the only squirrel we know of is a single flat example that relates to the bird on twig weights. These are all flat motifs in low, flattened-crowned weights with filigree torsades and flat, strawberry-diamond-cut bases that suggest St. Louis.

The point is we simply do not know as yet. Convenience is our temptation for attributing to Pantin whatever is left uncatalogued, and in the process we are likely to want to place at Pantin's door more paperweights of differing internal features such as leaves and flower forms than are likely to have been developed by glass artists of a single period working in a single factory.

Colné considered Baccarat the most important exhibitor, Clichy the second most important. Yet, in the matter of Pantin compared to Baccarat production in 1878, it is significant that Colné mentions no paperweights from Baccarat or

Fig. 163. Rose on opaque white ground, possibly Pantin. *Courtesy Sotheby & Co.*

Fig. 164. Crocus, possibly Pantin. *Courtesy Sotheby & Co.*

Fig. 165. Lily of the valley, possibly Pantin. *Courtesy Bergstrom Art Center and Museum.*

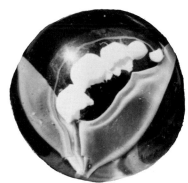

163   164   165

from Clichy. He says of Baccarat, "The reputation of this house is as good as ever, but it cannot be denied that some of the other glassworks around Paris are producing goods fully equal, and sometimes superior." Perhaps Pantin was only one of many places around Paris where glassworkers revived the popularity of paperweights in the years after 1878.

NOTES

[1] *Journal of Design and Manufactures,* 1849, vol. 1, pp. 194–95.

[2] James Barrelet, *La Verrerie en France,* Paris, 1953, p. 131; Eugène Péligot as quoted by Imbert and Amic (p. 66) credits St. Louis with being the first French glasshouse to take up overlay.

[3] Yolande Amic, *L'Opaline Française au XIXe Siècle,* Paris, 1952.

[4] Barrelet, *op. cit.,* p. 131.

[5] Great Exhibition 1851, *Jury Reports,* pp. 528, 529.

[6] Apsley Pellatt, *Curiosities of Glass-making,* London, 1849, pp. 42, 43.

[7] Albert Christian Revi, "The 'Fourth' French Paperweight Factory," *Bulletin,* 1965; *Spinning Wheel,* Oct., 1966, pp. 10, 11, 45.

[8] *U. S. Commission Reports 1878,* vol. 3, pp. 252, 253.

[9] *Ibid.,* p. 295.

[10] *Ibid.,* p. 266. Patented snowstorm paperweights were made in the United States in the 1930's with a black bakelite base. Today they are being made in Japan.

ABOUT THE ENGLISH MAKERS

THE CONCEPT OF THE GLASS PAPERWEIGHT as a decorative motif rendered more vivid and yet more mysterious by the magnifying and light-refracting properties of a thick, glass-covering lens became a possibility with the introduction of lead glass by Ravenscroft in the 1670's. But the realization of the glass paperweight as a novelty item to be sold along with other merchandise in stationers' shops and what the English called fancy shops had to await not only the inventive, progressive times of the mid-nineteenth century but also the repeal of the Glass Excise Duty in 1845.

In 1700 nearly one hundred English glasshouses were making lead glass. Then in 1745 the Glass Excise Duty became law, taxing glass by weight. Increased by the further acts of 1777, 1781, and 1787, the noxious tax had the effect of stifling English production of solid, heavy glass forms and particularly of flint (lead) glass. Bohemia, France, and Ireland usurped England's dominant position in the glass world. The 10½ pence-per-pound weight tax was lowered in 1825, but the last sixpence of the tax was not removed until the repeal of the excise duty in 1845, having thus trammeled English glass production for precisely one hundred years. 1845! Millefiori paperweights were already being made in Bohemia—Silesia, in Venice—Murano, and in France.

The removal of the excise duty led to an explosion in the English glass industry and the results of this explosion were on view six years later at the Great Exhibition in London. Millefiori paperweight production, never as extensive in England as in France, attained quality during those years, its finest efforts being on a par with those from St. Louis. Production of millefiori paperweights continued after 1851, and at Whitefriars it has gone on sporadically right to the present day. English millefiori paperweight production of the Classic period, confined almost entirely to London and Birmingham, derives stylistically from the concentrics of Baccarat, St. Louis, and Clichy.

Though, compared to the Continent, England began late in the making of millefiori weights, she can lay fair claim to having made the first non-millefiori weights, which are also probably the first glass paperweights from any source. They were the green glass weights, the earliest of which date from about 1829. They were made by Kilner of Yorkshire and by many other bottle factories. The Kilner examples continued to be made for nearly one hundred years after 1829.

Beginning in the early 1920's, when almost nothing was known about paperweights, the first English research into the subject made a number of false assumptions, whose subsequent establishment as fact was misleading to later students. These included assumptions of paperweight production at Bristol, Nailsea, and Stourbridge, where there was no solid evidence of such production. These questions will be considered in Chapter Eleven.

151

9

BACCHUS AND ISLINGTON

Bacchus

THE NAME OF BACCHUS, GREEN & GREEN, owners of the Union Glass Works on Dartmouth Street, Birmingham, first appears in the city directory of 1818, continuing under that listing until 1833, when the name was changed to George Bacchus & Co.[1]

This same year we also find listed Rice Harris & Company and W. Gammon & Company. Harris and Gammon had been together in 1822 as Harris Gammon & Company, but in 1834 we find William Gammon together with George Joseph Green and John Ogdin Bacchus, the son of George Bacchus, sharing Patent No. 6671.[2] They say in their patent:

> Now, the object of the Invention, consists in keeping clear a surface on the metal (molten glass) in the pots by means of rings which, lying on the surface of the metal, prevent the impurities which rise all around the sides of the pots from entering into the interior of such rings . . . and thus the metal may be drawn from the surface within the rings with but little hazard of taking up impurities.[3]

The patented Bessemer glass furnace of 1848 and the Henry Howard furnace of 1849 made further progress toward a clearer glass, yet the Glass Jury for the Great Exhibition of 1851 noted that English glass was still "charged with the defect of colour, of striae, of globules, and of undulations."[4]

George Bacchus died on September 6, 1840. An obituary in Aris's *Gazette* (September 21) describes him as "one of the most excellent and deservedly esteemed inhabitants of the town." The next year the firm name was changed to George Bacchus & Sons, listed in the directory as "Union Glass Works, Dartmouth Street and Tokenhouse Yard, London. Glass manufacturers (plain & cut)." Retitled Bacchus & Sons in 1858, the directory entry two years later reads "Stone Fawdry & Stone, (plain and cut) late George Bacchus & Sons, Union Glass Works, Dartmouth Street."[5]

The removal in 1845 of the last sixpence of the Glass Excise Duty brought a surge to recover markets lost to Bohemian and Continental glassmakers—the output of Bohemian style glass in the Birmingham-Stourbridge area was tremendous.[6] Like many other glasshouses Bacchus made primarily domestic glass, including table glass, cut, enameled, engraved, and cased glass in such forms as vases, jugs, decanters, sugar basins, and heavy glass rolling-pins. Soon they began to make glass "in the Venetian manner." Experimentation was encouraged and friggering was rampant. Among these experiments and friggers were glass paperweights which Bacchus exhibited at the Society of Arts in 1848. Commenting upon them the next year, the *Art-Union Monthly Journal of the Arts* had this to say:

> Glass Paper Weights—The introduction of these ingenious and pretty ornaments from Bohemia has induced some of our glass manufacturers to turn their attention to the production of similar objects. We have seen a large number of home manufacture, which, for beauty and variety of color, are equal to the best imported; and in design are superior to them. Mr. Bacchus, an eminent glass manufacturer of Birmingham, has produced some that deserve special notice for their novelty and elegance.[7]

The notion that Bacchus paperweights may have been based upon Bohemian imports rather than French models is not in accord with what we know of paperweights from those two countries, and the writer implies as much in his suggestions about their "novelty" and superior design, but it is significant as an indication of the hold of the *façon de Bohême* upon England (as upon France) at this time. As the *Art Journal* elsewhere comments,

> The contributions of Messrs. Bacchus & Sons, in plain and coloured glass, are all of very considerable excellence. . . . Messrs. Bacchus are among those manufacturers who have been labouring, and with success, to rival the productions of Bohemia . . . . Birmingham took the lead in this process, and, we rejoice to learn has kept it.[8]

In 1849 Bacchus showed its wares at the Exhibition of Manufactures and Art in Birmingham, sponsored by the British Association. The exhibition was held in Bingley Hall, the first building erected in England specifically to house exhibitions, and the exhibition was so extensive that another temporary building had to be constructed.[9] Some 102 glass articles, singly and in pairs, were exhibited on Table No. 62 of the exhibition. Item 91 in the catalogue of Bacchus articles is "Letter weights," an early and short-lived term for paperweights. Most of the Bacchus exhibits comprised cut, engraved, gilded, painted, and enameled overlay vases, toilet bottles, tea bells, water and milk jugs, wine coolers, candlesticks, and goblets, indicating that paperweights were a minor item.

Minor but not entirely ignored, for though the accent was on *façon de*

Bohême and glass "in the Venetian manner," we find the *Journal of Design and Manufactures* commenting:

> It were to be wished that Messrs. Bacchus had been a little earlier in the manufacture of their GLASS PAPER WEIGHTS, for the specimens we have recently seen of their works are quite the equal in transparency, color, skillful arrangement of parts, and ingenuity of make, to the foreign works with which stationers' and fancy shops have been and are so crowded.[10]

At the Great Exhibition of 1851 Bacchus glass similar to that shown at the 1849 Birmingham exhibition was on view, but no paperweights are mentioned, though doubtless a few were included, and the factory took a prize medal for its cut glass. Writing a century later, Haynes reflected that:

> Bacchus of Birmingham, it may be, could surely have done much more. The firm made a number of patterned millefiori weights, the best of which have definite merit. The colors are pallid and disappointing after cross channel brilliancy. But regard their pastel colors as a novelty and their restraint as a merit, and you may perceive their charm and acquire a taste for them. And remember that you will see 20 or 30 times as many French as period Bacchus weights.[11]

Actually, Haynes understates their scarcity. London is the paperweight capital of the world, and yet in the shops of antiques and paperweight dealers there in the summer of 1964 were four Bacchus weights. Of these one was fine, another good, a third adequate, and a fourth poor, a ratio typical of most factories. A check of auction catalogues since World War II from Sotheby in London and Parke-Bernet in New York, a period when most of the world's great paperweight collections came on the market, shows only a few dozen Bacchus weights, even allowing for possible misattributions. Probably no more than three or four hundred were made.

Bacchus Paperweights

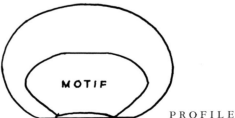

Heavy though they may feel in the hand, Bacchus weights show only a medium refractive index (see Chapter Nineteen). With few exceptions they are magnums by definition, averaging over 3¼ inches in diameter, and it is their size that accounts for their weight. Beginning at the top of the wide dome, the rather gentle profile curve becomes pronounced as it drops to the waist and moves quickly under to a flat basal rim that measures ⅛ inch to as much as ½ inch wide. The basal concavity, though especially shallow in relation to the bulk of the weight, usually touches the bottom ends of the peripheral canes. While often sugary, the glass in the crown is bright and clear; and while it is sometimes possible (for study purposes) with the aid of a strong light and a ten-power loupe to discover considerable flotsam and jetsam inside the cushion (probably the detritus of cullet), it is ordinarily invisible and in no way mars the beauty of the weight.

In most Bacchus weights the motif is a large, hassock-shaped cushion that springs from the concave base and extends from one-half to two-thirds of the way to the top of the weight, the lower half of this cushion sheathed in a peripheral ring of canes that draws down and under, to almost the center of the base, leaving a rather small opening which is likely to repeat in microcosm at least part of the paperweight design. Shaped like a cup, this outer sheath of canes is a characteristic that helps distinguish Bacchus from other paperweights, except Gillinder.

Canes

There are four basic types of Bacchus cane: the star [59], the ruffle [60A], the crimp [60B], and the cog [61]; and the combinations of their assembly make for a variety not seen in other English paperweights. There is also the hollow tube, but this is most often used as a container or frame for other canes.[12] I have before me as I write this a close millefiori that is a lexicon for Bacchus canes. All those mentioned above appear in it, but in a variety of sizes and colors. Take the simple star cane: in this weight the stars appear large in white with blue centers and the reverse; they appear in plain red, and they appear as bundles of tiny, white-topped, mauve stars. The same variety is found for the other canes. There is also the hollow tube, but this is most often used as a container for other canes. One large Bacchus tube encloses a potpourri of up to forty other canes greatly reduced in size. Occasionally the extent of the reduction in size is difficult to conceive. In one fine concentric, for example, the central motif is composed of what appears at first to be eight fair-sized pink canes with white centers. The white centers are nothing but solid, opaque white rods that take up about a quarter of the area of the cane. It requires a ten-power loupe to reveal that the other three quarters of the area of each cane are made up of no less than twenty-eight individual ruffled canes (not rods) that were drawn out until each was thinner than the shaft of a pin (Col. Fig. 74). But one seldom sees canes this fine, for many, especially the large ruffled central canes of the motifs, are simple and bold. Fortress (square) and triangular canes are sometimes seen.

Colors include the primaries plus pale thalo, viridian, and tourmaline greens,

[59]

[60A]

[60B]

[61]

aquamarine, various pinks, lilac, mauve, and, of course, opaque white. White is the basic containing element and color modifier. By modifier I mean that the variety of color shading is determined by the degree of thickness of a color coating over the opaque white. What appears to be a rich red may in fact be a very thick coating of pink, and what appears over the opaque white as pink may in fact be a thin coating of red. Subtle colors in Bacchus are often achieved through the very close juxtaposition of two colors, as, for example, a salmon pink created by the proximity of custard yellow to red, or a warm cerulean blue created by pale green next to pale cobalt blue. Actually, Whitefriars uses many more colors than Bacchus, yet the opposite appears true. This making of much from little in both design and color is the essence of artistic sensibility.

No dated canes from Bacchus are known, but there is a silhouette profile of a lady, which appears infrequently as an odd cane in close millefiori weights or as the central cane of close millefiori and concentrics. This may actually be the same cane used by William T. Gillinder in weights from that Philadelphia company. (See Chapter Fifteen.)

Paperweight Types and Characteristics

CLOSE MILLEFIORI—Many of the canes are apt to be large, compared to their counterparts in other factories, and the whole collection is enclosed in a peripheral ring of canes, usually crimped, that cup under to the center of the base (Fig. 166). One example is faceted with sixteen printies, another is swirl faceted.

CONCENTRICS—Most Bacchus weights are concentrics, with an average of five concentric rings of canes about a large central floret, the outer ring again usually of crimped canes cupping down to the center of the base, though sometimes star, ruffled, or other canes are seen (Figs. 167, 168, 169). This large cushion forming the motif is a flattened dome that rises from a half to two-thirds of the total height of the weight, so high, in fact, that when viewed from above, it appears to fill the entire weight almost to bursting. Viewed from the side, the profile of the cushion may appear perfectly smooth and even, or it may show an irregular edge, the cane tops appearing and disappearing as in a heat wave above the crown of a road, an effect that may be due to an actual break in the refractive index of the glass, or to a thin air pocket between the tops of the canes and the skin of glass with which they were covered before the final dippings were made, the air pocket producing the same silvery effect it does upon a

Fig. 166. Bacchus close millefiori. *Private collection. Photograph by Taylor & Dull.*

Fig. 167. Bacchus red, yellow, and blue concentric. *Private collection. Photograph by Taylor & Dull.*

Fig. 168. Bacchus concentric, large central floret. *Private collection. Photograph by Taylor & Dull.*

Fig. 169. Bacchus concentric, ruffled canes. *Courtesy Sotheby & Co.*

166

167

168   169

sulphide. Whatever the consistency of the cushion curvature, the large, bold central floret is usually flat in profile.

Upon close inspection it frequently appears that the ruffling or scalloping in the design of this large floret is apparently supported by very thin wires, visible as they emerge from the top of the floret. In florets with wide, open centers there may be a naked wire like a flower pistil topped by a tiny bubble. Perhaps the idea was that these tiny wires would be consumed by the heat during composition and perhaps where they do not appear they were consumed. But when the big central floret is viewed again in profile, little whitecaps or snowdrifts, probably caused by the opaque white glass adhering to the wires, can be seen as breaks in the flat top surface. Such wires occasionally show up in other ruffled canes but are usually too small to see.

The evenness with which the concentric rows are set is about on a par with that from France, but mention should be made of a dissimilar or maverick cane which sometimes crops up in a ring of otherwise identical canes. The assumption springs to mind that the creator, having miscalculated the number of canes he could accommodate in a given row, or not having cut enough slices from the cane intended for that row, filled the gap with a different cane that was handy. Yet the explanation may be that, like the oriental rug weavers, he made a slight variation in the pattern to avoid monotony.[13] Molas made by the San Blas Indians of Panama show such breaks in rigid geometric design codes, which avoid monotony and are the result of relaxed and happy inspiration.

Haynes called the colors pallid. What makes Bacchus weights so often appear pallid is not the colors so much as the fact that the top rims of the canes are usually opaque white, which tends to dilute the effect of the surrounding colors. Color for color and tone for tone one might be looking at a Turner or a Constable sky (Col. Fig. 75). Where the intensity of the color overlay is diluted, it was no doubt meant to be, perhaps as an unconscious antidote to overstuffed Victorian color. A very dry, mat, opaque white that resembles plaster is the moderator at Bacchus, which imparts an almost Georgian restraint to the concentrics. In one lovely example, the big, opaque white central floret, over an inch in diameter, sits like a plaster or marble patera amid rings of canes in palest lavender and thalo green, pale lake red and scarlet, a cotillion of delicately colored canes—one might be looking in at the Assembly Rooms at Bath. One incredible concentric is a double, that is, the central motif of the concentric is not a large floret but another tiny, tufted concentric, like a double skyrocket burst.

The work of individual, unknown artists is easily discernable among the concentrics. One sees examples belonging to a series featuring stars or stiff ruffles, a series where the color scheme of the whole weight is carefully calculated for balance, or a series like delicate powder puffs with the canes bleeding their colors into each other. Alone, these might be considered accidents, but several of each are found. While many Bacchus concentrics are not particularly exciting, the finer examples hold their own with the French concentrics, and a few rival anything produced by St. Louis (Col. Figs. 76, 77).

PATTERNED MILLEFIORI—Including the usual Bacchus outer ring of crimped or other canes, these weights space from four to eight square, circular, or triangular clusters of canes (identical in form and color within each cluster but differing from cluster to cluster) about a central large floret or a roughly star-shaped group of canes. The clusters of canes are sunk in what at first glance appears to be a solid color ground of a peculiar opaque but fuzzy white-like dense fog, or, as someone aptly called it "sodden snow."[14] Closer inspection shows it to be not a ground at all, but an arrangement of thick rings like cotton wadding set tangent to, and blending with, one another. One can see down into the gaps among the clusters as if the canes were intaglios, when, in fact, they are sunken relief (Fig. 170, 171). In one fine example the arrangement of clusters

Fig. 170. Bacchus sodden snow. *Courtesy Christie's.*

Fig. 171. Bacchus sodden snow, red central floret. *Private collection. Photograph by Taylor & Dull.*

170

171

and rings suggests a marbrie festooning like one of the rare St. Louis carpet grounds. One amazing weight has, instead of the clusters, large red and white florets like paterae surrounded by the "sodden snow" (Col. Fig. 78). In others, the sodden snow is a custard yellow or green. One wonders if there is a specimen with a silhouette at the center of the motif?

[62]

MUSHROOMS—There are not many of these massive 3¾-inch weights. In the half-dozen examples seen, the sides rise steeply from a wide base to a flattened crown [62]. The motif is a concentric mushroom surrounded by a torsade of flat spirals in cerise, magenta, or royal blue (over opaque white, the white visible on the inside of the spiral) about a many-stranded, opaque-white chaplet bead twist. The feathery canes in soft mauve, red, pink, blue, viridian green, and white give the effect of a skyrocket bursting, but without the bang (Col. Fig. 79). The center of the motif, as in the concentrics, usually shows a flat profile. The best of these rare weights are superbly done, and one fabulous example without the torsade appears in a weight cut with printies and vertical flutes (Col. Fig. 80).

CARPET GROUNDS—I have seen only two of these, one of pink and white canes, the other of viridian and white canes, both poorly done. Some close millefiori show a predominance of one cane form or color but are not strictly carpet grounds because they contain a scattering of fortress, sodden snow, and other canes (Fig. 172).

PEDESTAL—One pedestal is known, a lovely faceted concentric, the green, pink, and pale blue canes set in an opaque white basket extending to the footed base. A superb weight.

ENCASED OVERLAYS—A double overlay basket containing a tufted or egg-shaped, close millefiori collection of canes is in turn encased in clear glass. In two instances the opaque white basket is overlaid with a lattice of another color (one in pink, the other in mauve) seen in reverse: that is, the lattice is opaque white while the interstices are colored (Fig. 173). Both baskets have handles of the same reverse lattice. In two other specimens the basket is a solid cobalt blue or lapis blue over opaque white, the opaque white interior of one decorated with sky blue spirals. One basket is turquoise blue. About a half-dozen encased overlays are known and these are usually mistaken for St. Louis (Col. Fig. 81).

Related Millefiori

TOILET BOTTLES—A pair is known, the bases containing concentric arrangements of canes.

Fig. 172. Bacchus carpet ground spotted with pink. *Courtesy Christie's.*

Fig. 173. Bacchus encased double overlay basket with Victoria silhouette. *Courtesy The New-York Historical Society.*

Islington

The general history of the Islington Glass Works as it concerns us closely parallels Bacchus. In 1803 we find the Birmingham city directory listing "Owen Johnson, glass and glass toy manufacturer, dealer in cornelians, Islington."

During the period 1818-33 the name changes to Johnson, Berry & Harris. After 1839 it becomes, successively, Rice Harris, "Flint and cut glass manufacturer, Islington" (1839-45); Rice Harris, Islington Glass Works, Sheepcote Street (1845-55); Rice Harris & Son, Islington Glass Works, Sheepcote Street (1855-58); London & Birmingham Flint Glass and Alkali Company, 46 Sheepcote Street (1858-60); and finally in 1860, Islington Glass Company (Limited), H. C. Ensell, manager, Sheepcote Street.

Like Bacchus, Islington showed at the Exhibition of Manufactures and Art, Birmingham, 1849. The exhibition ran for fifteen weeks from September 3 through December 15, and netted close to 100,000 visitors. The Rice Harris exhibits were displayed on Table No. 64 and included much the same wares as those shown by Bacchus, but with a stress on ruby, canary, violet, and opaque green glass colors. No paperweights were listed among the 108 items shown, but they were certainly being made at this date because they are mentioned in that year.

> We have been much interested in examining some specimens of colored, threaded, and engraved glass, the productions of the Islington Glass Works, Birmingham, in which colours as brilliant and designs as elaborate as any seen in the Bohemian specimens were produced. The articles we have seen consisted of compound millefleur paperweights, coloured and engraved goblets, carafes, and glass slabs of a most beautiful character in green and silver, adapted for finger plates and similar purposes. The whole of these specimens were little, if anything, inferior to the most choice productions of the Continent.[15]

The "compound millefleur" sounds interesting but doesn't tell us much.

The catalogue of the Great Exhibition of 1851 lists for Rice Harris & Son "specimens of threaded or Venetian glass." This, of course, means latticinio and does not include paperweights which, it should be noted, were considered in those days to derive from Bohemian or French models. The *Illustrated London News* for May 10, 1851, has an interesting comment to make with regard to the removal of the glass excise tax in 1845:

> Had this exhibition taken place seven years ago, the examples of glass manufacture on the British side would have been so ridiculous as to have provoked contempt .... Messrs. Rich Harris & Son, of Birmingham, exhibit a series of most elegant specimens of cut and pressed glass in a variety of colors, gilt, enamelled and engraved, as also examples of threaded or Venetian glass.

For all the "compound millefleur" paperweights Islington may have made we have documentation of only two. One rather small weight, just under 2¾ inches in diameter, is a close millefiori dome that includes arrow, star, and whorl canes, a cane like a three-bladed propellor, a silhouette cane of a draft horse, and an opaque white lozenge bearing the initials IGW, obviously for Islington Glass Works. The other example, also signed and containing a horse silhouette, has a muslin ground. The promise shown in these two weights makes us hope more will turn up for study.

NOTES

[1] The 1833 listing is given by Harry J. Powell, *Glassmaking in England,* Cambridge, 1923, p. 104.

[2] Patent Library of The New York Public Library.

[3] Patent No. 6671, p. 2.

[4] G. Bernard Hughes, *English, Scottish and Irish Table Glass,* New York, 1956, pp. 68, 69.

[5] These entries supplied me by the Birmingham Reference Library, Birmingham, England.

[6] Bernard and Therle Hughes, *After the Regency,* London, 1952, p. 142.

[7] *Art Union Monthly Journal,* 1849, p. 343.

[8] *Art Journal,* vol. II, 1849, p. 314.

[9] Kenneth W. Luckhurst, *The Story of Exhibitions,* London, 1951, p. 82.

[10] *Journal of Design and Manufactures,* vol. I, Mar.–Aug. 1949, p. 95.

[11] E. B. Haynes, *Antique Collector,* Dec., 1953.

[12] The tube, of course, is filled with clear glass—it only appears to be hollow.

[13] Christopher Dunham Reed, "Rugs of Turkestan," *Antiques,* Jan., 1966, p. 97.

[14] J. P. Boore, "Some Little Known English Makers," *Bulletin,* 1959.

[15] *Art Journal,* vol. II, Feb., 1849, p. 65.

10

WHITEFRIARS

Whitefriars Street slopes out of Fleet Street down to the river through the centre of a district that used to be occupied by a Carmelite monastery and its garden. By the time of James I the monastery had disappeared, but the area that belonged to it retained the ancient right of sanctuary that was granted to religious houses and their precincts, and the streets that had replaced the monastery and its garden were a secure retreat for debtors, cutpurses, highwaymen, and all the blackguards of the town, for the law had no right to pursue them once they had escaped into that privileged quarter.[1]

THE MONASTERY of the White Friars was torn down in 1538, and it was on these grounds, with their easy access to the Thames, that a glasshouse was erected about 1680.[2] A map of 1682 labels the location of the glassworks. Even after the revocation of the privilege of sanctuary in 1697, Whitefriars remained a tough and sinister labyrinth where "the visit of a tax collector was resisted by the brandishing of blow-irons headed with red hot glass."[3] Angus-Butterworth quotes the Whitehall *Evening Post* of 1732 to recall that "Yesterday a Press Gang went into the glasshouse in White Fryars [sic] to press some of the men at work there, but they were no sooner got in but the metal was flung about 'em, and happy was he that could get out first, and in hurrying out they ran over their officer, who was almost scalded to death."[4]

By 1700 there were eleven glass factories in London, including Whitefriars, making lead glass.[5] The first products were tableware, especially the increasingly popular clear glass decanters used for the fashionable port wine. "At the Flint Glass House in White Friars," runs an advertisement of 1710, "are made and sold by Wholesale and Retail, all sorts of Decanters, Drinking Glasses, Crewitts, etc., or glasses made to any pattern of the best Flint, as also all sorts of common Drinking Glasses and other things made in ordinary Flint Glass at reasonable rates." Sand for the glass came from the Forest of Fontainebleau.[6]

164

James Powell (1774-1840) was a glassmaker in Bristol, where flint glass had been made from the middle of the eighteenth century. Bristol had been a center for window and bottle glass, and was famous for the opaque white glass fashioned and decorated in imitation of popular porcelains and soft pastes. But by 1800 Bristol was declining as a glass center, and in 1835 James Powell moved to London and James Powell & Sons became another of a series of owners of the Whitefriars glasshouse.

During the nineteenth century Whitefriars kept pace with foreign as well as domestic demands; it supplied the home market with cut and engraved crystal and made such foreign shipments as thick telescope glass for the optician Dolland, watch dials for the Swiss, and a pair of girondoles presented to Queen Adelaide (1837).[7] From the 1830's, Whitefriars carried a wide range of colors for the production of stained glass windows.[8]

At the Great Exhibition of 1851 James Powell & Sons was listed both as exhibitor and as glass associate, and was awarded a prize medal for its "fine crystal." Richardson, Bacchus, and Pellatt were also awarded medals.[9] In his report on the work of the French Commission to the Exhibition, Eugène Péligot notes of Whitefriars that "The Messrs. Powell at London have made some very white crystal pieces with sand from Lynn, in the county of Norfolk, or the Isle of Wight."[10] Typically no glass paperweights were mentioned, but this is true of the exhibition as a whole, and Whitefriars paperweights, which were being made as early as 1848, were probably on view there.

By the time of the Great Exhibition every conceivable thing was being done with and to glass. For some time there had been a scientific interest in techniques of ancient and modern glassworking, encouraged by Pellatt and Chance. In 1845 the repeal of the Glass Excise Duty reopened the door to lead glass and the limitless possibilities for imitation of Bohemian overlay work, cutting, and engraving. All sorts of styles from other times and other lands were appropriated, while parallel to these currents ran the Anglo-Irish tradition; and to these, after 1851, was added a new intellectual view that glass should be worked in terms of the material itself as against superimposed decorative form, a view propounded by Ruskin and others of the intelligentsia. These forces are mentioned because Whitefriars steered an interesting course between them, pursuing some aspects, rejecting others. In the area of stained glass such artists as Rossetti and Burne-Jones came to Whitefriars. In 1859 William Morris commissioned the architect Philip Webb to design table glass, which was subsequently made by Whitefriars, and glasses were again made for Morris in 1874 to the design of the architect T. G. Jackson. It is interesting to note that a policy of collaboration with artists has also been followed at Orrefors in Sweden and Steuben in America.

The presence of Whitefriars seems to have been a rather quiet one at the various exhibitions following 1851, and the next major prize won was only a silver medal at the Paris Exposition of 1878. Here Pantin and the Venice-Murano Company were awarded gold medals, and Baccarat and Thomas Webb the Grand Medal. However, under the direction of H. J. Powell (1853-1922),

Whitefriars "began to recover an English tradition of hand-made blown glass," showing Venetian and English medieval influences, produced in addition to its line of glass cut and engraved in the Anglo-Irish tradition.[11] Following the death of Powell, Whitefriars moved from London, where it had been for some 240 years, to Wealdstone, Middlesex, where it was known until recently as James Powell & Sons (Whitefriars) Ltd.; now as Whitefriars Glass Ltd., it is still operating.

Paperweight Production

Unfortunately but typically, very little record appears to have been kept at Whitefriars of paperweight production which, evidently and again typically, was considered a relatively unimportant sideline, "extra to normal production lines." Correspondence with Whitefriars has furnished me with the following morsels of fact and conjecture. Millefiori paperweights were made there on and off from 1848; also the popular inkwells and decanters, but rarely anything else in the millefiori line. Whitefriars has very few examples of their work put aside, and these are "nearly all examples made over the last ten years" as experiments or friggers. Until 1965, when about four hundred were made specially, only "some four or five dozen have gone on the market."[12]

How continuously or sporadically they were made from 1848 we do not know, but we do know that they were being made in the 1960's, and we do know that some 600-700 concentrics with a central cane, in which is inscribed E. II R., 1953," were made to commemorate the coronation of Queen Elizabeth II in 1953. Recently a Whitefriars weight with a paper label stuck to the base came up for auction in London. This label, which shows a white-robed monk holding a sign reading Whitefriars and around him the words "Powell's English Glass," first made its appearance in the late 1930's, so the London paperweight must date from then or later, the label having remained the same for some years (Fig. 174).

And there is one other shred of evidence. About ten years ago, in several places in Massachusetts, Whitefriars inkwells, wine glasses, and decanters began turning up in antiques shops. In form they were all concentrics of fine heavy lead glass, and the wine glasses had a good ring to them. Their shapes, canes, and the degree of their wear marks were so similar as to provoke the suspicion that they were all from the same batch. And sure enough, an inquiry here and there unearthed the rather delightful explanation collectors dream of, namely that they had all come from the same New England dealer, and that he had found them in an old factory warehouse in England (I believe it was even in Wealdstone) among boxes of merchandise that had remained unopened since they were made "many years before." This enticing story convinced me then and it convinces me still, my only qualification of it being, for "many years before" read "1930."

Whitefriars Paperweights

PROFILES

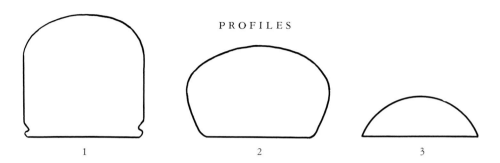

1   2   3

The most striking aspect of Whitefriars paperweights is their persistent similarity in the 120 years they have been produced. The record does not tell us whether they were made continuously or sporadically, yet in all that time two basic types of millefiori predominated; close millefiori and concentrics. Examples may be footed or plain. Nevertheless, there are some important differences within this overall similarity; differences in profile and in execution.

There are three typical Whitefriars profiles. In Type 1, the sides rise straight and vertical to a high dome. In Type 2, the profile curve more nearly resembles that from other factories but is extremely wide based. In Type 3, the base is wide but the shallow dome is spanned in an unbroken curve. Since the profile of most paperweights from any given factory and period is standardized, the profiles illustrated seem to represent work of different times and creators. As the individual creators are unknown, we must consider the profiles temporally, and here the inkwells are of some help. All the inkwells in the Massachusetts group, that is, in the crated and unused group made around 1930 or thereafter, show tall, nearly straight sides, the lower or well part of the inkwell having a profile corresponding to Type 1. We have only to add a neck and stopper to the Type 1 paperweight to achieve the modern Whitefriars inkwell. Side by side, an inkwell and paperweight of this profile look like a desk set, as if they were made at the same time to go together. I would therefore say that the high-domed, straight-sided weights are comparatively recent, fifty years old or less.

I would place Type 3 profile in the Classic period and later. It should be noted here that, regardless of paperweight profile, the millefiori motif is set low on a broad, rather rough and wrinkled base. The base is composed of two sections, an inner core containing the motif, with a jagged pontil mark as its center, and a thick outer casing. In most instances the bottoms of the canes actually touch the base, and this and the joining of the two sections can be seen and often actually felt with the fingers. Since the Type 3 profile represents the initial steps in making an inkwell, it would seem that weights having this low profile, particularly those of magnum diameter, were made at the same time as and to accompany inkwells. The unsuccessful examples were carried no further, but merely covered with a low dome and let go at that. Many of the inkwells dated

1848 show a sloppy placement of crude canes, and it is likely that the low-domed and sloppy paperweights were made at the same time. Dated examples corroborate this. I would assume that low-domed but finely executed examples might date from the time of the Great Exhibition when there were foreign examples to copy. And it would seem logical that the many excellent examples of the Type 2 profile appeared only after execution of the motif was perfected and the magnifying properties of the glass from other paperweight sources well understood. But it is certainly possible that some of the many poorly executed low profiles represent a time late in the nineteenth century, when a revival of the technique was undertaken by other enthusiasts such as the English-controlled Venice-Murano Company. In a desert of information and record, these hypotheses must serve until further research proves them to have been oases or mirages.

Whitefriars Canes and Colors

If one accepts a difference in paperweight profiles over the span of a century, the minor variations in cane structure follow naturally and are, in fact, barely enough to account for the variety usually seen in the work of a single glasshouse. The canes are generally limited to single rods or tubes, or tubes enclosing single rods. There are some trefoil and quatrefoil rods, some star rods, and much crimping, ruffling, or cogging of the tubes, but very little else. It is the coloring that gives the illusion of multiplicity. Just as in the case of Baccarat dating it was possible with five rods and three colors to get over two hundred color-rod combinations, so here the possibilities are legion and immense variety results from but a few cane types. Some Whitefriars weights may appear predominantly a forceful red, a cold blue, a rich pink, or a delicate white or yellow, but individual cane colors run the gamut from the palest yellow to deepest eggplant and include just about every variation known to St. Louis, as well as many olive greens, golden ochres, powder blues, and other colors unknown to French paperweight-making. Yet this variety is given unity by the simplicity of the concentric design.

Unusual canes include the large, opaque white, sitting rabbit of the early weights and inkwells, and the hearts, diamonds, clubs, and more elaborate motifs of the weights and inkwells made after about 1935. One very Near-Eastern-looking motif that has turned up several times recently and appears throughout whole rows of canes is actually nothing more than a trefoil, about which are stationed four rods in square formation, but when the cane was made, the trefoil had slipped to touch the surrounding hollow tube, and the multiple repetition of the error gives the illusion of some rare and esoteric motif. The phenomenon is similar to those "C" canes in Clichy that are merely slipped rods.

The only dating of Whitefriars millefiori products comes in examples from 1848 and 1953. The 1848 is composed of four separated rods [63]. The 8 rods

[63]

Fig. 174. Whitefriars label on base of weight. *Courtesy Christie's.*

are really double, that is, they are two white tubes with colored centers that have been fused together. The 4 rod looks more like a curved sword or an upside-down f than a 4. The 1953 date, contained in one large cane, was made to commemorate the coronation of Queen Elizabeth II, and reads "E.II R. 1953."

Paperweight Types and Characteristics

CLOSE MILLEFIORI—These are mainly the old Classic period weights and inkwells, particularly the matching desk sets with pairs of inkwells or pairs of weights and matching inkwells. Canes are close set and there is no muslin stuffing underneath, such as we find in France. These weights are likely to contain about every cane in the house in a soft riot of gorgeous, delicate colors—an English garden of color, with strawberry, peach and coral, Naples, lemon, and chartreuse yellows, powder blue, violet, opal, turquoise, moss green, eggplant, and ruby. Some examples are so deeply and intricately faceted as to suggest an English garden gently blurred by the wind. Scent bottles, wine glasses, and decanters also are known, and some sets of the latter. In a few weights and inkwells the sitting white bunny makes his appearance. This bunny, incidentally, is no cousin to the lithe, running hare of American and Bohemian weights.

CONCENTRICS—These are the chief Whitefriars paperweights, ranging in diameter from about 2¼ inches to 4½ inches, and containing from three to ten or more concentric rings of close-set canes (Fig. 175). As with the close mille-fiori, the design is set very low at the base of the weight and has a low-domed, extraordinarily even profile. Coloring may be subtle and varied, or it may be rather hard and monotonous, with row after row of nearly identical canes and colors, like a mouthful of false teeth. Center canes are usually somewhat larger and occasionally considerably larger, though they lack the keystone impact of central canes from Bacchus. In this and other aspects one can see the strong dissimilarity between the work of the two houses, something that would probably have been less pronounced if the paperweight-making rival Bacchus had been located in Stourbridge instead of in London. For symmetry and color harmony a small number of concentrics are, however, in a class apart. I recall one that is all white except for a row of the palest pink and the turquoise central floret. A 4½-inch magnum combines ultramarine blue with chartreuse yellow, scarlet and pink with a translucence that catches and reflects colors like the rose window in Reims Cathedral (Fig. 176; Col. Fig. 82).

CHEQUERS—A number of unsuccessful attempts were made at chequers with gauze partitions in pink and blue, but this demanding form proved unmanageable—canes would dwindle, leaving great gaps of clear glass, and tubes of gauze would pile up like log jams. Still, there must be a satisfactory example somewhere (Fig. 177).

[64]

INKWELLS—Show two general profiles; one, early [64], the other, late [65]. In the early profile, the footed body is squatter and more curved. The stopper mushroom is thick, tall, and knopped. In the late profile, also footed, the sides rise nearly vertically from the base, and the stopper is flatter, lower, and unknopped. The motif in both types is set right at the base. Early examples may be close millefiori or concentric, and are frequently elaborately faceted or panel cut. Late examples are unfaceted concentrics, with the pontil usually ground off. Though canes and coloring are usually monotonous in late examples, some show hearts, diamonds, clubs, and other more interesting canes in carefully selected juxtapositions of pastel shades (Fig. 178).

[65]

DECANTERS AND GLASSES—May also be early or late. Decanter canework is generally good in both vintages, but in the old glasses, which include both wine and shot glasses, the smaller ground area has apparently been a problem and the canes are often sloppily arranged. In a series of wine and shot glasses made about 1953, the very reduced canes are closely set but covered only with a thin dome, which gives them the tinselly appearance of Christmas tree ornaments.

DOORSTOPS—A few enormous examples. In two of them, five complete millefiori concentrics appear, four ranged vertically about the sides and a fifth on top, floating like sea anemones in the massive crystal. One doorstop is dated 1848.

OVERLAY—Only one example is known to me, a single white overlay that is a remarkable but not entirely successful paperweight (Col. Fig. 83). The motif

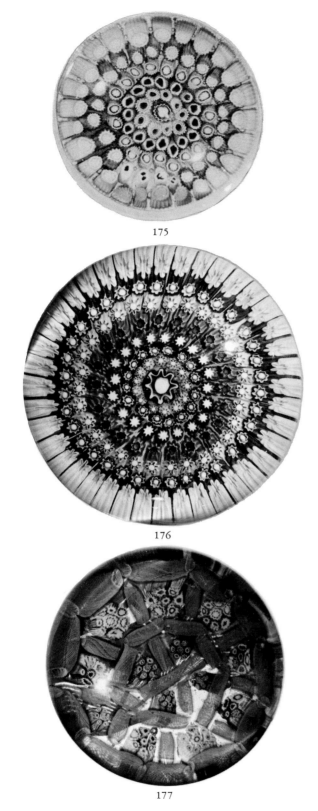

175

176

177

Fig. 175. Whitefriars concentric dated 1848. *Courtesy Parke-Bernet Galleries, Inc.*

Fig. 176. Whitefriars magnum concentric. *Private collection. Photograph by Taylor & Dull.*

Fig. 177. Whitefriars chequer. *Courtesy Christie's.*

Fig. 178. Whitefriars modern inkwell, heart and club canes. *Courtesy Christie's.*

is a cushion of coral red, orange and blue canes, a mushroom cap without the stem. The weight is faceted overall with printies, but the thick white overlay covers only the lower half. However, the inner surface of the white overlay is striped with radiating blue spokes which, seen through the printies, show up as a marbrie festoon. The mushroom cap is not set high enough in the weight to benefit from the printies and the interior is a bit dim. As an overall conception it doesn't quite come off, though it was a noble attempt and a proof that Whitefriars could be daring.

NOTES

[1] St. John Adcock, *London Memories,* London, n.d., p. 111.

[2] L. M. Angus-Butterworth, *British Table and Ornamental Glass,* London, 1956, p. 29 *et seq.*

[3] *Ibid.,* p. 30.

[4] *Ibid.*

[5] E. Barrington Haynes, *Glass Through the Ages*, Baltimore, 1964, p. 196.

[6] Anon., "The Glass Blowers of Whitefriars," *Arts & Decoration,* Nov., 1938, pp. 9, 10.

[7] Angus-Butterworth, p. 30.

[8] Letter from G. P. Baxter, Whitefriars designer.

[9] Great Exhibition, 1851, *Jury Reports.*

[10] Péligot, *Travaux de Commission Français sur l'Industrie des Nations,* Paris, 1854, vol. 6, XXIV Jury, pp. 1–58.

[11] W. B. Honey, *Glass, A Handbook,* London, 1946, pp. 124, 125.

[12] Quotes and information are from correspondence with G. P. Baxter, Whitefriars designer.

11

OTHER ENGLISH FACTORIES

Bristol

IN THE YEARS leading up to and including the Great Exhibition enough was written about English paperweights to establish their production, particularly by Bacchus and Islington, both of Birmingham. Production at Whitefriars in London is established in the continuity of paperweights, including dated examples. Aside from this, nothing has come to light that would indicate substantial paperweight production from other English glasshouses during the middle and latter years of the nineteenth century. Not from Nailsea, nor from Bristol, nor from Stourbridge, to name the three areas most commonly and persistently claimed as sources of paperweights.

Only after 1900 do we begin to come upon assertions that production did occur in these places. By 1920 the assertions have been taken for fact and we find articles identifying Baccarat paperweights as Bristol because they are signed with a "B." The fixation of Bristol as a paperweight center has had a long life. As recently as 1965 a weight made by Paul Ysart of Scotland was identified in an article as Bristol. The late Mrs. Bergstrom in her marvelous book unwittingly added fuel to the Bristol fire when she illustrated a concentric supposedly from Bristol which had a center cane with the date 1831. This, she said, was an "English fake . . . probably made for one of the expositions in Paris or London which were held during the height of the paperweight popularity," which would mean around 1851.[1] This weight has turned out to be one of the many millefiori concentrics made at Baccarat by old Mr. Dupont before his death, about 1933. And it seems likely that the pansy, likewise attributed to Bristol by Mrs. Bergstrom (1948 edition, p. 65), who apparently made a distinction between it and pansies she knew to be nineteenth-century Baccarat, was also made by Dupont.[2] Having expressed my disinclination to regard Bristol as a paperweight-making center to Mr. Hugh Wakefield, noted authority on British glass and author of *Nineteenth Century British Glass*, I received a reply containing the following sentence. "I am very suspicious of any attributions to Bristol, since I know how readily dealers attribute all coloured English glass to that city, whereas in fact, glass making was dwindling very rapidly there in the middle of the 19th century."[3] Other reliable correspondents have been equally discouraging. Claims have been widely made that all sorts of weights, including flowers, millefiori, butterflies, snakes, etc., were made at Bristol. Usually the weights themselves are freakish examples difficult to track down, and perhaps some of them were made in Bristol. But no extensive or important production has been reliably associated with that city.

Nailsea

We next turn our attention to Nailsea, which was, after all, only nine miles from Bristol. The Nailsea Glass Works was founded in 1788 by John Robert Lucas and, under successive owners, including Robert Lucas Chance, was engaged in the manufacture of crown and sheet glass. In 1824 Robert Lucas Chance moved to Spon Lane, Birmingham, where, with the help of Georges Bontemps, formerly of Choisy-le-Roi, he continued and perfected the manufacture of the sheet glass that was used to sheathe the Crystal Palace of the Great Exhibition. The Nailsea works closed down in 1873.[4] Elville says of it that in the debris of the factory "no colours have so far been unearthed," and that there is "no positive evidence that any coloured glass was ever made there."[5] Elville describes in some detail the ovoid or bullet-shaped green glass paperweights so persistently assumed to have been made at Nailsea. He says of them:

> As green paperweights of the type described above were easy to make, and were formed from the cheapest glass, most bottle factories throughout the country produced them up to comparatively recent times. It is, therefore, extremely difficult to distinguish the early specimens from those of later manufacture; nor is it possible, as some writers claim, to decide from its colour where a bottle-green weight was made.[6]

Yet the myth of Nailsea paperweights persists. Perhaps a sentence in a letter written to me recently by Sir Hugh Chance, descendant of Robert Lucas Chance of Nailsea, will lay the myth to rest. Sir Hugh speaks of an article he has just completed for *Connoisseur* on the history of the Nailsea glassworks. Then he says, "What I can say with certainty is that Nailsea can never have produced paperweights."[7]

Stourbridge

It has long been fashionable to label as "Stourbridge" concentric weights and inkwells that are slightly more elaborate than those from Whitefriars, and no distinction in paperweight attribution has been made in so offhand and cavalier a fashion. Yet the fact is that no evidence of any substantial or important paperweight production from Stourbridge has yet come to light. In terms of glass manufacture, the Stourbridge area is and has long been extensive, and a few of those whom I consulted in preparation for this book have indicated a belief that paperweights must have been made in the area. Belief, but no proof.

For example, Mr. C. J. Share, curator of the Stourbridge Town Council Glass Collection writes, "It is my opinion that Richardson produced paperweights during the latter part of the nineteenth century." Elsewhere in the same letter he says, "I have carried out a little research here and can report no proof that paperweights were made at Spon Lane (Stourbridge, sic.)."[8] Glass expert G. W. Beard describes in a letter to me an inspection he made of the archives of Thomas Webb & Sons where his father-in-law was production manager. "They certainly made paperweights, but the documentation is almost non-existent. I only found one record of a paperweight being made and that only occurred in the archives because it had a gilded badge set within it and a cost for the gilding was incurred."[9] This would imply a special order rather than a production line.

In Guttery's book on the Stourbridge glass industry there is a single statement that might be construed as relating to the making of paperweights. Referring to the period immediately after 1845 when colored glass "had squeezed through," Guttery says, "The many cribs, which grew up in the Stourbridge district when the Excise century ended, made the stock bottles and phials, but some specialized in small coloured canes which they supplied to the glasshouses."[10] We are not told to which glasshouses they were supplied, whether to glasshouses in the Stourbridge area or to the glasshouses of Bacchus and Islington in nearby Birmingham. In any event it is unlikely that these semioutlawed cribs with their limited facilities would have been able to compose their canes into the more elaborate forms required for the supposed Stourbridge paperweights, and it is still less likely that they could have made paperweights.

Barely fifteen years ago Bacchus weights, which were as yet unresearched and whose provenance was unknown, were classified as Stourbridge. Yet how different they look from those which today are still being classified as Stourbridge. It seems likely that most of the latter will soon be accepted as coming from Whitefriars, unless someone with time for thorough research and easy access to the Stourbridge neighborhood comes up with more solid evidence of production there than has been found so far. Such a possibility is certainly to be hoped for and might also shed more light on the hollow weights discussed later in the chapter.

Kilner and Others

Actually, it has been known for some time that many of the soft green weights with the flowerpots and sulphides inside were made in the West Riding section of Yorkshire, not far from Leeds, as an after-hours by-product of bottle manu-facture. Castleford, where there was a glassworks, has repeatedly been men-tioned as a source. However, the nearby town of Wakefield is pinpointed by labeled examples as an unchallengeable source. One such weight in the Wells collection at Old Sturbridge Village, Sturbridge, Massachusetts (not to be con-fused with Stourbridge, England), has a glass wafer label on the bottom like the wafer on old wine bottles, which reads "J. Tower, Maker, Wakefield." But most labeled weights read "J. Kilner, Maker, Wakefield."

In 1829 John Kilner (1792-1857) and four other men formed a partner-ship at Whitwood Mere for the manufacture of glass bottles. After a few years the group split up and Kilner moved to Thornhill Lees (now Dewsbury, near Wakefield) where, with the help of his sons, he established the Providence Glass Works, also known as J. Kilner & Son, then as J. Kilner & Sons, contin-uing the bottle trade. In 1844 the company became known as Kilner Brothers and remained so until just before World War II when it was absorbed by the Glass Trust. Prosperity, especially after the repeal of the glass excise in 1845, seems to have been continuous through the nineteenth century and Kilner prod-ucts from the smallest vial to the biggest carboy were shipped to the remotest reaches of the far-flung British Empire, the United States, South America, and Europe. A plant was added at Conisboro in 1863, and there were warehouses, offices, and sample rooms in London.[11]

Mr. C. A. Kilner is a great-grandson of the founder John Kilner, and a col-lector of Kilner weights. Thanks to him we are able to piece together a compre-hensive picture of paperweight-making at the Kilner works. Mr. Kilner says they were made from what the people of the region called "dumps," that is, molten glass left at the end of the day which would otherwise have been dumped out.[12] About one in twelve is labeled on the bottom, which provides remarkable documentation. The labels are glass seals about an inch in diameter, found where the pontil mark appears in unlabeled examples. The earliest labels read "J. Kilner, Maker," and must therefore have been made in 1829 or during the three or four years after 1829 before his sons joined him in the business. Those labeled successively "J. Kilner & Son" and "J. Kilner & Sons" must date from about 1832 until 1844, when the name was changed to Kilner Brothers. This means that they are easily the earliest recorded paperweights made in Eng-land, and probably the earliest known in quantity from any source, though of course they are not millefiori.

Looking at them in this light it is suddenly easy to recognize in the mon-ochromatic simplicity of their conception and the crudity of their execution the northern prototype of the paperweight. The weights vary in size and shape from small and large flattened spheres to 8-inch high, bullet-shaped ovoids. A few have a footed base, which is a downward extension of the crown. Color varies from cool, pale green to deep, warm green, with many shades in between. While signed examples were undoubtedly made for advertising purposes, most were probably made as the spare-time friggers of self-amusement, or as gifts. Yet enough seem to have been made so that they were frequently cited as being used to line garden paths in Yorkshire, a concept that has something mysterious and druidical about it.[13] And from the holes drilled in some of them they may have been used as newel posts or bedstead knobs.

The basic theme of these green, underwaterish creations is the three-dimensional, upright flowerpot, from which springs a stem with one, two, or three tiers of blossoms. Pot, stem, and blossoms are distinguishable from the surrounding glass by a coating of myriad, infinitesimal air bubbles said by Elville to have resulted from touching the glass to a marver powdered with chalk.[14] It seems equally plausible that the pot and flower might have been subjected to a refined version of the bucket of cold water into which glass is plunged to achieve the crackle effect: perhaps a jet of steam or a fine water spray. In any event, the separate stages of constructing these weights are as clearly marked by contour lines as a topographical map, suggesting that an appreciable amount of time must have elapsed between stages or coating. In some examples, one sees an inner core of extremely sugary glass, the result of hasty work when the glass was already losing its ductility, and this in turn covered with a clear, crown coating free from striae. Is it inconceivable that a number of pots and flowers were made at one time, then let cool and stored away perhaps even for days, before reheating and reworking, until a fine film of dust settled over them?

It must not be thought from what has already been said that these bottle glass weights were all made before 1844—far from it. The simple form of them must have been repeated over the years, as we can tell from the variation in the treatment of the flowerpot motif and from the sulphides inserted in many examples. Once the flowerpot motif was developed to three tiers of ten or more blossoms, gilding the lily could be tried in the form of silver foil blossoms. These silver flowers would seem to be a later form, especially since so many of them are about these days. Some of the sulphides can be roughly dated from such Victorian subject matter as busts of Disraeli and Gladstone, a little girl with a bundle on a stick over her shoulder, cherubs, a hand holding a spray of flowers, a Scotch thistle with leaves, Chanticleer, etc. A plaque with lions rampant and titled "Jubilee" must date from Victoria's Diamond Jubilee of 1897. But sulphides were made well into the twentieth century, as, for example, the bust titled "Queen Alexandra." Alexandra was crowned queen in August, 1902, and lived until 1925. Some of the many other sulphide subjects include a boy riding an elephant, a brown-colored, lifelike dog, and a pair of large, round flower-bordered sulphides, one reading "Merry Christmas," the other "Happy New Year," that could have been made anytime (Figs. 179, 180).

In addition to the flowerpots and sulphides, weights featuring fountain-like sprays of elongated bubbles and weights with just plain big, flattened bubbles were made in all sizes up to huge, ten-pound doorstops. A high proportion of

Fig. 179. Green glass weight, Prince of Wales feathers sulphide. *Courtesy Bergstrom Art Center and Museum.*

Fig. 180. Green glass weight, boy riding elephant sulphide. *Courtesy Bergstrom Art Center and Museum.*

179

180

green glass weights of all sizes shows signs of having received a good deal of
rough treatment over the years, and the bottoms of some appear to have had
their pontils attacked with an ice pick. Yet, rough or smooth, crude or skillful,
these soft green weights from Kilner and the many other bottle factories where
they must have been made are a source of quiet charm and gentle mystery.

Pinchbeck and Painted Weights

As a concept, and in their materials and construction, Pinchbecks stand apart
from the mainstream of paperweights discussed in this book, whose medium is
glass through and through. As an item of Victorian decorative art they have
been largely ignored and very little has been found out about them. Christopher
Pinchbeck (1670–1732) was a well-known watch and musical clock-maker of
London, who lived for a time in St. George's Court (now Albion Place, off St.
John's Lane) and then moved to Fleet Street. He was the inventor of an alloy
simulating gold that was reported to consist of 83 parts copper and 18 parts
zinc. The alloy was used for watch cases, jewelry, and trinkets, hence the use of
the term "pinchbeck" to denote flashy imitation jewelry or, as Webster puts it,
"something that is counterfeit and spurious." Christopher Pinchbeck had two
sons, Christopher, a clockmaker, and Edward (1713–66) who, because of imitations of the alloy, issued the warning that he "did not dispose of one grain of
his curious metal, which so nearly resembles gold in colour, smell and ductility,
to any person whatsoever."[15]

    In the best piece written on the subject, Mrs. Bergstrom says that Pinchbeck
paperweights were very popular about 1850,[16] a date that quite obviously
excludes any possibility of such paperweights having been made by Christopher
Pinchbeck or his son. The term "Pinchbeck paperweight" refers loosely to any
paperweight whose large design in relief is made of a metal leaf incorporating
or giving the effect of incorporating some of the Pinchbeck copper-zinc alloy,
which design is set in a pewter or marble base, screwed (in the case of the
pewter) or cemented (in the case of the marble) to a flat-round magnifying
glass lens, the lens projecting beyond the base. Other bases are made of copper,
tin, alabaster, even cardboard, and all metal ones may be covered with velvet or
leather. The large alloy relief, which fills the entire ground surface of the
weight, was probably pressed and burnished into a female mold made from the
original relief design. As Mrs. Bergstrom points out, the skills of jeweler,
chaser, and glassmaker are all required here, and it is unlikely that a Pinchbeck
paperweight was the work of one artisan or even one factory. The fine workmanship and remarkable detail of the subjects, together with the mysterious effect
created by the magnifying lens, make these weights at least as interesting and
successful decorative objects as the sulphides, though the advantage of the sulphide from our standpoint is that it is completely encased in glass in such a way
as to create the illusion of metal where none exists.

Subject matter covers a wide variety of scenes and portraits, including Queen Victoria (the relief here is painted), Wellington, a mountain village, a cavalier and the hunt, ladies on horseback, a carousing scene, Silenus riding an ox attended by satyrs, Leda and the Swan (signed "Thev"), the finding of Moses, the Nativity, a music lesson, and a number of other religious, domestic, and outdoor scenes, some of them probably copied from paintings or relief sculpture. Duplicates are known, especially the Moses and Wellington (Figs. 181, 182, 183).

Aside from a weight signed "G. & S. Lobmeyer, Wien," which shows a lion about to pounce on two horses drinking from a pool,[17] Pinchbeck weights have been attributed to no particular factory and were probably made on the Continent (where the Pinchbeck alloy jewelry was popular), as well as in England.

In the basic form of a base affixed to a magnifying glass top there exist several paperweights in which the subject is painted on an opaque white glass

Fig. 181. Pinchbeck, domestic scene. *Courtesy The New-York Historical Society.*
Fig. 182. Pinchbeck, man leading horse. *Courtesy The Art Institute of Chicago.*
Fig. 183. Silver Pinchbeck, music lesson. *Courtesy The New-York Historical Society.*

181

182

183

ground, the form relates them to Pinchbeck while the painting style relates them to miniature painting. Three large weights with painted putti on metal bases are known, and there is one on an alabaster base showing a portrait of a lady in an English turbaned costume that dates almost precisely from 1847 (Fig. 184).

Other Weights

A variety of other paperweights were made. There was the weight showing the Crystal Palace made for or by Berens Blumberg & Company of London, that has already been mentioned in Chapter Four. There were the "crystal cameo" weights mentioned by Hughes as having been made from about 1875 by John Ford and Company of Edinburgh. Hughes also mentions "composition cameos" of Queen Victoria embedded in glass cubes for her Diamond Jubilee in 1887.[18] And we have the reference in the Colné report of 1878 crediting James Green and Nephew, of London, with "paperweights cut and engraved," but without further specification. Probably they were not millefiori.

But one hesitates to discuss those paltry little souvenir weights in which a colored engraving on paper of Exeter Cathedral, the pier at Brighton, or the Dyspeptic Women's Reformatory at Piddle Hinton-on-Tyne is stuck to the basal concavity of a crown of glass.

Hollow Weights

Though there is as yet no evidence to support such a contention, it seems reasonable to propose that one type of unidentified paperweight may well be English and just possibly from the Stourbridge area. Like the St. Louis crown weights, these are hollow, but there the resemblance ceases, for while the motif of the St. Louis crowns derives from a fusion of individual ribbon and filigree members, the motif of the hollow weights appears to have been impressed intaglio into the inner face of the clear glass casing, showing up as a cased relief. Inside its rather thick outer casing the weight may be completely hollow, or it may contain an inner, colored cushion in red, royal blue, or gold that nearly fills the inner cavity, almost but not quite touching the outer intaglio shell. In both instances the inner air space created by the intaglio impression and the consequent break in the refractive index of the glass imparts a silvery quality to the motif.

Three motifs are known. The simplest is a honeycomb above an impression of rays that draws under to the center of the base. When the honeycomb surrounds no interior colored cushion, the effect is of mercury glass. In some examples the effect is complicated by a gold or ruby cushion, with the ruby particularly effective. A second motif is a very large bee above the aforementioned raying. The bee may appear in clear glass or above a royal blue cushion. The third known motif shows the royal British seal of lion and unicorn and the words "Dieu et Mon Droit" above the royal blue ground (Fig. 185). Hence the

184

185

Fig. 184. Painted weight, c. 1847, alabaster base. *Private collection. Photograph by Taylor & Dull.*

Fig. 185. Molded weight, blue ground, British royal coat of arms. *Courtesy Bergstrom Art Center and Museum.*

suggestion that the weights may be English. As successful specimens of mold-pressed glass, their appearance suggests the art glass period of the late nineteenth century, and it is possible that they may have been made by the Webbs or Richardsons, of Stourbridge.

Sizes run from miniature to $3\frac{1}{2}$ inches, and some are doorknobs.

NOTES

[1] Evangeline Bergstrom, *Old Glass Paperweights.* second edition, New York, 1948, plate 43 and pp. 65, 66.

[2] Baccarat had a small retail shop on the Rue Montalembert, which from 1930–34 sold Baccarat undated garland, concentric, and pansy paperweights in three sizes. My authority for this is Miss O. D. Dahlgren who lived in Paris during those years and went frequently to the shop. On her last visit in 1934 there were no more weights, Mr. Dupont having died, and the secret with him. Dated examples, including unbelievable dates such as 1811, 1831, 1815, are so similar to the undated that I have assumed Dupont made them but sold them on the side. See Chapter Eighteen.

[3] Letter to me dated March 28, 1966.

[4] Sir Hugh Chance, "Records and the Nailsea Glass Works," *Connoisseur,* American edition, July, 1967, p. 171.

[5] E. M. Elville, *Paperweights and Other Glass Curiosities,* London, 1954, p. 50.

[6] *Ibid.,* p. 42.

[7] Letter to me dated January 22, 1967.

[8] Letter to me dated March 14, 1967.

[9] G. W. Beard is the author of *Nineteenth Century Cameo Glass.* At one time he had intended to write a book on glass paperweights but abandoned the project.

[10] D. R. Guttery, *From Broad-Glass to Cut Crystal,* London, 1956, p. 134.

[11] "Fifty Years of The Glass Bottle Trade," reprinted, Chicago, 1940, from *The British Trade Journal,* Dec. 1, 1894, p. 2, *et seq.*

[12] Letter to B. H. Leffingwell and me from C. A. Kilner, June 13, 1966.

[13] C. A. Kilner mentions this, but there are many other references to this use.

[14] Elville, p. 41.

[15] Letter to me dated Feb. 14, 1967 from N. W. Bertenshaw, director of the Department of Science and Industry, City Museum and Art Gallery, Birmingham, England. Proportions of copper and zinc given vary with the source.

[16] Evangeline H. Bergstrom, "Pinchbeck—But Precious," *American Collector,* Nov., 1945, p. 6.

[17] *Ibid.,* p. 19.

[18] Bernard and Therle Hughes, *After the Regency,* London, 1952, p. 150.

VENETIAN

1.

BOHEMIAN

2.

BACCARAT

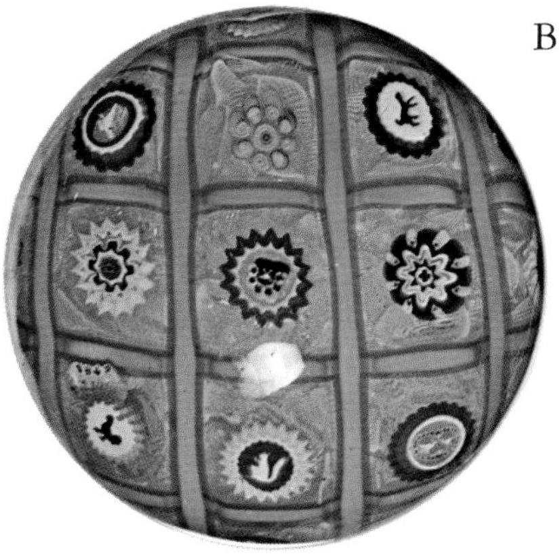

3.   4.

Fig. 1. Venetian plaque with gondola. *Courtesy Bergstrom Art Center and Museum.*

Fig. 2. Bohemian crown weight. *Sinclair Collection, Courtesy New-York Historical Society.*

Fig. 3. Baccarat chequer, B. 1849. *Courtesy Sotheby & Co.*

Fig. 4. Baccarat concentric mushroom. *Courtesy Bergstrom Art Center and Museum.*

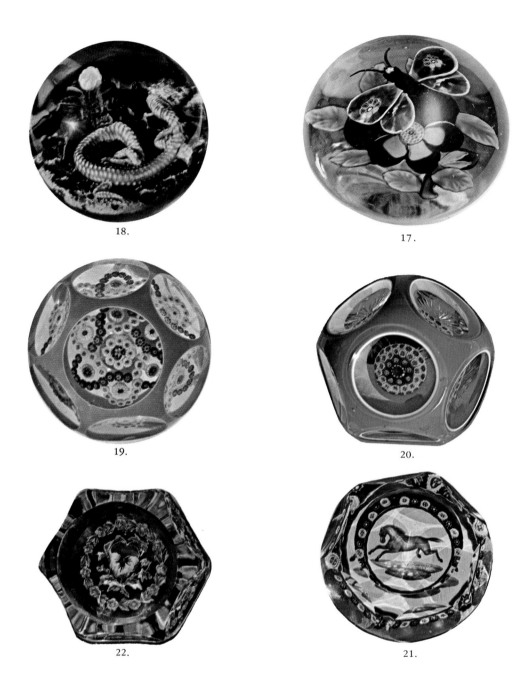

18.

17.

19.

20.

22.

21.

Fig. 17. Baccarat butterfly over second type pansy. *Courtesy Sotheby & Co.*

Fig. 18. Baccarat coiled green lizard on sand ground with white aloe. *Courtesy Bergstrom Art Center and Museum.*

Fig. 19. Baccarat rose double overlay of interlocked trefoils. *Courtesy Bergstrom Art Center and Museum.*

Fig. 20. Baccarat blue double overlay, mushroom with variation of Clichy rose. *Courtesy Bergstrom Art Center and Museum.*

Fig. 21. Baccarat plaque of galloping horse. Printies create arcs of light. *Courtesy Bergstrom Art Center and Museum.*

Fig. 22. Baccarat pansy etched and painted on base. *Courtesy Bergstrom Art Center and Museum.*

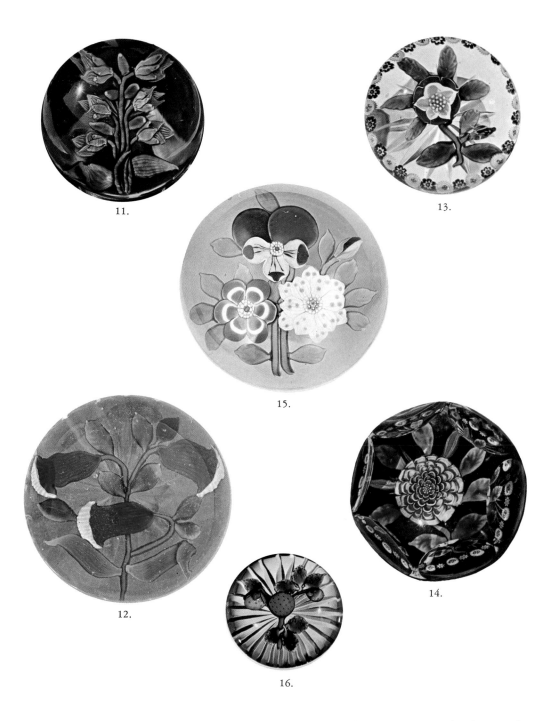

11.

13.

15.

12.

14.

16.

Fig. 11. Baccarat clematis buds arranged in symmetrical tiers. *Courtesy Bergstrom Art Center and Museum.*

Fig. 12. Baccarat blue and white buttercup with bud. *Courtesy Bergstrom Art Center and Museum.*

Fig. 13. Baccarat blue fringed gentian. *Courtesy Sotheby & Co.*

Fig. 14. Baccarat copper camomile with circle of canes. *Courtesy Bergstrom Art Center and Museum.*

Fig. 15. Baccarat pansy, red primrose, white polka-dotted wheatflower. *Courtesy Sotheby & Co.*

Fig. 16. Baccarat strawberry, one green berry. Note bract leaves. *Courtesy Corning Museum of Glass.*

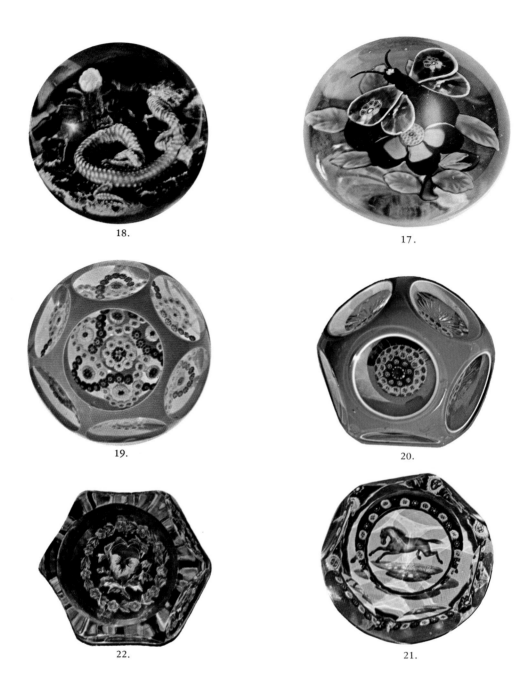

18.

17.

19.

20.

22.

21.

Fig. 17. Baccarat butterfly over second type pansy. *Courtesy Sotheby & Co.*

Fig. 18. Baccarat coiled green lizard on sand ground with white aloe. *Courtesy Bergstrom Art Center and Museum.*

Fig. 19. Baccarat rose double overlay of interlocked trefoils. *Courtesy Bergstrom Art Center and Museum.*

Fig. 20. Baccarat blue double overlay, mushroom with variation of Clichy rose. *Courtesy Bergstrom Art Center and Museum.*

Fig. 21. Baccarat plaque of galloping horse. Printies create arcs of light. *Courtesy Bergstrom Art Center and Museum.*

Fig. 22. Baccarat pansy etched and painted on base. *Courtesy Bergstrom Art Center and Museum.*

VENETIAN

1.

BOHEMIAN

2.

BACCARAT

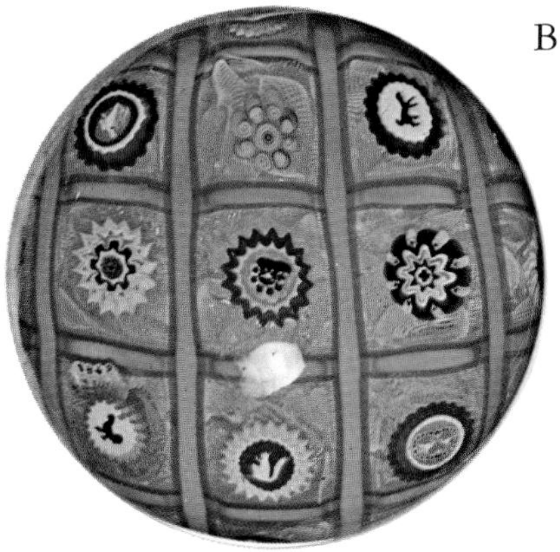

3.   4.

Fig. 1. Venetian plaque with gondola. *Courtesy Bergstrom Art Center and Museum.*

Fig. 2. Bohemian crown weight. *Sinclair Collection, Courtesy New-York Historical Society.*

Fig. 3. Baccarat chequer, B. 1849. *Courtesy Sotheby & Co.*

Fig. 4. Baccarat concentric mushroom. *Courtesy Bergstrom Art Center and Museum.*

Fig. 5. Baccarat white stardust carpet ground. *Courtesy Bergstrom Art Center and Museum.*

Fig. 6. Baccarat blue carpet ground with cane clusters. *Courtesy Bergstrom Art Center and Museum.*

Fig. 7. Baccarat garland on stardust carpet ground. *Courtesy Sotheby & Co.*

Fig. 8. Baccarat blue honeycomb carpet ground. *Courtesy Corning Museum of Glass.*

Fig. 9. Baccarat upright bouquet. Note disappearing torsade. *Courtesy New-York Historical Society.*

Fig. 10. Baccarat rare primrose-related flower, multiple petals. *Courtesy Sotheby & Co.*

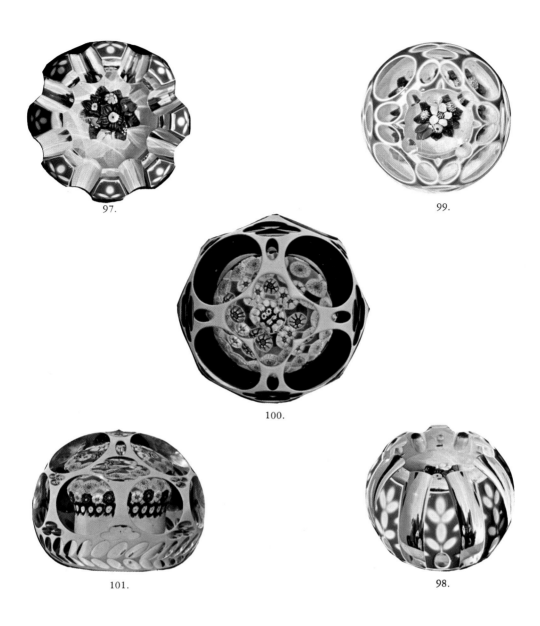

97.

99.

100.

101.

98.

Fig. 97. New England Glass Company melon-cut double overlay with upright bouquet (top view). One of the great paperweights. *Sinclair Collection, Courtesy New-York Historical Society.*

Fig. 98. New England Glass Company, same as Fig. 97 (side view).

Fig. 99. New England Glass Company elaborately Bohemian-cut double rose-red overlay with upright bouquet. *Courtesy Bergstrom Art Center and Museum.*

Fig. 100. New England Glass Company white overlay with open concentric mushroom (top view). *Courtesy Bergstrom Art Center and Museum.*

Fig. 101. New England Glass Company, same weight as Fig. 100 (side view), showing capstan-like mushroom.

95.

92.

91.

96.

93.

94.

Fig. 91. New England Glass Company mushroom (side view). *Private collection.*

Fig. 92. New England Glass Company posy and fruit on cane-cut base. *Private collection.*

Fig. 93. New England Glass Company cross of leaves with floral center on latticinio. *Courtesy Bergstrom Art Center and Museum.*

Fig. 94. New England Glass Company finely. executed flower with typical NEGC leaves. *Sinclair Collection, Courtesy New-York Historical Society.*

Fig. 95. New England Glass Company bird on leaves that are typically NEGG. (Bird actually faces the opposite way.) *Sinclair Collection, Courtesy New-York Historical Society.*

Fig. 96. New England Glass Company magnum upright bouquet with fruits on latticinio. Leaves again typically NEGC. *Courtesy Bergstrom Art Center and Museum.*

105.   106.   103.

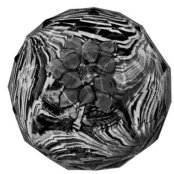

104.   107.   102.

Fig. 102. Sandwich yellow and blue weedflower with missing left leaf tip. *Private collection.*

Fig. 103. Sandwich blue poinsettia on red and white jasper ground. *Private collection.*

Fig. 104. Sandwich red and blue weedflower on rare red-white-blue chip ground. *Private collection.*

Fig. 105. Sandwich striped flower with "Clichy" rose center. *Private collection.*

Fig. 106. Sandwich rose bush. *Sinclair Collection, Courtesy New-York Historical Society.*

Fig. 107. Sandwich faceted marbrie with flower motif. *Courtesy Bergstrom Art Center and Museum.*

GILLINDER

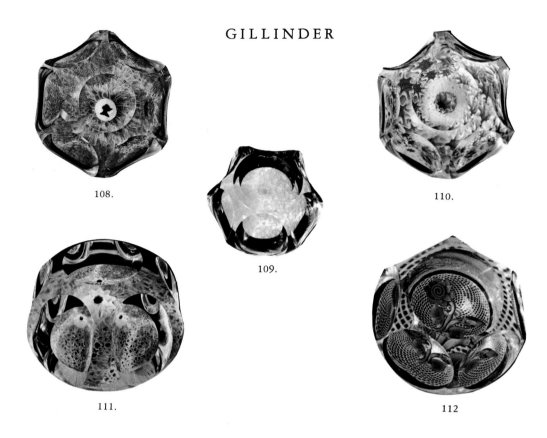

108.

109.

110.

111.

112

PORT ELIZABETH

113.

114.

Fig. 108. Gillinder aqua blue carpet ground with silhouette profile. *Private collection.*

Fig. 109. Gillinder white carpet, domed ground. *Private collection. Photograph by author.*

Fig. 110. Gillinder pink-white-blue concentric of ruffled canes. *Private collection.*

Fig. 111. Gillinder aqua blue carpet echoed in cutting that creates a fascinating design. *Sinclair Collection, Courtesy New-York Historical Society.*

Fig. 112 Gillinder rose with bud on double spiral latticinio. *Private collection.*

Fig. 113. Port Elizabeth bird on yellow ground. *Private collection.*

Fig. 114. Port Elizabeth or Millville magnum flowers in basket, powdered glass. *Private collection.*

MILLVILLE

115.

116.

MT. WASHINGTON

117.

120.

119.

118.

Fig. 115. Millville rose of delicate pink. *Private collection.*

Fig. 116. Millville water lily. *Sinclair Collection, Courtesy New-York Historical Society.*

Fig. 117. Mt. Washington lavender rose with buds, butterfly, fruit. *Courtesy Bergstrom Art Center and Museum.*

Fig. 118. Mt. Washington giant rose with buds and leaves. *Sinclair Collection, Courtesy New-York Historical Society.*

Fig. 119. Mt. Washington poinsettia with leaves and petals similarly veined. *Courtesy Bergstrom Art Center and Museum.*

Fig. 120. Mt. Washington orange dahlia with leaves. *Sinclair Collection, Courtesy New-York Historical Society.*

121.

122.

123.

Fig. 121. Mt. Washington superb floral flat weight, stems tied with ribbons. *Private collection.*

Fig. 122. Mt. Washington floral plaque hobnail-diamond base. *Courtesy Bergstrom Art Center and Museum.*

Fig. 123. Mt. Washington large strawberry weight. *Sinclair Collection, Courtesy New-York Historical Society.*

BACCARAT

124.

125.

CLICHY   ST. LOUIS   CHINESE

126.   127.   128.

KAZIUN

129.   130.

Fig. 124. Baccarat Madonna and child sulphide, ruby ground. *Courtesy Bergstrom Art Center and Museum.*

Fig. 125. Baccarat sulphide of Joan of Arc on green ground. *Courtesy Bergstrom Art Center and Museum.*

Fig. 126. Clichy sulphide of Napoleon on blue ground. *Courtesy Bergstrom Art Center and Museum.*

Fig. 127. St. Louis magnum floral weight about 1953. *Private collection.*

Fig. 128. Chinese painted landscape on white ground. *Private collection.*

Fig. 129. Kaziun apricot-colored double overlay with deep red rose. *Private collection.*

Fig. 130. Kaziun turtle on goldstone and amethyst ground. *Private collection.*

YSART

131.

132.

134.

MURANO

135.

133.

Fig. 131 Ysart butterfly in garland of canes. *Courtesy Bergstrom Art Center and Museum.*

Fıg. 132. Ysart buttterfly on blue fiiligree cushion (side view). *Private collection.*

Fig. 133. Murano goldfish with fronds. *Private collection.*

Fig. 134. Murano pedestal with zinnia. *Private collection.*

Fig. 135. Murano single deep thalo blue cane. *Private collection.*

12

BELGIAN FACTORIES

IN THE CONTEXT of mid-nineteenth-century paperweight-making over a large part of the continent of Europe, it is not surprising that paperweights were made extensively in Belgium. Specifically, they are known to have been made at the Verrerie Bougard (Fig. 186) and at the Verreries Nationales (Fig. 187) in Jumet, which is near Charleroi; at Chênée (Fig. 188) near Liège, and also in the region of Laeken (Brussels) and Namur.[1] The Bougard example illustrated dates about 1850, the Verreries Nationales example about 1880, and the Chênée sulphide of Christ at the end of the nineteenth century. As the photographs show, the weights are crude in comparison with French and Bohemian work. But it was at Val St. Lambert, probably the greatest of all Belgian glassworks, that the finest and probably the greatest number of Belgian weights were made.

Val St. Lambert was founded in Seraing, near Liège, in 1825, the same year the Boston & Sandwich Glass Company was founded. Originally, it occupied the grounds and buildings of an old Cisterian Abbey. There were twelve workers. Its first catalogue, issued in 1829, included pressed ware, which, incidentally, had been introduced by Jarves at Sandwich two years earlier.[2] In 1835 Val St. Lambert exhibited candelabras and a "Vase Médicis" of huge proportions.[3] The company prospered from the beginning and, from time to time, bought and absorbed other factories. In 1878 it employed 1,600 workers and by 1896 the number had risen to 7,872.[4] Raymond Chambon concludes that its crystal always conformed to the taste of the moment, but A. C. Revi says, "The Cameo Glass productions of the Val St. Lambert factory in Belgium are well known to collectors. Their cased glass bodies were lavishly cut with the wheel and acid-engraved into beautiful expressions of Cameo Glass."[5] This famous factory is still turning out crystal for the table and, judging from its current products, its "taste of the moment" is somewhat antediluvian. Interestingly enough, in its own glass museum there are no Classic period paperweights.

186

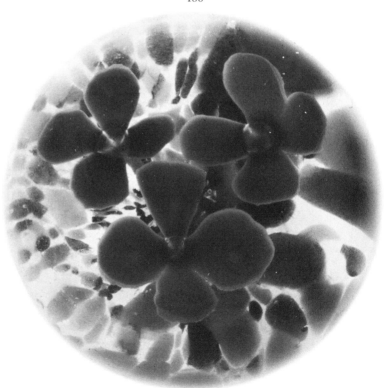

187

Fig. 186. Verrerie Bougard weight about 1850. *Courtesy Musée du Verre, Liège, Belgium.*
Fig. 187. Verrerie Nationales weight about 1880. *Courtesy Musée du Verre, Liège, Belgium.*

Fig. 188. Chênée sulphide of Christ on the cross. *Courtesy Musée du Verre, Liège, Belgium.*

Val St. Lambert Paperweights

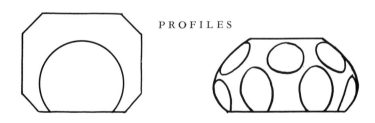

PROFILES

There are at least two typical profiles: the one on the left used for overlays, and the one on the right for ordinary weights, but there are also shapes in between. The bases are usually flat, but in some instances reveal the amalgamation of an inner motif section to an outer casing similar to the procedure employed at Whitefriars and discussed in Chapter Ten. The lightness of the glass suggests that it contains little or no lead. Though usually fairly clear, it is frequently of a grayish or yellowish cast and is likely to be sugary with striae and polluted by foreign matter and bubbles.

These paperweights do not turn up very often at European or American auctions; so one must assume that, unless they are secreted in great numbers in Belgian households, not very many were made. However, where only one or two of a given common type have come to light, it would seem logical that others must have been made. Such a conjecture is reinforced by the presence from this factory of the more advanced and difficult types of weight and the dearth of simpler types. Generally, it can be said that there is something of the ice cream parlor about Val St. Lambert weights.

Val St. Lambert Canes

Canes include star rods, crimped canes, and an assortment of pastry molds. At first glance they vaguely resemble Clichy canes, but after more careful scrutiny they are easily distinguishable. Cane coloring is, if anything, even more brilliant, and we are likely to find pinks, reds, and yellows in close proximity. Barber-pole twisted rods in two or more colors are used extensively as design elements and borders, while infrequently one finds lace rods shaped to resemble tied ribbons and festooning. The barber-pole twist rods run both clockwise and counterclockwise, come in short lengths, and are frequently given a slight loop or hook at the ends.

Val St. Lambert Paperweight Types

(In the sections to follow the number of examples seen by or known to me will be given after each type.)

SPACED MILLEFIORI (One example)—Canes spaced inexactly on a pale sky blue over opaque white ground.

CONCENTRICS (One example)—An overlay presentation weight. (See "Overlays.")

PATTERNED MILLEFIORI (Several examples)—These involve garlands, circles of canes, groupings of canes in square or other formations. In one, we see a star-shaped field of millefiori canes set in an opaque, sapphire-blue ground surrounded by a green twisted ribbon. In another, short lengths of twisted ribbon enclose the design in a square. A rare example has a translucent ultramarine ground, which centers a small sulphide of Joan of Arc on horseback, enclosed in a hexagon of counterclockwise barber-pole twists alternately in red and white, green and white. Parts of the sulphide are colored with pink and green powdered glass. This unusual weight is faceted with two rows of oval printies and a large, circular top printy (Fig. 189; Col. Fig. 84).

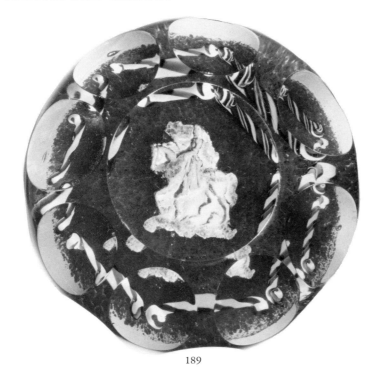

189

190

Fig. 189. Val. St. Lambert, Joan of Arc colored sulphide on blue ground. *Private collection. Photograph by Taylor & Dull.*

Fig. 190. Val St. Lambert, opaque white ground streaked in blue. *Courtesy F. Schuell.*

GROUNDS (Many examples)—These include lace (muslin), a number in opaque solid pink, opaque white, translucent magenta, ruby red, and ultramarine. The ultramarine ground is granulated with the granulation largely fused together. The chewing gum pink ground sometimes has a slightly fuzzy, blotter-like appearance. Grounds are set very low and weights are frequently flat bottomed (Fig. 190).

FLOWERS (Three examples)—These are so fine as to indicate that others must have been made before such a high level of execution was reached. In two cases, the flower, set in clear glass, has several ample scarlet-vermilion petals about a central cane with leaves and stem. Leaves are carefully arranged and very similar to Baccarat in shape, but a deep emerald green, with the white tube ends sometimes visible. In the third great example, the petals are composed of a brilliant, rainbow lamination of white, pink, turkey-red, green, and royal blue strips. Flower and leaves are set in clear but slightly smoky blue glass with a twisted ribbon torsade of the same colors. Base is cut with a big star (Col. Fig. 85). A realistic pansy appears on a pink ground with barber-pole torsade.

OVERLAYS (Six examples)—These large, flat-bottomed weights are single, translucent overlays; sapphire blue in four cases, olive-gold in a fifth. Faceting is elaborate; more so in Bergstrom color plate XIV than in the example illustrated here (Col. Fig. 86). Sides and top are table cut with the top window 2⅜ inches in diameter. There are six flat oval side windows, which are cut off by the base. Grounds are placed low. In the Bergstrom example the design of canes and filigree swags is intentionally punctuated with regularly spaced air bubbles, a rare occurrence when intentional. In Col. Fig. 87 the large blue florets are each encircled by a yellow and pink twist rod. In both weights the ground is opaque strawberry ice-cream pink, and the decorative wheel cutting is superior to anything inside the weight. Two other single overlays also exhibit fancy wheel cutting

Fig. 191. Val. St. Lambert, Fastre presentation overlay. *Courtesy The New-York Historical Society.*

but their interiors are clear glass devoid of any design. A sixth example is a ruby-gold overlay cut and engraved, but dated 1907.[6] In the olive-gold overlay example the great, magnum concentric is faceted in long oval printies alternating with vertical flutes. In the center a blue sulphide plaque reads "Nicolas Fastre, Ingénieur Honoraire" (Fig. 191). The canes in this weight are, for a change, excellently detailed and arranged meticulously.

INSCRIPTIONS (Several examples)—These are inscribed with the names of persons who presumably received them as gifts, or with homely mottoes. They usually stand out on color grounds, the lettering or accompanying twists sometimes punctuated with air bubbles. In one example the name is inscribed in red glass threads trailed in script. In another, a sulphide of a hand holding a rose is inscribed with "Amitié." The sulphide rests on a jelly-red translucent cushion about which is a red, white, and blue spiral ribbon (Col. Fig. 87).

NOTES

[1] Letter from Joseph Philippe, Secrétaire Général des Journées Internationales du Verre.

[2] Ruth Webb Lee, *Sandwich Glass,* sixth edition, pp. 89, 449, 450.

[3] Raymond Chambon, *L'Histoire de la Verrerie en Belgique.*

[4] *Ibid.*

[5] A. C. Revi, *Nineteenth Century Glass,* New York, 1959, p. 168.

[6] Musée du Verre, Liège, Belgium.

ABOUT THE AMERICAN MAKERS

American visitors to the Great Exhibition of 1851 in London may have brought back as souvenirs a paperweight or two made by Clichy of France, or Bacchus or Whitefriars of England. But the first substantial look at these foreign novelties probably came with the exhibition at New York's own Crystal Palace in 1853, during whose run Horace Greeley commented at length in a piece in the *Tribune* upon paperweights exhibited by Clichy, and where, as the McKearins suggest, the popularity of the French and Austrian displays of cased and overlay glass provided the stimulus to American manufacturers to make what they termed "Bohemian Glass."[1]

The first American paperweight appears coeval with or in the years immediately following the Great Exhibition in London. The date 1825 in some Sandwich weights may commemorate the founding of the Boston & Sandwich Glass Company, or it may be an error in which the last two digits of the year 1852 were reversed, but it is certainly not a date when paperweights were being made in America or Europe. The hexagonal plaque weight from the New England Glass Company, commemorating the Great Exhibition and dated 1851, is the first reliable dating of an American paperweight. Other weights from Sandwich or the New England Glass Company are dated 1852. There is no doubt that by 1860 American paperweights were an accepted commonplace. There is, for example, a portrait painted by William Sidney Mount in 1860 that shows Susan T. Marsh, a child of about five, standing amid her playthings. One of these is a glass paperweight of what appear to be fruits and berries in a French-derived American arrangement.[2] But production of paperweights did not cease in the 1860's. Indeed it has continued with intermissions right up to the present, with much recapitulation of old forms and a few innovations.

European domination of American styles of paperweight-making during the Classic period derives from a headstart of a decade and a millefiori tradition of some eight centuries. The little we know of the men who made paperweights in this country indicates that most were born and glass trained on the Continent or in Britain. They came to America not as apprentices but as gaffers, bringing with them the foreign concepts and know-how. A few eventually formed their own glassworks, and trained workers in the European tradition. Though the international character of such foreign influences on American work as Venetian blown fruits, Bohemian canes and overlays, cannot be ignored, most influences, including subject matter, design schemes, the extensive use of flowers both singly and in groups, grounds, and special forms like the mushroom, are either French or refined through French practice. In comparison with France the scope of American paperweight output is limited. Consequently, while only some of the many features of French paperweights are discernible in American work, these involve the bulk of American production.

192

Yet despite their European heritage, American paperweights are easily distinguishable from their European counterparts. They bear the imprint of local enterprise and homespun fancy. They stand halfway between the practicality of the whale oil lamp and the memento of the sailor's valentine (imported, incidentally from Barbados). Frequently primitive beside French weights, they become the more endearing because of their flaws. Compared to the elite bonbons of Clichy and Baccarat, American millefiori canes may seem pale, but they are peppermint and they sting. American paperweights are as American as the foreigners who made them became in the new air of their adopted land.

NOTES

[1] George S. and Helen McKearin, *American Glass,* New York, 1956, pp. 33, 34.

[2] The Painting is in the Suffolk Museum, Stony Brook, Long Island, New York.

13

THE NEW ENGLAND GLASS COMPANY

OF THE MANY GLASS ENTERPRISES located in nineteenth-century Cambridge, Massachusetts, by far the most successful and longest-lived was the New England Glass Company, referred to for the sake of convenience as the NEGC or, simply, Cambridge. It came into being in November, 1817, when the property and effects of the defunct Boston Porcelain & Glass Company, formed three years previously, and its successor, Emmet, Fisher & Flowers, were purchased at public auction by Amos Binney, Edmund Monroe, Daniel Hastings, and Deming Jarves. These were men of vision and standing in the community and they were not about to let the new venture founder for lack of proper materials and know-how. They incorporated February 16, 1818, as the New England Glass Company of Lechmere Point, East Cambridge, Massachusetts, and with forty men, a six-pot furnace, and one other furnace, began making decanters, tumblers, salts, globes of all sizes and kinds, electrical apparatus, convex clock faces, and a variety of other items, all of the finest flint glass.[1] Already in its first year it was called "one of the most extensive flint glass manufactories in the country. Two flint furnaces and twenty-four glass-cutting mills, operated by steam, and a red-lead furnace capable of making two tons of red lead per week, enabled them to produce every variety of plain, mould, and the richest cut glass, as Grecian lamps, chandeliers for churches, vases, antique and transparent lamps, etc. for domestic supply, and exportation to the West Indies and South America."[2]

Like many glasshouses, but more than most, the NEGC was to employ men who later went into business for themselves and made glass history. Two of the first were Richard Fisher and John L. Gilliland, who left after the first year to found Fisher & Gilliland in New York, and some years later each owned his own glassworks, Fisher in New York and Gilliland in Brooklyn.[3] Before they left Cambridge, Fisher's brother John and Gilliland did the cutting on a large, cut-glass bowl or urn intended for President Monroe and exhibited later in the Capitol in Washington.[4] Another early employee was James B. Barnes, who

194

was hired by Deming Jarves to design and supervise construction of the furnaces and pots.[5] Barnes stayed with the NEGC until 1844 when he went to Wheeling, West Virginia, to cofound Hobbs, Barnes Company, later Hobbs, Bruckunier & Company of Wheeling Peachblow glass fame.[6] Jarves himself left Cambridge in 1825 to found the rival Boston & Sandwich Company, and William T. Gillinder, who later founded Gillinder & Sons, was there briefly in 1854.

Two years after the exhibition of the cut bowl, in 1827, a silver medal was awarded the NEGC by the Franklin Institute in Philadelphia.[7] The company was exporting pressed glass and had a wide sales territory. By mid-century it had some five hundred employees and was doing a $500,000 business a year. The factory worked around the clock five days a week, furnaces were uniquely fed from beneath, and its main chimney rose 10 feet higher than the Bunker Hill monument.[8] Cambridge glass rivaled Sandwich in a wide line of tableware, lamps, and other items so similar as to invite close comparison. Though most of the Cambridge pieces of the Victorian deluge are only slightly less florid than their Sandwich counterparts, the comparison is invidious to Sandwich because of the high lead content of the Cambridge work, which was maintained in the face of competition from cheaper soda-lime glass.

In the 1870's the company nearly foundered because of the combined impact of such problems as the high cost of lead glass, the increasing cost of fuel supply in the form of coal hauled over long distances, labor troubles, the theft of glass by the company's own glassblowers, accusations of mismanagement, and rumors of bankruptcy. To save the company, in 1878 the directors leased it to William L. Libbey, who had been agent of the New England since 1872, having come from Jarves and Cormerais. In 1880 his son Edward Drummond Libbey became a partner, and the company was known as the New England Glass Works, Wm. L. Libbey & Sons, Props. After his father died in 1883, Edward Drummond Libbey continued management of the company until 1888, when in answer to a strike, he closed down the works and moved to Toledo, Ohio, taking with him about one hundred of the glassworkers, including Andrew Long, head of the local branch of the striking union, and the rabble-rousing union organizer Michael J. Owens, who was later to turn his talents to running Libbey's plant and to inventing a bottle-making machine that revolutionized the industry.[9]

Paperweight-making at Cambridge

We are fortunate that glass paperweights have been kept by the descendants of the men who made them or who worked beside the men who made them at the New England, for the physical evidence has made it possible at this late date to reconstruct a reasonable picture of paperweight-making at the NEGC over a thirty-year period, approximately 1850-80. It seems historically unlikely that any paperweight was made in the United States before 1850.

The first dated paperweight made at the New England Glass Company is the one presumably made to commemorate the Great Exhibition. It is a flat, hexagonal clear glass weight, slightly over 3 inches in diameter, 1 inch thick, whose motif is a double portrait of Victoria and Albert taken from an English medal. The medal was designed by W. Wyon, R. A., as Council Medal of the Great Exhibition, 1851, in London, was struck by the Royal Mint, and given to reward some "important novelty of invention or application . . . or originality combined with great beauty of design."[10] For its paperweight version, the NEGC must have made a mold impression of the medal; the mold in turn used to make a cameo die, which was used to impress the glass of the weight, for the details of the medal and the American weight are identical and the portraits in the glass weight appear impressed intaglio into the bottom (Fig. 192A). Even the Royal Mint imprint can be seen. The weight is dated (as was the medal) MDCCCLI (1851), and the area covered by the medal is treated to a mat finish by hydrofluoric acid, though it may be that the whole weight was immersed in the acid and the top and sides later polished.

It is not known specifically who made this weight, though "in 1931 it was owned by a niece of Thomas Hopkins, a Cambridge blower."[11] At least three Hopkinses were at the NEGC. One D. J. Crowley began working at the New England in 1869 and "remembers distinctly that millefiori paperweights were made there by a glassworker whose name was John Hopkins."[12] If John Hopkins made millefiori weights in 1869, it is at least possible that Thomas Hopkins was his father and that he made the 1851 medallion weight, which became the prototype for others he may have made during the 1850's.

Then we have the Leightons. It was Thomas Leighton (born, Birmingham, England, 1786; died, Cambridge, Massachusetts, 1849) who evaded the British law forbidding glassworkers from leaving the country by feigning a fishing expedition to France. Thomas Leighton became a gaffer at the NEGC in 1826. Of his seven sons, five became glassworkers at Cambridge.[13] One son, William Leighton, was an all-around glassman. In 1849 he came up with an original formula for the popular ruby glass. Leighton family tradition has it that William Leighton made at least one paperweight, which, fortunately, has been illustrated in *American Glass and Glassmaking*.[14] Judging from the illustration and Mrs. Watkins' description of it, this superb, faceted, rose-red-over-white double overlay mushroom is not only on a par with the finest from Clichy but, far more significant, it provides insight into the quality and variety of NEGC paperweight-making that has been largely ignored until now. The quality of this one weight is proof enough that William Leighton must have made many others before he achieved such perfection.

Frank Pierre, the one usually associated with millefiori paperweights at Cambridge, was born François Pierre in France in 1834, received his early training at Baccarat, probably at ten or twelve, and came to the New England in 1849 at the age of fifteen, where he was even then listed in the Cambridge directory as a fancy glassworker. Mrs. Watkins says his health was not good and so during the winter months he "travelled with a group of glassblowers to the

Fig. 192A. New England Glass Company, Victoria and Albert intaglio, 1851. *Private collection.*

tropics giving exhibitions. At these exhibitions the blowers fashioned the glass birds and ships, with decorations of spun glass . . . so often displayed under a glass dome."[15] Perhaps it was François (Frank) Pierre, then, not Lutz, who made the hollow-blown paperweight with the glass stag, the swan with pink wings, and the basket of roses. (See Chapter Fourteen.) In any event, Pierre was known to have made "paperweights and other fancy articles of colored glass about 1853," as told to Edwin Atlee Barber by none other than Andrew Long of East Cambridge who worked at NEGC at the same time and who later went with Libbey to Toledo.[16] Pierre was quite probably the Frenchman who continued for William T. Gillinder the instruction in paperweight-making Gillinder had begun in Birmingham, England. Gillinder was briefly with the NEGC in 1854. At the New York Exhibition of the Industry of All Nations in 1853, the NEGC was listed as exhibiting "plain, pressed, cut, or decorated glassware."[17] It exhibited pitchers, goblets, wine glasses, decanters, vases, decorated colognes, door handles, and all sorts of fancy glass, including paperweights. "The Venetian paper-weights manufactured here," runs a contemporary report, "are very excellent examples of their class." Some of these millefiori weights must have been the work of François Pierre, who also made many of the blown fruit weights for which the factory became famous. Pierre worked all his adult life at Cambridge and died about 1872 at the age of thirty-eight.

Paperweight production during the 1850's and '60's was a regular part of company merchandise, and not something done sneakily at three o'clock in the morning. For weights were exhibited at the twenty-fifth exhibition of the Franklin Institute, Philadelphia, in 1856,[18] and again the same year at the Charitable Mechanics' Association exhibition in Mechanics' Hall, Boston, where it was said that "the medallion paper weights deserve particular notice."[19] Barber says that Edward Drummond Libbey, by this time (before 1915) president of the Libbey Glass Company, told him that when he was a young man working at the New England in the 1850's and '60's a "large business was carried on in the manufacture and sale of glass paperweights until 1874 when the manufacture of this variety of glass was discontinued. Many metal moulds for making the filigree rods were in use, which included multicolored designs of flowers, stars, scrolls, animals, letters, and figures, from which an infinite number of combinations could be obtained."[20] Libbey's statement that paperweights were discontinued in 1874 is challenged by a letter written by Henry Leighton to his father John H. Leighton in 1877. "For Tom's paper-weight goods I think I shall get between six and seven dollars according to Mr. Brown's estimate."[21] Perhaps though, Libbey was only thinking of millefiori and flowers, while Leighton's "paper-weight goods" may refer to such things as the black glass and white glass bulldogs and the Plymouth Rock weight probably made about the time of the Centennial in 1876, where the NEGC also exhibited.

We have mentioned the names of Hopkins, Leighton, Gillinder, Pierre, and the mysterious Tom as known and assumed makers of weights. And there was another: George Dale, born in Leith, Scotland, in 1810. At the age of twelve he made a contract with William Bailey Company, glass manufacturers in Edinburgh, for an apprenticeship of seven years. The first year he was to be paid 4 shillings a week, working up to 8 shillings a week in the seventh year. One of the witnesses to the contract was Thomas Leighton.[22] It was Leighton who later, as gaffer at the NEGC, encouraged Dale to come to Cambridge. In August, 1829, Dale completed his apprenticeship. The excise tax had closed many of the shops and glass jobs were few. George Dale moved to Liverpool, and then in 1830 he and his twin brother Robert sailed for America.

Robert Dale served in the Civil War and died in 1862 in Baton Rouge, Louisiana, but George Dale never left the Cambridge works, though whether he stayed until it closed in 1888, when he would have been seventy-eight, is not known. He died at East Cambridge in 1897. During his years at the New England, George Dale is known to have made many paperweights, among them scrambleds, fruits, and a crown weight, now in the possession of his lineal descendants.

New England Glass Company Paperweights

PROFILE

There is no single profile, but in general it may be said that NEGC weights have a relatively broad base, an irregularly fashioned basal rim, sometimes resembling the bottom of an old jelly glass, and the deepest basal concavity of any paperweights. Occasional profiles are low, but the profile usually rises more steeply than at Sandwich to a higher crown, presumably raised to accommodate faceting. The top center of the crown may show a cowlick left from the gathering of the glass. Faceting includes side flutes alternating with printies, a top quatrefoil of interlocked printies, such as one finds in the double overlay lamps from Cambridge and Sandwich, little crowsfeet used between larger printies, and elaborate Bohemian-style cutting on some of the overlays. In other words, Cambridge weights include those that up to now have been attributed to Gilliland. The frequently very clear but sometimes slightly grayish or pinkish, and sometimes sugary, lead glass is heavier than that found at Sandwich. In some of the cruder examples the pontil mark has not been ground off.

Dates and Canes

Only three dates are known. The date 1851 is seen in Roman numerals on the Victoria and Albert intaglio-pressed weight. Mrs. Watkins refers to one millefiori weight dated 1854. There are several dated 1852.[23]

Cambridge canes, whose bottoms are nearly always chopped off very irregularly, are almost indistinguishable from those at Sandwich, an indication that either their rod elements came from the same source, or that the tastes of the artists were similar. In form they have a Bohemian-Baccarat ancestry. The star rod (usually many-pointed) and the cog rod enclosed in tubes is the basis of New England canework. These tubes are assembled in bundles of six or more, set in a circle about another star tube, thus constituting a cane or floret. Tubes are usually square edged from being forced together, and are characteristically of alternating colors. Occasional unusual canes are nothing but rod elements enlarged to cane size, and this must be understood if the viewer is not to be misled as to provenance [66]. The lovely colors include crimson, a wild carmine, opaque peppermint pink, salmon, orange, sulphur, butter and chartreuse yellows, lettuce, apple, moss, sap, and thalo greens, pale, royal, and inky blues, lavender, amethyst, eggplant, black, and opaque white. The chief difference from Sandwich work is that more white shows in the individual Sandwich colored cane and the Sandwich motif tonality is white, whereas at Cambridge there is usually a distinct color tonality to each weight. Also, at Sandwich only scrambled millefiori were made to any extent, whereas at Cambridge many patterned millefiori were made. All Cambridge canes are characteristically uneven on the bottom.

[66]

Figure canes include many like those from Sandwich, the thick Greek cross, the heart, bee, running rabbit with the pink eye, dog and eagle, canes that appear in somewhat altered form in Bohemian weights. The rabbit cane is particularly interesting, because it is often almost disintegrated, which suggests that perhaps it was of an imported composition alien to fusion in American glass. In Bohemian weights the same rabbit appears without distortion.

Paperweight Types and Characteristics

MEDALLIONS—These hexagonal, 3½ inches in diameter, clear glass weights feature portrait profiles pressed into the underside of the weight and frosted with hydrofluoric acid. Portraits include the Victoria and Albert already referred to, a profile of Daniel Webster taken from a medal signed "Wright," a double profile of Abbot and Amos Lawrence who founded Lawrence, Massachusetts, Henry Clay, Lafayette, and a scene based on a commemorative medallion of a treaty with the Indians in the 1850's. In this scene a white man and an Indian stand against an American flag in an agricultural setting with ox and plow, and beneath, a ribbon reading "Labor-Virtue-Honor." It is signed "J. Willson." The subjects were taken from medals of which a cast was made, a relief probably made from the cast, and this in turn pressed into the hot glass. The weight was then given an acid bath, and sides and top were subsequently polished, leaving the bottom frosted. The portraits are actually intaglios, that is, impressions left in the glass, but looked at from above they appear as cameos. They recall the earlier intaglio work of James and William Tassie who used a similar process (see Chapter Seventeen).

SCRAMBLED—These differ from their Sandwich counterparts in the greater lead content and in the variety of colored fragments of cane and especially brightly colored twisted ribbon (Col. Fig. 88). They are also likely to be more fully stuffed with cane and filigree, and may include parts of the small fruits. These rather casual weights are likely to be very sugary when seen in profile. Unusual examples include rather makeshift color grounds of what looks like blue fuzz in two cases, and brown and green fuzz in another.

CLOSED CONCENTRICS—These uncommon and delightful little weights have been largely ignored as minor examples from Gilliland or Bristol. Averaging 2½ inches in diameter, they feature four concentric rings of identically colored star-tube canes about a central cane, the rings contrasting in color. The rather low-domed bed of canes is set about halfway up the weight, with the bottom edges of the canes characteristically chopped off very irregularly. Though the canes here are close packed, there is no filigree stuffing underneath and there are gaps where clear glass shows and bubbles form, rather upsetting the effect. A few are large faceted weights (Fig. 192B).

OPEN CONCENTRICS—These contain two separated rows of identical canes about a central cane, the rows contrasting in color, and set above a double-swirled latticinio ground. This ground differs markedly from its St. Louis counterpart in two respects. First, the lattice, though similarly created from the collapse of a cylinder of latticinio, retains both ends of the cylinder in the form of a long stem reaching to the bottom of the weight and a stem reaching up to support the central cane. Attenuation of the lattice tube ends gives a rather Gothic, sometimes Moorish effect to the lattice, like the tracery of the

Fig. 192B. New England Glass Company, faceted closed concentric. *Private collection. Courtesy Albany Institute of History and Art.*

Venetian palazzos. Second, the collapsed latticinio ground is distinctly indented and warped, and sometimes even broken by the canes, which rest almost ¼ inch above it. This distortion is apparently the result of a thick but uneven coating of the bottom of the cane rows when the canes, whose bottoms were cut off unevenly, were lying face down in the form, plus the partial hardening of the glass in that distortion before the latticinio was applied. The latticinio itself varies in opacity and whiteness from a skimmed-milk white to a very opaque porcelain white. Occasional grounds have a translucent cranberry red or pale lettuce green flash between the latticinio layers (Col. Fig. 89). (See "Color Grounds.") Some concentrics are faceted, with intersecting quatrefoil printies and crowsfeet.

S P O K E   C O N C E N T R I C S—Open concentrics are frequently set off by four or five canes evenly spaced outside the rings, giving the motif the appearance of a star or spoked wheel (Fig. 193). Aside from this they are identical with other open concentrics. Some concentrics of both types have a central silhouette cane.

M U S H R O O M—Several of these rare and remarkable weights are double overlays. The thick mushroom of opaque white glass rises on a columnar stalk from the base to a broad, rather flattened cap, and serves as a mushroom-shaped ground into which are studded various spaced millefiori canes, occasionally centering a flat bouquet with florets and leaves. The overlay colors include a bluish off-white, a soft powder blue, and cocoa over white. Faceting is elaborate but does not obscure the motif (Col. Fig. 90). The composite skills of cane-making, lampwork bouquet-making, overlaying, and cutting have been coordinated to achieve a flawless result. In one not overlaid the very tall mushroom is open in the middle from cap to base. The sides of the stalk are composed of alternate

Fig. 193. New England Glass Company, open concentric, quartrefoil faceted. *Courtesy Old Sturbridge Village. Photograph by James C. Ward.*

blue and white, long pulled canes, the outer rim of the mushroom cap formed by a ring of cut canes. A flat bouquet and two rings of canes complete the motif. Probably this was intended to be overlaid, but the mushroom rose too near the crown to permit cutting (Col. Fig. 91).

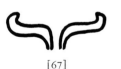

[67]

CUPPED WEIGHTS—A variation on the mushroom is the three-dimensional, cup-shaped motif of several large, faceted weights. The motif is open at the top like a large blossom, and centers a flat bouquet [67]. Faceting may be concave, brilliant cut or done with small, oval printies widely spaced about the sides (Fig. 194).

CROWN—These small (about 2¼ inches-2½ inches diameter), but finely executed weights resemble their St. Louis models, except that they are looser, that is, they leave a bit more clear glass showing between the twisted ribbons and filigree, and the ribbons show a variety of colors in a single weight, and some of the filigree itself may be pink or blue. The casing is thicker than the French casing, with the motif less close to the outer upper surface. Some are bold, most are gay, and one very delicate all-white filigree example, which centers a rabbit cane, has the filigree arranged as in a Clichy swirl, making it a crown swirl.

COLOR GROUNDS—One of these very rare weights is a spoke concentric. Between the double swirl of the latticinio ground is a cranberry red (Fig. 195;

Col. Fig. 89). Another is a flat bouquet within a ring of canes, with the same latticinio ground internally flashed with lettuce green. A third example has for its motif five flat bouquets, punctuated with florets, about a central cluster of canes, all set above a dome-shaped aquamarine ground (Fig. 196). Reminiscent of similar color grounds from St. Louis, it suggests a familiarity with this French paperweight.

CARPET GROUNDS—A few remarkable specimens show a carpet of hollow crimped tubes of one color about a central floret. An all-malachite-green carpet ground at Corning centers a Greek cross cane, while a red carpet at Old Sturbridge Village centers a rabbit cane (Fig. 197). Crimped tubes are shorn off unevenly on the bottom; and there is no muslin underneath to make the field completely opaque, a factor also noted in the closed concentrics.

Fig. 194. New England Glass Company, cupped weight with flat bouquet. *Private collection. Courtesy Albany Institute of History and Art.*

Fig. 195. New England Glass Company, spoke concentric on latticinio over cranberry *Private collection. Photograph by Taylor & Dull.*

Fig. 196. New England Glass Company, five flat bouquets on smoky aqua ground. *Private collection. Courtesy Albany Institute of History and Art.*

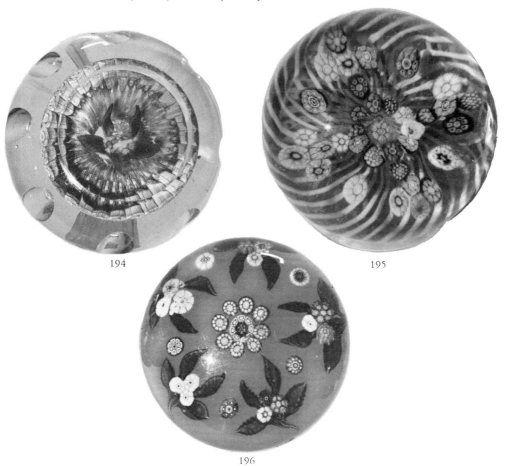

194

195

196

Fig. 197. New England Glass Company, red carpet ground, white rabbit center. *Courtesy Old Sturbridge Village. Photograph by James C. Ward.*

FLOWER WEIGHTS

[68]

Flat Bouquets—Identical in concept with, but stiffer in treatment than, those from St. Louis, these are made up of three florets in a clump surrounded by four rather stiff leaves, two up and two down, like the ears of a pair of listening animals. The stiff green and usually bright leaves are delicately impressed on top [68] in a series of parallel arcs whose ends point toward the tip of the leaf, the arcs frequently marked by a series of tiny air bubbles commonly referred to as dewdrops (Col. Figs. 94, 95). When these occur naturally in the grooved arcs they are left for decorative and suggestive purposes. A fair number of these three-cane flat bouquets appear in clear glass miniature weights, but most float above double-swirled latticinio grounds, frequently surrounded by a ring of canes, with the weight faceted (Fig. 198). One rare example, dated 1852, has five bouquets over an aquamarine ground (Fig. 196). (See "Color Grounds.") Another flat bouquet surrounded by fruits is elaborately faceted and has a base cut like the caning of a chair (Col. Fig. 92). One of the loveliest of all NEGC weights.

Faceting takes two main forms. One is a series of circular or oval side printies punctuated with vertical flutes, a single circular printy on top. The other may involve similar side cutting, but shows a quatrefoil of intersecting printies on top, such as are often seen in Cambridge and Sandwich overlay lamps. In the better examples there is often a ring of rabbit canes, but the canes are as often as not fused and disintegrated almost beyond recognition.

Fig. 198. New England Glass Company, flat bouquet on double swirled latticinio. *Private collection. Photograph by Taylor & Dull.*

Cross of Leaves—These large, rare weights have as a motif a cross of cool green leaves, mauve or white petals, or petals impressed as leaves, with a flower or a cane at the crossing point, above a double-swirl latticinio ground (Col. Fig. 93).

Poinsettia, Clematis—Only a very few of these in salmon pink or mauve on double-swirl latticinio ground, and they are beautifully done (Col. Fig. 94). The leaves (see "Flat Bouquets") and the deep basal concavity are the features that identify them as Cambridge, not Sandwich or French. Latticinio is thick and very opaque white (Figs. 199, 200).

Fig. 199. New England Glass Company, pale yellow clematis on double swirl latticinio. *Old Sturbridge Village. Photograph by James C. Ward.*

Fig. 200. New England Glass Company, poinsettia with bud. *Private collection. Photograph by Taylor & Dull.*

199   200

Buttercup—Only a few of these and they are not strictly buttercups. The blossom is enclosed in buttercup sections à la Baccarat, but the blossom may be a heraldic rose or a camomile. One on latticinio, another on jasper ground.

Upright Bouquet—Not very many of these either (Col. Fig. 96). A very rare example is overlaid in a rich brick red or dusky rose red over an opaque white, then melon cut with vertical flutes and elaborate leafage that permit exciting glimpses of the interior. The subtle red overlay is a trademark of NEGC, and appears in several other overlay weights. The red-white-blue upright bouquet stands crisp and bright in the white interior of this almost unbelievable tour de force (Col. Figs. 97, 98).

O V E R L A Y S—In addition to the mushrooms and the upright bouquet, there are other overlays, most in that special red over white, with elaborate faceting and cutting in the Bohemian style so popular in the mid-Victorian years, including the quatrefoil cutting of the top (Col. Figs. 99, 100, 101). Most are simple flat bouquets centered in two-ring concentrics. But one very rare weight is simply cut with printies in Baccarat style. The overlay is a cool, almost acid cinnabar green over white, with a motif of spaced canes on muslin and a large central cog cane featuring rods dated 1852, plus three rabbits.

FRUIT   WEIGHTS

Fruits in Latticinio Basket—Like Sandwich fruits, except that the basal concavity is deeper, the dome higher, the latticinio basket smaller, but with thicker, whiter lattice; the fruit may be pinker and the leaves more acid green. Most of these were not made very well (Fig. 201).

Before we leave these small fruits, mention must be made of a possibility raised in Francis Edgar Smith's book *American Glass Paperweights,* published privately in 1939 and the first book published on glass paperweights. This pioneering work was written at a time when knowledge about paperweights was still largely in the mythological or alchemical stage, which perhaps is why Smith's book has been generally ignored. Yet the fact remains that early in the twentieth century Smith interviewed some of the glassmen who had once worked at Cambridge and Sandwich. He refers several times to an interview with a former Cambridge glassworker who by the time Smith wrote his book had already "passed away many years ago." The unnamed man was eighty-nine when interviewed. He showed Smith his first attempt at paperweight-making, a partially completed radish or turnip weight with the motif set in clear glass. He then showed Smith what the latter refers to as "His Prize," made after twelve tries "in the heyday of his working life." From the look of it, anyone today would not hesitate to call it a St. Louis fruit in latticinio basket. Then Smith asked this eighty-nine-year-old man to make him a fruit weight. The man did. Looking at the illustration of this weight in Smith's book, no one today would hesitate to call it a Cambridge-Sandwich fruit weight.[24]

Fig. 201. New England Glass Company, fruit in latticinio basket. *Courtesy Corning Museum of Glass.*

Not all the information imparted in his book is so carefully documented as this little story, but the book should be read with a questioning mind by every serious student of paperweights.

Blown Fruits on Base—By contrast with the little basket fruits, these life-sized blown fruits were the NEGC's forte. Fruits include apples, pears, quinces, most of them fused to rather simple, clear glass "cookie" bases, which were made separately. The bases are usually round but sometimes square, and occasionally the glass was glopped on to suggest folds of cloth (Figs. 202, 203). Most probably the opaque white fruits were dipped before and during blowing into pots of various reds, pinks, yellows, and ambers, or sometimes streaked or spattered with colored glass, the bloom and mottling becoming increasingly realistic in the distention of the blowing and the flowing of the colors when the fruit was reheated. The fruits are fused at an angle to the bases, usually blossom up, stem down, and touching the base. The blossom is usually a dark brown, green, or black wad of glass, but also frequently an opal filigree, broken off unceremoniously, which may have acted as an extension of the pontil rod at some stage of the blowing, perhaps when the stem was affixed to the other end. Occasional superbly mottled fruits are freestanding, and these, curiously, have clear glass stems. The color effects of some of these fruits may well have suggested the ideas for Peachblow, Burmese, and Amberina; patterns they antedate by a good fifteen years.

The idea of blown glass fruits did not originate at Cambridge or Sandwich.

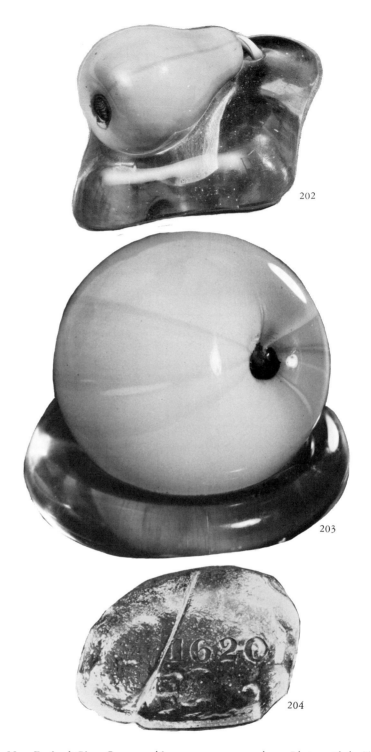

202

203

204

Fig. 202. New England Glass Company, blown pear on square base. *Photograph by Taylor & Dull.*

Fig. 203. New England Glass Company, blown apple on round cookie base. *Courtesy Old Sturbridge Village. Photograph by James C. Ward.*

Fig. 204. New England Glass Company, or Providence Inkstand Company "1620" weight. *Private collection.*

In an inventory of Ettore Bigaglia, Murano, made in 1714, *70 frutti di diversi sorti* are mentioned.[25] They are very pleasant-looking glass fruits with buds and leaves, now in the Museo Vetrario in Murano. In the same museum are late eighteenth-century fruits and, one assumes, they were also made in Murano during the nineteenth century, for they are being made there today, including apples, pears, even green and red peppers. Like the Cambridge fruits, the glass of these is shiny, but a peach is known with an outer glass coating realistically simulating the fuzz.

SILVERED GLASS WEIGHTS—These were presumably made after 1855 when William Leighton secured a patent for silvered glass doorknobs. The hollow weights are perforated at the bottom, silvered inside, and engraved on top with leaves and flowers. One such is in The Brooklyn Museum.

OTHER WEIGHTS—Three other types of weight are known: the Plymouth Rock clear glass weight, made apparently in conjunction with a similar product from the Providence Inkstand Company, the sitting bulldog in oval base in black and in opaque white glass, and the clear glass bubble weights composed of many rows of evenly spaced bubbles, an effect achieved with a mold similar to the iron maiden (Fig. 204).

INKWELL—One Cambridge inkwell is known, a two-row concentric in clear glass.

SULPHIDES—(See Chapter Seventeen.)

NOTES

[1] Lura H. Watkins, *Cambridge Glass*, 1930, pp. 5–12.

[2] Watkins, p. 11, quotes from Bishop, *History of American Manufacturers*.

[3] McKearin, *American Glass*, New York, 1956 edition, p. 595. Also, *New York Directory*.

[4] McKearin, *Two Hundred Years of American Blown Glass*, New York, 1958 edition, p. 62.

[5] Watkins, *op. cit.*, pp. 12, 13.

[6] McKearin, *American Glass*, p. 141. Barnes seems to have collected some paperweight memorabilia from the NEGC, though he must have acquired a fruit weight and a seal long after he left there.

[7] Watkins, *op. cit.*, p. 15.

[8] *Ibid.*, pp. 18–26.

[9] Watkins, *op. cit.*, pp. 26–38; also see *Forbes*, June 1, 1967, p. 30.

[10] *The Great Exhibition of 1851 Commemorative Album,* Victoria and Albert Museum, London, 1950, fig. 207, p. 138.

[11] Watkins, "Medallion Paper Weights," *Antiques,* Aug., 1941, p. 94.

[12] Edwin Atlee Barber, "Mosaic and Millefiori Glass," Bulletin of the Pennsylvania Museum, July, 1915, p. 40.

[13] Leighton information from Watkins, *op. cit.,* p. 163 ff.

[14] Watkins, *American Glass and Glassmaking,* London, 1950, Plate 24 C, p. 78. At one time Mrs. Watkins owned this weight.

[15] Watkins, *Cambridge Glass,* p. 171.

[16] Barber, *op. cit.,* p. 39.

[17] *Official Catalogue of the New York Exhibition of the Industry of All Nations,* first revised edition, New York, 1853, p. 83.

[18] McKearin, *American Glass,* p. 592.

[19] Correspondence with Mrs. Watkins.

[20] Barber, *op. cit.,* p. 40.

[21] Watkins, *Cambridge Glass,* p. 138.

[22] Correspondence with Roland Barker, grandson of George Dale.

[23] Watkins, *Cambridge Glass,* p. 138.

[24] Francis Edgar Smith, *American Glass Paperweights,* Wollaston, Mass., 1939. All information in this paragraph was obtained from pp. 12–14 and Plates One and Two.

[25] Gudmond Boesen, *Venetian Glass at Rosenborg Castle,* Kobenhavn, 1960.

14

SANDWICH

THROUGH MOST OF THE NINETEENTH CENTURY the generally but not always
friendly rivalry between the New England Glass Company and the Boston &
Sandwich Glass Company formed an important part of the American glass
economy, until in 1888 both companies, faced with the unsurmountable problems
inherent in the vicissitudes of progress, closed their doors, practically speaking,
in unison.

Sandwich, to call it by its familiar contraction, was sprung from the womb
of the New England in the person of Deming Jarves. The name of Jarves was
an anglicized version of Gervais, a family of Huguenots who left France for the
Channel Island of Jersey after the edict of Nantes, 1685. John Jackson Jarves,
Deming's father, came to America in 1787 and became a cabinet-, chair-, and
clock-case-maker in Boston. Deming Jarves was born in Boston about 1790. By
the time he was twenty-three he was already a merchant, first in dry goods, then
in crockery.[1] By 1817 he was moving toward glass, first as "clerk" with the
short-lived and fading Boston Porcelain & Glass Company, East Cambridge,
Massachusetts, and then, in 1818 as cofounder of the New England Glass Company, which bought it out. The other cofounders were three established merchants, and Deming Jarves seems to have been chosen to attend to the glass end
of the business.[2] His title there was "agent," which meant sales or general manager, but Jarves was a born organizer who really wanted a factory of his own.
His backing came in 1823 when his father died, leaving him the better part of
$25,000.

Two years later Jarves left that training ground of glasshouse founders to
start the Sandwich Manufacturing Company, very soon retitled the Boston &
Sandwich Glass Company, of Sandwich, Massachusetts, and known the glass
world over simply as Sandwich.

An advertisement signed by Jarves and appearing during the first months
of operation reads "The subscriber informs his friends and the publick that his

Flint Glass Manufactory in Sandwich, is now in full operation, and is ready to receive and execute orders for any article in that line—particularly Apothecaries, Chemical and Table Wares. Also, Chandeliers for Churches and Halls, Vase and Mantle Lamps, Lamp Glasses, and all other articles usually made in similar establishments; and on as favorable terms. Orders directed to Sandwich, Mass. will receive prompt attention."[3]

Though very little is known of Jarves himself, company records are copious and indicate he must have picked Sandwich partly for its location in the midst of abundant stands of pine that would make ideal fuel, and partly for its easy access by water to the Boston market, though sand used for the glass came from the Berkshires. Sandwich itself, founded in 1637 near the entrance to Cape Cod, was a settled farming community. To some extent Jarves was to make it a company town. He began with an eight-pot furnace and seventy men turning out $75,000 worth of glass a year. By 1854 with four ten-pot furnaces, five hundred men were making $600,000 worth of glass, about the same figures as shown by the rival New England.[4] Jarves enlarged the factory, constructed a small railroad to the docks, improved harbor facilities, built houses for the workers and saw to their basic needs, supplied the town with gas, and generally monopolized the life of everyone concerned.[5]

In 1828 Jarves secured a patent for "Pressing Melted Glass into Molds" which, though not the first use of molds for pressing, was an improvement that put the Boston & Sandwich Glass Company on the map in the new world of pressed-glass technology and mass production.[6] Sandwich pressed glass is too multifarious and too well known to bear discussion here, but it is significant in the light of paperweight-making at Sandwich and Cambridge to note that many other products made by both companies are to this day as easily confused as their paperweights. This was due partly to the tastes of the times and to the reasonably easy intercourse between the two companies, which several times made price-fixing and other agreements on the marketing of almost identical products.

Like other glass manufacturers, Jarves got his glassmen wherever he could find them. Some followed him from Cambridge, others came from South Boston, where in 1837 he started the Mt. Washington Glassworks for his son George; and later he brought them over from England, Ireland, Belgium, and France.[7] Jarves combined business know-how with a thorough knowledge of glass. As "agent" he had considerable autonomy, but he was frequently at odds with the board of directors and five times threatened to resign.[8] His fifth resignation was accepted in 1858 and Jarves left Sandwich to form the Cape Cod Glass Company (incorporated 1864), a few blocks away, for his son John.[9] But John Jarves died in 1863 and Deming went on alone, a frustrated man in his seventies. In 1869 the Cape Cod Glass Company closed down, Deming Jarves died, and a new man came to work at the Boston & Sandwich.

Nicholas Lutz was born in St. Louis, France, in 1835.[10] In 1845, at the age of ten he began his apprenticeship with the Cristalleries de St. Louis presumably for at least five and perhaps seven years, when he would have been due for his service in the French Army. Lutz worked at several factories in Europe, including Murano, where he may have gotten the taste for goldstone we find in some of his weights.[11] In 1860, on the invitation of Christian Dorflinger, another St. Louis graduate, Lutz and six other French glassworkers came to New York where Dorflinger had established the Green Point Glass Works in Brooklyn.[12] In 1863 Dorflinger went to White Mills, Pennsylvania, where in 1865 he founded the Wayne County Glass Works. While Nicholas Lutz was working for Dorflinger at White Mills, he made paperweights and decanter stoppers with flowers enclosed, like those he had seen made at St. Louis in France.[13] In 1867 Lutz went to work for the New England Glass Company, and on October 13 of that year he became a United States citizen.

In 1869 when Lutz came to Sandwich, Jarves was already dead. But Lutz was apparently not the first to make paperweights at Sandwich for there are the dated weights to consider. These are invariably scrambled weights bearing the dates 1825, 1852, or both in the same weight. The 1825 has always been considered an error involving an involuntary reversal of the last two figures of 1852, the logic behind this notion being that no weights were made in 1825. Yet it has not occurred to the logicians that the 1825 might be intended to celebrate the Sandwich founding date, or that where both dates appear in a single weight, the weight might have been made in 1852 and the two dates included intentionally. Frances Edgar Smith, author of *American Glass Paperweights,* says on page 25 of his book that one Sandwich scrambled is dated 1825 in six places and contains a "Liberty Head" on the back of the weight. It was made, he says, by Edmund Rice and came down through Rice's descendants. Elsewhere it has been said that one Timothy Collins, another European import, made for Deming Jarves "paperweights and other remarkable presentation pieces to valued clients, friends, and relatives of officers in the company," and that Jarves considered Collins his most skilled workman.[14]

Perhaps it was Collins who made the dated scrambled weights. In any event, Lutz, though his son has said he brought canes with him from France, seems to have concentrated on flower and fruit weights. Lutz worked at Sandwich from 1869 until its closing in 1888. At one time there was concentrated in the Lutz family a large selection of weights and also the lampwork ingredients of weights and related objects made by Nicholas Lutz. These weights and lampwork, fruits, leaves, and flowers have appeared widely over the years in books and articles by Ruth Webb Lee and others, and there is no doubt whatever of their origin. Many of them are now in museums and private collections. For example, a pair of vases with paperweight bases containing cherries, pears, blue plums, and turnips made by Lutz (1870-80) as a gift to his wife is now in the Bennington Museum, Bennington, Vermont, along with a large double vase of marbrie festooning that bears a striking resemblance to the rare Sandwich marbrie weights. Lutz's career did not end with the closing of the Boston & Sandwich. In 1892 he moved his family to New Bedford, where he worked at the Mt. Washington Glass factory. In 1895 he moved on to the Union Glass factory at Somerville and worked there the last years of his life. He died in 1904 and is buried at Sandwich.[15]

In its final years the Sandwich factory faced labor problems, competition from a vastly expanded American glass industry, geographical isolation, and the rising costs of fuel transported over long distances. After it was closed down in 1888 by its directors in Boston, an unsuccessful attempt was made to get it going again. The buildings remained for many years and were the delight of small boys on treasure hunts and wrecking sprees. One Jarves relative remembers salvaging a rare blowpipe, plaster molds, cylindrical slugs of colored glass, and lamp globes which he tried in vain to use as fishbowls. Much of the excavation work done at Sandwich is now in the glass museum there and in the Smithsonian in Washington, D.C. Imperfect paperweights were found among the cullet.

Sandwich Paperweights

PROFILE

Amid considerable variation there is one preponderant Sandwich paperweight profile. It shows a low outline, with the curvature springing almost imperceptibly from the base to a low, somewhat flat crown. The concave base is usually quite shallow, and the basal ring varies from hair thin to medium broad as weights go. One frequent, though by no means preponderant, clue to Sandwich identification is a whorl or cowlick found at the apex of the crown and presumably caused by rotation of the weight and/or the severance of a tail of glass at this point in the final stages of production, much as the frosting applied to a cake or the meringue of a lemon pie might settle. It is not impossible that in a majority of instances where it does not appear it was marvered out.

There were several grades of flint glass said to have been used at Sandwich and the degree of lead used in the paperweights seems to have been low; in fact, the refractive index of Sandwich paperweights was the lowest of all old makes of paperweights tested by the author, though admittedly few weights were tested, and the index range was considerable. Compared to most weights, and particularly to those from the New England Glass Company, Sandwich weights feel light in the hand. Authorities on glass from the two companies such as Watkins have indicated to me that Cambridge glass of any sort is likely to feel heavier than a comparable piece from Sandwich. Quality of paperweight glass varies widely, from limpid clarity to a sugaring that obscures the image even from above.

Dates and Canes

Canes bearing the dates 1852 and 1825 have already been discussed in connection with Nicholas Lutz, who only arrived on the scene in 1869. They appear in scrambled weights, and the navy blue and white canes dated 1825 may not be an erroneous reversal of the last two figures of the date 1852, but a celebration of the year of the company's founding. Only one signature has been found and this is from Lutz, with the letters trailed like tendrils among the foliage of one weight.[16]

Sandwich canes again are very similar to canes from the New England Glass Company. Though one must generally seek origins in the rods, here again the similarity is striking. Ultimately one is forced to distinguish Sandwich weights from New England weights on the basis of lightness as opposed to heaviness, type of motif, and family ownership. Initially, one really has to work the process backward from family ownership. It has been said that Nicholas Lutz brought canes with him when he left France, and perhaps he did, though they certainly bear no resemblance to St. Louis canes. The assumption is implicit that they were French canes, and here I demur. For the rod elements making up those canes are almost all many-pointed star rods of the type associated with Bohemian canes, though the results are strictly American. My thought is that the general structure of the canes was based on Bohemian prototypes and not French, but that the canes themselves, wherever the 'rod glass may have come from, were all made here in molds that were nearly identical in Sandwich and Cambridge.

Figure canes at Sandwich include a thick Greek cross, heart, bee, running rabbit, eagle, and occasional initials such as a large capital "B." A rabbit cane was found in the Sandwich factory dump. The rabbit may be white or inky blue black, but usually has a red eye. Most of these canes are also used in Cambridge weights, again showing the closeness of the two companies. More surprising is that the eagle, rabbit, and bee are found in somewhat different drawing in Bohemian weights.

Sandwich canes are of many lovely colors, including crimson, a fine, opaque peppermint pink, a wild carmine, salmon, and orange, sulphur, butter and chartreuse yellows, lettuce, apple, moss, sap, and thalo greens, pale, royal, and inky blues, lavender, deep eggplant, and black. Yet the first thing one notices in comparison with the French weights is the predominance of white—a dense, very opaque, chalky bone white. While in the flower weights its function is to give life to the colors superimposed, in the millefiori, where the color coating is thin, it is the basis of cane design. White, white, white; it gives the peppermint sting to Sandwich weights. Only slightly less prominent are the blacks and inky blues, which with the white form the silhouette canes and give to some weights the funereal finality of black crepe on snow-washed Vermont white marble.

Paperweight Types and Characteristics

SCRAMBLED—There are many of these topsy-turvy concoctions, and a fair number are dated 1852, occasionally several times in one weight. Execution is usually indifferent, with the jumbled and highly distorted sections of rod, barber-pole twists, and filigree often widely dispersed among large bubbles and annealing cracks in indifferent, sugary glass. Parts of fruits are found, as if they had been diced for a mixed salad. Silhouette canes are often so distorted as to be unrecognizable. Most are the unattractive work of amateurs. One example, however, has two separate layers of scrambled canes, one above the other.

PATTERNED MILLEFIORI—Very few of these were made, most examples of what have been called Sandwich are high-domed concentrics from the New England Glass Company. If there are any Sandwich concentrics or examples with a single ring of millefiori canes about a central cane all on a latticinio ground, they were made before Lutz's time, that is 1850-69.

FLOWER WEIGHTS—These were made by Nicholas Lutz and possibly others, 1869-88, and constitute the bulk of the better Sandwich weights. Two of them, for example, a white poinsettia and another flower were exhibited in the Boston and Sandwich display at Mechanics' Hall, Boston, in 1878, as shown in a glass, stereopticon slide (Fig. 205), which certainly dates them.[17] Lutz's flower work, some of which exists in specimens never put into paperweights, is well known and documented. The deeply serrated leaves with their sawtooth edges are almost identical with St. Louis leaves; their color, however, runs from an acid thalo to moss and forest greens, and the color layer is apt to be thin and washed out over the opaque white leaf form. Two different leaf and stem greens are frequently seen in the same weight. The stems have the St. Louis curve at the end and the placement of the leaves is careful though natural looking. Yet, curiously, one often sees leaves and flower petals that for all the care taken in their execution are cracked. This probably happened when the fragile flowers (very flat and thin) were being covered with glass and it was too late to do anything about it, for some of the leaf and petal tips are completely separated from the rest by a quarter-inch or more. In one example the leaf tip is missing, and must have broken off before the unit was immersed in glass (Col. Fig. 102).

Poinsettia—One of two common flowers appearing usually in clear glass but also on latticinio and jasper. Five or more long, pointed, unstriped petals are evenly placed with five or more additional petals appearing in the interstices. Colors are poinsettia red, rich cobalt blue, pale blue, white, or, rarely,

Fig. 205. Boston & Sandwich Glass Company, table at Mechanic's Hall, Boston, 1878, two
        weights at edge of table (see above the letter "S" of "Sandwich" and "G" of "Glass").
        Courtesy Sandwich Historical Society.

BOSTON & SANDWICH GLA

alternate-colored petals such as red and blue (Fig. 206). Overcooked reds have a brownish or orange tinge. Flower centers are typical Sandwich-Cambridge canes, except in some Lutz examples, which show his predilections for a version of the Clichy rose with close-cropped petals and translucent red center cane, and for stippling the petals immediately outside the center with spots of goldstone. Some Lutz center canes have goldstone centers, an idea he may have got when he was in Murano. The poinsettia motif characteristically appears well off center in clear glass examples, but better centered in jasper grounds of red-white, blue-white, and, less commonly, green-white, the flower color contrasting with the jasper color, except in one striking instance where both are red (Col. Fig. 103). One clear glass weight has two poinsettias with Clichy-like rose centers. Lutz must have gotten the jasper idea from St. Louis but he improved upon it, for the Sandwich jasper is generally finer in texture. The thin flower rests flush with the ground and follows its curve, but in clear glass examples the flower is sometimes absolutely flat. Flower petals are often punctuated with nicely placed and sized air bubbles, sometimes even covering the entire shape of the outer row of petals. Quality in poinsettias ranges from downright sloppy to superb.

Weedflower—For want of a better name, this is the other common Sandwich flower and appears to be a pure Lutz botanical invention. Like the pansy in form and shape, it consists of two larger upper and three smaller lower petals, but there the similarity ends, for these lower petals are gaily striped in all sorts of color combinations to set off equally gay upper petals. Whatever its initial spark, the weedflower is strictly American. One daring example has a ground of glass chips of the same pinks and blues as the flower petals. Clear glass or latticinio ground (Col. Fig. 104).

Wheatflower—Another makeshift name, but these are almost exactly like their counterparts from Baccarat, with pale blue dots on white petals.

Striped Flower—These are like poinsettias with striped petals. One marvelous example with blue stripes on white petals has an inner row of goldstone petals about a green and white Clichy rose (Col. Fig. 105). Like most Sandwich flowers these appear in clear glass.

Cross Flower—Found in clear glass and on grounds of jasper and alternating red and white latticinio, this unusual symbolic flower has stems in the shape of a cross, with small florets at the extremities and primary leaves in the angles, with two regular leaves below. In well-executed examples it has a strange, hypnotic power that fixes the eye (Fig. 207).

Rose Bush—This extremely rare and perhaps unique weight (Col. Fig. 106) is another example of Sandwich daring in ideas which do not always come off. The tiny roses are put together like pasta, the stem of the bush pulled like chewing gum, and that's that.

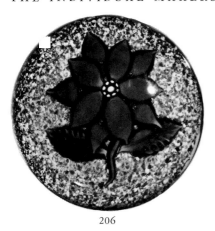

206   207

Fig. 206. Sandwich blue poinsettia on red jasper. *Private collection. Photograph by Taylor &*
Dull.

Fig. 207. Sandwich cross flower, clear glass. *Courtesy Parke-Bernet Galleries, Inc.*

Basket of Flowers—In these, the roses and other anonymous flowers are similar
to those just described and they line the top of a basket made of thin tubing of
yellow or green, trailed to suggest the basket weave. This woven effect is part of
a Victorian predilection stemming from Venetian practices, but perfected in
English and American frigger work that included such concoctions as glass
ships, birds-in-the-fountain,[18] and other fantastic assemblages usually made to
fit under glass bells. The basket rests just above a lattice of opaque white glass,
indenting the lattice sharply (Fig. 208). Lee says that the process of making
milk glass was taught to Sandwich by an expert from Rice, Harris of Birmingham, England, who was paid $5,000 plus expenses for his instruction.[19] The
results indicate that the gentleman from Rice, Harris got the better part of the
arrangement, for the latticinio used in Sandwich paperweights is apt to resemble
skimmed milk.

Fig. 208. Sandwich emerald green basket of rose. *Private collection. Photograph by Taylor &*
Dull.

Upright Bouquet, Large Floral Arrangements—It has consistently been claimed that these rare and impressive paperweights on latticinio swirl grounds were made at Sandwich. Perhaps they were, and by Nicholas Lutz or someone else with a St. Louis background. If I had to choose one of the two types as Sandwich, I would choose the upright bouquets, simply because of their red-white-blue predominance and the white that permeates the florets, that Sandwich bone white. The large floral bouquets certainly have the St. Louis feeling, but the leaves are Cambridge (see Chapter Thirteen), and the execution seems a bit too good for Sandwich.

FRUIT WEIGHTS

Fruits in Latticinio Basket—These were made at Sandwich and at Cambridge, and the experts have made various tentative distinctions between them, such as that the latticinio basket in which the fruit rests is larger and paler at Sandwich, or the fruit is pinker at Cambridge. I would only add the suggestions that the leaf types, lead content, and base form may eventually shed light on the problem. Sandwich leaves are like St. Louis leaves. Sandwich weights are generally lighter. Sandwich bases are usually quite regular, with a shallow basal concavity and an even, uniform basal ring. New England weights are in these respects quite the opposite. The archetypal fruit weight has a motif of four pearlike fruits, arranged blossom up about a central fifth fruit. The pattern forms a Greek cross and the gaps are filled with another Greek cross of leaves and what look like radishes. The form is almost invariable, but there are some Lutz and possibly other examples where the fruit, including what could pass for plums and turnips, is loosely set in clear glass, with various stems and tendrils. The pair of paperweight vases Lutz made for his wife is of this type. Of all the Lutz fruits, perhaps the most effective are the clear glass weights—sometimes they are lovely red pears, sometimes cherries, sometimes blue plums—that show two fruits on stems with four naturally placed leaves that are obviously St. Louis leaves and were possibly brought over by Lutz from France.[20] All the Sandwich fruits appear to have been blown first and then flattened during lampwork assembly.

Blown Fruits on Base—These are life-sized, realistic blown single fruits with an outer coating of two or more colors bled over the inner opaque white glass. After blowing they are fused at an angle usually stem down, blossom up to a cookie-shaped pad of clear glass. Lutz made some, but most were made at the New England.

FAUNA WEIGHTS—There is no way of telling if these are Sandwich or New England. They derive from the techniques described immediately above. And one example, as a matter of fact, shows the same basket of roses, but standing upright in full three-dimensional form. These weights are hollow, the blown and faceted top and upright motif being glued to the base it encloses. Motifs also include a blown white glass stag, and a blown white swan with pink wings and bill.

CROWN—There was some filigree glass made at Sandwich as a variant of the *façon de Venise,* and some crown weights inspired by the St. Louis model were probably also made. But examples that appear to be Sandwich are not very successful and a much better job was done at Cambridge.

MARBRIE—Derived in feeling if not method from the old witchballs, a few of these in red festooning over opaque white blown glass were made at Sandwich, probably by Nicholas Lutz who is known to have made a two-tiered vase with similar festooning (Col. Fig. 107). One example is in the Chrysler Museum, Provincetown, Massachusetts. Similar festooning also appears in a few large single flower weights that Lutz may have made later at Somerville.

RELATED OBJECTS—These include a pair of candlesticks with paperweight bottoms, a pedestal mantel ornament with the flat flower set upright in clear glass, numerous doorknobs with poinsettia motif, decanter stoppers, and a large number of glass pens that Lutz made to give to friends.

NOTES

[1] Ruth Webb Lee, *Sandwich Glass,* New York, 1947, pp. 1–12.

[2] Lura Woodside Watkins, *Cambridge Glass, 1818–1888,* Boston, 1930, pp. 7, 8.

[3] *Ibid,* p. 68.

[4] Deming Jarves, *Reminiscences of Glass Making,* 1854.

[5] Lee, *op. cit.,* pp. 60–65.

[6] *Ibid.,* p. 82.

[7] Mabel M. Swan, "Deming Jarves and His Glass-Factory Village," *Antiques,* Jan., 1938.

[8] Lee, *op. cit.,* pp. 79–132.

[9] Watkins, *op. cit.,* p. 175, notes that "After the era of the versatile Jarves, the agent was business manager only and a 'gaffer' was engaged as factory foreman."

[10] This and subsequent data on Nicholas Lutz, except where otherwise specified, comes from correspondence with his son Victor Lutz.

[11] Correspondence with B. H. Leffingwell. But the goldstone is my idea.

[12] Victor Lutz places Dorflinger at White Mills, Pa., in 1861, but several other sources have him founding the glassworks there in 1865.

[13] Correspondence with Victor Lutz who was told so by his old friend John Dorflinger, son of Christian Dorflinger's cousin.

[14] Charles Woolsey Lyon, "Glass Paper Weight Collecting," *Avocations,* Oct., 1937, p. 37.

[15] Correspondence with Victor Lutz.

[16] Don Nesbitt discovered it.

[17] Photographs and engravings of the New England Glass Company's showrooms of 1875 show no paperweights.

[18] There is a fine example in the Pilkington Museum, St. Helens, Lancashire, England.

[19] Lee, *op. cit.,* p. 166.

[20] Victor Lutz said his father brought over "pieces of cane and other decorative material." Lee, *op. cit.,* p. 488.

15

GILLINDER

EXCEPT FOR THE COMPARATIVELY EARLY AGE at which William T. Gillinder died, his life might serve as a model for the successful, peripatetic glassman; in fact, it closely parallels the lives of many of his contemporaries. Gillinder was born in 1823 at Gateshead near Newcastle-on-Tyne, England, and spent the early part of his life in the Birmingham glass area. Typically, he first went to work in a glass-house at the age of eight. At sixteen he was delivering lectures in chemistry to his fellow workmen; at twenty he was gaffer in a first-class shop. The records show many different addresses as he moved about the Stourbridge-Birmingham area, and he became well known as one familiar with the technical side of glass-making, its labor problems and working conditions. In 1851 his talents were rewarded as he became central secretary of the National Flint Glass Makers Society of Great Britain and Ireland, a post he held for only two years because by then he had negotiated for a position as gaffer in the head shop of the New England Glass Company in Cambridge, Massachusetts. As a token of esteem for his labors at the society he was presented with a gold watch, a bound volume of the society's publications during his tenure, and a purse of 40 guineas. In the fall of 1854 he sailed for America with his wife and children in the ship *Canadian*.[1]

But work at the New England was slack just then and Gillinder was not offered the position he had negotiated for.[2] His stay there was limited, but for the purposes of this book important. Before Gillinder left Birmingham he had made paperweights, and it is significant to what was to come later from the Gillinder factory that he should have learned the art in the town of Bacchus & Sons. At the New England he learned more about making paperweights from "a Frenchman who was working there at the time,"[3] probably François Pierre, who had come to the New England in 1849 after training at Baccarat.

After a brief time at the New England Gillinder moved about considerably. He went first to Pittsburgh, working there at the O'Hara Glass Works where he made improvements in the pots they were using. Then on to St. Louis, Missouri, where for a time he worked in a bottle factory that made common amber glass. In the next two years he was to make six more moves. In 1859 he returned to the O'Hara works in Pittsburgh, and then pushed on to Baltimore where he started a small factory. When it did not prosper he once again returned to O'Hara, but not for long. He next went to Philadelphia, working first at the Philadelphia Glass Works on the Schuylkill River at South Street, and then, when this factory failed, at the Kaighms Point Glass Works near Camden. Finally, in 1861 he returned to Philadelphia and started a small factory to make the lamp chimneys which were beginning to come into demand.[3]

No one knows where Gillinder got the money to buy the old Samuels bottle factory at the southeast corner of Howard and Oxford Streets, which at first was called the Franklin Flint Glass Works. But this time he was successful. He added a chemical factory across the street and began making chemical glassware. In 1863 he was joined by Edwin Bennett, whom he had met in Baltimore and who was one of the founders of the Bennett Pottery, East Liverpool, Ohio, and for the next four years the firm was known as Gillinder & Bennett. A business card of that period proclaims them "Mfrs. of plain, moulded and cut glass table ware—all styles. Patented annealed lead-glass chimneys, peg and hand lamps, chemical apparatus, etc."[4] About this time another factory, the Philadelphia Flint Glass Works, located on Maria Street between 4th and 5th Streets, was added. It produced "Fancy colored glass, Silvered Glass Table Ware, Door Knobs, curtain pins, apothecaries, chemical and philosophical glass." Gillinder & Bennett now had a New York salesroom at 46 Park Place; later moved to the Para Building at Church and Warren Streets.[5] In 1867 Gillinder bought out Bennett's interest and the company became known as Gillinder & Sons. Upon his death in 1871 his sons James (age twenty-seven) and Frederick (age twenty-six) took over the business.[6]

At the Centennial Exposition in Philadelphia in 1876, Gillinder & Sons made exhibiting history by erecting their own building. "It was a complete establishment, showing the processes of melting, blowing, pressing, cutting, etching, and annealing. The product was sold as souvenirs and realized $96,000."[7] Among the Gillinder souvenirs sold were molded clear glass paperweights of different kinds, including the Lincoln and Washington, various animal weights, and weights showing several buildings of the Centennial.

In 1888 or 1890 the Gillinder pressed-ware department moved to Greensburg, Pennsylvania, where it was later merged with the U. S. Glass Company and ceased making tablewares.[8] An undated company catalogue (circa 1900) shows the Philadelphia factory making a wide and hideous selection of globes for incandescent, Argand, and electric lamps.[9] At this time the company had a salesroom in Philadelphia and representatives in New York, Chicago, and Boston. In 1912 the three sons of James Gillinder withdrew from Gillinder & Sons to found Gillinder Brothers, Inc. at Port Jervis, New York. This company is still in business, but the Philadelphia factory closed in 1930.[10]

Gillinder Versus Gilliland

Of all the material perused in research for this book, one of the most haunting documents is a letter written by James Gillinder to Evangeline Bergstrom on June 30, 1948. James Gillinder of Gillinder Brothers, Inc., Port Jervis, was the grandson of William T. Gillinder. On this occasion he has just finished reading Mrs. Bergstrom's pioneering book and he congratulates her "on a very splendid addition to a library on glass." He continues:

> In 1861 my grandfather founded his own company in Philadelphia and during the 1860's made a great many different types of paper-weights at the Gillinder factory. I had an opportunity to visit the factory and found a room that was not being used. In the room was a box of rods that he had used[,] probably 200 pounds or more. These were of a great variety—stars, millefore, figures, etc. Unfortunately, fire a short while later destroyed the room and its contents.[11]

The meaning of this passage was clear enough to me, but the specifics were tantalizing. Two questions were inherent. First, what different types of paperweights did William T. Gillinder make in the decade between 1861 when he founded the company and 1871 when he died? And second, were the 200 pounds of rods consumed by fire the only existing rods?

The answer to the first question was as simple as it was providential. A phone call to Gillinder Brothers at Port Jervis put me on the trail of members of the Gillinder family. Yes, they did know what kinds of paperweights William T. Gillinder made and yes, they would show them to me and let me show them in this book.

The answer to the second question was obtained in a far more roundabout way. In the *Bulletin of The Pennsylvania Museum* (now The Philadelphia Museum of Art) for July, 1915, there is an article by Edwin Atlee Barber entitled "Mosaic and Millefiori Glass." Toward the end of this piece Barber, then editor of the museum's *Bulletin* and a pioneer American student of glass, gives a brief survey of American millefiori, using as illustrations two photographs of what he labels "Cut sections of millefiori rods, cut and grouped for insertion in paperweights, silhouette of Queen Victoria in center, from the Gillinder Glass Works, Philadelphia." The canes are crimped and ruffled in a manner reminiscent of work from Bacchus of Birmingham.

When I first saw this illustration I knew I was on the scent. The name Barber kept reasserting itself until it came to me that in a catalogue issued on the occasion of an exhibition of glass of the New England Glass Company at The Toledo Museum of Art, Toledo, Ohio, in 1963, several of the paperweights were noted as ex-collection: Edwin Atlee Barber. In subsequent correspondence with Millard F. Rogers, Jr., then curator of American Art at The Toledo Museum, I obtained a copy of the cataloguing by Barber of the paperweight acquisitions paperweights known to have been made by the New England Glass Company, and this comfortably encompasses any type heretofore attributed to Gilliland, and any examples except those likely to have been made by William T. Gillinder when he was under the spell of the New England and before he reverted to what he had remembered of Bacchus of Birmingham.

Before we come to a discussion of paperweight types and characteristics, mention must be made of Challinor. Charles Challinor was born in 1841 or 1842 and died in 1932 at the age of ninety. The sixty years of his life spent in the glass business began with his apprenticeship at Gillinder & Sons about 1867. Challinor's son Frank says of his father that he became a skilled "offhand worker, that is, he did not use molds. He would take a daub of glass on the end of a blowpipe or punty and fashion it into something useful or ornamental." Then he adds, cryptically, "He made several paper-weights."[14] His instructor in the paperweight art was undoubtedly William T. Gillinder, for their work bears an inescapable similarity in canework, coloring, and cutting. How long Challinor stayed at Gillinder & Sons and whether he later joined Taylor in Challinor-Taylor of Tarentum, Pennsylvania (circa 1880-90) is not clear.[15]

Paperweight Types and Characteristics

PROFILE

This typical early Gillinder profile shows a high-domed weight. The white, medium lead-content metal is cut with long, deep oval printies, usually six about the sides and one circular printy on top. Basal concavity varies from very shallow to medium, and from broad in cases where no flat rim exists to narrow diameter where there is a wide basal rim. In the best examples the glass is entirely free from striae and sugaring, though black foreign matter exists in varying quantities at the base below the motif. Late Gillinder profiles dating from the Philadelphia Centennial are either flat and circular, oval or hexagonal, or molded in the three-dimensional form of birds and animals.

Canes

Typical Gillinder canes consist largely of crimps and ruffles, with an occasional star or spoke (Fig. 209). Of the figure rods mentioned by James Gillinder, who

paperweights known to have been made by the New England Glass Company, and this comfortably encompasses any type heretofore attributed to Gilliland, and any examples except those likely to have been made by William T. Gillinder when he was under the spell of the New England and before he reverted to what he had remembered of Bacchus of Birmingham.

Before we come to a discussion of paperweight types and characteristics, mention must be made of Challinor. Charles Challinor was born in 1841 or 1842 and died in 1932 at the age of ninety. The sixty years of his life spent in the glass business began with his apprenticeship at Gillinder & Sons about 1867. Challinor's son Frank says of his father that he became a skilled "offhand worker, that is, he did not use molds. He would take a daub of glass on the end of a blowpipe or punty and fashion it into something useful or ornamental." Then he adds, cryptically, "He made several paper-weights."[14] His instructor in the paperweight art was undoubtedly William T. Gillinder, for their work bears an inescapable similarity in canework, coloring, and cutting. How long Challinor stayed at Gillinder & Sons and whether he later joined Taylor in Challinor-Taylor of Tarentum, Pennsylvania (circa 1880-90) is not clear.[15]

Paperweight Types and Characteristics

PROFILE

This typical early Gillinder profile shows a high-domed weight. The white, medium lead-content metal is cut with long, deep oval printies, usually six about the sides and one circular printy on top. Basal concavity varies from very shallow to medium, and from broad in cases where no flat rim exists to narrow diameter where there is a wide basal rim. In the best examples the glass is entirely free from striae and sugaring, though black foreign matter exists in varying quantities at the base below the motif. Late Gillinder profiles dating from the Philadelphia Centennial are either flat and circular, oval or hexagonal, or molded in the three-dimensional form of birds and animals.

Canes

Typical Gillinder canes consist largely of crimps and ruffles, with an occasional star or spoke (Fig. 209). Of the figure rods mentioned by James Gillinder, who

Gillinder Versus Gilliland

Of all the material perused in research for this book, one of the most haunting documents is a letter written by James Gillinder to Evangeline Bergstrom on June 30, 1948. James Gillinder of Gillinder Brothers, Inc., Port Jervis, was the grandson of William T. Gillinder. On this occasion he has just finished reading Mrs. Bergstrom's pioneering book and he congratulates her "on a very splendid addition to a library on glass." He continues:

> In 1861 my grandfather founded his own company in Philadelphia and during the 1860's made a great many different types of paper-weights at the Gillinder factory. I had an opportunity to visit the fac-tory and found a room that was not being used. In the room was a box of rods that he had used[,] probably 200 pounds or more. These were of a great variety—stars, millefore, figures, etc. Unfortunately, fire a short while later destroyed the room and its contents.[11]

The meaning of this passage was clear enough to me, but the specifics were tan-talizing. Two questions were inherent. First, what different types of paper-weights did William T. Gillinder make in the decade between 1861 when he founded the company and 1871 when he died? And second, were the 200 pounds of rods consumed by fire the only existing rods?

The answer to the first question was as simple as it was providential. A phone call to Gillinder Brothers at Port Jervis put me on the trail of members of the Gillinder family. Yes, they did know what kinds of paperweights William T. Gillinder made and yes, they would show them to me and let me show them in this book.

The answer to the second question was obtained in a far more roundabout way. In the *Bulletin of The Pennsylvania Museum* (now The Philadelphia Museum of Art) for July, 1915, there is an article by Edwin Atlee Barber en-titled "Mosaic and Millefiori Glass." Toward the end of this piece Barber, then editor of the museum's *Bulletin* and a pioneer American student of glass, gives a brief survey of American millefiori, using as illustrations two photographs of what he labels "Cut sections of millefiori rods, cut and grouped for insertion in paperweights, silhouette of Queen Victoria in center, from the Gillinder Glass Works, Philadelphia." The canes are crimped and ruffled in a manner reminis-cent of work from Bacchus of Birmingham.

When I first saw this illustration I knew I was on the scent. The name Barber kept reasserting itself until it came to me that in a catalogue issued on the occasion of an exhibition of glass of the New England Glass Company at The Toledo Museum of Art, Toledo, Ohio, in 1963, several of the paperweights were noted as ex-collection: Edwin Atlee Barber. In subsequent correspondence with Millard F. Rogers, Jr., then curator of American Art at The Toledo Museum, I obtained a copy of the cataloguing by Barber of the paperweight acquisitions from him and, sure enough, not only were there paperweights specified as Gillinder, but there was a collection of Gillinder canes (Fig. 209). A few days later I traveled to see the Gillinder family paperweights. They showed many of the same canes, including the cane silhouette of Queen Victoria. The mystery of what the 1861-71 Gillinder paperweights really looked like was at least partially dissolved.

But we must return now to the letter James Gillinder wrote to Mrs. Bergstrom, for in his next paragraph the mystery appears to deepen once again. He writes, "You may be interested to know that the Encyclopaedia Britannica showed a paperweight made by him. If you are interested I shall be glad to write in more detail."[12] There appears to have been no further Bergstrom-Gillinder correspondence because a couple of months later James Gillinder became ill and soon after died. The illustration he refers to appears in the *Encyclopaedia Britannica,* 14th Edition, Vol. 10, Plate XVII, Fig. 7, p. 412, and is a paperweight from The Toledo Museum attributed to William T. Gillinder, Philadelphia, 1850-60. It is unlike most of the Gillinder weights owned by the Gillinder family, and looks for all the world like a floral bouquet on spiral latticinio generally attributed to Gilliland, Brooklyn, New York.

The solution to this apparent dilemma is provided partly by William Gillinder's short paperweight apprenticeship with François Pierre and other paperweight-makers at the New England Glass Company and the influence of their styles and subject matter upon him. But it is equally explained by the apparent and persistent myth of paperweight production at John L. Gilliland & Company in Brooklyn. A modicum of data exists with which to form a picture of Gilliland's life, particularly his early life and his glassmaking activities, first at the New England, then with Fisher in Manhattan, and later when he had his own company in Brooklyn. But no one has come up with any evidence of paperweights made by or at Gilliland beyond the bald assertion that they were made there. The myth sprang, I think, from a very simple and understandable confusion between the two names: Gillinder and Gilliland. It was Deming Jarves of Sandwich who set the scene for the confusion when, in both the 1854 and 1865 editions of his famous *Reminiscences of Glassmaking,* he referred to John L. Gillerland. Spelling until the twentieth century was, after all, a casual and very personal matter. Subsequent writers, including Mrs. Bergstrom, borrowed the error.[13] The error was officially corrected by B. H. Leffingwell who checked the records, but there are still many experts, including the author, who are apt to say Gillinder for Gilliland and vice versa, or even to combine the two as Gillerland.

Finally, to set the record straight, it was Gillinder of Philadelphia that made the paperweights. It may have been Gilliland of Brooklyn too, especially at a time when almost everyone was making paperweights, but there has been to date no evidence to indicate it. Chapter Thirteen discusses fully the range of

Fig. 209. Gillinder canes. *Gift of Edward Drummond Libbey, 1917. Courtesy Toledo Museum of Art.*

may have been speaking collectively of one figure, only the silhouette head illustrated is known to me. While Edwin Atlee Barber described it as representing Queen Victoria, the concave line of the nose and the absence of a tiara would seem to indicate otherwise. Yet the silhouette is like that in some Bacchus weights and may actually be the same cane. A suggested possibility, that the silhouette is that of Jenny Lind has been checked. It isn't. The illustration gives no indication of the extreme delicacy of Gillinder canes when enclosed in glass. Cane coloring includes a lovely cool pink, the palest lemonade yellow, chartreuse yellow, pale thalo green, lettuce green, deep malachite green, pale cobalt blue, rich aquamarine, mauve, and white. The silhouette of the lady may be deep green, black, or white.

CONCENTRICS (1861-71)—In this basic Gillinder weight a large central cane reminiscent of Bacchus or the silhouette of the lady is enclosed in concentric rings (from two to several) of canes set in a high dome, which rises from the base to about one-half the height of the weight. Each ring may consist of identical or alternating types of canes in alternating colors. In some examples the silhouette of the lady also appears as an alternate cane. The bottom of the motif touches the basal concavity, and here the cane ends may often be felt with the fingers. Some bottoms show radiating trails of black flakes, but these in no way affect the view from above. Tall and very deeply cut oval printies are the rule, and the edge of the circular top printy is often beveled. In the unfaceted examples the canes may be misshapen or jumbled, but it is safe to say that some of the faceted examples represent the very finest in American paperweight-making and the equal of the finest from France (Fig. 210; Col. Fig. 108).

CARPET GROUNDS (1861-71)—These masterpieces are like the finer concentrics described above, except that they are carpet grounds of canes identical in form and color, an effect that makes them even more stunning. The small all-white carpet in Col. Fig. 109 with a large central lemon yellow ruffled cane, and beveled top printy is purity itself. The large example in Col. Fig. 110 has a carpet of feathery, ruffled canes in rich aquamarine with the central silhouette in a perfect ring of deep raspberry crimped tubes. Execution and cutting are superb in every detail. These are two of the finest carpet-ground paperweights ever made. Three other all-white carpet grounds each center a large pink Catherine wheel cane.

An unusual unfaceted carpet ground has the relatively low Bacchus profile as well as the large red central cane. The solid ground is of ruffled white canes that are packed as tightly as the nap on a fine oriental rug, and the peripheral blue ring of canes draws in to the center of the base exactly in the Bacchus way. When I first saw this weight I was sure it was a Bacchus, but the dealer informed me it had come to him from someone in the Gillinder family. Perhaps it was one William had made when he was in Birmingham, and his descendants, seeing that it was unlike the others, had thought it was not a Gillinder and had put it up for sale.

Fig. 210. Gillinder, faceted concentric probably by Charles Challinor. *Private collection. Photograph by Taylor & Dull.*

Except for the few—perhaps a half-dozen—faceted concentrics that Challinor made, all the faceted concentrics and carpet grounds were made by Gillinder himself (Col. Fig. 111). In their character, detail, and soft coloring they show the influence of Bacchus upon Gillinder. Even the drawing-in of the outer ring of canes to the center of the base is a Bacchus trait. These weights are a spectacular demonstration of the taste and restraint shown in much of the other Gillinder glass of this decade before he died and everything went flamboyant (Fig. 211).

F L O W E R   W E I G H T S—There are at least two that Gillinder may have made which show the influence of the New England Glass Company: a rose on double spiral latticinio ground (Col. Fig. 112). Everything about one—the brilliant color, the flower itself, the placement on the ground, the bold latticinio (as fine as anything from St. Louis), and the faceting—is superb. The other is less well done and has a large bubble in the latticinio.

L A T E R   W E I G H T S (1876)—A wide variety of clear glass weights from Gillinder & Sons was made at the time of the Philadelphia Centennial to commemorate that event.

P O R T R A I T S—These are flat, clear glass weights about ¾ inch thick and 3½ inches in diameter. Shapes are circular or octagonal. Portrait heads of Washington, Franklin, and Lincoln were intaglio-impressed into the bottoms and then bathed in hydrofluoric acid while the clear glass top and sides were either masked or repolished later. Sometimes, as in the case of the Washington, the sides were molded and treated with the acid, but the top surface is always clear to show the

Fig. 211. Gillinder, faceted white carpet ground of ruffled canes, Victoria silhouette. *Courtesy Bergstrom Art Center and Museum.*

portrait. Some, like the Lincoln, are inscribed "Gillinder & Sons, Centennial Exhibition, Phila. 1876." The Gillinder sons may have gotten the idea from New England, which had made a similar portrait weight of Victoria and Albert in 1851.

B U I L D I N G S—A similar treatment of various buildings at the Philadelphia Centennial similarly inscribed, but appearing in long oval glass. These were the forerunners of what are known as trade weights, those blocks of glass made to advertise companies or products and bearing inside or in decalcomania on their backs lurid primitive pictures of factories or merchandise.

M O L D E D   F L O R A   A N D   F A U N A—These molded creatures, including dogs, cats, lions, peacocks, sit in sculptural relief on top of blocks of glass. Like the portrait weights these also may have been inspired by the New England Glass Company, which made similar weights, but frequently in black or opaque white glass.

It is easy enough to trace the decline of paperweight-making at Gillinder, which paralleled the decline in handcrafted glass generally. But in the matter of paperweights made in its earlier days Gillinder has remained unknown to all but those intimately connected with the factory. It is time that the millefiori work of William Gillinder was recognized, for it was not bettered in this country.

NOTES

¹ Account written by James Gillinder in 1938, and other personal memorabilia. Gillinder birth date from Paul J. Fitzpatrick, Ph.D., "Gillinder & Sons at the Philadelphia Centennial," *Spinning Wheel,* July–Aug., 1965.

² In a letter to Evangeline Bergstrom, June 30, 1948, James Gillinder says of William T. Gillinder, "He took the position of head gaffer in the New England Glassworks." But in the 1938 account James Gillinder says, "He was not given the position offered as work was very slack." Whatever the facts, William T. Gillinder was not there long.

³ Account by James Gillinder, 1938.

⁴ Business card in possession of Gillinder family.

⁵ Business card in possession of Gillinder family.

⁶ Account of James Gillinder, 1938.

⁷ Paul J. Fitzpatrick, Ph.D., "Gillinder & Sons at the Philadelphia Centennial," *Spinning Wheel*, July–Aug., 1965. Fitzpatrick here quotes James Gillinder, *History of American Glass,* 1895.

⁸ McKearin, *American Glass,* p. 613.

⁹ Catalogue No. 9, on file in The New York Public Library.

¹⁰ McKearin, *op. cit.,* p. 610.

¹¹ Letter of James Gillinder to Evangeline Bergstrom, June 30, 1948.

¹² *Ibid.*

¹³ And how curious it is to note in passing that Francis Edgar Smith, who wrote the first book on glass paperweights and made so many errors in it, never even mentions the names Gilliland or Gillinder.

¹⁴ Information is taken from Frank Challinor's article, "A Glassman's Collection." *Antiques,* April, 1947.

¹⁵ There was also a (David) Challinor Taylor & Co. in Pittsburgh. *Antiques,* April, 1937.

16

OTHER AMERICAN FACTORIES

Dorflinger

THE BIOGRAPHIES OF MOST SUCCESSFUL nineteenth-century American glassmen are so similar that they read like slightly altered versions of the same success story. The man is likely to be born in Alsace-Lorraine, get his training early either at Baccarat or St. Louis, come to the United States, move around a bit in the restless American way, and finally settle down and establish his own glassworks which, of course, brings him fame and fortune. The success story of Christian Dorflinger was no exception.

Christian Dorflinger was born in the Canton de Bitsche, Alsace, on March 16, 1828. From the age of nine to eighteen (1837-46) he learned glassmaking at the Cristalleries de St. Louis, where he became interested in the decoration of glass, particularly etching, engraving, enameling, and gilding.[1] In 1846 Dorflinger came with his family to Indiana and worked as journeyman blower for a Philadelphia firm specializing in druggists' ware—a line he was to continue at White Mills. In 1852 at twenty-four, he shared ownership with his brother Christopher of the Long Island Flint Glass Works in Brooklyn, New York, and by 1860 he had established there the Green Point Glass Works.[2] This was the year he invited Nicholas Lutz (who had come to St. Louis for his apprenticeship the year before Dorflinger left) and six other French glassworkers to come to Brooklyn to work for him.

Ill health in 1863 forced Christian Dorflinger into temporary retirement, which he spent in White Mills, Wayne County, Pennsylvania. But two years later he again formed his own company, the five-pot Wayne County Glass Works (also known as the Dorflinger Glass Works), which was to become for White Mills what the Boston & Sandwich Glass Company had been for the town of Sandwich. Dorflinger made it a glass community, putting up the money for fifty workers' houses and providing the town with stores, schools, churches and, in 1867, a large hotel. "Old Chris" became the great benefactor to all the workers. He praised the men who fathered many sons and he entered these sons on the factory rolls at ages nine, ten, and eleven.[3]

In addition to a line of druggists' wares and lamp goods, the Dorflinger Glass Works became famous for its fine flint tableware and toilet ware. The McKearins say, "The crystal metal made by Dorflinger is superb. We must confess that, given pieces of equal thickness and simple forms, we can detect no tremendous difference between the metal of the Dorflinger pieces and modern crystal, including that of Steuben and Orrefors."[4] Dorflinger glass was rewarded with a prize at the Centennial Exposition of 1876, and the quality of its glassware was manifested in White House tableware made for eight Presidents from Lincoln through Theodore Roosevelt, as well as other crystal for assorted tycoons and foreign potentates. Christian Dorflinger died in 1915, but the Dorflinger family, who had grown up in the business, carried on until the firm closed down in 1921.[5]

Paperweight-making at Dorflinger

In 1924 John Dorflinger, a nephew of Christian, opened a small museum and shop devoted to the exhibition and sale of Dorflinger glassware. Among the exhibits were paperweights made by Nicholas Lutz, Ralph Barber, Emil Larson, the great Swedish glassworker, Ernest W. von Dohln, and a man named Tobias Hagberg, known locally as "the Swede." Von Dohln said that Larson was the first local gaffer to make a high-crowned (tall) weight. Lutz made weights and decanter stoppers whose motif was a flower set in clear glass, similar to the poinsettias he was to make later at Sandwich. Examples he made at Dorflinger are exquisite in workmanship and coloring and show none of the cracking and sloppiness associated with Sandwich work. Lutz seems always to have avoided latticinio grounds in his weights. Emil Larson, the only one of four Larson brothers to make paperweights, began making his rose weights while at Dorflinger, and continued to make them later at Mt. Washington and at Durand in Vineland, New Jersey, in the early 1930's. Tobias Hagberg's work at Dorflinger is identified by a small flower that he placed in the base of each piece, which could be seen only by turning the weight over. The main flower motif of his weights and inkwells are large, four-petaled lilies of deep rose over white, with a spatter of yellow, green, and blue in the center. These appear to be prototypes of weights made later at Steuben in Corning, New York, where Hagberg is thought to have gone after the closing of the Dorflinger Works. It is important to note that at Dorflinger paperweights were absolutely not a part of the regular company merchandise, but were made by the men during their lunch hour, the only time they could have been made because the work at the plant went around the clock.[6]

In terms of paperweights, White Mills was a stop along the way for Lutz, Barber, and Larson, and one associates their work not with Dorflinger but Sandwich, Millville, and Vineland.

Millville

Like the loose term "Sandwich," the term "Millville" in the paperweight lexicon refers not to a factory but to a place, Millville in southern New Jersey. The story of glassmaking at Millville has its origins in nearby Port Elizabeth, New Jersey, where, shortly after 1800, James Lee and several Philadelphia business associates established a works for making window glass. By 1806 Lee and his associates had built a new window-glass factory at Millville. Sometime before 1828 this property was taken over by a firm of druggists from Philadelphia, and it subsequently changed hands several times until in 1844 it was acquired by the Whitall brothers, who ten years later purchased another glasshouse in South Millville. In 1849 it became known as Whitall Brothers & Company, and in 1857 as Whitall Tatum & Company, the designation implied in the term "Millville."[7]

The works at Millville produced pharmaceutical wares in green glass and opaque white glass. In 1854 it exhibited green glassware at the twenty-fourth exhibition of the Franklin Institute. In 1863 a wooden mold department was opened for the seamless fashioning of chemical and pharmaceutical wares, including laboratory equipment and the drug-store glass in which Millville had a virtual monopoly.[8] Whitall Tatum & Company received an award at the Centennial in 1876 for "chemists, druggists and perfumers wares of lime and green glass."[9] At one time or another every American boy strolling down the road or alongside the railroad tracks must have found a discarded green or clear glass telephone line insulator stamped "Whitall Tatum & Co." These were made in the millions. Today one sees them in the more flea-bitten antique shops, particularly the clear glass insulators whose manganese content turned them amethyst when exposed to long years of sunlight. The name of Whitall Tatum & Company ceased to exist when the factory was bought by the Armstrong Cork Company, but the factory still operates in Millville where it makes common glass for Armstrong.

Paperweight-making at Millville

Edward Minns, whose thorough and definitive research of Millville paperweights (done thirty years ago when it could still be done) included detailed information from relatives of the men who worked at Whitall Tatum, said that the skilled men of the wooden mold department were "noted for their ability to produce practically any article of glass by hand, regardless of the difficulties entailed." Minns says that soon after the department opened in 1863 the cruder types of paperweights appeared as offhand work. These included the weights in which the image lay flat, the first crude lily, the fountain and the devil's fire.[10]

BIRD WEIGHTS—Minns illustrates a paperweight showing a blue-colored bird on a branch, all on a light-colored ground, the color not specified, which, he says, was made at the Port Elizabeth works before the wooden mold department was started at Millville; that is, before 1863.[11] (Col. Fig. 113) is a similar blue bird on a canary yellow ground. It is not clear whether Minns was referring to the window-glass works founded at Port Elizabeth by James Lee, which continued in operation till 1885,[12] or to the other glasshouse near Port Elizabeth founded by Stanger and Shough.[13] In any event, these two rare bird weights, whose motif and ground were formed of powdered glass probably placed on a metal or a wooden die, were the prototype for the later Millville weights featuring pictures (Fig. 212; Col. Fig. 114).

MOTTO WEIGHTS—In general the weights with horizontal motif feature a ground of partially bled (fused) glass chips of many colors, above which float such slogans and cautions as "Friendship" (with clasped hands), "Rocked in the Cradle of the Deep" (with clipper ship), "Hope" (with anchor and wreath), "Remember Mother," "Remember the Maine" (with warship and dated Feb. 15, 1898), "Remember Me" (with wreath, leafy branch, and fruit), "Home Sweet Home," "No Place Like Home" (with house and paths) (Fig. 213). The lettering and illustrations were cut in iron dies, the usually white powdered glass swept into the die cuts, and the motif then picked up, adhering to a blob of glass on the end of the pontil rod, after which the whole was carefully marvered and shaped before being covered with more glass. Other subjects include emblems of Masons, Elks, etc., and presentation weights of a personal nature with names such as Maude S. (with a horse) and Kizzie Pepper. These weights appear to have been made from 1863 on and vary a good deal in workmanship. Most of them are reminiscent in subject matter and some in the cruder feeling of the American pictorial and historical flasks, which tradition they continue.

FLOWER WEIGHTS

Roses—Millville has become famous chiefly for the upright roses made by Emil Stanger, Marcus Kuntz, Ralph Barber, and John Rhulander. The Barber rose is generally thought to be the finest, but Minns discovered that all of these men made fine roses and that an actual ownership of a rose weight was the only way of telling who made which rose.[14] The red, pink, mauve, white, and yellow roses were made with a hand-forged iron crimp that looks a bit like a half-opened rose. The colored glass over opaque white was supposedly stuck in a wad on the ball of clear glass that formed the bulk of the weight and forced up into it with the crimp, which at the same time gave it the basic shape. The ensemble was then coaxed and marvered until the petals spread out. The Ralph Barber roses—and probably those by the others mentioned above—were made between 1905 and "sometime before 1912," when Barber "left Whitall Tatum to become plant superintendent of the Vineland Flint Glass Works at Vineland, New Jersey."[15] The roses made by these men come upright or tilted, with or without leaves and bud, in globular, almost spherical weights with or without

212

213

Fig. 212. Port Elizabeth magnum floral bouquet in powdered glass. *Private collection. Photograph by Taylor & Dull.*

Fig. 213. Millville dog, "Our Prince." *Private collection. Photograph by Albert "Kayo" Harris & Associates.*

footed base, and sometimes above a pedestal consisting of a base and baluster stem (Figs. 214, 215). For several years Barber encountered great difficulty in finding a ruby glass with the proper expansion coefficient. At Vineland he seems to have encountered even greater difficulties and his paperweight efforts there were aborted, though the efforts of Emil Larson (formerly of Dorflinger) in making rose weights at Vineland seem not to have been in vain. A rose is a rose is a rose, but these paperweight flowers for the most part resemble nothing so much as oversized ivory salt spoons or those ladle-like botanical freaks that the Italians use as funeral decorations. The rose on pedestal has been copied unsuccessfully by the Chinese and in recent years by Murano. While the Venetian attempt looks more like a half-opened peony with its ball of center petals still furled, it is about as successful as the Millville efforts. However, one Jersey rose with three pale moss green petals, probably made by Larson at Vineland, has about it the ineffable mystery of all great paperweights (Col. Fig. 115).

Fig. 214. Millville group of roses, pair of clipper weights. *Courtesy Parke-Bernet Galleries, Inc.*

215   216

Fig. 215. Millville pedestal with fitted rose and leaves. *Courtesy Parke-Bernet Galleries, Inc. Photograph by Taylor & Dull.*

Fig. 216. Millville water lily. *Courtesy Parke-Bernet Galleries, Inc.*

Tulip, Water Lily—The Millville pink tulip is really a rose with a single row of jagged-topped petals and a yellow stigma. Far more interesting than the rose or tulip is the great waterlily, one of the boldest and most powerful of all presentations under glass (Fig. 216; Col. Fig. 116). These rare specimens vary somewhat in appearance, but have an outer row of leaves inside which the tuberous petals reach up almost to the top of the weight, or spread out like candelabra. The Bergstrom example has also an outer row of large white petals and a canary yellow stigma. They have been called Millville, but there is an assurance about them that suggests they may have been made by Larson at Vineland.

Lilies—In my view the most fanciful paperweights made at Millville were the lily weights and inkwells made by Emil Stanger and Marcus Kuntz. These were umbrella-like creations of opaque white glass, appearing as if sprinkled with, but actually rolled in, chips of colored glass, forced (like the rose) with a crimp into the ball of clear glass, pierced with a pick to form the stem, and finally pulled into shape by a hooklike device. The stoppers of these inkwells contain a reduced version of the same motif (Fig. 217).

SCENES—But the most ingenious paperweights at Millville were those upright scenes derived from iron or steel dies (as described above) and made by Michael Kane. In paper-thin colored glass pictures as delicate as if they had been etched, Kane shows a hunter and his dog flushing a covey of quail (Fig. 218), a yacht, a clipper ship (Fig. 214), or the American eagle (white against a translucent red ground) in a superb series of vignettes that sets the pulse to beating with chauvinistic nostalgia. These large, clear, heavy, handsome weights come plain, footed, on pedestals, and, occasionally, as with the clipper ships, in pairs that were probably used as mantel ornaments. One can sense the vestige of Bohemian engraving through flashed glass, but these vertical colored pictures, that catch the light from behind, are strictly and completely American.

Mt. Washington

The history of what may be referred to loosely and inclusively as the Mt. Washington Glass Works is so long (1837-1958) and complicated, particularly in view of the scant information about paperweights made there, that to relate it in all its mystifying detail would distort its importance in relation to the other American glasshouses considered in this book. Instead, a brief synopsis will suffice.[16]

1837—Deming Jarves founds Mt. Washington Glass Works in South Boston for his son George D. Jarves, aged twelve. In view of his youth and the fact that he died in 1850 at the age of twenty-five, George D. Jarves probably saw little service with the glassworks.

1837-55—Factory superintended by Luther Russell.

1846—Glassworks also known as Labree and Jarves.

1847—Glassworks also known as Jarves and Cormerais.

1851—William L. Libbey becomes bookkeeper at Jarves and Cormerais' Boston office.

1856—Timothy Howe becomes clerk at Mt. Washington Glass Works.

1860 or 1861—Libbey and Howe take over "Mt. Washington Glass Works, Manufacturers of Kerosene Lamps, Lanterns, Glass and Kerosene Shades, Chimneys and Glass Ware in all its varieties."

1866—Howe dies. Libbey becomes sole proprietor.

1869-70—Libbey buys up New Bedford Glass Company, formed by striking workers from Sandwich (1866-67), and moves Mt. Washington to New Bedford.

1870-71—Firm known as W. L. Libbey and Company.

1871—Libbey sells out to Mt. Washington Glass Works stock company.

1872—Libbey becomes agent of the New England Glass Company.

1876—New Bedford factory known as Mt. Washington Glass Company.

1894—Mt. Washington becomes part of Pairpoint Manufacturing Company.

1929—Depression affects Pairpoint.

1938—Glassworks purchased by I. N. Babbitt and Robert M. Gundersen, and known as Gundersen Glass Works.

1952—Known as Gundersen-Pairpoint Glass Works.

1957—Moved to East Wareham, Massachusetts, as Pairpoint Glass Works.

1958—Operations suspended.

Though more exaggerated than most, the tangled history of the Mt. Washington enterprise gives a striking idea of the peripatetic nature and manifold activities of such great glassmen as Deming Jarves and William L. Libbey, whose movements have been traced in other chapters of this book.

Paperweight-making at Mt. Washington

Almost nothing is presently known about work at the South Boston factory besides what has been listed in advertisements and directories, but practical glassware is supposed to have been the chief output. The assumption

Fig. 217. Millville "lily" inkwell. *Courtesy Parke-Bernet Galleries, Inc.*

Fig. 218. Millville hunter and dog by Michael Kane. *Courtesy Bergstrom Art Center and Museum.*

217

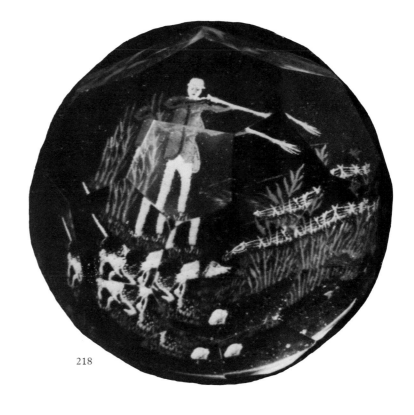

218

has been that very few Mt. Washington paperweights were made at the New Bedford works, which had ample facilities for elaborate work and where, in the last quarter of the nineteenth century, such fine art glass as Pearl Satin Ware, Coralene, Rose Amber, Burmese, and Crown Milano was made by men of great imagination and technical skill. Nicholas Lutz is known to have worked at Mt. Washington in New Bedford between 1892 and 1895, when he moved on to Somerville,[17] though it is doubtful that his style changed noticeably, since what he made earlier at Dorflinger and at Sandwich is substantially the same as what he probably made at Somerville after leaving Mt. Washington. However, Lutz's presence at New Bedford may have sparked others to try a hand at paper-weight-making. Emil Avinwell worked at New Bedford with Lutz and also went on to Somerville. Emil Larson was also at Mt. Washington (then called Pairpoint), sometime between 1918 when he left Dorflinger and 1925 when he went to work at the Durand Works in Vineland, New Jersey.[18]

LAVA—Albert Steffin and Frederick S. Shirley were men who also might con-ceivably have made weights at Mt. Washington, especially Shirley who received so many patents for his varieties of art glass. In 1878 Shirley received a patent for Lava glass, of which lava was an actual constituent.[19] I have seen one weight, described by the old dealer who had it as a lava weight made at New Bedford. The black glass extended almost to the surface where it showed a mat finish and was inlaid with a mosaic, cross-shaped design in opaque red, white, and blue glass. Was this perhaps something made by Shirley or someone under him?

FLOWER WEIGHTS

Rose—Whoever made these extraordinary weights was a master at flower-making. Unlike the Millville roses, these are horizontal motifs meant to be looked at from above and set in relatively low-crowned broad weights whose diameter runs about 4½ inches. Nevertheless, the rose and its bud appear in high relief, like a flower that has been laid on a tabletop and has flattened out on the bottom yet retains the elevation of its petals. The large blossom, possibly a portrait of an unusual climbing rose, hovers curiously between the realistic and the fantastic like some vividly dreamed-of-hybrid. The petals unfurl with a botanical exactitude, yet their puckered edges and highly mottled coloring sug-gest more the parrot tulip than any rose. The leaves are naturalistic in varying degrees and the bud or buds are as convincing as the glass flowers made by the Blaschkas, yet the one, two, or three moths that hover about most of the roses are moths of the Douanier Rousseau. In some examples, a pink hand that might be the work of some bemused pastry cook grasps a stem as large, relative to it, as a rake handle. The rose, whose petals come in pure white, pink, a combination of corals and yellows, or the dead purple and white of the well-known English and American Victorian slag glass, may have a goldstone center, and the third finger of the hand that grasps the stem may have a goldstone ring. To this mingling of the real and the surreal may be added the presence in one slag-petaled rose weight of small blueberries and yellow and red berries that may very well be fruits brought by Nicholas Lutz from Sandwich. But afterward, when he went to Somerville, did he once again regress to the single flowers he had made over and over at Sandwich? It is not known. One open rose rests on an opaque white ground and is ringed by small flowers in the Somerville manner. Another rose weight has a relatively small top printy and three small side printies (Fig. 219; Col. Figs. 117, 118).

Poinsettia—In the one example known to the author, leaves and petals are traversed by the same veins, which is at least true of the poinsettia flower itself, but here suggests a shortage of lampwork parts. Perhaps Lutz left these parts behind when he left New Bedford and someone else finished this poinsettia, just as someone had put the Lutz fruits in with his own purple slag rose to fill out the composition (Col. Fig. 119).

Dahlias (Two known examples)—The big Mt. Washington dahlias, to be sure, have the poinsettia petals in great quantities, but they also have a flower center composed of shorter, cupped, and close-packed petals that, since they also appear in the roses and the poinsettia, suggest the inspiration of one man. Though some of them are afflicted with extraneous bubbles, these huge, powerful flowers have an impact that puts St. Louis and Clichy dahlias to rout (Col. Fig. 120).

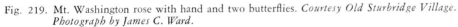

Fig. 219. Mt. Washington rose with hand and two butterflies. *Courtesy Old Sturbridge Village. Photograph by James C. Ward.*

Fig. 220. Mt. Washington floral plaque weight. *Private Collection. Courtesy Sotheby & Co.*

Floral-fruit Group (Two known examples)—These large weights show a casual grouping of multipetaled flowers in white, amber, saffron yellow, faded mulberry, and scarlet, along with a large bunch of blue grapes that could be taken for Nicholas Lutz's plums. These flowers have the centers composed of small closed petals found in the Mt. Washington dahlias and roses.

Large Floral Plaque Weights (Four known examples)—These bouquets, as rare as they are remarkable, are set in rectangular clear glass plaques about an inch thick and 5 inches by 3½ inches. Corners and upper edges of the plaque are beveled like the NEGC medallion weights, while the flat base may be plain, frosted (Col. Fig. 121), or hobnail-diamond cut (Fig. 220; Col. Fig. 122). The bouquet like all other Mt. Washington floral motifs is flat on the bottom but modeled in high, upright relief. The many large natural-looking flowers, buds, and leaves grow from stems which are tied together at the bottom by prominent, tightly plaited ribbons in one or two colors. One of only three known examples contains seven full flowers, four buds, and thirty-seven leaves. The amount of complicated lampwork involved in assembling such a floral spray can be imagined when one peeks behind and sees the network of stems binding the spray together. Here again the flower centers are distinctive and different from all non-Mt. Washington flower centers; consisting of a globelike berry of glass, presumably the seed pod, studded with small, pale seeds. They resemble gumdrops. One plaque includes four wild strawberries, and it is this inclusion that enables us to identify the strawberry weights described below as Mt. Washington. Leaf and stem colorings in these plaques vary from deep emerald to a pale, root-cellar green; the latter is also the color of the leaves in roses believed to have been made at Vineland by Emil Larson. The glass in these plaques feels heavy for the size, but varies in clarity. Three examples contain the many bubbles attendant upon the covering of three-dimensional flowers, and one of them also includes a quantity of other extraneous matter noticed in other weights from this source.

STRAWBERRIES (Several known examples)—In addition to strawberries in a plaque weight, there are several large weights in which the strawberry and its blossoms form the entire motif. These berries have a thick, translucent coating of juicy red studded with tiny flakes of clear glass (probably cullet), an effect similar to the flower centers already discussed. The mouth waters just to look at them (Col. Fig. 123). The blossoms are white with yellow centers and some leaves are emerald green, while others are the same pale green mentioned in connection with the plaques, tentatively suggesting either the Larson touch or that of Avinwell, who is known to have made strawberries at Somerville. At one time the strawberries with the dark leaves were said to be Sandwich, and there was talk of a dozen light-green-leafed copies having been made somewhere else. The "somewhere else" probably refers to the strawberry weights made by Emil Avinwell at Somerville after he left New Bedford, though it is likely he began making them at Mt. Washington. In size and in the construction of the three-dimensional motif, the strawberry weights bear no relation to Sandwich, while in these particulars they do resemble other Mt. Washington weights.

Along with the best of the New England Glass Company overlays and the Gillinder carpet ground concentrics, the flower weights from New Bedford represent the finest in American paperweights.

Pairpoint

Footed Spirals

These distinctive weights comprise a solid glass sphere whose motif is an upright, two-colored spiral roughly in the shape of an egg, the sphere mounted on a base that may be plain, or engraved with leaves, or simple crosshatching. Spiral colors are opaque white and either cobalt blue or ruby red. The sphere in which the spiral is enclosed is often polka dotted close under the surface with evenly formed and spaced bubbles produced by a sort of iron-maiden mold studded with short spikes (Fig. 221).

In view of the fact that these weights are usually considered as having been made at Pairpoint, it is worth bearing in mind that the Pairpoint Manufacturing Company, at one time one of the country's largest manufacturers of plated silver, did not come into existence until 1880 and did not take over the Mt. Washington Glass Works until 1894.[20] The weights must therefore have been made after 1894, and were probably made after 1910, because the footed bases were engraved by Carl Banks of Pairpoint, who was born sometime around 1885. Many years later Banks remembered so well the work he had done that he was able to duplicate the engraving in spite of being unable to find an old spiral paperweight to copy.[21] The spiral weight was again attempted by Pairpoint not long before it closed, but the results are disappointing. Kaziun says, "A man named Lilljaquist had in his possession some of the old Mt. Washington leaves and may possibly have made weights."

Fig. 221. Pairpoint pair of footed spirals with bubbles. *Courtesy The Art Institute of Chicago.*

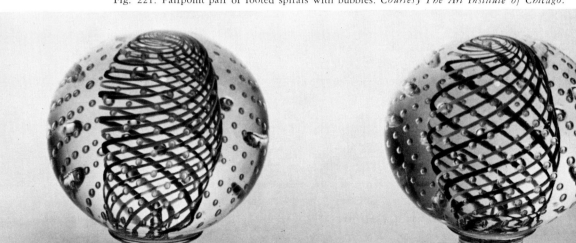

Somerville

The Union Glass Company, Somerville, Massachusetts, was founded by Amory Houghton, Sr. and Jr., in 1851. The McKearins say Houghton, Sr. "was considered one of the ablest mixers of his time," while, "Amory Jr., who was associated with him, was imbued with the scientific approach to the multiplicity of problems inherent in glassmaking and devoted the major portion of his time to laboratory experimentation."[22] In 1864 the Houghtons left Somerville for Brooklyn, where they acquired the Brooklyn Flint Glass Works.

The Union Glass Company exhibited "glass shades, monuments and cylinders" at the Centennial in 1876.[23] The McKearins illustrate a handsome Somerville goblet of about 1860 with a red-white-blue corkscrew twist in the stem.[24] But perhaps the most popular and attractive glass was the Kew Blas and other art glass made in the 1890's, which parallels the Tiffany and Carder efforts. A photograph taken in 1893 shows William S. Blake, of whose name Kew Blas was an anagram, standing in a room crammed with goblets, vases, and bowls which constituted the first batch of this glass.[25] The Union Glass Company closed in 1927, reopened, then closed again in 1929. The cutting shop, however, remained open several more years.

Paperweight-making at Somerville

As at most glassworks, paperweight-making at Somerville was an offhand, off-hours labor of love. Edward J. Mazerski of Somerville, who began work as an apprentice at the Union Glass Company in 1923 and later served until its closing as "first gather," has furnished me with photographic prints of Somerville glassmaking taken from company archives and information about the men he knew there who made paperweights. One can only wish that such information were available from associates of the men who made paperweights at Baccarat, for instance.

Glass at Somerville was made in large furnaces of twelve pots each, each pot containing 3,600 pounds of glass. The glory hole, where the glass was reheated while being worked, was located conveniently near the gaffers' chairs. Large art pieces were annealed in kilns heated by fruitwood which was stacked beside them. (The company also made reflectors, cruets, decanters, perfume bottles, and a variety of other glass.) Smaller items such as tumblers, doorknobs, stoppers, and paperweights were annealed in a kiln or leer heated by oil and moved on a hand-operated conveyor. The oil left a film on the glass, which had to be brushed or buffed off. If the object was later sent to the cutting room, acid polish removed the film. One photograph shows Philip Bunamo in his attic at home, making over a Bunsen burner the pigs, birds, and flowers he would later take to the factory and incorporate in his paperweights. Bunamo worked at Somerville from 1900 until 1929. Another photograph (unfortunately, these are not of reproduction quality) shows Emil Avinwell and a group of employees. Avinwell, whose name originally may have been Avinelli, made many of the flower weights and, Mazerski says, rose weights and strawberries. He was a protégé of Lutz, who ended his long glassmaking career at Somerville. When the Union Glass Company closed, Avinwell went on to Pairpoint.

Somerville Paperweight Types and Characteristics

Generally speaking, the very heavily leaded and extremely clear, striae-free glass of these 4-inch, well-proportioned, flat-bottomed weights contrasts with the rather nervous, crude, sloppy execution of the motifs inside them. Some weights contain so much lead that they have a faintly yellowish cast.

FLORAL GROUPS AND ANNIVERSARIES—These well-proportioned weights generally show a wide circle of as many as ten single blossoms of alternating colors with leaves set in a flattened-dome shape in clear glass, the match-head flower centers reminiscent of St. Louis but the workmanship far below St. Louis level. Flower colors are a dull scarlet, thinly applied over the opaque white, an equally dead cobalt, and a pale but solid opaque green (not over white). Leaf colors run from pale cinnabar green to deep emerald. The commodious center space may be occupied by another flower, or by the name, date, and insignia of some special occasion. These floral and commemorative weights were made in dated examples from about 1910 through 1920 by Philip Bunamo and Emil Avinwell. Names of recipients such as Mabel A. Collins, 1918; Clark, Schwartz, and others in initials appear in white block capitals. The author has seen four examples dated 1917, and one of these bears the initials "D. A. C." above crossed French and American flags. One weights says "Happy New Year, 1920." Some weights were made as wedding gifts.

FLORAL MARBRIE—In this single instance (and there must be others) a central flower is enclosed by a poorly executed red and blue marbrie festooning in the clear glass.

ROSES—These small, high-crowned weights were made by Philip Bunamo and are probably his best work. Somewhat reminiscent of the roses said to have been made by John Degenhart of Cambridge, Ohio, and of the Millville tulips, these Bunamo roses without leaves rise directly from the flat base, nearly filling the glass. The petals are a soft, mottled rose-red, with a soft, wavy top outline. A most successful and attractive weight.

PIGS—These were also made by Bunamo, and one is dated 1908. In these weights, from one to as many as five crudely made opaque white pigs point toward a central flower or loll about a ground composed of crude, colored chips.

In one, a sulphide sow lies upon her side, her dugs prominent. A boar is also known.

B I R D S   A N D   N E S T—These similar weights show three opaque white birds about a nest filled with eggs on a similar chip ground. The birds were once claimed to have been broken off the tops of glass pens made in Japan, but this seems unlikely, since the birds were the lampwork of Bunamo, who also made glass pens. Again the chip ground.

S T R A W B E R R I E S—According to Mazerski, Bunamo also made strawberries, though whether these are the ones claimed to have been copies of the Mt. Washington strawberry is a moot question. The Mt. Washington strawberries form an arrangement of berries with leaves and blossoms that is certainly typical of Somerville, and perhaps Bunamo outdid himself on these occasions, leaving as an identifying mark those with the pale green leaves mentioned above.

C H I P   G R O U N D S—Mazerski says some of the weights with the chip grounds were made by Connie Mahoney.

L U T Z   W O R K—An indication that the paperweight work of Nicholas Lutz did not change appreciably from Sandwich through Somerville are a few weights whose flowers are identical with his Sandwich work but are Somerville-size weights bearing names in block capitals. One such poinsettia that is unmistakably Lutz reads above the flower "Eva St. Martin." Leffingwell says that Lutz made butterfly, fruit, and flower weights while at Somerville.[26] I have found no example of the butterfly.

Tiffany Paperweights (1885-1938)

Because Tiffany glass is very much in vogue and Tiffany paperweights are very few in number, they have been valued far beyond their merits as paperweights. One frequently hears the term "paperweight vase" applied to those Tiffany vases and bowls which incorporate inside the glass walls crude, daisy-like flowers in white and yellow, presumably in the hope that the linking of the two magic words Tiffany and paperweight will doubly enhance the market value of these fine pieces. Splendid examples of floral motifs in art glass, they bear only a vague relation to paperweights and should be left to speak for themselves as glass.

As in the so-called paperweight vases so in the Tiffany paperweights themselves one senses an attempt to create new effects, underwater effects, within this strict form. One feels that the flowers on their long, waving stems in the vases exist not within the glass walls of the vase but are immersed in the water that fills the vase. In the paperweights too, glass has been made to stand for water and we peek into an underwater world of mute sea creatures and waving fronds. The effect in both the vases and the weights is remarkable enough in itself to suggest a new direction for forms in glass. However, when placed alongside samples of Favrile glassware, representative of the major Tiffany output, the differences are obvious. For where the Favrile vase, goblet, or bowl is an object lesson in the successful union of surface texture and color to form, the paperweights and paperweight vases manifest stolidity of execution, in which the subject matter is imprisoned. The glass is simply too thick and heavy; the paperweight becomes a doorstop. One is reminded of the coagulated rhythms of Chavin ceramics, or of the small play afforded stained glass locked in massive Norman masonry. And yet, in their static bulk are trapped the seeds of a whole new concept of paperweight-making, which is only just now beginning to be practiced by glass craftsmen in Scandinavia and the United States.

Steuben

Frederick Carder was born in Brierley, Staffordshire, in the heart of the Stourbridge glass district, in 1863. Passing up an acceptance at both Oxford and Cambridge, he chose to shovel coal at his father's pottery works. Before he was twenty he became a designer of art glass and later an international salesman for the firm of Stevens and Williams. In 1903 with T. G. Hawkes he founded the Steuben works in Corning, New York, bringing over glassblowers from Sweden, France, and England. Shortages and essential industry priorities during the First World War forced the company to close in 1918, but it was then acquired by and became a subdivision of the Corning Glass Company, with Carder as its art director until 1934, when he retired. Carder continued his interest in glass and the glassworks until his death in 1963 at the age of one hundred.[27] The variety and excellence of his colored and decorated art glassware, including such famous patterns as Aurene, Jade, Cluthra, and Cintra are comprised in a body of creative glasswork the equal of any. Carder made some millefiori bowls and bottles after the Roman fashion, but is not known to have made any paperweights.

Paperweights were made at Steuben during the lunch hour but were never official products and never put on the market. No record of them was kept, though the "Home Sweet Home" type and a flower appear in the families of gaffers. John Sporer is said to have made paperweights whose motif is a large attractive, five-petaled flower that fills the 4¼-inch weight. The lily-like flower opens over a green mushroom, its petals purple edged with blue, blue edged with red, or green edged with orchid, a large bubble forming the flower center. One of these weights is signed "Steuben" (Fig. 222).[28] It is possible that they were made not by Sporer but by Tobias Hagberg, who is believed to have gone to Corning from Dorflinger when that factory closed in 1921. My reason for this assumption is that Hagberg's flower work at Dorflinger in both paperweights and inkwells could pass as the prototype for the Steuben weights.[29]

Fig. 222. Steuben lily signed on base "Steuben, Nov. 1941." *Courtesy Bergstrom Art Center and Museum.*

Other American Sources

In addition to the sources already considered in detail, glass paperweights were made widely in the last years of the nineteenth century in New York, New Jersey, Pennsylvania, Ohio, and Indiana.[30] Several patents for various paperweight designs, some of them the lily type, were secured. The lily form was very popular and so were those beds of granular chips of colored glass that formed the background for presentation and anniversary weights. There were also sulphides, forms pressed in molds, and some blown creations. But most of what was turned out was crude, tawdry, or oversentimental. The case of Fowlerton is a cautionary example.

The B. F. Leach Glass Company of Fowlerton, Indiana, was turning out paperweights from 1896 to 1898.[31] They were said to have been made by Leo. J. Ernst and Jean Annamaugh, of whom Leach said, "Ernst had the idea but Annamaugh was the artist."[32] Presentation weights bearing the inscriptions "To Mother," "My Father," "Home Sweet Home" were made from broken colored glass (much of it pink and yellow) bought from other factories at one cent per pound. Annamaugh used mineral ink to write names and inscriptions on the nameplates that were slices cut from white glass lampshades. The weights were shaped with a basswood mold. The clue to the quality of these weights lies in production statistics. Weights were sold at $2.50 per dozen. On a good day 150 weights could be made, and a total of some 20,000 to 25,000 were made.[33] They made them so fast they didn't even have time to grind off the pontil marks. Ettinger says, "Fowlerton also made mold-pressed weights of McKinley

and Bryan, the Presidential candidates of 1896."[34] Anyone who has seen a
Fowlerton weight will see the connection between production figures and
finished product—particularly the lily or fountain type. It would be difficult to
find a cruder, more unattractive weight. Fowlerton weights look as if they were
made under a leaky truck crankcase with the sole tool a tire air hose.

Canadian Paperweights

Though both quantitatively and qualitatively insignificant in comparison with
American production, there was considerable paperweight activity in Canada
during 1885-1915, particularly in Ontario and Quebec. Canadian and American
glassblowers frequently crossed the border to work in factories when there were
rush orders or breakdowns and a number of them acquired the knack of making
the simple lily and presentation weights and doorstops. Weights were made in
the Hamilton Glass Works, Hamilton, Ontario, by George Gardiner, William
McGinnis, Patrick Wickham, and George Mullin. "Nix" Daley made the big lily
doorsteps there.[35]

NOTES

[1] Helen and George S. McKearin, *Two Hundred Years of American Blown Glass,*
New York (ninth printing), 1958, p. 137.

[2] *Ibid.* The dates here are approximate and differ slightly with the source.

[3] Helen Barger, "The Two Dorflingers Who Cared," *The Glass Club Bulletin,*
Dec., 1966, p. 4.

[4] McKearin, *op. cit.,* p. 137.

[5] Barger, *op. cit.,* p. 4.

[6] Conversation and correspondence with Mrs. Barger. Janet Foster Newton, "Dorflinger Glass," *Antiques,* Jan., 1944, pp. 27–29.

[7] McKearin, *American Glass,* New York, 1956 edition; pp. 164, 165, 587, 588.

[8] Edward W. Minns, "Paperweight Making As Done At Millville," (Part I),
American Collector, Nov., 1938, p. 8.

[9] McKearin, *American Glass,* p. 588.

[10] Minns, *op. cit.,* p. 8.

[11] Minns, *op. cit.* (Part II), Dec., 1938, p. 10.

[12] McKearin, *American Glass,* p. 587.

[13] *Ibid.,* p. 164.

[14] Minns, *op. cit.* (Part I), pp. 8, 9.

[15] *Ibid.*

[16] Information in this synopsis is based on Kenneth M. Wilson, "The Mount Washington Glass Works And Its Successors, 1837–1958," *Antiques,* July, 1958, pp. 46–48. Wilson, glass expert and curator of the Corning Museum of Glass, is writing a book on the Mt. Washington.

[17] Letter to me from Victor Lutz.

[18] William E. Cross, *The Glass Club Bulletin,* Dec., 1954, p. 4. Cross and his wife had a large collection of paperweights. Also McKearin, *Two Hundred Years of American Blown Glass,* p. 326.

[19] A. C. Revi, *Nineteenth Century Glass,* p. 120.

[20] Wilson, *op. cit.,* p. 48.

[21] This information comes from Charles Kaziun.

[22] McKearin, *Two Hundred Years of American Blown Glass,* p. 140.

[23] McKearin, *American Glass,* p. 608.

[24] *Ibid.,* plate 68.

[25] Copy of a photograph from the company archives.

[26] B. H. Leffingwell, "Glass-Making at Somerville," *Hobbies,* Oct., 1962.

[27] *Frederick Carder And His Steuben Glass, 1903–1933,* The Rockwell Gallery, Corning, New York, 1966.

[28] Information comes from Robert F. Rockwell, a friend of Frederick Carder and owner of The Rockwell Gallery, Corning, N.Y. Sporer information was given by Anthony J. Hawkins to Paul Jokelson, who ran it in *The Newsletter of the Paperweight Collectors' Association,* Dec., 1965.

[29] Letter from Mrs. Frank Barger, who knew John Dorflinger and descendants of other workers.

[30] For example, The Brooklyn Museum has a dozen glass rods from the Clyde Glass Works, Clyde, New York, said to have been used to make paperweight designs.

[31] *Bulletin of the Art Institute of Chicago,* Sept.–Oct., 1938, p. 74.

[32] S. E. Leonardson, "Fowlerton Paperweights, B. F. Leach Glass Co.," *Hobbies,* Feb., 1944.

[33] *Ibid.*

[34] F. Sumner Ettinger, "Another Episode In Glass Paper Weight History," *Hobbies,* Nov., 1935, pp. 71, 72.

[35] *The Edith Crown Pierce and Gerald Stevens Collection of Early Canadian Glass,* Royal Toronto Museum, 1957.

17

SULPHIDES

WHILE IT MAY SEEM PUZZLING to paperweight students and enthusiasts that sulphides have not been considered in the chapters dealing with the factories making them, the reasons for a separate chapter lie in the special nature of the sulphide itself and in its antecedent history. A paperweight may contain a sulphide, but a sulphide itself is not a paperweight. Furthermore, most sulphides appear in objects other than paperweights, such as pendant plaques, scent bottles, tumblers, decanters, jewel boxes, knife rests, vases, ice plates, pitchers, and candlesticks.

The little white clay medallion relief plaques variously termed sulphides, cameos, cameo incrustations, or *crystallo-ceramie* would seem to have originated in Scotland, England, and Bohemia at roughly the same time in the last third of the eighteenth century, as expressions of the various neo-classicisms that were upon Europe at that time. To sense the reaction to the Baroque and Rococo, one has only to recall the excavations of Pompeii and Herculaneum, Robert Adam's return to Roman sources of design, the work of Wedgwood, particularly the invention of jasperware in 1774 and Wedgwood's copy in 1790 of the Barberini-Portland vase.[1] But it is probably to James Tassie of Edinburgh (1735–99) that credit for the first British sulphides is due. In 1763 Tassie had gone to Dublin where, with Dr. Henry Quin, he had invented a vitreous (glass) paste with which to imitate the ancient gem intaglios. These imitations were accomplished in a four-step process involving a relief impression in sulphur, taken directly from the intaglio gem, a plaster of Paris intaglio made from the sulphur relief, Quin's vitreous paste relief made from the plaster intaglio, and finally the resulting paste intaglios. In 1766 Tassie moved to London, where he made glass paste gems, both cameo (relief) and intaglio, which were then set by jewelers. He supplied molds to Wedgwood and made the first plaster casts of the Portland vase for Wedgwood. And he did many portraits from life in wax which were transformed by a similar but reverse process, in which the enamel paste could be made to resemble marble or precious stone in the final relief version. The extent of his production was noted in the Raspe catalogue of 1791—some 15,800 items. His work was carried on by his nephew William Tassie

(1777–1860).[2] And Honey says that after 1765 John Wilson also "made origi-nal portraits and copies of engraved gems in a white vitreous paste."[3] It is interesting to note that the Jews made artificial paste gems as early as the twelfth century,[4] and that as late as 1836 lead glass used for artificial gems was still known as "Jews Glass."[5]

James Tassie probably never left Great Britain, yet his influence on the neo-classic trend was felt on the Continent. Pazaurek in his *Die Gläser der Empire-und-Biedermeierzeit* mentions Tassie as one of several working to improve the shaping of "glass castings," which were beginning to supplant the older German forms.[6] And Honey refers to an engraved tumbler attributed to Saxony, which is "remarkable for a decoration of green and ruby paste gems set in its surface."[7] But it was Apsley Pellatt who credited a Bohemian manufac-turer with being the first to incrust in glass "small figures of greyish clay. The experiments which he made, were in but few instances successful, in conse-quence of the clay not being adapted to combine with the Glass."[8] That is, as Hughes put it, "distortion or cracking was always liable to occur during cooling, as the glass and clay possessed unequal powers of expansion and contraction."[9]

If the first attempts to enclose small clay medallions in glass originated in Bohemia, the idea must have traveled quickly from England and/or Bohemia to France, where the interest in the *verres de Bohême* was being superseded in the struggle to duplicate the English lead crystal, incidentally, a glass more enhanc-ing to whatever foreign matter might be embedded in it. At first the objects made appear to have been not much more than the clay medallion and the glass immediately enclosing it. The first known dated examples from France are a goblet in the Ceramic Museum at Sèvres, made by Henri-Germain Boileau in 1790 or 1796, in the bottom of which is embedded a sulphide of Voltaire, and a pair of medallions from the Boileau factory at Gros-Caillou near Paris whose sulphide profiles show, respectively, Franklin and Voltaire, who met in 1778. The medallions are inscribed "PB 1798." Boileau, incidentally, was making fili-gree and twist candlesticks in 1796.[10]

Sulphide cameo figures were incrusted in all sorts of glass objects with increasing frequency from 1800 until about 1830 when, under Louis-Philippe, there was a falling off in number and quality. During the Second Empire (1852–70) they disappeared completely.[11] Made as an adjunct to prints, sulphides served to reiterate the changing political attitudes, commemorative events, and the personages of the days before the firm establishment of the daguerreo-type. Models for the sulphide medallions were intaglio castings made from medals by the great engravers of the time such as Andrieu, Dubois, Duvivier, Gayrard, and Masson whose names, where they have not been trimmed off by the sulphide-maker in the separation of the portrait from its background, appear usually along the bottom edge of the sulphide. Though experiments in sulphide-making were many, the first recorded patent for perfecting (not for inventing) appears to have been secured in France in 1818 by Pierre Honoré Boudon de Saint-Amans (1774-1858). Saint-Amans' description of the process reads:

Prepare a copper mold, whose size and depth depends upon the size and thickness of the cameo to be incrusted. The first workman pours in molten crystal from his dipper; a second levels the surface with his copper palette knife and puts in the cameo, face downwards; a third workman pours more molten crystal on the back of the cameo, which is thus between two layers of crystal; the second man with his palette knife gently presses the mass in the mold. An apprentice carries the hot mold in a pair of tongs to the oven. Two minutes' baking generally is sufficient to set the crystal, no matter of what size the object.[12]

Compared to the method used by Apsley Pellatt, whose patent was acquired the next year, Saint-Amans' process sounds rather crude. Pellatt's Patent No. 4424, December 18, 1819, calls for "incrusting into glass vessels and utensils, white or other coloured, painted, or otherwise ornamented figures, arms, crests, cyphers, and any other ornaments made of composition metal, or other suitable material," for use in such solid glass bodies as "stoppers of bottles, decanters, door knobs, handles and knobs of vases, bellpulls, pillars, of candlesticks, and columns for clocks and other ornaments."[13] Pellatt describes his method in detail and it is worth transcribing here:

The figure intended for incrustation must be made of materials that will require a higher degree of heat for their fusion than the glass within which it is to be incrusted; these are china clay and super-silicate of potash, ground and mixed in such proportions as upon experiment harmonize with the density of the Glass.[14]

It is important to note that by "super-silicate of potash" is meant "sand exposed at high temperature in a crucible, with a small portion of carbonate of potash, sufficient to fuse it partially, for grinding into an impalpable powder." So we have as the composition of a sulphide, china clay mixed with sand and a flux of potash, in other words, a clay-glass paste. A sulphide cameo is not, as many used to think, a mysterious silver composition. The silvery look is imparted to the cameo by the pocket of glass, in which it is enclosed in the following process described by Pellatt. He says that the clay and super-silicate of potash mixture,

when moulded into a bas-relief or bust (in plaster of Paris moulds) should be slightly baked, and then suffered gradually to cool; or the cameos may be kept in readiness till required for incrustation, for which purpose they should be carefully reheated to redness in a small Stourbridge clay muffle. A cylindrical flint glass pocket is then prepared, one end adhering to the hollow iron rod, M, with an opening at the other extremity, into which the hot composition figure is introduced; the end, N, is then collapsed and welded together by pressure, at a red heat, so that the figure is in the center of the hollow glass pocket or muffle. The workman next applies his mouth at the end of the tube, O, while rewarming the glass at the other extremity; but instead of blowing, he exhausts the air, thus perfecting the collapse, by atmospheric pressure, and causing the Glass and composition figure to be of one homogeneous mass, as P.

INCRUSTATION METHOD

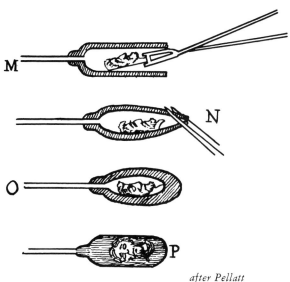

after Pellatt

The source of Pellatt's china clay is not mentioned, but the white sand he used in his glass is said to have been carried as ballast on the return voyages of wool-laden ships from Sydney, Australia.[15] So much for the composition of the sulphide and for the process of incrustation itself.

In addition to Saint-Amans, French sulphides were made by artists working mostly before the time of paperweights. One was the Parisian sculptor Desprez, associated with the pottery works at Sèvres (circa 1773–86), who moved to Paris about 1792, opening a factory for the manufacture of cameos and porcelain on the Rue de Recollets. Robiquet says that Desprez fils was making cameos for necklaces before 1806 and that in 1819 he put the cameos in glass.[16] Barrelet, however, credits the elder Desprez with incrusting sulphides in glass after 1792, which were first exhibited in 1806.[17] Mont-Cenis, La Vilette, and Creusot (before Baccarat and St. Louis teamed up in 1832 to close down Creusot) were all making sulphides. William E. Cross, who had a famous collection of paperweights, claimed that Creusot made sulphide paperweights.[18] And Martoret, a glasscutter and engraver, is said to have made cameo incrustations after 1823. A sulphide paperweight, signed "Martoret" on the reverse, shows a view of the building for The Great Exhibition of Industry of All Nations in London, 1851, with sky and lettering in powder blue. This rare weight is also signed "A.B. à

Paris." All these effects were sold along the Rue de la Paix and in the Palais-Royale by such leading dealers as L'Escalier de Crystal, Acloque, Schmitt, and Feuillet. Sometimes the name of a dealer or maker of sulphides appears on the back of the sulphide itself. Names in blue found on the beveled bottom edge of the portrait in paperweights are the names of the portrait subjects.

It must be remembered that only a small proportion of sulphides made in France and England were ever incorporated in paperweights. Pellatt himself made a few of what he called "letter-weights"—the early and short-lived term for paperweights—but these have flat 8-inch bases topped with an upright plaque containing the sulphide, flanked by large obelisks, and look more like overgrown knife rests than paperweights. Furthermore, in Pellatt's work the sulphide is always close to the surface, not deeply embedded as it is in a true paperweight. The sulphide work of Pellatt and most of his English and French contemporaries up to about 1840 does not even appear in paperweights and certainly has nothing to do with paperweights of the Victorian era. On the contrary, its neo-classic character is evident in both the imperial aspect of the sulphide reliefs themselves, even to the dress, coiffure, and bearing of the subjects, and in the formal style of the cutting of the glass, which is so inseparable an enhancement to the sulphide. Ray and strawberry diamond-cutting carried over to the paperweights of late Louis-Philippe, Napoleon III, and the Victorian Age, but the paperweight sulphide encircled by florets on a colored ground is a very different aesthetic creation from the neo-classic Empire or Regency sulphide medallion pendant or scent bottle.

The most complete study of French sulphides was made by J. P. Emperauger in a monograph of 1909 entitled "Embedded Glass and Crystal" and is recommended to the reader for what is necessarily eliminated from this present consideration. We will now proceed to a consideration of the sulphide paperweights of various countries.

French Sulphide Paperweights

EARLY EXAMPLES—Perhaps one of the earliest French sulphide paperweights is that of Madame de Sévigné, taken from a medal dated 1816 by Gayrard. Illustrated in Mrs. Bergstrom's *Old Glass Paperweights* as Fig. 36 in the 1948 edition, it shows the complete medallion, a practice usually abandoned in later paperweight-making where the head appears on cutout and the name of the sulphide maker is substituted for the medal engraver. The sides are cut with alternately plain and diamond-cut raised leaves to complete the neo-classic feeling—a superb sulphide and a superb paperweight, which the style of cutting would tend to place before 1830, though its success as a paperweight would indicate a later date.

A 4-inch magnum of clear but very sugary glass contains a large sulphide medallion commemorating the Baptism of L'Hip. Alb: Comte de Paris, 2 Mai,

1841, that is, Louis Philippe Albert, nephew of Louis-Philippe (1830–48). The sulphide is excellent but the weight itself shows inexperience in manipulating such a quantity of glass.

B A C C A R A T—Sulphide subjects include Aescalapius, Chateaubriand, Duc d'Orleans, Franklin (?), Hunter and Dog, Joan of Arc, Lamartine, Louis Napoleon, Louis-Philippe, the Madonna (with and without child; Col. Fig. 124), Napoleon I, Daniel O'Connell (1775–1847), St. Cecilia (on a cloud, playing the portative organ), St. Therese, St. Vincent de Paul, Czar Nicholas I, Victoria, Washington, and possibly Chopin, and others. Weights are about equally divided between clear glass and color grounds that include rich cobalt blue, translucent cranberry, translucent ruby, moss green, and possibly light opaque green. A few examples, particularly the Napoleon III and Victoria, have a circle or two of canes, but most are plain, and this is what chiefly distinguishes them from Clichy (Fig. 223).

The Joan of Arc (Col. Fig. 125) and the Hunter and Dog (Fig. 224) deserve special attention as perhaps the finest sulphides ever made. In these large (usually magnum), color ground weights something of the neo-classic feeling has been preserved in the triangular faceting, which extends from the flat top table to just above the base, where it cuts sharply inward to form a flat-bottomed pedestal base that is also faceted. The rather flat, translucent ruby, blue, or emerald ground occurs just at the point of deepest cutting, but do not think from this that the base is fused to the crown; it is not. Lying flush with the ground, a sulphide scene of the most remarkable delicacy, far removed from the old sulphide medallion, shows a hunter with gun accompanied by his stalking dog in a rural scene that includes two trees and considerable vegetation. The workmanship recalls the best of Bohemian (or any other) engraving, and we have to look closely to see that this is no engraving cut through ruby glass to clear glass, but a sulphide in which each leaf and reed is delineated as if by the most skillful glass engraver, or silhouette artist using scissors and paper. The effect is uncanny. How such perfection was nearly always achieved (I know of one cracked Joan of Arc) is a mystery. The Joan of Arc sulphide scene is equally wonderful (Fig. 225). Joan stands with head bowed, hands clasping her sword. Behind her is the plinth of a column, and about her a wreath of oak leaves and acorns, neo-classical devices that symbolize her agrarian background. It is simple, it is quiet, it evokes meditation on the event. In other respects the weight is similar to the **Hunter and Dog**, except that the **green ground** is sometimes a mossier tone. **Examples of both are known in clear glass.**

Other fine sulphide paperweights are the very few magnum double overlays in blue over white and deep rose over white, whose sulphide subject is Victoria or Victoria with Albert. Cutting in the former includes up to twenty-six printies, most of which reiterate the star-cut base, creating a feeling of great opulence. Victoria's profile appears as if in the pale, secluded light of a great pantheonic rotunda. In the blue over white Victoria-with-Albert examples, this effect is

223

224

225

diminished by the cutting away of the overlay between the top printies down as far as the girdle of the weight. Instead of being outside the rotunda, we are looking into a doll's house with the roof removed—the whole effect is lost.

Baccarat is also credited with embedding such other devices in paper-weights as a golden lyre, the Legion of Honor medal with and without ribbon, the arms of Pius IX, and other memorabilia appearing in clear glass with or without a circle of canes. These are actually made of gold leaf to which enam-eled colors have been applied. They are not sulphides and they are not the actual medals either. They are very small reproductions, as can be seen from the reverse side.

MODERN BACCARAT SULPHIDES—(See Chapter Eighteen.)

ST. LOUIS—Sulphide subjects include bouquet of flowers, carp, Josephine (?), Louis Napoleon (1848–52), Lamartine, Piux IX (one with green laurel wreath), and Czar Nicholas I (with laurel wreath) (Fig. 226). These weights sometimes include a circle of canes or spiral torsade, but are set in clear glass, and one wonders why St. Louis did not compete with Baccarat and Clichy in this area. Nevertheless, St. Louis did create its own form with the sulphide placed as the central motif of paneled carpet grounds. These include a few delicious small weights with miniature rectangular or circular, stippled-edge, sulphide medal-lions painted with bouquets of flowers (see Fig. 88), and two or three large carpet grounds featuring a sulphide profile cutout of what looks to be Josephine. In these absolutely spectacular weights the sulphide is enclosed in a thick, blood-red, jelly-like tube that imparts to the tiny sulphide head a surrealistic sen-sation of being both alive and dead, like a severed head. It is the surrealistic overtones coupled with the patriotic red-white-blue of the carpet panels of two of these weights that has urged upon the author the notion that the lady may not be Josephine at all but the spirit of France in the Revolution of 1848. This notion is mitigated somewhat by the third example, in which the crimped canes of the carpet ground are arranged in festoons suggesting the St. Louis marbrie weights.

The carp is a long, three-dimensional, silvery sulphide that floats straight across the weight. Examples are known in clear glass, on a mottled ground of blue or green, and with a double overlay of blue or green over white. The over-lay, cut with niches, covers only the bottom half of the weight, and the top half is a plain dome, a feature also noted in the large blue St. Louis clematis weights. The long fish usually has in its bite a tiny, bright red fish, which is typical carp behavior.

CLICHY—Sulphide subjects include Chateaubriand, Princess Eugénie, Alfred de Musset, Louis Philippe, Marie Antoinette, Napoleon I (Col. Fig. 126), St. Elizabeth, St. Eugénie, St. Palmire, St. Réné, St. Vincent de Paul, and Victoria

Fig. 223. Baccarat sulphide, Victoria. *Courtesy Sotheby & Co.*
Fig. 224. Baccarat sulphide, hunter and dog. *Courtesy Sotheby & Co.*
Fig. 225. Baccarat sulphide, Joan of Arc. *Courtesy Sotheby & Co.*

Fig. 226. St. Louis sulphide, Napoleon III, attractively faceted. *Courtesy Sotheby & Co.*

(Figs. 227, 228). There may be other subjects commonly attributed to Baccarat such as Franklin, Lafayette, and Washington (Figs. 229, 230). The distinguishing feature of Clichy sulphides is their presence in color grounds of pale, smoky green, apple green, sky blue, deep aquamarine and thalo blue, deep purple, ruby, and, most unusually, black, and in about half the examples a circle of large florets that is usually punctuated with Clichy roses. A superb magnum of Marie Antoinette, her coiffure resplendent, is set in a translucent green ground with a circle of twenty-four Clichy roses, six all-white and eighteen green and white. Napoleon I appears both in profile and in a full figure representation of the characteristic pose, hand in vest—an awesome weight. The sulphide of Victoria as a young woman appears in clear glass and in a stunning black ground surrounded by canes, a very formal yet fetching weight.

All opaque Clichy grounds, it should be noted from below, are perforated at the center.

British Sulphide Paperweights

Sulphide subjects include only a small portion of the portraits known to British sulphides generally. One sees chiefly Albert, Victoria, and Wellington (deep blue ground), the latter a product of Allen & Moore[19] signed "A & M." Early, neo-classic sulphides include a number of circular and octagonal sulphide double medallions that are cemented back to back, with a profile from antiquity on one side and a classical Greek or Roman scene on the other, the medallions fre-

Fig. 227. Clichy sulphide, Alfred de Musset. *Courtesy Parke-Bernet Galleries, Inc.*
Fig. 228. Clichy sulphide, Marie Antoinette. *Courtesy Corning Museum of Glass.*
Fig. 229. Clichy sulphide, George Washington. *Courtesy Parke-Bernet Galleries, Inc.*
Fig. 230. Clichy sulphide, Benjamin Franklin. *Courtesy Parke-Bernet Galleries, Inc.*

227

228

229

230

quently painted with a thin blue or acid green border. These weights are small, very heavy, and attractively cut. One example shows traces of the rougelike substance that was frequently used as a means of preventing the sulphide from adhering to the mold. Another Allen & Moore weight made to commemorate the Great Exhibition is a sulphide circular medallion whose upper panel shows a view of the Crystal Palace topped by the words "The building at London for the International Exhibition, 1851," the lower panel with a tiny profile portrait of Victoria and Albert, flanked by putti, the panels divided by the inscriptions "J. Paxton, Esq. Architect" and "Allen & Moore" (see Fig. 13). The sulphide appears in clear glass up to 3 inches in diameter and also on blue or amber translucent grounds. Another signed "Allen & Moore product" contains a circular sulphide medallion with a full portrait of Edward VII as a boy in naval costume beside an anchor, the inscription reading "Britain's Hope, The Prince of Wales." Hughes says that from about 1875 John Ford & Company of Edinburgh made "exquisite crystal cameo paperweights" and other items "closely resembling that of the Apsley Pellatt glass of 1820." And that sulphide cameos of Victoria were embedded in cube paperweights to commemorate her Jubilee of 1887, "but the majority display a slight flaw in the cameo."[20] The author has not seen them. Hughes also lists a series of medallion paperweights (not sulphides) in which portraits of Victoria, Albert, Robert Peel, and the Duke of Wellington were impressed into glass, leaving an intaglio impression which was then dipped in hydrofluoric acid.[21] These, he said, were made by William Kidd of 12 Poland Street, London, and by F. & C. Osler and Lloyd & Summerfield of Birmingham. Their subject matter and the elaborate cutting of the borders would distinguish them from Gillinder products.

Belgian Sulphides

Subjects include Joan of Arc, Charles X (with barber-pole spiral from Val St. Lambert), Christ on the Cross (on mottled ground from Chénée, end of the nineteenth century, see Fig. 188), a hand holding a rose inscribed "Amitíe."

Bohemian Sulphides

Sulphides are known in goblets about 1830, but no paperweights have come to light.

Czechoslovakian Sulphides

This country is territorially coextensive with the old Bohemia. Many sulphide paperweights were made here during the brief period of the Czechoslovakian Republic (1918-35). These are large, flat-bottomed, high-domed (3½-4 inches), faceted weights of slightly yellowish-brownish lime-potash glass containing few swirls but myriad tiny bubbles. The sulphide motif, which may be a doe, stag, bear, lion, dog, two dogs, rooster, eagle, monkey, swan, elephant, bust of a lady, or dwarf, is usually big and always three-dimensional and varies in workmanship between simple and crude. It always rests upon a cushion (sometimes high) of multicolored glass chips laced with veins of another color. The simplicity or crudity of its detail is enhanced or masked by the flat faceting of the weight, which gives it the aspect of a huge gem. In some weights the outer glass at the base is decorated with repeated festoons in such gaudy colors as orange, cerise, and magenta which fairly scream the weight's presence.

Scandinavian Sulphides

There is the possibility of sulphide work here after 1820, though the scent bottles and other glass trinkets may have been made in France. One large paperweight is known to me; its subject, a thick sulphide medallion of King Carl XIV Johan of Sweden and Norway (1818-44), which rests on a moss green and red spatter ground. The medallion, signed "Parse F.," is based on a medal cut in 1821 by the French medalist Jean Jacques Barre and struck at the personal expense of Carl Johan, who had a collection of similar sulphides.[22]

American Sulphides

These include portraits of Victoria, with and without Albert, Kossuth of Hungary, and a double portrait of Harrison and Monroe (on black ground) all said to be from the New England Glass Company (Figs. 231, 232). I have found no evidence of this, though it seems a plausible attribution. From Pairpoint comes a profile portrait of General Nathan Forrest and another of Robert E. Lee, both on a small red-white-blue spoke ground. Bakewell, Page & Bakewell in Pittsburgh made sulphides as early as 1839, but whether they later made sulphide paperweights is not known.[23] American sulphide paperweights abound that cannot be pinpointed. Some feature Washington, Lincoln, and Harrison. Others show a bird with a goldstone eye on a mottled chip ground. The workmanship of most of these is very poor and the glass resembles stagnant water.[24]

Two sulphides in The Art Institute of Chicago are fascinating (Figs. 233, 234). Both are heads of women modeled in high relief, wearing the coiffure and bonnets of the 1850's, with details such as the eyes, eyebrows, ribbons, and bonnet flowers painted amateurishly in color. There is a carnival atmosphere in these weights with the well-fed, mannequin faces thrust forward in the magnifying glass. It is as if their creator had said, "You think you've seen sulphides? Ladies and gentlemen, they are as nothing compared with my *big, individual, lifelike, three-dimensional, portrait heads!* Looka them expressions! Looka them hairdos!"

Fig. 231. New England Glass Company, sulphide, Victoria and Albert. *Courtesy Parke-Bernet Galleries, Inc.*

Fig. 232. New England Glass Company, sulphide, Monroe and Harrison. *Courtesy Sotheby & Co.*

Figs. 233, 234. American sulphides. *Courtesy The Art Institute of Chicago.*

NOTES

[1] *The Story of Wedgwood, 1730-1930,* Cambridgeshire, 1930, pp. 25, 27.

[2] John M. Gray, *James & William Tassie,* Edinburgh, 1894, pp. 6–11, 26.

[3] W. B. Honey, *Glass,* Victoria and Albert Museum, 1946, p. 120.

[4] *Ibid.,* p. 3.

[5] J. A. Knowles, *Journal of the Royal Society of Arts,* Vol. LXII (1914), p. 570.

[6] Pazaurek, *Die Gläser der Empire-und-Biedermeierzeit,* p. 293.

[7] Honey, *op. cit.,* p. 90.

[8] Apsley Pellatt, *Curiosities of Glass-Making,* London, 1849, pp. 28, 29.

[9] G. Bernard Hughes, "English Crystal Cameos," *Country Life,* June, 1949, p. 1304.

[10] James Barrelet, *La Verrerie en France,* pp. 135, 203, where differing dates are given. Pazaurek, *op. cit.,* p. 294.

[11] J. P. Emperauger, "Embedded Glass & Crystal" (published Paris, 1909, as "Verres et Cristaux incrustes"), *Bulletin,* 1959, Chapter Two.

[12] Mary Martin, "The Crystal Cameos of France," *House and Garden,* Dec. 1926, illus.

[13] British Patent Records.

[14] Pellatt, *op. cit.,* pp. 119, 120. The whole explanation is contained in these pages.

[15] Bernard and Therle Hughes, *After The Regency,* London, 1952, p. 148.

[16] Jacques Robiquet, *L'Art et le Goût Sous la Restauration, 1814–1830,* Paris, 1928.

[17] James Barrelet, *op. cit.,* Paris, 1953, p. 173.

[18] *The Glass Club Bulletin,* No. 37, Dec. 1954, p. 3.

[19] Allen & Moore were not makers of paperweights. They are listed in Kelly's Post Office London Directory for 1854, p. 687, as "manufacturers of buttons, vesta boxes, candle lamps, ink stands and fancy articles in metal, papier mache etc. and medallions, 60 Aldermanbury." They were probably merely the distributors of these weights.

[20] Hughes, *op. cit.,* p. 150.

[21] *Ibid.,* p. 151.

[22] Ida Polak, "Sulphides & Medals," *Journal of Glass Studies,* Vol. VIII, 1966, pp. 116–19.

[23] William E. Cross, "Paperweights," *The Glass Club Bulletin,* No. 37, Dec., 1954, p. 4.

[24] Perhaps these are the ones Mrs. Bergstrom thought were made by Washington Beck during the 1870's at the Curling & Pierce factory in Pittsburgh. She both commends and disparages them. Evangeline Bergstrom, *Old Glass Paperweights* (1948 ed.), New York, p. 94.

18

MODERN PAPERWEIGHTS

THE IMPLICATION OF THE USE of new techniques embodied in the so relative term "modern" makes it difficult to discern with any precision the onset of a modern period of paperweight-making. We enter the first decade of the twentieth century with an inherited residue of paperweight-making that derives from the Classic period and continues right up to the present. Upright flowers from Millville, though different in appearance and in the fact that a crimp was used, are still in the old tradition. One sees the first evidences of new technical approaches to glass in the paperweights of Tiffany (see Chapter Sixteen) and in those of Maurice Marinot in France, an example of which is in the Corning Museum of Glass. Marinot (1882-1960), once a Fauve painter, turned to glass in 1911. Working in that medium through the late 1930's, he exploited the deficiencies of the material at his disposal in a glass bottle factory, combining rough glass with metallic oxides and artificially induced bubbles.[1] His paperweight shows a complete break with Classic tradition.

But as is so often the case with innovators, the signposts of Tiffany and Marinot were unheeded and the new road untraveled—instead of adventure we had a return to Victorian orthodoxy.

Czechoslovakia

During the period of the Czechoslovakian Republic (1918-38) a fair number of big, tall (3½ inches), flat-bottomed, sulphide paperweights were made in which the upright, three-dimensional, rather crude but very effective sulphide was set on a flat ground or raised cushion of partially bled, colored glass chips. Though the somewhat light glass is apt to be yellowish in cast and filled with myriad, infinitesimal bubbles, the fauna subject matter (described in Chapter Seventeen) and the overall flat faceting of these weights (as if they were huge gems) are appealing. One might almost be looking at a branch of folk art. Considerably less appealing are the ones whose upright motif is a black and white or sepia photograph of Thomas Masaryk (Czechoslovakia's founder and first President), or anonymous persons transferred to a ceramic plaque. These lack the charm of the American Civil War daguerreotypes and look like icons from the parlor of a psychic medium. Czechoslovakia today is producing smaller but tall, bullet-shaped weights with the same facet treatment, in which the motif is three or more long-stemmed flowers springing from a colored chip ground or a flowerpot. The sometimes soft, sometimes rather hard, colors are appealing and the execution of the flowers is good but the glass appears to be cullet with a dark cast to it (Fig. 235).

The return to Classic style paperweight-making in the late 1920's and early 1930's could hardly be called a Renaissance in the historical, artistic sense of the word; it was nothing more than a desire on the part of clever and farsighted

Fig. 235. Czech faceted flower weight (1920–25). *Courtesy Museum of Industrial Art, Prague Czechoslovakia.*

manufacturers to make paperweights that would be taken by an ignorant public for old. Nor was there anything new about such an attempt. "Art collecting," writes the famous French auctioneer Maurice Rheims, "involves a permanent conflict between what the eye sees and what it reads, between instinct and scientific research."[2] Rheims is speaking of art forgeries. He says that instinct may detect the fake where in cases of clever forgery, even scientific tests may not. For the forger of something antique can never quite duplicate or recapture the fashion of a previous day. Of course, modern weights passed off as old by some ignorant or eager dealer are not forgeries in the counterfeiting sense of close imitation, for the simple reason that close imitation has not been possible with the knowledge and equipment available to modern would-be fakers. In fact, the secret ingredient of the spurious "old" weight has been public ignorance.

Baccarat

The millefiori garland and pansy weights made by Dupont at Baccarat in the late 1920's and early 1930's are a case in point.[3] Dupont was obviously working at that factory under the protection of the management. His work shows that he was doing everything he could to recapture the spirit if not the letter of the Classic Baccarat weights, and his near success is testimony to his skill. Yet the trained eye spots the difference immediately—the color schemes of the canes, magnifying properties of the glass, shapes of the weights, all are different. The lower petals of the pansy, for example, are amber instead of yellow. Baccarat sold these weights through a small retail shop next to the Hôtel Montalembert until about 1933 or 1934 when Dupont died. But it is significant to note that those millefiori and pansy weights in which Dupont, through ignorance or pure whim, inserted canes bearing such impossible dates as 1815, 1837, etc., were not sold in this shop. Revelli says Baccarat pansies were still being made in two sizes as late as 1941.[4] And in its most recent revival of millefiori techniques Baccarat has been most careful to date its weights properly and to see to it that the new figure canes cannot possibly be confused with the old.

The revival began about 1947 with the making of a few simple millefiori weights by Georges Brocart, but got its impetus in 1951 with the discovery of a Baccarat weight dated 1853 in the cornerstone of the bombed-out church at Baccarat. In 1953 a suphide, the first of a continuing series, was made to commemorate the coronation of Queen Elizabeth II. By 1957 millefiori production was under way, first with the close millefiori of Brocart and later of Roland Guignon. These contain modern simplified approximations of the old canes interspersed with rather modern canes bearing signs of the zodiac and a figure 8, intended to protect the unwary from dealers who might be inclined to pass them off as old weights. Though pleasantly colored, with an overall tonality of pinks sprinkled with pastel blues and greens, the close millefiori are uninteresting, with no distinction to the individual canes, no lovely passages such as one always finds in the old weights from Baccarat. In addition to this "large economy" line of close millefiori there is a smaller "standard" line of spaced concentrics with small, thin, pastel-colored canes that bleed and swim a bit before the eyes.

The company has, meanwhile, put out an astonishing roster of sulphide subjects, beginning with the attractive signs of the zodiac series, first on a woolly, pale blue ground and later on a rich, cathedral-window, cobalt-violet, flat, translucent ground. Sulphide profiles, more than twenty of them, have included such assorted subjects as Washington, Jefferson, Lee, Lafayette, Franklin, Lincoln, Pope Pius XII, Pope John XXIII, Churchill, Eisenhower, Martin Luther, Sam Rayburn, Prince Philip with Queen Elizabeth, and, of course, Kennedy. (Not to be outdone by Baccarat, Murano has come up with a plausible sulphide head of President Kennedy inappropriately overlaid in pink and baby blue.) The Baccarat sulphides come on color grounds and with a variety of simply and elaborately faceted single and double overlays too numerous to describe. The sulphides were made from reliefs by medalists Gilbert Poillerat and Albert David, and painter Dora Maar. Though the faces of the old historical characters are more precisely chiseled than the faces of the recent great, all are more or less simplifications verging on caricature (*e.g.* Franklin's wattle and Jefferson's bowsprit nose), and the sulphide surface itself looks more like magnesium or mat aluminum than silver. One of the more attractive is the three-quarter-view bust of Lafayette by Poillerat—a younger, trimmer Lafayette than the portly profile we are accustomed to see in the old sulphides. The flat bases of these and most other modern Baccarat weights are lightly etched with a small circle enclosing the words "Baccarat, France," and a decanter flanked by a tumbler and goblet. A specified but easily adequate number is produced of each sulphide subject and type of weight treatment, following the completion of which the molds are ceremoniously disfigured.[5]

St. Louis

For a short period beginning in 1952 St. Louis revived the old styles of paperweight-making from its Classic days. Like Baccarat they made a sulphide of Queen Elizabeth II for her coronation. Other productions include a number of superbly executed millefiori concentrics, concentric pedestal weights with latticinio and twist ribbons, flowers singly and in pairs set in clear glass or on mottled color grounds accompanied by a dragonfly, mixed fruits and cherry sprigs in loosely woven latticinio double-swirl baskets, a shot cup signed and dated 1953 with crown paperweight base. One brilliant weight shows bright orange carrots in a real three-dimensional blue basket on a parrot-green, translucent ground. An enormous magnum encloses a riotous bouquet in high relief (Col. Fig. 127). Still another fruit weight shows green pears and ultramarine blue cherries in the usual basket. Fruits and flowers come in unusually bright, almost fluorescent colors. The petals of a single flower, for example, may be alternately ruby and wild, chartreuse yellow. The latticinio is wide and bold, tightly knit in the best examples, but often loose, off center, and sloppy. A small SL and the date 1952 or 1953 appear in numerous examples. St. Louis made double overlays in deep green, red, and rich cerulean blue whose motif is a very tightly formed, thin-stemmed, close millefiori mushrooms composed of very small canes, the canes pulled down to form the tapering stem. Though finely done, the pale canes are really too small to see. Some examples are elaborately faceted, the whole top of the weight being a deeply cut star.

Easily the finest postwar St. Louis productions, far superior to anything appearing from Baccarat and on a technical par with Classic examples, are the modern upright bouquets. One clear glass magnum dates from about 1953 (Col. Fig. 127). The most recent, signed and dated 1965, are remarkable indeed for their rich color and precision. One example is faceted in a modern manner, another overlaid with a deep aqua flash, a third double overlaid in cerulean over white. Small rods show the cross of St. Louis.

China

Unlike Baccarat and St. Louis, which have only been turning out modern versions of and variations on their own former products, China during the 1930's produced a number of genuine fakes. According to Robert A. Elder, Jr., of the Smithsonian, who made a study of modern Chinese paperweights, ". . . several American import dealers, who had direct contact with Chinese sources, sent fine old weights to China for the express purpose of having them copied during the 1930's when the better Western items were becoming scarce."[6] Elder goes on to describe the light, yellowish, greasy-to-the-touch, soda-lime glass unforgettable to anyone who has ever held and felt a Chinese weight. The types copied included the Baccarat pansy, Millville rose, Sandwich poinsettia, the New England bouquet, and a rare yellow and copper-petaled flower, also from Baccarat. The bouquet on double-swirl latticinio ground from Cambridge is faceted with a quatrefoil of interlocking printies in the New England way, but the Chinese made the mistake of applying the Cambridge faceting to the Baccarat pansy. No student of paperweights could mistake the copies for the originals. The motif appears through a fog of "sick" glass, flower colors are garish, and the latticinio watery. The "Millville rose," touching the bottom of the weight, is likely to be waxy or muddy looking, and the Chinese outdid themselves when they made a blue rose.

Other Chinese weights include a variety of millefiori concentrics and clusters on a convoluted double cushion of opaque yellow or white latticinio swirl (the canes ranging from delicate to crude), a sea anemone in a small cube-shaped weight, three birds in a coral-red tree (faceted with touching square printies), a lotus in vermilion and yellow bursting from an opaque white pot calligraphically streaked with red, green, and blue, and a doorstop with an African daisy above several tiers of Chinese-vegetable green leaves from a similar pot. This flower comes in coral, mauve, and dirty yellow. Painted weights embrace a variety of scenes and landscapes painted in the oriental manner with colored inks on white ground (the ground inside the weight). One shows a grasshopper in a thicket, another a full-rigged clipper ship with waves, that harks back to the days of the China trade (Fig. 236). Miniature painted sulphides are a frog and two ducks.

Later Chinese weights, probably made until recent years, include an enormous number of close millefiori, concentrics, and scrambled weights in Chinese-vegetable green, vicious orange, and bilious yellow, though occasionally they are found in pale pink, mauve, and green.

The glass enclosing Chinese weights is so poor, probably from too much alkali, that a pleasant motif is obscured. But one painted floral motif on a bright white ground is enhanced by a lens of limpid glass and rivals French work (Col. Fig. 128).

Japan

The only thing worse than the late Chinese weights are the contemporary Japanese. These are of three types: small lilies rising from an amorphous colored ground, macerated slices of cane floating aimlessly in clear glass, and the snowstorm weights in which plastic figures are caught in a momentary snow flurry of green detergent.

America

United States paperweight production in modern times has been enormous. Yet, with the exception of the work of Charles Kaziun, American paperweight-makers have produced little of aesthetic value since the days of Millville, Somerville, and Steuben.

Prolific but uncomplicated production has come from such places as the Gentile Glass Company of Star City, West Virginia, Degenhart's Crystal Art Glass of Cambridge, Ohio, Glass Handicrafters of Corydon, Indiana, and other

Fig. 236. Chinese clipper ship. *Private collection. Photograph by Taylor & Dull.*

Midwestern sources.[7] A wide range of subject matter from homely mottoes in the old Millville tradition, flat subjects such as butterflies, flying geese, the American flag, to various upright lily forms, punctuated with large bubbles, leaves the viewer unexcited. A few items, such as the Degenhart and John Gentile roses, which are similar to the earlier roses of Philip Bunamo of Somerville and are mottled variations of the Millville rose and crocus, show an effective restraint. The same is occasionally true of a rather thin, watery, but delicate lily in a cube weight flashed with amber, blue, or purple that was made by John Degenhart and also at Ravenna, Ohio (Fig. 237). But generally one may say that the motif is rather primitive and the colors either bland or garish.

Also operating are a number of makers whose individual predilections among the simplest of approaches can be identified only with difficulty. Most of these are apparently content with the "ice pick" method of insertion in the pseudo-floral motifs whose festooned and lily-like forms may be seen in the gift shops, along with other American weights and penholders featuring a symmetrical arrangement of bubbles, and those epidemic creations from Murano.

Fig. 237. Degenhart or Ravenna cube weight, blue flash. *Courtesy The Art Institute of Chicago.*

Technically far superior to all this, though still retrograde, is the work of Hacker, Thompson, Whittemore, and Hansen. Harold J. Hacker of Bueno Park, California, has imprisoned in glass beautifully made small lampwork lizards that appear alive on sand grounds. The offhand weights of George Thompson at Steuben approximate but do not equal the old Steuben lilies, while his regular paperweight work for that company is necessarily limited by the company's proscription against the use of color. F. D. Whittemore, Jr., of Lansdale, Pennsylvania, a glassblower with twenty years' experience blowing chemical and medical glass, some of it tiny scale models, has turned to paperweights, particularly to the problem of the rose, which Kaziun solved years ago, and whose early work Whittemore's resembles. Whittemore roses in several colors, accompanied by leaves and signed "W" on the bottom of the motif, are set in footed weights and perfume bottles, some of which are engraved. In some instances, crocus-like flowers appear in bottle stoppers whose graceful taper plays interesting tricks with the image. Ronald E. Hansen of Mackinaw City, Michigan, is another relative newcomer to paperweights. Unlike Whittemore, who works to perfect each type of blossom before attempting the next, Hansen has tried everything almost at once. Using rather hard colors and not very luminous glass, Hansen has overrun the lush fields of flowers and fruits on color grounds and has even coupled the apple with the serpent. Occasionally the workmanship is good and the coloring sensitive, but the weights are generally too low in the crown, which gives them a stunted appearance, and the faceting is poorly done.

There are, nevertheless, a few hopeful signs in American paperweight-making. Dominik Labino of Grand Rapids, Ohio, is tinting his metal various colors. And there are a number of young glassblowers who, like Harvey Littleton of Verona, Wisconsin, began as potters, and who have carried over into glass, including paperweights, some of the free forms of the Raku pottery tradition. Their weights are apt to be asymmetrical in shape and to contain large bubbles and spongelike concentrations. Finally, in another direction, there is Bill Sydenstricker of Brewster, Massachusetts, whose main production is plates and bowls of laminated window glass. His paperweights are laminated, five-decker sandwiches of colored glass, sometimes enclosing thin slices of millefiori rod, copper screen wire, or other abstract design elements, and are fired in a kiln for several hours at 1500 degrees before fusion of the layers takes place.

KAZIUN—We are fortunate to be able to see in our time the successive accomplishments of a great craftsman as they come from the annealing kiln, for the technical excellence—one may justifiably call it perfection—of Kaziun's paperweights is on a comfortable par with fine work from the Classic period. Like all boys with the creative urge, Charles Kaziun was a self-taught eavesdropper, learning his art from a family of traveling glassblowers who came each year to the fair in Brockton, Massachusetts, Kaziun's hometown. After he finished high school in 1937, Kaziun's knowledge of glassblowing got him a job blowing ampules in a small establishment in New York. Returning to Brockton, he went in business for himself, blowing scientific glass, until a dealer in antiques brought him a "paperweight" button to copy. His glassblowing ability brought him a job with the very family of blowers on whom he had eavesdropped, and his buttons brought him to the attention of James D. Graham, "the best blower of scientific instruments in this country," whose assistant Kaziun became.[8] Graham encouraged Kaziun to continue making and selling his paperweight buttons, and when Kaziun met Emil Larson and saw his first Larson rose, he must have known what his life's work would be. Kaziun made his first Kaziun rose in 1942.

The range of Kaziun's paperweight work, probably greater than that of any individual among the glass artists of the Classic period is, like the man himself, enormous. It includes, in addition to the paperweight buttons, weights of all sizes up to 3 inches, plain, footed, and pedestal, millefiori concentrics on muslin, goldstone, and other grounds of such unusual colors as amethyst and forest green, weights with snakes, flower weights, perfume bottles, and double, even triple overlays in all colors, including orange and yellow (Col. Fig. 129). A triple overlay of red over white over an inner turquoise blue is duplicated only by St. Louis. So delicate and sure is the touch of this huge man that he has made a double overlay complete with minuscule interior motif that measures only half an inch in diameter. Kaziun's millefiori work is spiced with silhouette canes of his own design: the little vermilion heart, the outlined sitting rabbit, the turtle (Col. Fig. 130), the golden bee, the whale, and of course his own signature "K," sometimes surrounded by yellow rods tipped with orange hearts, which invariably appears on the bottom side of his motifs (Fig. 238).

After perfecting his various roses, Kaziun went on to make a series of flower weights, both flat and upright, that rival the finest from Classic France. There are the pansy, its lower petals marked with the crowsfoot (arrow) as in the same from Baccarat—so simple looking and so difficult to make; the opaque yellow and white daffodils (though Kaziun works "off the rod," he does not, as has been speculated, use Chinese opaque yellow rods); the hibiscus, the pleated petaled dogwood, the tulip, pond lily, crocus, the blue-and-white striped morning glory, trailing naturally about a white trellis on a violet-purple ground, its pollen sampled by the golden bee. In the pedestal weights the flowers are tilted about 45 degrees for easy viewing. Kaziun's control of color is extraordinary— he regrets the acceptance with which mistakes in color, as for example a rose pink that turns bluish red, are considered rare and become a fad. In his flower weights one sees subtle petal coloring at its best. Not earthbound to nature, because the flower centers are usually millefiori rods or canes, the flowers breathe the air that angels breathe.

It took a week for the old New England weavers to make enough yarn for a yard of material. It takes Kaziun a week to make enough muslin for the ground of one weight. Prolific though he is, everything is done with loving care. Even his glass is a special formula (close to Clichy), arrived at after diligent research. He finds it easier to homogenize than lead glass and free of the cordes and striae that result from difficulty of a proper lead mix and its corrosive effect upon the surface of the pot.

If there could be any criticism of Kaziun's work, it would be that it is con-

Fig. 238. Kaziun perfume bottle. *Courtesy Bergstrom Art Center and Museum.*

temporary but not modern. One sees small pedestal after pedestal turned out with monotonous perfection. Difficult as the procedures may be for mortal man, they are clearly too easy for Kazuin. One wishes he would turn his creative imagination toward the new possibilities of design inherent in the technical knowledge and facilities he possesses and come up with something of our time for our time.

Scotland

For many years there has been considerable paperweight activity in Scotland, beginning with the work of Paul Ysart (described below) and continuing in the work of his brothers. Ysart Brothers of Perth, Scotland, made cheap paper-weights in the Paul Ysart manner but lacking the technical perfection of those fine weights. The company was called the Vasart Glass Company, and during the 1950's and early '60's all manner of millefiori concentrics from miniature to large were turned out. Miniature weights frequently appeared glued to metal shafts as bottle openers, stirring spoons, corkscrews, and other bar equipment. The light, frequently tinted glass covered small, crudely simple canes of a porce-lanous opacity tinted with thin coatings of pale pastel colors and set in grounds textured like felt. At the end of 1964 the Vasart Glass Company was re-formed as Strathearn Glass Ltd. and moved to Crieff, Scotland. "The new company," a brochure reads, "employs the same craftsmen under the guidance of Mr. Vincent Ysart, and will continue the old tradition of hand made glassware and Millefiori specialties."

The Strathearn weights are a distinct improvement over the Vasart. The contours of the canes are more definite and though they still have a bone-dry look, they are coated with exquisite colors of a range unique in the history of paperweight-making. The motifs, usually radiating from a hub cane in the Paul Ysart manner, are precisely organized and set on colored grounds of great variety from the palest gray through deep maroon, navy blue, and black. Some weights are obviously made in molds in the shape of a star, and one suspects that others are at least partially molded.

Y S A R T—Paul Ysart, whose father and grandfather were master glassblowers, was born in Barcelona, Spain, in 1904. Moving with his family to France, Paul Ysart got his apprenticeship at St. Louis. The father moved to Scotland in 1915, where he joined the Leith Flint Glassworks in Edinburgh and Paul later assisted him there, specializing for a time in scientific glass, much as Kaziun had done.[9]

In range and quality, Ysart's work closely parallels that of Kaziun, though the stamp of his personality upon the motifs is completely different and Ysart does not appear to have become interested in three-dimensional flowers, prefer-ring designs that are flush with the ground. The majority of the weights are pat-terned millefiori, with a somewhat lesser number devoted to single flowers and bouquets, butterflies, dragonflies, fish, and a large cross made of flower petals like the one from Cambridge. The flat motifs are set somewhat above mottled, translucent grounds in deep blues, purples, reds, and greens, but absolutely flush with smooth or mottled opaque grounds in a variety of colors ranging from pastel pinks and blues to sand color and wild orange. Millefiori canes are a sim-plification of the St. Louis canes, composed of crimped, cogged, and petaled rods and are arranged in a variety of concentric and other patterns whose most notable characteristic is an alternation of canes with short lengths of colored fili-gree rod, set like the spokes of a wheel. Though lengths of colored filigree are seen in uncommon Clichy chequer weights, their use by Ysart as a design ele-ment equal in importance to the canes themselves is unique in paperweight-making. They do not form the ground as in Clichy but are sunk into it intaglio, which gives the filigree a three-dimensional life and sparkle it would not otherwise have. A signed cane bearing the initials "PY" appears in many but by no means all of the finer weights sent to the United States; it seldom shows up in weights sold in Europe. Flat flowers of the clematis and daisy type stand out well against the rich, brilliant grounds. Occasional tiny bouquets are seen well above the ground and framed in a circle of florets. The butterflies and dragonfly, similar to but much bolder than the French, are also better executed (Col. Fig. 131). Bodies may be red- or green-coated goldstone, antennae are thick but absolutely symmetrical, and wings are shaped canes. The flat fish with open mouth, goldstone fins and tail is equally well done. The fish and particularly the flowers are sometimes enclosed by a three-dimensional basket of white or pale yellow filigree tubes that form a hemisphere from the base of the weight.

A variation of this attractive form appears in one of the most remarkable paperweights I have ever seen. It features a bold butterfly with pink and amber wings, orange body, and pea-green antennae, surrounded by a circle of red and white canes. This ensemble is placed upon a tall cushion that fills the weight (Col. Fig. 132). This fantastic cushion is composed of an opaque white chambered nautilus whose hemitubed chambers are neatly and exactly filled with continuous, blue, spiral filigree rods, the filigree passing under the circle of canes as they spiral downward to an intricate pattern on the bottom of the weight. The contrast of bold butterfly against gossamer filigree is breathtaking. This is adventuresome paperweight-making and one would like to see more of it from both Ysart and Kaziun, the only two artists alive who are capable of such feats.

Germany

Before the First World War the Germans made a few small millefiori weights in which the crude canes in red, a dead blue, and bile yellow were poorly set in the lowest grade of cullet. Today they are making clear glass weights with a yellowish cast, enclosing lily-like agglomerations of colored chips, neatly formed and placed, but very uninteresting.

Holland

Some not very successful experimentation here with new paperweight shapes formed of glass casually seeded with color and long ovoid bubbles.

Venice

The visitor to Venice does not have to seek out paperweights, they seek him out. They are everywhere: in the countless glass shops that stay open until eleven at night, even for sale on a table set up on the grass in front of the old cathedral on Torcello. In his thoroughly delightful book on Venice James Morris says, "The important thing to know about the Murano glass-makers is that almost everything they make is, at least to my taste, perfectly hideous. This has always been so." Describing factory salesrooms, he says, "Upstairs the products of the factory are laid out horribly for your inspection, as in some nightmare treasure cave; feathery candlesticks, violent vases, tumblers of awful ostentation, degraded glass animals, coarse images of clowns and revellers."[10] How well I remember that glass drunk climbing that glass lamppost! It is, unfortunately, with the products of Venice and Murano that one gets a good idea of what most contemporary paperweights are like and likely to be until adventurous designers and glass craftsmen cure the public of its Victorian fetishism.

Before World War II Murano had been making close millefiori and concentric weights in small, lumpish canes in raw colors. The surplus canes were shipped to glass distributors in the United States, presumably for use as gangsters' tie tacks. Soon after the war Murano began exporting thousands upon thousands of weights with large cogged canes in howling primaries and orange and green; one still sees them in the windows of junk shops whose proprietors swear they are very old because they were purchased in Europe several years ago or came from the house of a lady who was eighty-nine.

But in the late 1950's a change for the better was apparent. The muggy crown glass began to clear and slightly more intricate canes showed up in pleasing colors: soft pinks, wine reds, sea greens, mauve, and sky blue. However, to judge the new Venetian weights fairly it is necessary to observe the ones sent to the United States, because the Italian government apparently holds back the horrors for the Venetian tourists. In 1964 I saw one really attractive weight in Venice. It was made by Pauly & Company, the concern for whom Franchini and Moretti in 1869 made the portrait rods now in the Smithsonian.[11] The weight was a carpet ground of white canes divided into quadrants by a crossed green ribbon whose axis was a single red cane. Yet in New York today one sees all sorts of pleasant Victorianoid weights from Murano with rather competent filigree work, crown ribbons, flower-like florets, all in a variety of shapes and sizes from miniatures to doorstops, and ovoids to breadloaves and bookends. There is a fine goldfish swimming among very convincing green fronds (Col. Fig. 133), a massive pedestal mantel ornament, one with a peony-like rose that is about as successful in its own terms as the Millville creation, and another with a three-dimensional zinnia tilted toward the viewer (Col. Fig. 134). A series of weights with a ground of shattered gold leaf over goldstone shows various insignia such as a big "N" surrounded by a wreath (for Napoleon) and the coat of arms of the town of Palermo. Another attractive gold-foil weight, made by the Gilliano Ferro Company of Murano, is a flat glass tile whose shattered gold foil outlines an ancient tile design on an amber ground. Some weights on the verge of the experimental show a single enormous cane or a crown of twisted ribbons about a blue or amber ball (Col. Fig. 135). One has to admire these departures from what has been for so long a tradition of mediocrity and to hope that from the fine designers of Pauly and Venini will come new paperweight ideas for the glassblowing gymnasts of Murano.

Scandinavia

In Norway the item next in national popularity after the ubiquitous rubber trolls seems to be the "brevpress" or paperweight, a clear crystal in the three-dimensional shape of owls, penguins, seals, and other Arctic and sub-Arctic species.

Sweden has done better. Though the Strömbergshyttan green algae in clear crystal is rather inconsequential, another unnamed company has let the crystal fall in coils over a perforated green and white double overlay interior suggesting seaweed. The result is new and effective. And F. M. Konstglas of Ronneby has fashioned a weight whose motif suggests a sea urchin, with spines of pink glass over black. Naturally based, the abstract motif is one of the finest specimens of modern work.

Glass production began at Orrefors in 1898 as a sideline to a bog iron ore foundry, but important glassmaking was not begun until 1913 when, under new ownership, veteran glassblowers, cutters, engravers, and artists were put on the payroll. (One is reminded of the great Frederick Carder, a decade earlier, importing Swedish glassmen to Steuben.) Since 1913 there has been constant collaboration between artist-designer and glass craftsman. Part of the Orrefors motto is "Trust the Artists," and this has paid off in imaginative design. Illustrated are rather simple clear glass weights by Gunnar Cyrén and Ingeborg Lundin (Figs. 239, 240). Cyrén's weights feature spare symbols of heart, cross,

Fig. 239. Gunnar Cyrén heart. *Courtesy Orrefors Glasbruk, Sweden.*
Fig. 240. Gunnar Cyrén cube weight. *Courtesy Orrefors Glasbruk, Sweden.*

239

240

and crown centered in flat, square, and circular weights. A cube weight enclosing a circular tube about a single bubble might be a symbol for our time. Yet, perhaps the most effective Orrefors weight is the crystal block used for advertising purposes and adorned only with the incised name of the company in black.

An older Swedish glasshouse is Kosta, founded in 1850, where the variety of forms is evidence of great experimentation with new possibilities for glass. Here the most exciting Swedish paperweights are made. In 1964 and '65 a number of cylindrical weights were made and signed by Mona Morales at Kosta. They are formed of concentric cylinders coated in two different colors and then cut on opposite sides with a concave oval window, so that one can see through the outer to the inner color. It is as if one were looking down a woodland path, for the effect is one of great depth. A smaller, unfaceted cylinder, when held a certain way, makes a third color from the overlapping of the other two. Another fascinating Kosta weight signed "W.G." has the heavy, clear glass sprinkle coated with a black overlay the texture of graphite. The surface has been etched with abstract foliage that has been given an acid finish. It recalls a prehistoric pictograph or a rare mineral with fossil.

It is weights like these that point in the direction paperweight-making should take if it is to free itself from the shackles of Victorianism, from a style, color sense, and facility of execution it can never hope to and should no longer try to duplicate.

NOTES

[1] Information supplied by the Corning Museum of Glass.

[2] Maurice Rheims, *The Strange Life of Objects,* New York, 1961, p. 3.

[3] For a description of these weights see Chapter Five. My information comes from Miss O. D. Dahlgren, who lived in Paris during those years and who visited the Baccarat factory.

[4] Yvonne Sohn Revelli, *Hobbies,* Oct. 1941, p. 71.

[5] For complete documentation of modern Baccarat millefiori weights see Guillaume Chaumeil, "The Rebirth of Millefiori at Baccarat," *Bulletin,* 1965, pp. 39–41.

[6] Robert A. Elder, Jr., "Chinese Paperweights," *Bulletin,* 1958.

[7] Mrs. F. J. Sisson, "Modern American Weights," and Albert Christian Revi, "Modern Glass Paperweights," both in *Bulletin,* June, 1961.

[8] Factual information on Kaziun comes from an interview with Mr. Kaziun and from Caroline Hyde Swift, "Charles Kaziun," *Bulletin,* 1956.

[9] Biographical information from Paul Jokelson.

[10] James Morris, *The World of Venice,* New York, 1960, pp. 289–91.

[11] Albert Christian Revi, "Miniature Portraits in Glass Rods," *The Glass Industry,* June, 1957.

III

Examination of Paperweights

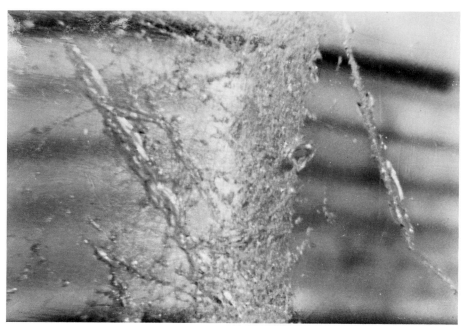

Fig. 241. Long scratches crossing basal rim provide excellent testing ground for refractive index liquids. *Photograph by Dr. Seymour Z. Lewin.*

Fig. 242. Matte surface of abrased basal rim maintains inconclusive appearance and is poor testing ground for refractive index liquids. *Photograph by Dr. Seymour Z. Lewin.*

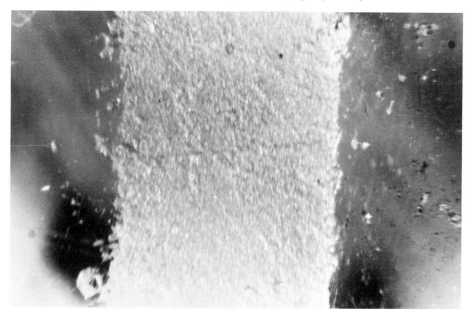

19

TESTING FOR REFRACTIVE INDEX

UP TO NOW THE CHIEF CONCERN of everyone associated with glass paperweights has been factory identification, with some further emphasis on classification of types. There has been almost no concern with paperweights as physical, chemical glass objects, whose study in this direction might aid in the identification and classification desired. Attempts to determine the provenance of glass paperweights by physical means have been largely confined to two methods: 1) direct visual observation, which has accounted for almost everything learned about paperweights that cannot be credited to historical research, and 2) observation of fluorescence under ultraviolet (UV) light. A third procedure, determination of specific gravity, was pursued some years ago by Lloyd J. Graham, who at the time was chemist at the U.S. Radio Logistical Laboratory in San Francisco.[1] To the methods of study already attempted another may now be added: determination of refractive indices of glass paperweights. But since these tests were decided upon by the author as a result of dissatisfaction with UV light usage, a preliminary discussion of that dissatisfaction is in order.

Fluorescence, the phenomenon associated for the purposes of this discussion with the long wave UV light, is an electromagnetic visible radiation emitted by a substance excited by an outside source of shorter wavelength than that of the emission. To put it another way, "Fluorescence is caused by the absorption of radiant energy and the emission of this energy in the form of visible light."[2] Observation under ultraviolet light of paperweights whose origin, on the basis of ordinary daylight observation, is said to be unquestioned, has led to the assignment of simple fluorescent colorations of the crown or dome glass to various important factories; deep blue to Baccarat, peachy pink to St. Louis, greenish blue to Clichy.[3] One obvious trouble with these simple color attributions is that they are not so simple. Another student of paperweights, for example, has found the colors to be pale lavender for Baccarat, peach for St. Louis, and lime green for Clichy,[4] while still other observers have found some Baccarat a peachy pink and some Clichy a bright sea green, or even sulphur yellow. In fact, the more weights one subjects to UV light the more color variety one finds within a given factory and the more similarity between factories.

I remember examining a large collection for several nights in darkness with the UV lamp as the only light source. Sometimes I examined simultaneously many weights from the same factory, sometimes I mixed the factories. The results were inconclusive, some weights from different factories fluorescing similar tints, while weights from the same factory showed a variety of tints. Furthermore, the pale, subtle coloring of a given weight might change before the eyes as other weights were added to or removed from the group. As a professional artist I knew that one color can only be judged in the context of other colors, yet that the very juxtaposition of one color with another affects the appearance of both. I couldn't understand how the experts could be so confident in assigning specific fluorescent colorations to particular factories.

Three things would seem to account for these imprecisions: first, the imprecision of human evaluation of color; second, the concentration in glass of fluorescent material upon which that evaluation is based; and third, the basic question of what is asked from fluorescence and what is answered by it.

To most of us, reactions to color are highly subjective and therefore unreliable as objective diagnostic criteria. As to the second point, Harley and Wiberly say that "the intensity of the light emitted by a fluorescent material is dependent upon the concentration of that material."[5] While in a single cane, one among many in the interior design of the paperweight, the fluorescent concentration is often strong enough to emit a distinctive glow, in the batch of glass as a whole fluorescent material is necessarily dispersed and the resultant glow weaker.

As to the third point, there seems to have been confusion as to what is sought and what is found in paperweight fluorescence. What has been sought is an easy clue to origin through simple fluorescent color labeling. What paperweight fluorescence shows is actually a predominance in the spectrum of the chemical, mineral contents of the glass itself, a predominance of lead over soda, or soda over lead; and this predominance interfered with and confused by the presence of other chemical elements or mineral species somewhat modified by the glass, such as alkali, manganese, willemite, scheelite, calcite, scapelite, hyalite, autunite, or uranium compounds, which may fluoresce.[6] Willemite, for example, can fluoresce a pale green, while autunite can fluoresce a strong green yellow, colors approximating the glow attributed to Clichy paperweights. Only chemical analysis, which would require a damaging sample of the paperweight glass, could determine what specific elements are causing what colors.

Basically, however, what is answered by UV fluorescence is the question not asked of it by the UV paperweight testers, namely the question of lead content. Analysis of the chemical composition of glass, whether it be spectrographic fluorescent, spot testing with hydrofluoric acid and ammonium sulfide, measurement of density, specific gravity, or refractive index keeps coming back to this question of lead content, because lead is the element which has the most important effect on all these characteristics.

Thus the lead content of a paperweight seemed as likely an indicator as any of something basic about the glass which might reveal kinship among specimens thought to be from the same factory.

Under the instruction and guidance of Dr. Seymour Z. Lewin of the Conservation Laboratory of the Institute of Fine Arts, New York University, I undertook to find the refractive indices of a number of paperweights whose provenance could be reasonably assumed. A description of the tests and their results follows.

Refractive Index Tests

The index of refraction is the ratio of the velocity of light in the first of two media (in this case, air) to its velocity in the second (in this case, glass) as it passes from one into the other. As already noted, the refractive index of glass is an indicator of its lead content. Refractive indices work in reverse; thus an index of 1.500 means that light entering glass of that index travels $1\frac{1}{2}$ times slower than light traveling through air.

Equipment required for testing includes a low-power microscope (a stereomicroscope was used here), a set of refractive index liquids ranging from 1.500 to 1.600, a support suitable for paperweights, a solvent and tissue for removing the index liquids, and a good light.

The problem is to find the refractive liquid that exactly corresponds with the refractive index of the glass. If a drop of liquid is placed on a glass surface, the interface between the glass and the liquid will be visible so long as there is a difference in the refractive indices of the two materials. As the point of correspondence of the two refractive indices is approached, the interface becomes invisible. Since only the surface of the glass can be tested, a small area containing scratches is the best place to observe the effects of the liquids. Except for paperweights that have recently been repolished by a painstaking expert, most old paperweights show an abundance of surface breaks of one sort or another, usually along the basal rim. Surface breaks that may be invisible to the naked eye can easily be seen under the microscope at magnifications from 10X to 40X, though occasionally it may be necessary to make a small scratch with a carbon steel file, or with the rough edge of another piece of glass.

Procedure

The base of the paperweight is usually best for testing, though a scratch already on the dome can also be used. If the bottom is to be tested, the paperweight is cradled upside down directly under the microscope in a pillow filled with sand or lead filings, and a likely area of scratches brought into focus with the microscope. Scratches that resemble long, jagged-edged wounds (Fig. 241) are preferable to those mottled abrasions (Fig. 242) that are the result of even grinding, and the trick is to fill the wound with one liquid at a time, cleaning it out thoroughly between applications with a solvent. Acetone is an excellent organic solvent for the standard refractive index liquids. When the refractive index of the glass is found, the wound (scratch) appears completely healed, that is, invisible.[7] The glass rod applicator of the liquid bottles makes for proficient application of the tiny drop required to fill the scratch. Too much liquid either tends to create a dome of liquid that supports unwanted reflections, or the liquid runs off and is wasted.

Under the scrutiny of the microscope some effort may be required to select an area with good, sharp-edged scratches. When a scratch site is selected, the weight is tilted 10 to 15 degrees toward the light source and brought into sharp focus under the microscope. Too great a tilt means uneven focus and causes the liquid to run off. Many applications are usually required to arrive at the correct index of stubborn specimens, but when one appears to be lucky on the third or fourth try, it is wise to apply widely separated index liquids as a gauge of visual accuracy, and then to test the successful application in another area. Paperweight glass occasionally shows varying refractive indices. The time required for testing a single specimen varies from five minutes to two days. Occasionally no exact index can be arrived at, and here one has to settle for the nearest approach to invisibility. As a general aid, it is advisable between applications to memorize the effect of the preceding application. When one part of a rough area tends to disappear under the liquid but another remains, it usually means that the microscope is including a view of some imperfection beneath the surface of the glass, such as striae or bubbles that cannot be penetrated by the liquids.

Results of the Tests

Tests results of fifty-six weights from seven factories appear in Table I. Reading from left to right the table shows each factory and the number of weights tested, the refractive index range among specimens for each factory, the average refractive index for each factory, and the 95 percent Confidence Limit deviation carried to three decimal places. The meaning of the 95 percent Confidence Limit is that the chances are 95 out of 100 that any future refractive index readings for paperweights of these makes will fall within the ranges indicated in the table or, to put it conversely, there is only a 1-in-20 chance that they will fall outside the indicated ranges.

The broad range of lead content found within the glass of each factory is a graphic demonstration of the variation in glass from batch to batch in the mid-nineteenth century, while the overlapping of lead content ranges among factories is an indication of the unreliability of seeking factory identification on the basis of lead content, UV fluorescence, or any other single factor by itself.

Any additional unknown weight tested might come statistically within the lead content range of several factories. And yet, as shown in Table I, there is a different average lead content for each factory. Listed in ascending order these averages show clearly such things as the high and possibly closely consistent lead content of St. Louis weights (though the sampling has been admittedly very small) and the considerable difference between the averages of Sandwich and the New England Glass Company, which might aid in identification of questionable specimens where other criteria were not much help. It is interesting to note that Graham's independent and prior findings for specific gravity with a different set of weights show the same factory order.

More testing for refractive indices of weights of known factories is certainly to be desired—say 100 weights from each factory—in order to sharpen the findings recorded here. Until all methods of study, historical and scientific, are brought to bear on the problem, we may not be able to identify the source of many weights now classified as unknown.

TABLE I
Refractive Indices of Glass Paperweights

Factory	No. of Weights Tested	Refractive Index Range	Av. Refr. Index	Deviation— 95% Confidence Limit
Chinese	6	1.492–1.524	1.508	0.013
Sandwich	4	1.530–1.580	1.554	0.033
Clichy	12	1.508–1.578	1.555	0.016
Bacchus	10	1.548–1.572	1.561	0.005
NEGC	11	1.564–1.600	1.573	0.007
Baccarat	8	1.562–1.600	1.582	0.010
St. Louis	5	1.588–1.592	1.589	0.003

NOTES

[1] Lloyd J. Graham determined the specific gravity of 53 paperweights. His results were substantially similar to my own in the ranking of factories by average lead content.

[2] Harley and Wiberly, *Instrument Analysis*, John Wiley & Sons, Inc., New York, 1954, p. 113.

[3] E. M. Elville, "Art of the French Glass Paperweight," *Bulletin*, 1959.

[4] J. P. Boore, "Old Glass Paperweights, The Ultra-Violet Light," *Hobbies*, March, 1961, pps. 76, 77, 80. Mr. Boore is fully aware of the limitations of UV observation.

[5] Harley and Wiberly, *op. cit.*, p. 113.

[6] Increased presence of uranium compounds has been noted in glass made at the time of paperweights, that is, in the 1840's. Some Bacchus and Baccarat canes appear to contain uranium oxides or autunite (calcium uranium phosphate), but I have had several such weights tested in an atomic radiation laboratory and they were found not dangerous to humans.

[7] Cargille Index of Refraction Liquids supplied by Fischer Scientific Company, New York City, were used.

Bibliography

The *Bulletin of the Paperweight Collectors' Association* is referred to in the text as *Bulletin*. The *Bulletin of the National Early American Glass Club* is referred to in the text as the *Glass Club Bulletin*.

ADAMS, JANE FORD, and ALBERT, LILLIAN SMITH, "PW Means Paperweight Buttons," *Bulletin of the Paperweight Collectors' Association*, 1956.

"The Almanac," *Antiques*, August, 1937, p. 86, illus.

AMIC, YOLANDE, *L'Opaline Française au XIX Siècle*, Paris, 1952.

Ancient and Near Eastern Glass, The Toledo Museum of Art, no date.

ANGUS-BUTTERWORTH, L. M., *British Table and Ornamental Glass*, London, Leonard Hill, Ltd., 1956.

Art Journal, The, London, 1847 ff.

AVILA, GEORGE C., "The Pairpoint Glass Story," New Bedford, Mass., 1968.

BARAT, JULES, *Exposition de l'Industrie Française, Année 1884*, Paris, no date.

BARBER, EDWIN ATLEE, "Mosaic and Millefiori Glass," *Bulletin of the Pennsylvania Museum*, July, 1915, No. 51 pp. 31–40, illus.

BARGER, HELEN, "Two Dorflingers Who Cared," *Bulletin of the National Early American Glass Club*, No. 80 (December, 1966), pp. 3–5, illus.

BARRELET, JAMES, *La Verrerie en France*, Paris, Larousse, 1953.

"A Beautiful Modern Baccarat Millefiori Paperweight," *Bulletin of the Paperweight Collectors' Association*, 1960.

BEDFORD, JOHN, *Paperweights*, New York, Walker and Co., 1968.

BERGSTROM, EVANGELINE H., "B as in Baccarat," *Antiques*, Vol. XLIII, No. 4 (April, 1943), pp. 178–180, illus.

_____, *Old Glass Paperweights*, 1940, New York, Crown Publishers, Inc., 1947.

_____, "Paperweights, Rare and Not so Rare," *American Collector*, July, 1943, illus.

_____, "Pinchbeck but Precious," *American Collector*, November, 1945, pp. 6, 7, 19.

_____, "Steeple Weights," *Hobbies*, October, 1941, p. 73.

BOESEN, GUDMOND, *Venetian Glass at Rosenborg Castle*, Copenhagen, I kommission hos G.E.C. Gad, 1960.

BOORE, J. P., "Baccarat Silhouettes," *Bulletin of the Paperweight Collectors' Association*, 1964, pp. 16–18, illus.

_____, "Bergstrom Revisited," *Bulletin of the Paperweight Collectors' Association*, 1963, pp. 26–29, illus.

_____, "Glass Paperweights," *Hobbies*, Vol. 63, No. 3 (May, 1958), p. 72; Vol. 63, No. 11 (January, 1959), pp. 73, 74, illus.; No. 12 (February, 1959), pp. 72, 73, illus.; Vol. 64, No. 1 (March, 1959), p. 72, illus.; No. 2 (April, 1959), p. 72.

_____, "Glass Paperweights—Attribution by Association," *Hobbies*, Vol. 62, No. 12 (February, 1958), p. 84.

_____, "Glass Paperweights—What Is a Fake?" *Hobbies*, Vol. 63, No. 6 (August, 1958), p. 80.

_____, "Glossary of Terms Used by Glass Paperweight Collectors," *Bulletin of the National Early American Glass Club*, No. 56 (December, 1960), pp. 6–8.

_____, "Old Glass Paperweights," *Hobbies*, Vol. 66, No. 11 (January, 1962), pp. 82–84, illus.; Vol. 67, No. 7 (September, 1962), pp. 80, 92, illus.; Vol. 71, No. 4 (June, 1966), pp. 98F–98G, illus.

_____, "Old Glass Paperweights—Baccarat," *Hobbies*, Vol. 71, No. 9 (November, 1966), pp. 98L–98M, illus.

————, "Old Glass Paperweights—A Brief History of the Art," *Hobbies,* Vol. 66, No. 4 (June, 1961), pp. 90–91.

————, "Old Glass Paperweights—Clichy," Part I, *Hobbies.* Vol. 66, No. 6 (August, 1961); pp. 90–92, illus.; Part III, Vol. 66, No. 12 (February, 1962), pp. 88, 89, 92, 93, illus.; Part IV, Vol. 67, No. 4 (June, 1962), pp. 82–84; Part V, No. 6 (August, 1962), pp. 68, 69, 88, illus.

————, "Old Glass Paperweights, Some Little Known English Makers," *Hobbies,* Vol. 65, No. 12 (February, 1961), pp. 80, 81, illus.

————, "Old Glass Paperweights—The Ultra-Violet Light," *Hobbies,* Vol. 66, No. 1 (March, 1961), pp. 76, 77, 80, illus.

————, "Random Observations on Paperweights," *Hobbies,* Vol. 62, No. 11 (January, 1958), p. 81.

————, "Was There a Glass Conspiracy?" *Bulletin of the Paperweight Collectors' Association,* 1963, illus.

"The Bergstrom Paperweight Collection," *Antiques,* Vol. LXXIX, No. 5 (May, 1961), p. 486, illus.

BONTEMPS, GEORGES, *Guide du Verrier*, Paris, 1868.

BOZEK, MICHAEL, "Paperweights," *Treasure Chest,* May–June, 1961, p. 20, illus.

————, *Price Guide Handbook of Glass Paperweights,* Treasure Chest Publications, North Hollywood, Calif., 1961.

BROTHERS, J. STANLEY, JR., "How Glass Paperweights Are Made," *Antiques,* Vol. XXXII, No. 2 (August, 1937), pp. 60–63, illus.

————, "The Miracle of Enclosed Ornamentation," *Journal of Glass Studies,* Vol. IV, 1962, pp. 116–126, illus.

BROWN, DOROTHY FOSTER, "Buttons 'Modern Paperweights,' " *Hobbies,* Vol. 65, No. 12 (February, 1961), pp. 52–53, illus.

Bulletin of the Paperweight Collectors' Association, 1955–1965.

Catalogues of paperweight sales at Christie's, London; Sotheby & Co., London; Parke-Bernet Galleries, Inc., New York; Plaza Galleries, New York; and others.

CHALLINOR, FRANK, "A Glassman's Collection," *Antiques,* April, 1947, pp. 254, 255, illus.

CHAMBERLAIN, GEORGIA S., "Early American Portrait Medallions on Glass Paperweights," *Bulletin of the Paperweight Collectors' Association,* April, 1955, pp. 18–22, illus.

CHAMBON, RAYMOND, *L'Histoire de la Verrerie en Belgique,* Brussels, Edition de la Librarie Encyclopédique, 1955.

CHANCE, SIR HUGH, "Records—The Nailsea Glassworks," *The Connoisseur,* July, 1967, pp. 168–172, illus.

CHAUMEIL, GUILLAUME, "The Rebirth of Millefiori at Baccarat, 1957–1964," *Bulletin of the Paperweight Collectors' Association,* June, 1965, illus.

CHURCHILL LTD., ARTHUR, "The Applewhaite-Abbott Collection," *Glass Notes,* No. 12 (December, 1952), pp. 33–35, illus.

CLARKE, T. H., "The Guggenheim Collection," *Bulletin of the Paperweight Collectors' Association,* 1961.

————, "Notes on a Terminology for French Paperweights," *Bulletin of the Paperweight Collectors' Association,* April, 1955, pp. 9–17, illus.

"A Collection of Glass Paperweights," *Hobbies,* December, 1938.

"A Collection of Paperweights," *Bulletin of the Chicago Art Institute,* Vol. 63, No. 5 (September, 1938), pp. 72–74, illus.

COUSE, L. ERWINA, "Paperweight Buttons," *Hobbies,* October, 1941, p. 20.

COVALT, ZORA, "More on Paperweights," *Hobbies,* November, 1941.

CROSS, WILLIAM E., "Talk on Paperweights," *Bulletin of the National Early American Glass Club,* December, 1954, pp. 2–5.

Cyclopedia of Useful Arts and Manufactures, ed. by Charles Tomlinson, New York, c. 1854.

DAVIS, FRANK, "French 19th Century Glass Paperweights," *Illustrated London News,* Vol. 242, No. 6453 (April 20, 1963), p. 588, illus.

DAVISON, MARY E., "The Glass Industry of Cleveland, New York," *Antiques,* April, 1937, pp. 183–185, illus.

DEBETTE, M. L. P., "On the Manufacture of Glass in Bohemia," trans. from the *Annales des Mines,* December, 1843, for the *Franklin Journal,* Philadelphia.

Dickenson's Comprehensive Pictures of the Great Exhibition of 1851, London, 1852.

DILLON, EDWARD, *Glass,* London, 1907.

DIXON, ERIC, "Paperweights," *Antiques Dealer,* Vol. VIII, No. 12 (December, 1956), pp. 11, 30, illus.

DU CANN, C. G. L., "Allure of Old Glass Paperweights," *Collectors' Guide,* February, 1963.

DYER, WALTER A., "Millefiori, the Glass of a Thousand Flowers," *House Beautiful,* June, 1928, pp. 741, 784, 785, illus.

EHRENBERG, RAYMOND W., "Mystery Paperweight—The Telephone BlueBell," *Bulletin of the Paperweight Collectors' Association,* April, 1955, pp. 28–31, illus.

ELDER, ROBERT A., JR., "Chinese Paperweights," *Bulletin of the Paperweight Collectors' Association,* 1958, illus.

————, "The Colonel Guggenheim Paperweight Collection," *Bulletin of the Paperweight Collectors' Association,* June, 1960.

————, "The Lillie and Aaron Straus Paperweight Collection," *Bulletin of the Paperweight Collectors' Association,* 1961, illus.

————, "Modern Venetian Paperweights," *Bulletin of the Paperweight Collectors' Association,* 1959, illus.

ELVILLE, E. M., "Art of the French Glass Paperweight," *Country Life Annual,* 1959.

————, *The Collector's Dictionary of Glass,* London, Country Life Ltd., 1961, pp. 145–153, illus.

————, "English Glass Paperweights," *Country Life Annual,* 1954.

————, "French Paperweights," *Country Life,* June, 1953.

————, "Glass at the Great Exhibition," *Country Life,* April 27, 1951, pp. 1294, 1296, 1299.

————, "Glass Paper-Weights," *Apollo,* April, May, 1948.

————, *Paperweights and Other Glass Curiosities,* London, Country Life Ltd., 1957.

EMPERAUGER, J. P., "Embedded Glass and Crystal," Part I, *Bulletin of the Paperweight Collectors' Association,* 1958; Part II, 1959, illus.

————, *Verres et Cristaux Incrustés,* Paris, 1909.

ETTINGER, F. SUMNER, "Another Episode in Glass Paperweight History," *Hobbies,* November, 1935, pp. 71, 72.

"Exhibition of the Industry of All Nations, 1851," *Jury Reports.*

"Fifty Years of the Glass Bottle Trade, 1844–1894," reprinted from *The British Trade Journal,* December 1, 1894, for Messrs. Kilner Bros. Jubilee, pp. 4–48, illus.

FITZPATRICK, PAUL J., "Gillinder & Sons at the Philadelphia Centennial," *Spinning Wheel,* July–August, 1965, pp. 14, 15, illus.

————, "William T. Gillinder's Contributions to Glass-Making," *Spinning Wheel,* Vol. XXII, No. 5 (May, 1966), p. 22, illus.

FFRENCH, YVONNE, *The Great Exhibition,* 1851, London, no date.

"Foreign and Native Paperweights Pass in Review, a Comparative Study of Design and Craftsmanship," Part I, *American Collector,* February, 1942; Part II, March, 1942.

"French Paperweights," *Réalites,* March, 1957, pp. 4–9, illus.

GASPARETTO, ASTONE, *Il Vetro di Murano dalle origini ad oggi,* Venice, Neri Pozza, 1958.

Gems of the Centennial Exhibition at the Philadelphia International Exhibition of 1876, New York, 1887.

"The Gentile Glass Co.," *Bulletin of the National Early American Glass Club,* March, 1965, pp. 6, 7, illus.

GIBBS-SMITH, T. H., *The Great Exhibition of 1851, A Commemorative Album,* Victoria and Albert Museum, London, 1950.

Glass Bibliography, Steuben Glass, Inc., New York, 1947.

"The Glass Blowers of Whitefriars," *Arts and Decoration,* November, 1938, pp. 9, 10.

"Glass Paperweights," *Hobbies,* January, 1939.

"Glass Paperweights at the Edinburgh Festival," *The Connoisseur,* Vol. 126, November, 1950, p. 138.

"Glass Paperweights of Many Types," Anon., *Antiques,* October, 1938, p. 194, illus.

GRAHAM, LLOYD J., "Another 'Mystery' Paperweight," *Bulletin of the Paperweight Collectors' Association,* 1959, illus.

GRAY, JOHN M., *James and William Tassie,* Edinburgh, 1894.

GREPPE, PASCAL, "Propos d'un Collectioneur Napoléonisant," *Bulletin of the Paperweight Collectors' Association,* 1960.

GUTTERY, D. R., *From Broad-Glass to Cut Crystal,* London, Leonard Hill, Ltd., 1956.

HANSEN, RONALD E., "Hidden Facets of a Paperweight," *Bulletin of the Paperweight Collectors' Association,* June, 1965, illus.

————, "Lamp Work—Its Significance to Paperweights," *Bulletin of the National Early American Glass Club,* Christmas, 1965, pp. 10, 11, illus.

HARLEY, J. H., and WIBERLEY, S. E., *Instrumental Analysis,* New York, John Wiley and Sons, Inc., 1954.

HARMSWORTH, GEOFFREY, "Magic in Glass," magazine unknown, possibly *Hutton's Weekly,* 1947.

HARRINGTON, C. C., "Never Made for Sale," *American Home,* April, 1939, illus.

HAYES-CAVANAUGH, DORIS, "Early Glass-Making in East Cambridge, Mass.," *Old-Time New England,* Vol. XIX, January, 1929, pp. 113–122, illus.

HAYNES, E. BARRINGTON, "Baccaramania," *The Antique Collector,* December, 1953, pp. 252–253.

————, *Glass,* New York, Pelican, 1948.

"Herstellung der Millefiori-Briefbeschwerer," *Sprechsaal,* 1898, Vol. 31, p. 829.

HICKEY, MARGARET CONDON, "Signed with a 'K'," *Yankee,* November, 1966, pp. 97, 212, 215, illus.

HOBHOUSE, CHRISTOPHER, *1851 and The Crystal Palace,* London, 1937.

HOLLAND, VYVYAN, "Glass Paperweights," a lecture delivered on May 18, 1937, before a luncheon club, and reprinted in *Hobbies,* January, 1939, pp. 75, 76, illus.

HOLLISTER, PAUL, JR., "Bacchus and Other English Weights," Glass Paperweight Symposium, 1967, Bergstrom Museum.

————, "Foreign Influences in American Paperweights," talk given at Old Sturbridge Village, October 28, 1966.

————, "Foreign Influences in American Paperweights," *Bulletin of the National Early American Glass Club,* June 1968, pp. 3–5, illus.

————, "Glass Paperweights at Old Sturbridge Village," Old Sturbridge Village, 1969.

————, "The Modest Collector and the Snake in the Glass," *Bulletin of the Paperweight Collectors' Association,* 1965, illus.

"New Light on 'Gilliland,' Cambridge, and Gillinder Paperweights," *Antiques,* October, 1968, pp. 562–564.

————, "Outstanding French and American Paperweights in the Wells Collection," *Antiques,* February, 1966, pp. 265–269, illus.

HONEY, W. B., Glass, *A Handbook and a Guide to the Museum Collection,* Victoria and Albert Museum, 1946.

HOWE, FLORENCE THOMPSON, "A Paperweight Collection," *Antiques,* April, 1946, pp. 246–247, illus.

HUGHES, G. BERNARD, "English Crystal Cameos," *Country Life,* June 3, 1949, pp. 1304, 1305, illus.

————, *English Glass for the Collector,* London, publication date unknown.

————, "Old English Glass Paperweights," *Country Life,* May 10, 1946, illus.

————, "Old French Glass Paperweights," *Apollo,* March, 1953, illus.

————, "Some Victorian Paperweights," *Woman's Magazine,* March 1949, illus.

————, and THERLE HUGHES, *After the Regency,* London, 1952.

HUNT, ROBERT, *Handbook to the Official Catalogues,* 2 vols., London, 1851.

Illustrated London News, 1851; Christmas Number, 1949, illus.; July 12, 1952, illus.

IMBERT, ROGER, "Crystal Glass Paperweights" (Eng. trans.), *Connaissance des Arts,* August, 1955, illus.

————, and YOLANDE AMIC, *Les Presse-Papiers Français,* Paris, 1948.

"Initials on a Paperweight," *Country Life,* Vol. CXXV, No. 3252 (May 14, 1959), p. 1071, illus.

IRWIN, FREDERICK T. *The Story of Sandwich Glass and Glass Workers,* Granite State Press, New Hampshire, 1926.

ISRAEL, JAQUES, "The Art of Glass Paperweight Making," *Bulletin of the Paperweight Collectors' Association,* 1963, pp. 21–23, illus.

JARVES, DEMING, *Reminiscences of Glass-Making,* Boston, 1854.

JARVES, JAMES JACKSON, "Ancient and Modern Venetian Glass of Murano," *Harper's New Monthly Magazine,* 1882, Vol. 64, pp. 177–190, illus.

JENKINS, DOROTHY H., "Woman's Day Dictionary of Paperweights," *Woman's Day,* July, 1965, pp. 25–32, illus.

JOHNSON, GRACE, "Old Paperweights," *Hobbies,* May, 1946, pp. 53–55, illus.

JOKELSON, PAUL, *Antique French Paperweights,* 1955.

————, *One Hundred of the Most Important Paperweights,* 1966.

————, "Steuben Paperweights," *Bulletin of the Paperweight Collectors' Association,* 1965, p. 45, illus.

————, "Sulphides, The Art of Cameo Incrustation," Thomas Nelson & Sons, New York, 1968.

Journal of Design and Manufactures, London, Chapman and Hall, 1849.

Journal of Glass Studies, Vols. 1–8, Corning Museum of Glass, Corning, New York, 1959–1966.

KAHN, DOROTHEA, "Art in Paperweights," *Christian Science Monitor* (June 23, 1945), pp. 10, 11, illus.

KASEMEYER, JEAN, "The Paperweight Buttons of Weinman, Rutter, Israel, Kaziun and Erikson," *National Button.*

KAZIUN, CHARLES, "As Seen from the Glory Hole," *Bulletin of the Paperweight Collectors' Association,* June, 1962, illus.

————, "From the Gaffer's Chair," *Bulletin of the Paperweight Collectors' Association,* June, 1964, pp. 6–9, illus.; June, 1965.

KEARNEY, VIRGINIA A., "Cape Cod and the Sandwich Glass Museum," *Hobbies,* Vol. 64, No. 4 (June, 1959), pp. 70, 71, 86–88, illus.

KILNER, C. A., "English Glass Paperweights," *Hobbies,* October, 1941, pp. 71–72.

KING, HUBERT GRAHAM, "An Unsolved Case," *Antiques,* April, 1944, pp. 201–202, illus.

KNOWER, F. H. "Ohio Made Paperweights," Glass Paperweight Symposium, 1967, Bergstrom Museum.

LAIDECKER, SAM, "Old Glass Paperweights," *The American Antiques Collector,* April, 1941, p. 133, illus.

LAWRENCE, RONALD M., M.D., "The Estelle Doheny Paperweight Collection," *Bulletin of the Paperweight Collectors' Association,* June, 1965, illus.

LAWSON, MRS. ROBT. "Paperweights Inside and Out," *Bulletin of the National Early American Glass Club,* December, 1960, pp. 4–5.

LEE, RUTH WEBB, *Antique Fakes and Reproductions,* Wellesley Hills, Mass., Lee Publications, 1950.

———, "Medium-priced Paperweights," *Hobbies,* October, 1941, pp. 59–60, illus.

———, "Ralph Barber and the Millville Rose Paperweights," *American Collector,* April, 1938.

———, "Reproduction Millville Rose Paperweights," *American Collector,* August, 1939, illus.

———, *Sandwich Glass,* sixth ed., Northborough, Mass., 1947.

———, "Three Little Pigs Go to Market," *American Collector,* May, 1938, illus.

LEFFINGWELL, B. H., "A Beautiful Mystery Paperweight," *Bulletin of the Paperweight Collectors' Association,* 1959, illus.

———, "Glass-Making at Somerville," *Hobbies,* Vol. 67, No. 8 (October, 1962), pp. 84–85, illus.

———, "Gilliland Paperweights," *Bulletin of the Paperweight Collectors' Association,* 1959, illus.

———, "Glass Paperweights," *Antiques Journal,* Vol. 17, No. 2 (February, 1962), pp. 22–24, illus.

———, "Paperweights at Auction," *Hobbies,* Vol. 64, No. 11 (January, 1960), pp. 70–72.

———, "Paperweights for the Advanced Collector," *Antiques Journal,* Vol. 19, No. 3 (March, 1964), pp. 20–27, illus.

LEGGE, J. M. D., "Glass Paperweights of the 19th Century," *Shell Magazine,* April, 1954.

———, "Old Glass Paperweights," *Collectors' Guide,* May, June, 1965.

LEONARDSON, S. E., "Fowleton Paperweights, B. F. Leach Glass Co.," *Hobbies,* February, 1944, pp. 50, 52–54.

LICHTEN, FRANCES, *Decorative Art of Victoria's Era,* Scribner's, New York, 1950.

LUCKHURST, KENNETH W., *The Story of Exhibitions,* London, The Studio Publications, 1951.

LYON, CHARLES WOOLSEY, "The Beauty of Glass Paperweights," *Avocations,* January, 1939, pp. 232–236, illus.

———, "Collection," *House Beautiful,* August, 1936, pp. 19, 57, illus.

———, "Glass Paperweight Collecting as a Hobby," *Avocations,* October, 1937, illus.

McCAWLEY, PATRICIA K., *Antique Glass Paperweights from France,* London, Spink & Son, Ltd., 1968, illus.

McCLINTON, KATHARINE MORRISON, *A Handbook of Popular Antiques,* New York, Bonanza Books, 1945.

McGRATH, RAYMOND, and FROST, A. C., *Glass in Architecture and Decoration,* London, Architectural Press, 1937.

MacINTIRE, MRS. ALAN, "The Lafayette Cameo Paperweight," *Bulletin of the Paperweight Collectors' Association,* April, 1955, p. 27.

McKEARIN, GEORGE S. and HELEN, *American Glass,* New York, Crown Publishers, Inc., 1956.

———, *Two Hundred Years of American Blown Glass,* New York, Crown Publishers, Inc., 1958.

MALSBURY, SALLY, "Old Glass Paperweights," *Arts and Antiques,* Vol. 1, No. 1, 1965, illus.

MANHEIM, FRANK, *A Garland of Weights,* New York, Farrar, Straus & Giroux, 1968.

MARIACHER, GIOVANNE, *L'arte del Vetro,* Verona, 1954.

————, *Italian Blown Glass,* New York, McGraw-Hill, Inc., no date.

MARSH, MRS. WM. R., "Zachary Taylor Sulphide Paperweight," *Bulletin of the Paperweight Collectors' Association,* April, 1955, p. 23, illus.

MARTIN, MARY, "The Crystal Cameos of France," *House & Garden,* December, 1926, illus.

MAUST, DON, "Glass Paperweights," *Antiques Journal,* Vol. 21, No. 8 (August, 1966), pp. 19–21, illus.

MELVIN, JEAN SUTHERLAND (MRS. GEORGE J.), *American Glass Paperweights and Their Makers,* New York and Toronto, 1967, illus.

————, "Contemporary American Paperweights and Their Makers," Glass Paperweight Symposium, 1967, Bergstrom Museum.

————, "John Degenhart," *Bulletin of the Paperweight Collectors' Association,* June, 1965, illus.

MIDDLETON, L. I., "Paperweights of the Victorians," *The Antique Collector,* London, 1931, Vol. 2, pp. 432–434, illus.

MILLER, ROGER C. "Swirl and Sulphide Playing Marbles," *Spinning Wheel,* Vol. XXII, No. 11 (November, 1966), pp. 20, 21, illus.

Milwaukee Institute Bulletin, Vol. 14, February, 1940, p. 2.

MINNS, EDWARD W., "Paperweight Making as Done at Millville," *American Collector,* November, 1938, illus.; Part II, December, 1938, illus.

MOORE, T. B., "The First Hundred Are the Easiest," *Hobbies,* October, 1941, pp. 68–69.

MORRIS, JAMES, *The World of Venice,* New York, Pantheon Books, 1960.

NAGEL, FRED A. "A Date with Silhouettes," *Bulletin of the Paperweight Collectors' Association,* June, 1957, illus.

NAGEL, DR. J. DARWIN, "Door-Stops, Door Knobs, Newel Post Tops," *Hobbies,* March, 1944, pp. 50–52.

NAYMAN, HARRIET, "Artist in Glass," *The Boston Sunday Herald Magazine,* May 14, 1967, illus.

NERI, ANTONIO, *L'Arte Vetraria,* Florence, 1612. Also, English translation by Christopher Merret, 1662.

NEUBURG, FREDERIC, *Ancient Glass,* University of Toronto, 1962.

————, *Glass in Antiquity,* London, Rockliff, 1949.

New England Glass Co. 1818–1888, Toledo Museum of Art, 1963.

NEWTON, JANET FOSTER, "Dorflinger Glass," *Antiques,* Vol. 45, No. 1 (January, 1944), pp. 27–29, illus.

O'BRIEN, MARY A. and S. WELDON, "Old Glass Paperweights," *Antiques,* November, 1949, pp. 354–357, illus.

Official Catalogues of the following exhibitions: London, 1851; Dublin, 1853; New York, 1853; London, 1862; Paris, 1867, 1878, 1888; Philadelphia, 1876.

PATTINSON, LILLIAN G. "Aventurine Glass," *Bulletin of the National Early American Glass Club,* No. 57, March, 1961, p. 7.

————, "The Union Glass Co. of Somerville, Massachusetts," *Bulletin of the National Early American Glass Club,* No. 60, December, 1961, pp. 4–7, illus.

PAZAUREK, GUSTAV E., *Gläser der Empire-und-Biedermeierzeit,* Leipzig, 1923.

PÉLIGOT, E., "Travaux de Commission Français sur l'Industrie des Nations," Paris, 1854, Vol. 6, pp. 1–58.

PELLATT, APSLEY, *Curiosities of Glassmaking*, London, 1849.

PERROT, PAUL N., "The Ancient Millefiori Technique," Glass Paperweight Symposium, 1967, Bergstrom Museum.

————, *Three Great Centuries of Venetian Glass*, Corning, New York, Corning Museum of Glass, 1958, illus.

PEVSNER, NIKOLAUS, *High Victorian Design*, London, Architectural Press, 1951.

PHILLIPS, HOWARD, "Learning to 'Look' at Glass," *Antique Collector,* Vol. 30, No. 2 (April, 1959), pp. 63–68, illus.

PIERCE, J. B., and WHITMAN, W. M., "New Light on Old Paperweights," *Hobbies,* May, 1933, pp. 84–86, illus.

POLAK, ADA, "Sulphides and Medals," *Journal of Glass Studies*, 1966, pp. 116–119, illus.

PONCINS, J. DE, "The Story of Baccarat Figured Canes," *Bulletin of the Paperweight Collectors' Association*, 1956.

POWELL, HARRY J., *Glass-Making in England*, Cambridge, 1923.

Reports of the U.S. Commission to the Paris Exposition of 1878, Washington, D.C., 1880.

REVELLI, YVONNE SOHN, "Thoughts on French Paperweights," *Hobbies*, October, 1941, pp. 70, 71.

REVI, ALBERT CHRISTIAN, "English Patented Paperweights," *Bulletin of the Paperweight Collectors' Association*, June, 1964, pp. 42–46, illus.

————, "The 'Fourth' French Paperweight Factory," *Spinning Wheel*, October, 1966, pp. 10–11, 45, illus.

————, "Henry Miller's Designs for Paperweight Door Knobs and a Flower Vase," *Bulletin of the Paperweight Collectors' Association,* June, 1960.

————, "Millefiore, Filigree and Striped Glass," *Spinning Wheel*, Vol XIV, No. 1 (January, 1958), pp. 12, 14, 15, illus.

————, "Miniature Portraits in Glass Rods," *Spinning Wheel*, Vol. XIV, No. 2 (February, 1958), pp. 24–25, 35, illus.

————, *Nineteenth Century Glass*, New York, Thomas Nelson & Sons, 1959, illus.

RHEIMS, MAURICE, *The Strange Life of Objects*, New York, Atheneum Publishers, 1961.

ROBIQUET, JAQUES, *L'Art et le Goût sous la Restauration, 1814–1830,* Paris, 1928.

ROGERS, MILLARD F., "The New England Glass Co. Exhibition," *Bulletin of the National Early American Glass Club*, No. 68, December, 1963, pp. 11, 12, illus.

ROWE, BARBARA BASTIEN, "How We Found the Oscar Wilde Collection of Paperweights," *Hobbies*, October, 1941, p. 122.

Saint Louis, Cristal de France, 1767, commemorative anniversary album, Paris, 1967.

SAUZAY, ALEXANDER, *La Verrerie Depuis les Temps les Plus Reculés,* Paris, 1868.

————, *Wonders of Glass-Making in All Ages*, London, 1869.

SAVAGE, GEORGE, *Forgeries, Fakes and Reproductions*, London, Barrie & Rockliff, 1963.

SCHMIDT, ROBERT, *Das Glas*, Berlin and Leipzig, 1922.

SILLIMAN, BENJAMIN, *A Visit to Europe in 1851,* New York, 1853.

SISSON, BARBARA BOWLES, (MRS. F. J.), "Dated Paperweights," *Bulletin of the Paperweight Collectors' Association*, 1963.

————, "Modern American Paperweights," *Bulletin of the Paperweight Collectors' Association*, 1961, illus.

————, "Modern Paperweight Reproduction," *Bulletin of the Paperweight Collectors' Association*, 1962, illus.

————, "Sulphide Paperweights from 1850–1952," *Bulletin of the Paperweight*

Collectors' Association, 1964.

SLADE, GEORGE H., "Glass Paperweights," *Hobbies,* September, 1939.

SMITH, BARBARA A., "Part II—The Weights of History, 1800–1900," *Bulletin of the Paperweight Collectors' Association,* June, 1965.

SMITH, FRANCIS EDGAR, *American Glass Paperweights,* Wollaston, Mass., 1939.

SMITH, RAY WINFIELD, *Glass From the Ancient World,* Corning, New York, Corning Museum of Glass, 1957.

STANDINGER, PAUL, *Einiges über Millefiori-Glas,* Verh. Berliner Ges. Anthrop, 1902.

SWAN, MABEL M., "Deming Jarves and His Glass-Factory Village," *Antiques,* January, 1938.

SWIFT, CAROLINE HYDE, "Charles Kaziun," *Bulletin of the Paperweight Collectors' Association,* June, 1956, illus.

TALLIS, *History and Description of the Crystal Palace,* 3 vols., 1851.

TAYLOR, H., *The Identification of Stones in Glass by Physical Methods,* Glass Delegacy of the University of Sheffield, England, 1952.

TEALL, GARDNER, "The Glass of a Thousand Flowers," *House & Garden,* January, 1918, pp. 3–4, 6, 60–61, illus.

THACHER, THURSTON, "Incognito Collectors and Collections," *Hobbies,* October, 1941, p. 61, illus.

THORPE, W. A., "English Colored Glass, Part II," *Antiques,* Vol. XIX, May, 1931, pp. 380–382, illus.

TIMBS, J., *Yearbook of Facts on the Great Exhibition, 1851,* London, 1851.

TOMLINSON, CHARLES, ed., *Cyclopedia of Useful Arts,* New York, 1854.

TOMLINSON, JAY B., "Pinchbeck Paperweights," *Bulletin of the Paperweight Collectors' Association,* April, 1955, pp. 6–8, illus.

"Unrecorded Paperweights," *The Connoisseur,* (American edition), Vol. 131, April, 1953, p. 40.

V. H., "Glass Paperweights," *Hobbies,* January, 1939, pp. 75–76, illus.

VAN NOSTRAND, LEONARD G., "Dorflinger Glass," *The American Collector,* Winter, 1944, pp. 59–61, illus.

VAVRA, JAROSLAV R., *5000 Years of Glassmaking,* Prague, 1954.

VULLIET, ANDRÉ, "Facts Concerning the John Fitzgerald Kennedy Paperweight by Baccarat," *Bulletin of the Paperweight Collectors' Association,* June, 1965, illus.

WAKEFIELD, HUGH, "Glasswares by Apsley Pellatt," *Antiques,* January, 1965, pp. 85–89, illus.

WALLACE, MARY, "Paperweights," *House & Garden,* April, 1954.

WALLACE-DUNLOP, M. A., *Glass in the Old World,* London, no date.

WATKINS, LURA WOODSIDE, *American Glass and Glassmaking,* London, Max Parrish & Co., 1950.

————, *Cambridge Glass,* New York, Bramhall House, 1964.

————, "Medallion Paperweights," *Antiques,* August, 1941, pp. 94–95, illus.

WATKINS, MALCOLM, "Report on J. Cheney Wells Paperweight Collection at Old Sturbridge Village," *Bulletin of the National Early American Glass Club,* February, 1940, pp. 1–5; continued June, 1940, p. 4.

WAY, H. W. L., "Glass Paperweights," *The Connoisseur,* December, 1920.

WESTWOOD, MARY GLADYS, "Old Glass Paperweights," *Antique Dealer and Collectors' Guide,* London, 1948, pp. 30–31, illus.

WILSON, KENNETH M., "Early American Paperweights," Glass Paperweight Symposium, 1967, Bergstrom Museum.

————, "The Mount Washington Glass Works and Its Successors, 1837–1958," *Antiques,* Vol. LXXIV, No. 1 (July, 1958), pp. 46–48, illus.

_____, "Paperweights at Old Sturbridge Village," *Bulletin of the Paperweight Collectors' Association*, Vol. 2, June, 1957, illus.

WYATT, M. D., *Industrial Arts of the 19th Century*, 2 vols., 1853.

YAEGER, DOROTHEA, "Comments on Paperweights," *Hobbies*, October, 1941, pp. 62–67, illus.

_____, "The Known and the Unknown in Old Glass Paperweights," *Bulletin of the Paperweight Collectors' Association*, June, 1957.

ZARE, F. N. A., "A Reply" (to "Old French Glass Paperweights," by G. Bernard Hughes), *Apollo*, September, 1953.

Glossary

ARROW (also known as CROWSFOOT). Small, three-pronged motif found in rods from many sources.

AVENTURINE. Colored glass combined with tiny crystals or flakes of gold (fifteenth century), copper (from seventeenth century), giving the glass a lustrous sheen. Called GOLDSTONE when yellow or brownish.

BASAL RIM. Bottom rim in paperweights with concave base.

BASAL RING. Flange found on some English paperweights as a result of in-cutting just above the base. Not footed.

BASE. Bottom of paperweight; usually concave.

BASKET. 1) Funnel-shaped latticinio ground typical of St. Louis fruit weights; 2) Outer sheath of staves typical of Clichy; 3) Encased overlay with handle rare in Bacchus; 4) Latticinio or stave basket rare in St. Louis, China, and Bohemia.

BLOCK. Fruitwood block with handle, whose cup-shaped interior was used to shape crown of paperweight.

BOUQUET. Concentrated arrangement of canes or flowers, natural or stylized, with leaves.

BROKEN CANDY. See CANDY.

CABBAGE ROSE. Clichy rose resembling cross-section of cabbage cable. Tube of latticinio used as core of torsade.

CAMEO. See SULPHIDE.

CANDY. See SCRAMBLED.

CANE. A fused bundle of rods or mold-made stick, subsequently pulled out to great length and cut into slices that reveal the design in cross-section. Any short or thin segment of such a bundle or stick. Also called SETUP, or read: when large, FLORET. Initially, that is, before being pulled out and sliced up, the cylindrical cane may have a diameter up to six inches and a length from six inches to one foot.

CARPET. See GROUND.

CHAPLET BEAD. A spiral twist of latticinio threads.

CHEQUER. A scattered or patterned millefiori weight in which the canes are separated by white or colored latticinio twists.

CHOUFLEUR. See GROUND.

CHRYSOPRASE. Apple green.

CIRCLET. Small circle of canes, florets.

CLEAR GROUND. See GROUND.

CLOSE MILLEFIORI. Closely compacted overall arrangement of canes, usually of great variety. Any weight with such an arrangement.

CLOVER CUT. Intersecting printies, typical of New England Glass Company surface cutting.

CLUSTER. Close grouping of similar canes, typical of certain Clichy weights.

COLOR GROUND. See GROUND.

CONCENTRIC. Common paperweight design in which a single cane or group of canes forms the axis for a series of concentric circles of canes.

COOKIE BASE. Thick, cookie-shaped pad forming base for New England Glass Company fruit weights.

300

CRIMP. A metal tool for forming three-dimensional flowers by insertion, used especially at Millville for roses and lilies.

CRIMPED CANE. Vertically ribbed or corrugated cane.

CROWN. The clear glass dome above the design; the outer, upper portion or surface of a weight.

CROWN WEIGHT. A hollow-blown paperweight comprising a flattened ball, usually of vertical, twisted ribbons alternating with latticinio twists, and topped by a single cane. A St. Louis specialty, it was also made in Bohemia, with variations at Cambridge and possibly at Sandwich.

CROWSFOOT. Alternate term for ARROW.

CRYSTALLO-CERAMIE. *See* SULPHIDE.

CULLET. Broken glass remnants often added to the new batch.

CUSHION. Paperweight ground.

CUTTING. External embellishment done with an abrasive wheel.

DATES. Authentic dates are found from 1845 to 1858; spurious dates before and after these years. Somerville weights bear legitimate dates of the early 1900's. Some modern Baccarat and St. Louis weights are dated.

DESIGN. Internal paperweight decoration.

DEVIL'S FIRE. A mottled, swirling motif used at Millville.

DIAMETER. Commonest physical identifying measurement of a weight.

DOORSTOP. Very large weight, usually over 5 inches diameter.

DOUBLE OVERLAY. Two thin, external glass coatings of different colors, the inner usually opaque white.

ENCASED OVERLAY. A single or double overlay further enclosed in clear glass.

END-OF-DAY. *See* SCRAMBLED.

FACET. Decorative plane-cut surface having three or more sides.

FACETING. Cut surface decoration of a weight, done originally to enhance the design, but lately to obscure internal defects on old weights. Old faceting is usually sharper edged.

FESTOON. Cartouche, or swag in the design, especially on marble weights.

FILIGREE. Any rod composed of straight or spirally twisted opaque white or colored threads.

FLASH. A thin coating of colored glass applied to the crown as an overlay, or applied to the base as a ground color. Scratches and rubs off easily.

FLORET. (also, florette, *fleurette*). Large cane, sometimes superficially, not realistically, resembling a flower blossom. *See also* CANE.

FLOWER WEIGHT. Paperweight with one or more realistic or stylized flowers as the dominant motif.

FLUTE. Deep, narrow cut whose ends taper to a point.

FOOTED. Having a basal flange.

FRIGGER. Glass novelty made in free time as experiment or gift. Also called whimsey. Some paperweights were friggers.

GAFFER. Skilled glassman in charge of shop or "chair." A "chair," literally the glassblower's chair, refers to a team of three or four glassworkers.

GARLAND. Continuous or closely associated chain or chains of canes looped or intertwined in various patterns.

GLASS A RETORTI. Filigree glass whose threads form a varying pattern; a Venetian specialty occasionally seen in the vase section of vase paperweights and shotcups.

GAUZE. Another word for FILIGREE, LACE, MUSLIN. *See* GROUND.

GOLD FLAKE. *See* GROUND.

GOLDSTONE. *See* AVENTURINE.

GROUND. The cushion above, on or in which the design rests. Grounds include:

CARPET—A close, all-over pattern of identical canes. The term, according to Elville, was first used in 1855 to describe a ground of stars.

CHOUFLEUR—Carpet ground of canes somewhat warped in appearance, suggesting a cauliflower.

CLEAR—Clear glass ground, invisible when well done, foggy or bubbly when not.

COLOR—May be opaque or translucent, single or overlaid.

GAUZE—MUSLIN or LACE ground, the filigree strands jumbled together, laid in parallel lengths, or both. "A lovely, ethereal ground."—J. P. Boore.

GOLD FLAKE—Peculiar to modern Venetian work.

JASPER—Mottled ground composed of small particles, usually in two colors. Occasional St. Louis examples have filigree backing up inside cushion.

LACE—*See* GAUZE.

LATTICINIO—Composed of spirally radiating latticinio threads or bands, seen as double or latticed when it has been blown and collapsed upon itself. The ground may have a translucent colored glass filler between the latticinio layers.

MOSS—Clichy ground composed of green, mosslike canes, sometimes punctuated with tiny white star rods.

MOTTLED—Composed of partially fused or melted chips of colored glass.

MUSLIN—*See* GAUZE.

ROCK—Rough, irregular sandy ground, composed of several elements, possibly including unfused sand, pulverized sulphide, mica, nacreous fragments, and algae-like green glass. Found in Baccarat snake and lizard weights, and without motif in weights that appear to have been trial runs for serpent weights.

SAND—*See* ROCK.

SODDEN SNOW—False ground of opaque white glass.

SPIRAL LATTICINIO—*See* LATTICINIO.

STAR DUST—Composed entirely of white star rods usually found in compacted clusters (canes) with or without colored dot centers.

SWIRL (also DOUBLE SWIRL GROUND)—*See* LATTICINIO.

HAND COOLER. Egg-shaped millefiori or overlaid object, or one containing an upright bouquet or filigree strands.

HOBNAIL. Basal or crown cutting of V-shaped grooves intersecting at right angles.

HOLLOW BLOWN WEIGHT. Typically a crown paperweight, with a substantial internal air space, characteristically blown in a mold.

HONEYCOMB. Cane cross-section (Baccarat) resembling honeycomb.

INCRUSTATION. Sulphide. The act of incrusting a sulphide in glass.

INTAGLIO. Form of concave decoration usually pressed into the glass.

JASPER. *See* GROUND.

LACE. *See* GROUND.

LAMPWORK. Process in which flora, fauna, and other non-millefiori design elements are formed and assembled by means of a torch.

LATTICINIO (also, LATTICINO). From the Italian *latte,* meaning milk. Usually an opaque white glass, sometimes colored, appearing as threads or tapes in parallel, swirl, latticed, or spiral arrangements for use as paperweight grounds, torsades, or other decorative features.

LATTIMO. Milk glass, opaque white glass.

MACÉDOINE. *See* SCRAMBLED.

MAGNUM. Any weight over 3¼ inches diameter, not including a doorstop.

MANTEL ORNAMENT. Globular paperweight fused to or resting free on pedestal consisting of knopped and baluster stem, and base. Frequently seen in pairs.

M A R B R I E.   Overlay or encased overlay of opaque white glass decorated with trailed loops or festoons in one or more colors.

M A Z A R E N E   B L U E.   A deep, purplish blue like ultramarine blue, occasionally cited as ground or overlay color.

M E T A L.   Glass, especially in its molten state.

M I L L E F I O R I.   From the Italian *Mille*—thousand—and *fiori*—flowers—thousand flowers. "Ornamental glass usually of a floral pattern produced by cutting cross-sections of fused bundles of rods of various colors and sizes and often embedding them in clear glass." *Webster.* Any glass object decorated preponderantly with such bundles of rods (canes, florets, setups), especially (for our purpose) paperweights. More restrictively a paperweight with a ground of canes so close-packed as to resemble "a thousand flowers."

M I L L E F L E U R S.   French for millefiori.

M I N I A T U R E.   Any weight under 2-inch diameter.

M O S S.   *See* GROUND.

M O T I F.   Internal design, subject matter.

M U S H R O O M.   A mushroom-shaped tuft of canes whose tops with a close millefiori or concentric millefiori design. A paperweight containing a mushroom, usually surrounded by a torsade. Also called TUFT.

M U S L I N.   *See* GROUND.

N O S E G A Y.   A flat bouquet of stylized canes and leaves, typical of St. Louis and the New England Glass Company.

O P A L I N E.   Flat plaque weight of opaque or translucent opaline glass resembling opal, usually rectangular and sometimes shaped like a book, with a slightly raised oval, or other shaped medallion with nosegay, or other millefiori design. A specialty of Clichy.

O V E R L A Y.   1) A layer of opaque or translucent glass obtained by dipping, and later cut with windows, printies, or other decorative cutting and sometimes gilded or festooned. Single overlay—one layer of glass; double overlay—two layers of glass; triple overlay—three layers of glass; encased overlay—single, double, or triple overlay cut with windows, printies, or other design, then further encased in clear glass. 2) Any paperweight so finished.

P A N E L E D.   A weight whose internal design is divided into sections, each section composed of an enclosure of identical canes.

P A P E R W E I G H T.   Here used to include only paperweights made entirely of glass or enclosing sulphide or metallic designs. Also called WEIGHT.

In French: *boule, serre-papiers, presse-papiers.*

In German: *Briefbeschwerer.*

In Swedish: *brevpress.*

P A S T R Y   M O L D.   A cane (often large) with several prominent points or undulations; simply formed and flares at the base. Prominent Clichy cane.

P A T T E R N E D   M I L L E F I O R I.   A weight composed of canes arranged in a definite design or order.

P E D E S T A L   W E I G H T.   A weight raised on a broad cylindrical column and having rings, flanges, and other basal orders, frequently decorated with latticinio and spiral twists, staves, etc.

P E L L - M E L L.   *See* SCRAMBLED.

P I E D O U C H E.   French for PEDESTAL WEIGHT.

P I N C H B E C K.   A weight featuring an alloy plaque resembling gold or silver, modeled in relief and fixed to a clear glass crown.

P O N T I L   (also PUNTY; various other spellings).   A solid metal rod (usually iron) used for fashioning hot glass, to which it is attached by a button of glass first gathered on the end of the rod.

P O N T I L   M A R K.   The rough button left on the bottom of the paperweight when it is separated from (cracked off) the pontil rod. In most fine weights this is ground off, resulting in the basal concavity.

P R I N T Y.   Any circular or oval concave cut on the outer surface of a weight. This nineteenth century term is here substituted for the American term, "punty," to avoid confusion with the term "pontil," for which punty is also a synonym.

Q U A T R E F O I L.   Garland of canes or printy-cut (New England Glass Company) of four-leaf shape.

R I B B O N.   Flat, spirally-twisted glass rod or band of one or more colors, used in border or crown designs.

R I N G.   Row or circle of canes in concentric weights.

R O C K   G R O U N D.   *See* GROUND.

R O D.   Initial basic element of paperweight design from which canes, latticinio, or flora and fauna are created. Cylindrical stick of clear or colored glass.

R O S E   P O M P A D O U R.   Delicate pink ground seen in some Clichy weights and Sévres porrelain.

R O S E T T E.   Ornamental circular cluster of closely fitted canes, usually seen as a central motif symbolizing a flower.

S A L I V A.   Unwanted string or conglomerate of small bubbles that may be the result of insufficient expulsion of internal air or cooling of the gather during assembly.

S C A T T E R E D   M I L L E F I O R I.   *See* SPACED MILLEFIORI.

S C R A M B L E D.   Random jumble of canes with or without filigree bits.

S E T U P.   *See* CANE.

S I L H O U E T T E.   Any cane having as its cross-section a human, animal, or flower silhouette.

S P A C E D   M I L L E F I O R I.   Suggested term to replace scattered millefiori. My objection to the latter is that it implies being "marked by disorganized dispersion. Separated by or occuring at wide irregular intervals. Having no fixed or definite arrangement,"—*Webster*. In spaced millefiori there is the attempt, not always successful, to space the canes at even intervals in even rows or circles.

S P I R A L   L A T T I C I N I O.   Convex or funnel-shaped ground. *See* GROUND.

S P O K E   C O N C E N T R I C.   New England Glass Company concentric, whose design suggests spokes of a wheel.

S P O K E   W E I G H T.   Any weight whose overall design suggests a wheel of spokes. A St. Louis weight having a jasper ground of alternating colors divided by spoke-like tubes.

S T A R   C U T.   Many-pointed star cut into base. A Baccarat specialty.

S T A R D U S T.   *See* GROUND.

S T A R W E I G H T.   A weight whose overall design is star shaped. A Clichy specialty.

S T A V E.   Flattened tube used as basket-like enclosure in millefiori motifs.

S T R A W B E R R Y   C U T.   A basal cutting resembling a fine meshed graph of many polished cuts intersecting at right angles. A St. Louis specialty, it is sometimes called strawberry-diamond cut.

S T R I A E.   "An elongated imperfection in glass caused by variation in temperature of the furnace or by unequal density of materials used."—*Webster*. Viewed from the side these wavy, sugary threads or bands can cause a break in the image, like a heat wave, but are usually not troublesome seen from above.

S U G A R Y   (also, SUGARING). Descriptive of glass containing straie, giving the glass the appearance of water to which sugar has been added.

S U L P H I D E. Relief medallion made of china clay and supersilicate of potash for insertion in paperweights, scent bottles, decanters, knife rests, and a variety of glass objects. Any paperweight containing a sulphide. *Sulfure* in French.

S W I R L   W E I G H T. Weight with spiral rods of two or more alternating colors radiating from a central cane or group of canes. A Clichy specialty.

T A B L E   F A C E T. Flat circular or other cut on top of a weight.

T A Z Z A. Dish supported by a stem and foot, used to hold wax seals or other desk minutiae. Also called wafer dish. Bowl or paperweight base often millefiori.

T O R S A D E. Twisted, spiraled circular belt about the motif, particularly in mushroom and upright bouquet weights, but also in rare parrot, squirrel, dog, and other weights from St. Louis.

T R E F O I L. Garland or any other design element in shape of three leaves.

T R I C O L O R E. Referring originally to the red-white-blue of the French flag of 1789, it later described paperweights, especially those with flowers in these three colors, which supposedly gained popularity with the Revolution of 1848.

T U F T. Alternative for MUSHROOM.

T U R B A N   W E I G H T. Paperweight with large, turban-like cushion, uniformly studded with small bubbles and centered by a single large bubble. Origin presently unknown.

T W I S T. *See* TORSADE.

U P R I G H T   B O U Q U E T. Three-dimensional floral bouquet set vertically in a paperweight, handcooler, stopper.

V E N E T I A N   B A L L. Venetian scrambled weight in which the millefiori leftovers are rolled or kneaded into a ball and covered with glass.

W E I G H T. *See* PAPERWEIGHT.

W H I T E   G L A S S. Clear, colorless glass.

W I G   S T A N D. Tall, obelisk-shaped glass ornament supposedly used as peg for wigs.

W I N D O W. Any round or oval, flat, or concave cut through overlay that gives a view into the interior of the weight.

Some Museums Having Glass Paperweights

The Art Institute of Chicago.
Bennington Museum, Bennington, Vermont.
Bergstrom Art Center and Museum, Neenah, Wisconsin.
Birmingham City Art Gallery and Museum, Birmingham, England.
Brooklyn Museum, The, Brooklyn, New York.
Corning Museum of Glass, Corning, New York.
Chrysler Art Museum, The, Provincetown, Massachusetts.
Conservatoire National des Arts et Metiers, Paris.
Cristalleries de Saint Louis, Paris.
M. H. de Young Museum, San Francisco.
Edward L. Doheny Memorial Library, Camarillo, California.
Flint Institute of Arts, Flint, Michigan.
Glynn Vivian Art Gallery, Swansea, Wales.
Henry Ford Museum, Dearborn, Michigan.
Metropolitan Museum of Art, The, New York City.
Minneapolis Institute of Fine Arts, The, Minneapolis, Minnesota.
Musée des Arts Décoratifs, Louvre, Paris.
Musée du Verre, Liège, Belgium.
Newark Museum, Newark, New Jersey.
New-York Historical Society, New York City.
Old Sturbridge Village, Sturbridge, Massachusetts.
Pascack Historical Society, Park Ridge, New Jersey.
Peterborough Museum, Peterborough, New Hampshire.
St. Mary's Seminary, Perryville, Missouri.
Sandwich Historical Society Museum, Sandwich, Massachusetts.
Smithsonian Institution, Washington, D.C.
Toledo Museum of Art, Toledo, Ohio.
Victoria and Albert Museum, London.

A

Albert, Prince, 37, 124, 260, 261, 262
Alexandra, Queen, as sulphide subject, 178
Allen & Moore, 43, 262, 264, 267, n. 19
American Glass and Glassmaking, 196
American Glass Paperweights, 206, 213
American paperweights, 192–253; *see also*
    modern paperweights, U.S.
American sulphides and sulphide subjects, 265
Amic, Yolande, 47, 73
Angus-Butterworth, L. M., 164
Annamaugh, Jean, 251
Art Institute of Chicago, 90, 265
Art Journal, 15, 16, 42, 43, 146, 147, 152
Art-Union Monthly Journal of the Arts, 153
Austrian Industry Exhibition, 48
aventurine, 14
Avinwell, Emil, 242, 248

B

Baccarat, Compagnie des Cristalleries de,
    2, 3, 42, 47–83, 174, 190, 199, 272, 285,
    289
    canes, 51–53
    dates and signatures, 50, 51
    history, 41, 47–49
    Launay–Hautin as distributor for, 47, 123
    modern paperweights, 270, 271
    modern sulphides, 271
    sulphides and sulphide subjects, 259–261
    supression of Creusot, 47
Bacchus, George, 152
Bacchus, George & Sons (also known as
    Bacchus, Green & Green; George Bacchus
    & Co.; Bacchus & Sons; Stone, Fawdry &
    Stone), 2, 152, 170, 176
    glass at Great Exhibition, 36, 40
    history, 152–154
    paperweights, 154–160, 229, 230, 289
    related millefiori, 160
Bacchus, Green & Green; *see* Bacchus, George
    & Sons
Bacchus, John Ogdin, 152
Bailey, William, Co., 198
Bakewell, Page & Bakewell, 265
Banks, Carl, 246
Barber, Edwin Atlee, 197, 225, 229
Barber, Ralph, 234, 236
Barnes, James B.
    at Cambridge, 194, 195
    at Hobbs, Bruckunier, 195
Barrelet, James, 123, 146, 257
    La Verrerie en France, 146
Barthélemy, Abbé, 16, 21, 98
Battestini theory, 50, 51
Beard, G. W., 176
Belgian factories, 185–191
Belgian sulphides, 264
Bennett, Edwin, 224

Bennington Museum, 213
Berens Blumberg & Co., 43, 182
Bergstrom, Mrs. Evangeline, 174, 180, 190,
    226
Bergstrom collection, 75, 98, 239
Bergstrom Museum, 21, 125
Berkshires, sand from, 212
Bigaglia, Ettore, 15, 209
Bigaglia, Pietro, 14, 15, 19, 21, 48
Blaschka, Leopold and Rudolph, glass flowers
    of, 242
Bohemian–Silesian paperweights, 1, 26–34, 199,
    215
    canes, 215
    sulphides, 264
Boileau, Henri-Germain, 255
Bonaparte, Napoleon, 78
Bonaparte, Pauline, Princess Borghese, 88, 98
Bontemps, Georges, 13, 43, 47, 145, 146, 147
Boore, J. P., 54
Boston & Sandwich Glass Co., 2, 185, 192, 199,
    205, 206, 207, 233, 272, 288, 289
    display at Mechanics' Hall, Boston, 216
    history, 211–214
    paperweights, 241–222
Boston Porcelain & Glass Co., 194, 211
Briati, Giuseppe, 14
Bristol, 174, 175
Brocart, Georges, 270
Brooklyn Flint Glass Works, acquired by
    Houghtons, 247; *see also* John L. Gilliland
    & Co.
Brooklyn Museum, 209
Brückmann, 24
Brunel, Isambard Kingdom, 36
Bryan, William Jennings, as paperweight sub-
    ject, 252
*Bulletin of the Paperweight Collectors' As-
    sociation,* 62, 148
Bulletin of the Pennsylvania Museum, 225
Bunamo, Philip, 247, 248, 249

C

Cambridge; *see* New England Glass Co.
canes, 8, 9
    portrait, 15, 19, 20, 156, 228–229
Cape Cod Glass Co., 212
Carder, Frederick, 250, 281
Centennial of 1876, Philadelphia, 198, 224,
    228, 230, 235
Ceramic Museum at Sèvres, 255
Chaffers, William, 42, 146
Challinor, Charles, 228, 230
Challinor, Frank, 228
Challinor-Taylor, 228
Chambon, Raymond, 185
Chance, Sir Hugh, 175
Chance, Robert Lucas, 37, 175
Chanticleer, as sulphide subject, 178
Charitable Mechanics' Association Exhibition,
    197

Charleston, Robert J., 13
Chaumeil, Guillaume, 49
Chênée factory, 185
Chinese paperweights, 238, 289; *see also* modern paperweights, China
Choisy-le-Roi factory, 47, 48, 123, 145, 146, 147
Chrysler Museum, 221
Clay, Henry, as paperweight subject, 200
Clichy (Clichy-la-Garenne), 41, 42, 202, 243, 278, 285, 286, 289
    boracic glass, 124, 276
    history, 123–125
    Maës and Clemandot, 125
    paperweights, 41, 125–144
    rose, 126
    sulphides and sulphide subjects, 261, 262
Cole, Henry, 36, 37
Collins, Timothy, 213
Colné, Charles P., 15, 48
    report, 73, 76, 148, 149, 150, 182
Conservation Laboratory, Institute of Fine Arts, New York University, 287
Corning Museum of Glass, 41, 115, 126, 142, 268
Creusot (also known as Cristallerie Lambert et Boyer, Cristallerie de Saint Cloud), 47, 84, n. 5, 85, 257
Cross, William E., 257
Crystal Palace, London, 37–39, 40, 43, 44
Crystal Palace, New York, 124, 192
Curiosities of Glass Making, 13
Cyclopedia of Useful Arts and Manufactures, The, 43
Cyrén, Gunnar, 281
Czechoslovakian sulphides and sulphide subjects, 264, 265; *see also* modern paperweights, Czechoslovakia

D

Dahlgren, Miss O. D., 48, 49
Dale, George, 198
Daley, "Nix," 252
D'Artigues, 47
Das Glas, 12
David, Albert, 271
Debette, M. L. P., 25, 26
Degenhart, John, 248, 274
Degenhart's Crystal Art Glass, 273
Desprez, 257
Die Gläser der Empire-und-Biedermeierzeit, 255
Dieu et Mon Droit, as paperweight subject, 182
Disraeli, as sulphide subject, 178
Dohln, Ernest W. von, 234
doorstop paperweights, 170, 178, 252
Dorflinger, Christian, 213, 233
Dorflinger, Christopher, 233
Dorflinger Glass Works (also called Wayne County Glass Works)
    history, 233, 234, 238
    paperweights, 234, 242, 250
Dorflinger, John, 234
Dupont, 48, 49, 63, 174, 184, n. 2, 270
Durand Art Glass Co., 234, 242
Dutch paperweights; *see* modern paperweights, Holland

E

Edward VII, as sulphide subject, 264
Egermann, F., 25
Eighteenth Dynasty; *see* New Kingdom
Elder, Robert A., Jr., 272
Elville, E. M., 178
Emmet, Fisher & Flowers, 194
Emperauger, J. P., 258
Encyclopaedia Britannica, 226
Ernst, Leo J., 251
Escalier Crystal (Escalier de Crystal), 86, 147, 257
Exhibition, Charitable Mechanics' Association, 197
Exhibition of Austrian Industry, 48
Exhibition of 1853, New York, 197
Exhibition of Manufactures and Art, Birmingham, 153, 162
Exposition Universelle; *see* Paris Exposition of 1878

F

F. M. Konstglas glassworks, 281
façon de Bohême, 15, 30, 145, 152, 153, 154
façon de Venise, 12, 15, 24, 221
Fastre, Nicolas, 191
Fawdry, Stone & Stone, 152
filigree glass, 13–14
filigree rod, 8, 10
Fisher, Richard, 194
Fisher & Gilliland, 194
fluorescence in glass, 285, 286, 288
Ford, John & Co., 182, 264
Forest of Fontainebleau, 164
Franchini, G. B., 15, 19, 21, 126
Franklin, Benjamin, as paperweight subject, 230, 255
Franklin Flint Glass Works; *see* Gillinder & Sons
Franklin Institute, 195, 197
Fuss, Dr. W. E., 24

G

Gardiner, George, 252
Gasparetto, Astone, 14
Gayrard, Raymond, 258
Gentile Glass Co., 273
German paperweights; *see* modern paperweights, Germany
Gilliano Ferro Co., 280
Gilliland, John L., 194
Gilliland, John L., & Co., 42, 199, 226
Gillinder, Frederick, 224
Gillinder, James, 224, 225, 226, 228
Gillinder, William T., 151, 156, 195, 197, 223–226, 228
Gillinder & Bennett, 224; *see also* Gillinder & Sons
Gillinder & Sons (also called Franklin Flint Glass Works, Gillinder & Bennett, Gillinder Brothers)
    history, 223–228
    paperweights, 2, 155, 228–232, 264
    vs. Gilliland, 225, 226

Gillinder Brothers, 224; *see also* Gillinder & Sons

Gladstone, as sulphide subject, 178

Glass Excise Duty, 151, 153, 162, 165
 levy of, 151
 repeal of, 151, 153, 162, 165

Glass Handicrafters, 273

glass rod, 7, 8, 9

glassblowers
 Graham, James D., 276
 Littleton, Harvey, 275

goldstone, 14

Graham, James D., 276

Graham, Lloyd J., 285, 289

Great Exhibition (of the Industry of All Nations, London, 1851), 19, 36–44, 192, 196
 Crystal Palace of, 38, 39, 40, 43, 44, 175, 264
 Jury Reports, 40, 41, 42
  on English glass, 42, 152
  on St. Louis, 86
 medal awards, 165
 paperweights of, 257, 264

Greeley, Horace, 192

Green, George Joseph, 152

Green Point Glass Works, 213, 233

Gridel, Emile, 51, 53

Guide du Verrier, 13, 146

Guignon, Roland, 270

Guinand, 147

Guttery, D. W., 176

H

Hacker, Harold J., 275

Hagberg, Tobias, 234, 250

Hamilton Glass Works, 252

handcooler, 16, 18

Hansen, Ronald E., 275

Harley and Wiberly, 286

Hawkes, T. G., 250

Haynes, E. Barrington, 14, 154, 158

Hobbs, Brockunier & Co., 15, 195

Hoffnungstal Works, 24

hollow weights, 182, 184

Honey, W. B., 12, 255

Hopkins, John, 196

Hopkins, Thomas, 196

Houghton, Amory, Sr. and Jr., 247

housefly, as paperweight subject, 182

Hughes, G. Bernard, 182

I

Illustrated London News, 38, 44, 162

Imbert, Roger, 47, 73

incrustation, Bohemian art of, 26; *see also* sulphide

Islington Glass works (also called Johnson, Berry & Harris; Rice Harris; Rice Harris, Islington Glass Works; Rice Harris & Son; London and Birmingham Flint Glass and Alkali Co.; Islington Glass Co., Ltd.), 40, 42
 history, 161, 162
 milk glass at Sandwich, 219
 paperweights, 36, 162, 163

J

Jackson, T. G., 165

Japanese paperweights; *see* modern paperweights, Japan

Jarves, Deming, 16, 185, 194, 195, 211, 212, 226, 241

Jarves, George, 212

Jarves, James Jackson, 16, 22, n. 25

Jarves, John, 212

Jarves, John Jackson, 211

Jarves & Cormerais, 195

Joan of Arc, as sulphide subject
 at Val St. Lambert, 188
 at Baccarat, 259

Josephine works, 25

Journal of Design and Manufactures, 40, 145, 147, 154

"J"-weights, 29

K

Kaighms Point Glass Works, 224

Kane, Michael, 240

Karlsthal works, 25

Kayser, Martin, 51

Kaziun, Charles, 3, 246, 273, 275–277, 278, 279

Kidd, William, 264

Kilner, C. A., 151, 177

Kilner, J. & Sons (also known as Providence Glass Works; J. Kilner & Son; Kilner Brothers), 176–180

Kilner, John, 177

Konstglas, F. M., 281

Kosta Glassworks, 282

Kuntz, Marcus, 236, 239

L

La Verrerie en France, 146

Labino, Dominik, 275

"Labor—Honor—Virtue," as paperweight subject, 200

Lafayette, as paperweight subject, 200

Larson, Emil, 3, 234, 238, 242, 245, 276

latticinio, 13–15

Launay, 85, 123

Launay, Hautin & Co., 47, 85, 123

"lava" weight, 242

Lawrence, Abbot and Amos, as paperweight subjects, 200

Leach, B. F., Co., 251

Lee, Ruth Webb, 213

Leffingwell, B. H., 226, 249

Leighton, Henry, 198

Leighton, John H., 198

Leighton, Thomas, 196, 198

Leighton, William, 196, 209

"letter-weights," 36, 41, 153, 258

Lewin, Seymour Z., Dr., 287

Libbey, Edward Drummond, 195, 197

Libbey, William L., 195, 241

Libbey Glass Co., 197

Lincoln, Abraham, as Gillinder paperweight subject, 224, 230, 231; *see also* modern paperweights

Littleton, Harvey, 275

Lloyd & Summerfield, 264
Lobmeyer, C. & S., 181
Long, Andrew, 197
Long Island Flint Glass Works, 233
Lucas, John Rober, 175
Lundin, Ingeborg, 281
Lutz, Nicholas, 2, 14, 197, 213, 215, 218, 220,
    221, 233, 234, 242, 243, 244, 249
    apprenticeship at St. Louis, 212
    at Murano, 213
    goldstone, 218

M

Maar, Dora, 271
McGinnis, William, 252
McKearin, George S. and Helen, 192, 234
McKinley, William, paperweight subject, 251
Maës (or Maez), L. Joseph, 41, 123, 124, 125
Mahoney, Connie, 249
marbrie paperweight, 10, 115, 221
Marinot, Maurice, 268
Marsh, Susan T., 192
Martoret, 257
Mazerski, Edward J., 247, 248, 249
medallists
    David, Albert, 271
    Gayrard, Raymond, 258
    Maar, Dora, 271
    Poillerat, Gilbert, 271
    Wyon, W. A., 196
millefiori, 8, 9, 10, 12–22
    American, 192–232
    Belgian, 185–191
    Bohemian, 24–34
    English, 151–173
    French, 47–144
    origin of term, 8
    Venetian, 12–23
millefleurs, 13
Millville; see Whitall Tatum & Co.
Minns, Edward, 235
Minutoli, Lt. Gen. Heinrich von, 18, 25
Miotti family, 14
modern paperweights, 268–282
    Baccarat, 270, 271
    China, 272, 273
    Czechoslovakia, 268, 269
    Germany, 279
    Holland, 279
    Japan, 273
    Kaziun, 275–277
    Marinot, 268
    St. Louis, 271, 272
    Scandinavia, 281, 282
    Scotland, 277, 278
    United States, 273–277
    Venice, 279, 281
    Ysart, 278, 279
Monot & Co. (Monot, Père et Fils et Stumpf);
    see Pantin, Cristallerie de
Morales, Mona, 282
Morris, James, 280
Morris, William, 165
mosaic plaque, 8
Mount, William Sidney, 192
Mt. Washington Glass Works (also known as
    Labree & Jarves; Jarves & Cormerais; W. L.

Libbey & Co.; Mt. Washington Glass Co.)
    history, 240, 241
    paperweights, 241–247, 249
Mullin, George, 252
Murano, Italy, 3, 15–16, 209, 238, 280, 281
Murano rose, 238, 280
Museo Vetrario, 209

N

Nailsea Glass Works, 174, 175
National Flint Glass Makers Society of Great
    Britain and Ireland, 223
Nativity, as Pinchbeck subject, 181
Neuwelt factory, 25
New England Glass Co. (also known as New
    England Glass Works; or, familiarly,
    Cambridge; or NEGC), 2, 3, 15, 41, 192,
    211, 212, 213, 214, 215, 216, 220, 221,
    223, 225, 226, 231, 245, 272, 278, 289
    history, 194, 195
    paperweights, 195–210
New Kingdom, Eighteenth Dynasty of, 7, 8
Nineteenth Century British Glass, 174

O

O'Hara Glass Works, 223, 224
Old Glass Paperweights, 190, 258
Old Sturbridge Village, 177, 203
Orrefors Glassworks, 234, 281, 282
Osler, F. & C., 264
Owens, Michael J., 195

P

painted paperweights, 182
Pairpoint Manufacturing Co. (also known as
    Bundersen Glass Works; Gundersen-Pair-
    point Glassworks; Pairpoint Glass Works),
    241, 245, 246, 248
Pantin, Cristallerie de (also known as Monot
    & Co.; Monot, Père et Fils et Stumpf),
    48, 73, 76, 120, 148, 149, 150, 165
paperweight collectors, 2
paperweights, painted, 182
Paris, Comte de, as sulphide subject, 258
Paris Exposition of 1878 (Exposition Uni-
    verselle), 15, 48, 73, 87, 148
    jury report, 125
    medal to Whitefriars, 165
Pauly & Co., 280, 281
Paxton, Joseph, 37, 38, 264
Pazaurek, Gustav E., 25, 26, 255
Péligot, Eugène, 19, 41, 42
Pellatt, Apsley, 13, 18, 41, 42, 43, 147, 255,
    258
    incrustation process, 256
Pevsner, Nickolaus, 40
Philadelphia Flint Glass Works, 224
Philadelphia Glass Works, 224
Pierre, Frank (François), 196, 197, 223, 226
Pinchbeck, Christopher, 180
    inventor of alloy, 180
Pinchbeck paperweights, 180–182
Plymouth Rock paperweight, 198, 209
Pohl, Franz, 25
Poillerat, Gilbert, 271

portrait canes, 15, 19, 20, 156, 228–229
Powell, H. J., 165, 166
Powell, James, 165
Powell, James & Sons, 165; *see also* White-
   friars
"Powell English Glass" label, 166

Q

Queen Elizabeth II, as paperweight subject,
   166, 169, 270, 271
Quin, Dr. Henry, 254

R

rabbit cane
   in Bohemian paperweights, 29
   at Cambridge, 199, 202
   found in Sandwich dump, 215
Ravenna (Glass Works), 274
Ravenscroft, George, 1, 151
refractive index tests, 50, 278–289
Reminiscences of Glassmaking, 226
Revelli, Yvonne Sohn, 270
Revi, Albert Christian, 76, 120, 185
Revolution of 1848, 68, 145
Rheims, Maurice, 2, 270
Rhulander, John, 236
Rice, Edmund, 213
Rice Harris & Co.; *see* Islington Glass Works
Rogers, Millard F., Jr., 225
Ronneby, Sweden, 281
rose, cabbage, 29, 126
rose, Clichy, 126
Rossetti, Dante Gabriel, 165
Ruskin, John, 40

S

Sabellico, Marc Antonio, 12, 16
St. Louis, Compagnie des Cristalleries de, 2, 14,
   41, 182, 200, 202, 204, 206, 216, 220,
   243, 248, 276, 278, 285, 288, 289
   canes, 88, 89
   dates and signatures, 87
   elimination of Creusot, 85
   history, 85–87
   modern paperweights; *see* modern paper-
      weights, St. Louis
   paperweights, 87–122
   questionable attributions, 120
   sulphides and sulphide subjects, 261
St. Maude factory, 147
Saint-Amans, Pierre Honoré Boudon de, 255,
   256
Salviati & Co., 15
Sandwich; *see* Boston & Sandwich Glass Co.
Scandinavian paperweights; *see* modern paperweights, Scandinavia
Scandinavian sulphides and sulphide subjects,
   265
Schindler & Veit, 149
Schmidt, 12
Scottish paperweights; *see* modern paper-
   weights, Scotland
Seidel, Alwin, 25
Sévigné, Madame de, as sulphide subject, 258

Share, C J., 176
Shirley, Frederick S., 242
Sinclair Collection, 26
Smith, Francis Edgar, 206, 213
Smith, Ray Winfield, 8, 18
Society of Arts, exhibit by Bacchus at, 153
sodden snow paperweights, 159, 160
Somerville (Union Glass Co.), 213, 214, 221,
   242, 247–249, 273
Spinning Wheel, 148
Sporer, John, 250
Stanger, Emil, 236, 239
Steffin, Albert, 242
Steuben Glass Works, 3, 234, 250, 281
Stourbridge, 175, 176
Strathearn Glass, Ltd., 278
sulphide makers.
   Desprez, 257
   Martoret, 257
   Saint-Amans, Pierre Honoré Boudon de, 255,
      '256
sulphides, 254–267
   modern; see modern paperweights, Baccarat,
      Czechoslovakia
Sydenstricker, Bill, 275

T

Tassie, James, 200, 254, 255
Tassie, William, 200, 254
Thompson, George, 275
Tiffany paperweights, 249, 250, 268
toilet bottles, 120, 160
Toledo Museum of Art, 225, 226
Tom, 198
torsades, 13–14, 56–59, 96
Tower, J., 177

U

ultraviolet light, 285
Union Glass Co.; *see* Somerville
Union Glass Works, 152; *see also* George
   Bacchus & Sons

V

Val St. Lambert glassworks
   history, 185
   paperweights, 187–191
Vasart Co., 278
Venetian ball, 1, 18, 89
Venezia-Murano Co. (also called Venice-
   Murano Co.), 15, 16, 22, n. 25, 165, 168
Venini Co., 281
Verrerie Bougard, 185
Verrerie de Sainte Anne; *see* Baccarat
Verrerie en France, La, 146
Verreries Nationales, Belgium, 185
Vetrario, Museo, 209
Victoria, Queen, 39, 88
   and Albert, 41, 124, 128, 186, 199, 200, 231
   as cane, 225, 226, 229
   Diamond Jubilee sulphide, 178
   as Pinchbeck subject, 181
   as sulphide subject, 182, 259, 262, 264
Vineland Flint Glass Works, 236, 238

Voltaire, as sulphide subject, 255
von Dohln, Ernest W., 234

W

Wakefield, Hugh, 174
Wallace-Dunlop, M. A., 18
Washington, George, as Gillinder paperweight
    subject, 224, 230
Watkins, Lura Woodside, 196, 214
Wayne County Glass Works (Dorflinger), 213
Webb, Philip, 165
Webb, Thomas & Sons, 48, 176, 184
Webster, Daniel, as paperweight subject, 200
weights, hollow, 182, 184
Wellington, Duke of
    as intaglio subject, 264
    as Pinchbeck subject, 181
    as sulphide subject, 262
Wells Collection, 177, 203
Whitall, Tatum & Co. (also known as Whitall
    Brothers & Co. and colloquially as Mill-
    ville)

history, 235
paperweights, 235–240, 248, 272, 273, 274
Whitefriars (James Powell & Sons) (also
    known as Whitefriars Glass Ltd.), 156,
    174, 176, 185
history, 164–166
paperweights, 166–173
rod dates, 168
Whittemore, F. D., Jr., 275
Wickham, Patrick, 252
Wilson, John, 255
Wyon, W. A., 196

Y

Ysart, Paul, 174, 277, 278, 279
Ysart Brothers, 278

Z

Zenker works, 25